THE COMPLETE IDIOT'S GUIDE™ TO

Upgrading and Repairing PCs

Third Edition

by Jennifer Fulton

**alpha
books
Que®**

A Division of Macmillan Computer Publishing
201 W.103rd Street, Indianapolis, IN 46290

For Scott, who taught me how to fix just about anything on a computer with a screwdriver, a paper clip, or a hairpin (OK, I learned that one on my own).

©1998 Que® Corporation

Library of Congress Catalog Card Number: 98-84268

International Standard Book Number: 0-7897-1642-9

00 99 98   8 7 6 5 4 3 2

Interpretation of the printing code: The rightmost double-digit number is the year of the book's first printing; the rightmost single-digit number is the number of the book's printing. For example, a printing code of 98-1 shows that this copy of the book was printed during the first printing of the book in 1998.

Screen reproductions in this book were created by means of the program Collage Complete from Inner Media, Inc, Hollis, NH.

Printed in the United States of America

Executive Editor
Angie Wethington

Acquisitions Editor
Renee Wilmeth

Development Editor
John Gosney

Managing Editor
Thomas F. Hayes

Project Editors
Gina Brown
Linda Seifert

Copy Editor
Julie McNamee

Indexer
Chris Wilcox

Technical Editor
Jeff Sloan

Production
Cyndi Davis-Hubler
Maribeth Echard
Terri Edwards
Donna Martin
Carl Pierce

Book Designer
Glenn Larsen

Cover Designer
Mike Freeland

Illustrator
Judd Winick

We'd Like to Hear from You!

Que Corporation has a long-standing reputation for high-quality books and products. To ensure your continued satisfaction, we also understand the importance of customer service and support.

Orders, Catalogs, and Customer Service

To order other Que or Macmillan Computer Publishing books, catalogs, or products, please contact our Customer Service Department:

Phone: 800-428-5331

Fax: 800-835-3202

International Fax: 317-228-4400

Or visit our online bookstore:

http://www.mcp.com/

Thank you for choosing Que!

Contents at a Glance

Contents

23 Maxi-Infra-Mega Storage Solutions 355

24 Sensational Stereophonic Sound 373

25 Adding a Fax Modem 383

Introduction

You are an intelligent, mature adult. You can balance the department budget, plan the annual week-long sales meeting, and get the copier to collate (and staple!). Yet, there's something about a computer that makes you feel foolish.

But, hey, at least you learned how to use the thing for something other than a desk ornament. Somehow that should be enough, but now you're feeling silly again because you just tried to install a new program using the CD-ROM drive—and your PC doesn't have one.

Looks like it might be time to upgrade.

Or, maybe your PC has a CD-ROM, but you discover after attempting to install your program that the darn thing isn't working.

Looks like you might need a repair.

Or a replacement.

Who's to know? Well, read on...

Why Do You Need This Book?

With so many "upgrade and repair it yourself" computer books on the market, why do you need this one? Well, first off, this book doesn't assume that you want to become a computer technician in your spare time. Instead of overloading you with technical mumbo jumbo, it shows you how to do just about any repair or upgrade you would want to try, while guiding you along with simple-to-follow steps and illustrations.

With this book's help, you can perform many common repairs, including:

➤ Repairing low memory problems

➤ Getting your PC to start when it doesn't want to

➤ Fixing a broken keyboard or a finicky mouse

➤ Unjamming a printer

You'll also learn how to perform many upgrades, including:

➤ Adding more RAM

➤ Upgrading the CPU

➤ Adding a second hard drive

➤ Installing a new sound card or a CD-ROM drive

➤ Getting your new modem to work

➤ Upgrading to Windows 95 or Windows 98

How Do I Use This Book?

First, start with the problem. If a computer nerd tells you that your PC needs more RAM and you're not sure if he's talking about a football team or your computer, turn to Chapter 2, "What Makes Your Computer Tick, and What It Takes to Upgrade Each Component." Here, you'll find all the computer stuff that nerds assume you already know.

After you find out that RAM is the same thing as memory, you could jump over to Chapter 19, "Make Mine More Memory," to learn how to go about adding memory to your PC. Want some alternatives before you try an upgrade? Then check out Chapter 7, "Running Low on Memory? Unjam Your RAM."

The best part about this book is that you don't have to read anything unless you need to. Just find the chapter that talks about your problem and go to it. If you do choose to read this book all the way through, you don't necessarily need to read every chapter in order. If there's something you should have read that came before, I'll tell you about it so you can review that chapter if you need to.

The Complete Idiot's Guide to Skipping Chapters

Here's what's in store so you can skip things you don't have time to deal with right now:

Part 1: Upgrading and Repairing 101

This part's full of background info—the sort of stuff you'll need to know if you're not sure what kind of computer you have, or what's in it. Not sure what RAM is? Don't worry—you'll get the help you need to unravel all that techno-babble you've been hearing.

Here, you'll also find help on whether to upgrade, as well as some nifty alternatives to try. Not sure what the problem is, and whether it's time to replace a part? Check out the last part of Chapter 1, "Making the Call: When, Why, and If You Should Upgrade" for help deciding what to do.

The final chapter in this section is a must for anyone considering a serious upgrade. Here, you'll get step-by-steps for safely taking apart your computer and putting it together again.

Part 2: Upgrading and Repairing Windows

If you're thinking about upgrading to Windows 95 or Windows 98, there's a whole chapter full of hints that will make the entire process easier. And, if you're sticking with Windows 3.1 for a while longer, there are some tips in this chapter on how to make the going easier.

Or, if you've been experiencing problems with Windows in general, low memory, lack of hard disk space, or general weirdness, you'll find a chapter in this section that will guide you through the process of repairing the problem—without upgrading.

Also, if you've been meaning to take the plunge onto the Internet, you'll find detailed instructions in the final chapter in this section.

Part 3: Easy Upgrades and Repairs

If you want to give it one more try before you attempt your first upgrade, the first chapter in this section will provide all the tricks you need to keep those peripherals running.

Want to get your feet wet without drowning in a sea of upgrades? Try the replacements in this section first. You won't even break a sweat—I promise.

Part 4: Revving Up Your PC with More Skillful Upgrades

Here, you'll find step-by-step instructions for the most common kind of upgrades, including the CPU, motherboard, power supply, hard disk, memory, monitor, video, and floppy disk drives.

Was your neighbor the first one on the block with a video cam, a satellite dish, or a cell phone? Well, the last section of this part provides sweet revenge. Learn how to upgrade your PC with the latest and greatest (some of which you may actually use to get work done). For example, you'll learn how to install a CD-ROM or DVD-ROM drive, Zip or Jaz drive, a tape backup, a sound card, and a fax modem.

Part 5: Getting Your PC to Figure Out What You've Done

If you ever thought you were dumb, wait until you finally get your new part installed. You see, your computer's so stupid that it won't know what you've done until you actually *tell it*. So after making an upgrade, you can jump to this section to learn how to get your computer's internal BIOS, DOS, or Windows to recognize all your hard work. You'll even learn how to edit your configuration files when necessary (oh, joy).

Sometimes adding a new modem or a sound card causes a conflict with an existing device. When that happens, you may have to change some settings to get everything to live together peacefully. The last chapter in this section, "Fiddling with Ports, IRQs, Addresses, and Such," will show you how.

Quick Fix Guide

At the end of this book is an appendix that will enable you to solve the most common PC problems, and hopefully, avoid an upgrade altogether.

Special Reminders

As you use this book, watch out for these special reminders that help you find just what you need:

Technical stuff

Skip this background fodder (otherwise known as techno-twaddle) unless you're truly interested in nerdy details.

Check this out!

In these boxes, you'll find a hodgepodge of information, including easy-to-understand definitions, time-saving tips, hints for staying out of trouble, and amusing anecdotes from yours truly.

Acknowledgments

Thanks to the great people at Que, including Stephanie McComb, Renee Wilmeth, Angie Wethington, John Gosney, Gina Brown, and Linda Seifert. Also, I'd like to thank Lorene Ivanoski of STD Corporation for her help with the video graphics chapter. Also, I would like to thank both Julie Seidel and Scott Kear at Maxtor Corporation for their help with the hard drive chapter. In addition, I received help from the good people at Hayes Microcomputer and Seagate, which I really appreciate. Thanks, guys!

Trademarks

Part 1
Upgrading and Repairing 101

My brother-in-law always buys the latest and greatest gadgets. He bought a VCR, microwave, Ginzu knives, cellular telephone, Thigh Master, video cam, and a satellite dish before anyone else I know. It's ironic when he boasts that his dish or his beeper is only six months old, while, in the next breath, he complains his computer equipment is six months old already. If you're one of those people who always has to have the best, you'll find owning a PC pretty frustrating. After all, whatever's new in the computing world today will be history tomorrow.

If you think owning a PC is frustrating, upgrading one can be even more so. In this section, you'll learn how to tell when it's time to upgrade, and what you need to know before you attempt one yourself.

Chapter 1

Making the Call: When, Why, and If You Should Upgrade

In This Chapter

➤ Deciding whether you can get away with a simple repair job instead

➤ What you can and can't upgrade on your PC

➤ Deciding whether an upgrade is worth it

➤ What upgrading means if you own a laptop

I know. The only thing you've ever upgraded was your airline seat. Maybe the mere thought of upgrading your computer brings a vision of possible electrocution (or execution by your boss if you accidentally destroy your computer). Or, maybe the thought of an upgrade brings visions of another kind—of money flowing out of your pocket and into a big putty-colored metal box with a TV on top.

In this chapter, you'll learn what types of upgrades fit both your risk tolerance and your wallet. And, for those who are upgrade-intolerant, I'll start off with some ways in which you can make your current situation more livable, even without an upgrade.

Can I Avoid an Upgrade and Just Repair My PC Instead?

If your heart is set on an upgrade, you might want to ask yourself why. Is it because you're tired of the problems you've been having with your computer the way it is now? Or is it because your computer works, oh, all right, but those newer ones that have the CPU that comes from the purple dancing guys in the fancy RV rig look so much better? To the point: Is the problem with your PC or with your perception of it (or your neighbors' perception of it)?

If your main complaint is how slow your programs are, you can do something about it without upgrading your CPU or adding more RAM. In the next two sections, you'll be introduced to alternatives to upgrading that you'll find throughout this book.

Check This Out...

Repairing: the bare truth Time for me to 'fess up: You don't actually "repair" a PC. At least, you shouldn't try. I mean, if the hard drive is giving you trouble, you don't pop it open and start poking around with a screwdriver. Instead, you try running various utilities (as described in Chapter 8, "Fixing Hard Disk Hassles") that reorganize and resituate the files on the hard disk, which hopefully will fix the problem. If the problem can't be fixed with what I call "repairs," then you replace it (a process you could call *upgrading* because most likely, the new hard disk you install will be bigger and faster than the one you had). So, bottom line: When I talk about "repairing" something in this book, I mean trying some simple tricks that might fix the problem without actually replacing (upgrading) the problem part.

Upgrading and Repairing Windows

Because Windows is probably the operating system you use (that is, unless you're among the less than one percent of users who still use DOS), then it makes sense that by making Windows better you can make your PC better at the same time. In this section, you'll learn about simple repairs you can make to Windows that might just fix a problem you've been having (and help you avoid an unnecessary upgrade).

General Computer Problems You Can Fix

Sometimes your only complaint is an odd problem with no known origin, such as strange buzzing noises, tiny blips onscreen, occasional computer lock-ups, and so on. Sure, these things might have little to do with Windows, but you can never tell. So, when you notice a problem, keep in mind that it might be symptomatic of a bigger problem, or (if you're lucky) the problem might be something as simple as a loose cable. Who's to know? Well, instead of guessing, check out Chapter 5, "Fixing Common PC Problems—Windows Style."

If you know that the problem is with your keyboard, mouse, printer, CD-ROM, floppy drive, sound card, or monitor, but you're not convinced that you need to replace it, you might be right. Check out Chapter 11, "Easy Repairs for Peripherals," for tips on how to get your peripheral up and running again.

Dealing with the Need for Speed: Making Your Computer Run Faster

If you don't have any specific problem with your computer other than its general lack of speed, you can do several things to get the old thing to move quicker. First off, you'll want to get the most out of your operating system (uh, Windows) by streamlining it. See Chapter 6, "Repairing Your Operating System," for help in that department.

Next, to make Windows run faster, jump higher, and go farther, make the most of the memory your PC has. For help maximizing memory, see Chapter 7, "Running Low on Memory? Unjam Your RAM." Also, reorganizing the files on your hard disk can make it easier for Windows to retrieve them (and quicker, too!). See Chapter 8 for how-tos.

Getting By with Less "Closet Space" (Hard Disk Space)

If you're running out of space for all those files you download off the Internet, but you're scared of having to open up your PC to add a new hard drive, then it's time to rearrange your closet (hard disk). Chapter 8 is filled with many easy things you can do to grab that space you need, regardless of which Windows version you use: Windows 3.1, Windows 95, or Windows 98.

Managing the Memory Muddle: Making the Most of the RAM You Have

Earlier, when I was talking about ways in which you could make your PC faster without upgrading, I mentioned that you might begin by making the most of the memory your PC has. Why? Well, because everything your PC does—every program it runs, every calculation it makes—is placed in memory first, so the computer can manipulate the data. Each program, in turn, grabs its own share of memory that it uses to keep track of its own stuff.

Windows especially needs a lot of memory. By making sure that your PC uses its memory wisely, you'll provide as large a working area as possible for Windows. And, with a bigger working area, Windows will be able to get more things done at the same time. Wondering how to perform this memory miracle? Chapter 7 has the details.

You'll also find details in Chapter 7 for increasing memory by grabbing some unused hard drive space. Sound impossible? Well, with Windows, it's easy.

Repairing Programs and Getting Them to Behave in Windows

Some programs just don't know how to behave. One minute, you're working in a word processor, typing along, and suddenly the cursor will freeze, preventing you from continuing (and possibly from even saving all the hard work you've done). Before you throw the program in the trash, see Chapter 5 for some quick fixes to common problems.

Repairing an Erratic Mouse, Keyboard, or Other Peripheral

Accidents can happen to anyone. For example, even the neatest person in the world has accidentally spilled a drink now and then. It's when that drink ends up decorating your keyboard and not the floor that you might be in trouble. As tragic as this sounds, however, it's relatively easy to fix. See Chapter 11 for steps to repair these mishaps.

Got a mouse that's lost its pointer, or a printer that won't print? Chapter 11 might hold the answer to your mystery. Got a monitor that's fritzing out, a floppy drive that's acting flippy, or a CD-ROM, sound card, or modem that's on vacation? Well, before you begin shopping for a replacement, make Chapter 11 your first stop.

What Can I Upgrade?

There aren't many limits to how you can upgrade your computer. For instance, you can upgrade your PC by adding something new to it, such as a CD-ROM drive. Or, as the need arises, you can replace an old part with something that's better or faster.

But what, exactly, can you upgrade or replace? This list tells you about some of the more popular upgrades and whether they're possible for your PC:

Replace the mouse or the keyboard. One of the easiest upgrades around. See Chapters 12, "Repairing a Funky Keyboard," and 13, "Replacing a Mangled Mouse," for the details.

Add a printer. Now's the best time to add that printer you've been eyeing. Prices are down, so a laser printer is now affordable (along with inkjets), and so is a color printer, for that matter. Besides, it's a simple upgrade for any computer. Jump on over to Chapter 14, "Choosing and Installing a Painless Printer," and give it a try.

Add memory. If your PC is slow and you use Windows, adding memory is your best upgrade. You won't believe the difference another 8MB of RAM makes, even on an old dinosaur. Check out the advice in Chapter 19, "Make Mine More Memory."

Add another hard disk, a tape backup, or other storage. If your hard disk's crowded, instead of copying files onto disk and then copying them back again when you need them, just bite the bullet and add another hard drive. Hard drives are relatively inexpensive and LARGE! (I'm talking several gigabytes here—each gigabyte equals 1,000 megabytes, or twice the size of most hard drives sold about a year ago.) While you're at it, add a tape backup, Zip, or Jaz drive to make protecting all that data simple. See Chapters 18, "Hands-On Hard Disk Replacement," and 23, "Maxi-Infra-Mega Storage Solutions."

Add a CD-ROM drive or sound card. To get current with today's programs, you need a CD-ROM drive to install most of them and probably a sound card to hear them. See Chapters 22, "Adding a CD-ROM or DVD-ROM Drive," and 24, "Sensational Stereophonic Sound."

Replace the CPU. If you have a need for speed, replace the CPU. For example, if you replace an old 486 with a newer Pentium, you won't believe the difference in speed. It's like going from a Taurus to a Ferrari. Sometimes, however, it's easier to replace the entire motherboard rather than the CPU itself. See Chapter 15, "Getting Your PC to Go Fast with a New CPU," for help.

Add a modem. A world is out there, and it's waiting for you. With a modem and some kind of online service such as CompuServe, America Online, or Microsoft Network, you can blab with friends, grab free software, and get more advice than a couple on their wedding day. Or, connect to the Internet and grab a world of information. See Chapter 25, "Adding a Fax Modem," for details.

Replace the monitor and upgrade the video. If you work in high resolutions, you get sharper graphics, but the trade-off is tinier toolbar buttons and icons. So do your eyes a favor and get a bigger monitor. Of course, you'll probably need to add a better graphics (video) card while you're at it. See Chapter 20, "Taking Advantage of Modern Video Capabilities," for how-tos.

Improve the power supply. After adding a new hard disk, CD-ROM drive, or other peripheral, you might find that you need to upgrade your PC's power supply as well. See Chapter 17, "Powering Up the Power Supply," for details.

Add PC to TV presentation capability. You've put in a lot of work on your computerized presentation, and you might even be able to close that deal, if you could only display it somewhere besides your crummy laptop monitor. Lucky for you, connecting your PC to a TV is fairly straightforward, with most devices connecting to your printer port. See Chapter 20 for help.

Add a video capture board. After you videotape your son's football game, your daughter's birthday party, or your company's annual summer picnic, why not use your computer to smooth out your photographic technique? Many so-called video capture boards create still-frame images from your videotapes, and some of the more expensive ones create digital movies. With accompanying software, you can warp images, morph between scenes, or add titles. You can then send the final product back to videotape, or out onto a Web page, presentation page, or even email. See Chapter 20 for the nitty-gritty.

You can upgrade or replace even more components, as you'll see in upcoming chapters.

The Laptop Liability

A laptop is like a PC that's been left in the dryer too long. If you have a laptop, I'm jealous. It's a mini-miracle that you can take literally anywhere.

Also, if you have a laptop, I'm sorry. It's a major headache to upgrade.

Why? Because you can only upgrade most laptops with special *proprietary* (a computer word that means "expensive") parts designed specifically for your laptop's make and model. So when you finally locate the correct part, it'll cost you plenty. Then you're stuck with the problem of actually getting the part into the laptop.

If your laptop computer was manufactured after 1994, then generally, adding peripherals such as a fax/modem or a hand scanner isn't so difficult. That's because newer laptops come with fancy slots called PCMCIA slots, into which you slip PC cards—peripherals with PCMCIA-compatible adapters. *PCMCIA* is short for Personal Computer Memory Card International Association. Many manufacturers make things that fit into these slots, such as CD-ROM drive adapters, external hard disk controllers, memory cards, modems, and so on. Just buy one of these gizmos, shove it into the slot, and bammo, it's installed (well, more or less).

Nothing is that simple

PCMCIA is not the beauty it appears to be. Although many cards say they are PCMCIA-compatible, there are at least three types, of the PCMCIA standard (four, if you count the yet-to-be-made-official Type IV). There's no guarantee that a card will work with your laptop. The best solution is to check with the manufacturer to see whether anyone has ever used the card you want to buy in your particular brand of laptop. Luckily, most laptops have more than one slot of different types (two type IIs and a type III, for example.)

If you hear of something with a CardBus adapter, it will probably work in your laptop's PCMCIA (PC card) slot. The CardBus standard is the 32-bit version of a regular (16-bit) PC card. ZV (Zoomed Video) is a new type of card that also works in PCMCIA slots. The card contains video images that can be played smoothly on the laptop's display—consider ZV a competitive technology to DVD-ROM.

Is It Worth Fixing or Upgrading?

Actually, that's pretty much up to you to decide. However, you should first consider whether you want to bother upgrading at all. For most older computers (pre-486), it's simply easier to throw them away and start over (and cheaper, too). I know this probably goes against the grain; after all, you hung onto that old toaster for three years, and now it makes a darn good doorstop. But really, new PCs are just too inexpensive today for you *not* to consider buying one instead of upgrading your old geezer.

Your laptop might not be the easiest thing to upgrade.

Does your upgrade make the grade?

The best way to find out whether an upgrade might fail on your system is to contact the manufacturer—not of your computer but of your upgrade—by phone or through its Web site. If that doesn't help, use an Internet search engine to look up the name of your upgrade and the brand name of your PC, to see whether someone's posted a message on some cyber-something network stating he's had problems, too, and need help. While you're on the Net, check out the Internet newsgroups that begin with comp.sys.IBM.pc. hardware. something. Also visit these Web sites: www.cshopper.com, zdnet.com and www. microsoft.com.

Your second consideration is your own tolerance for things that might not want to work right out of the box. (A couple of aspirin and the helpful hints you'll find throughout this book should ease the pain considerably, however.)

➤ Some major-name PCs are somewhat more expensive and/or difficult to upgrade than just the average built-in-someone's-garage model. Cases in point include Compaq Presario, Digital Equipment (DEC) Celebris, PS/1, PS/2, and some of the first IBM Aptiva models, along with some Gateway 2000 models. These are all quality machines, but they are often so full of proprietary hardware that parts made by other manufacturers just don't jibe well with them.

➤ Of course, everything's relative, but in my opinion, the most difficult upgrades include CD-ROM drives, CPUs, floppy drives, hard disks, memory, motherboards, power supplies, sound cards, tape backups, and video capture boards. For these upgrades, you'll have to open up the PC (no mean feat), insert the thing properly (without shorting anything out), and get it to play well with all the other devices already in your PC (sometimes, quite a headache-producing task).

➤ Money's always an issue, so keep in mind that the most costly upgrades include motherboards, video graphic cards, monitors, Jaz drives, recordable CD-ROMs, PC-to-TV converters, and video capture boards. Also, depending on the age of your computer, memory and CPU upgrades can be almost cost-prohibitive.

Before you open your wallet, be sure to check out Part II, which contains several easy things you can do to speed up a slow PC by speeding up Windows. Best of all, these tricks won't cost you a thing!

Check This Out...

There's no tellin' where the money went Beware of what many people call the "upgrade cascade." Sometimes upgrading one thing causes you to upgrade something else because the old thing is no longer compatible, or it's stinky slow. For example, if you go multimedia and add a CD-ROM drive and a sound card, you better have at least 8 MB of RAM to get the thing to work right. If you have only 4 MB, you'll find yourself adding more. See how the upgrade cascade works? On an old PC, you can quickly end up spending *more* on upgrades than you would on a new PC. The bottom line is, it's cheaper to get all the goodies you want in a new PC than to add them later.

PCs That Just Aren't Worth the Trouble to Upgrade

Deciding to scrap a PC rather than upgrade it is often a personal decision, like deciding to buy a new car instead of keeping the old one a few more years. So I can't really tell you what to junk, but I'll give you some leading indicators of old age.

➤ If your PC is an 8086 (XT) or a 286 (AT), donate it to a museum.

➤ If you own a PCjr, send it back to IBM.

➤ If you have a 386SX or 386DX processor (or compatible), you might be able to upgrade it to a 486SX *if* the old processor can come out (in other words, if it isn't stuck to the motherboard, or "surface-mounted"). In addition, your 386 would need to be "upgradable," meaning that it came with the wider, 486-compatible socket. Upgrading to a 486SX will speed things up...a bit. If you do find a 486SX processor, it will be a used one, and it should cost you about $20. However, the time and trouble it would take to locate your upgrade wouldn't really make it worthwhile, in my opinion.

➤ If your PC is a 486, consider scrapping it if the upgrades you're considering will cost you more than $400. You might be able to install a Pentium Overdrive processor; they're still available even though they're no longer being manufactured. Or you might be able to replace your 486 with a Pentium. But the cost might still be prohibitive, considering the fact that an entirely new motherboard with a faster processor might not even be a few hundred dollars more.

➤ If your PC is a Pentium, most upgrades will make sense, especially if you add a graphics accelerator. Pentium-based motherboards were designed with interchange-ability in mind, and that includes the CPU. If your PC is a Pentium II, you might not need to upgrade much, but if you do, it'll be worth it.

The Least You Need to Know

Deciding whether to upgrade a particular PC is sometimes a difficult decision because many factors come into play. Consider these:

➤ With a few simple repairs and a bit of maintenance, you might be able to improve your PC enough so that you can live with it a while longer without upgrading.

➤ If the programs you use today work adequately now and are likely to work ad-equately tomorrow, then even a major CPU speed upgrade might not even be noticeable to you. This is especially the case with programs that make quick calcula-tions, such as checkbook balancers.

➤ Some PCs are so old you can't upgrade them. Others aren't worth the trouble or the expense.

➤ Some laptops are just as difficult to upgrade as old PCs, because replacement parts are either too expensive, too difficult to install, or unavailable.

➤ When deciding whether it's worth upgrading a particular part, be sure to consider the expense, the difficulty factor, and your tolerance level.

➤ Beware of the upgrade cascade, a phenomenon that causes you to buy additional parts just to get the first part to work. For example, adding a new hard disk might force you to upgrade the power supply or add an additional fan.

Chapter 2

What Makes Your Computer Tick, and What It Takes to Upgrade Each Component

In This Chapter

➤ What lurks inside your computer

➤ The truth about your PC's guts: RAM, the hard disk, and so on

➤ What's involved in upgrading a particular component

A person has many parts—a heart that pumps blood, a stomach that changes food into energy, and a brain that processes information (but, in my case, not before 10:00 a.m.). A computer also has many parts, each serving its own function. The *system unit* (the big box that everything plugs into) contains most of these parts. Here's a quick lowdown on what you normally find inside a system unit:

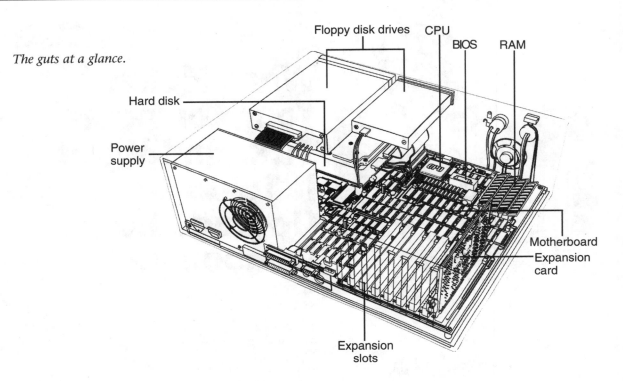

The guts at a glance.

Item	Description
Motherboard	Basically the "floor" of your system unit (that big beige box), the motherboard electronically connects all the other parts of the computer. In this way, you could think of the motherboard as being the nervous system of the computer.
CPU	Nicknamed the "brain," the Central Processing Unit performs all those fancy calculations. Upgrade this, and you can make your computer faster.
BIOS	If the CPU is the brain, then the Basic Input/Output System is the computer's "instinct." It's your computer's main program; it tells your computer how to run a program or read input from the keyboard or a disk drive. BIOS is also known as *firmware*, because it's the interface between the computer's hardware and its software.

Memory	Nicknamed "RAM(for Random Access Memory)," memory is the "work area" of the computer. Upgrade this, and the computer has a bigger area in which to work. A small part of your RAM is reserved for system use only; it's called system memory.
Data bus	This is the highway upon which data travels. Like all highways, your PC's interface has an inherent speed limit. To upgrade this, you have to replace the motherboard.
Hard disk	This is where the computer stores programs and permanent data stuff that you create and then save). Upgrade this and you can install more of those mega-do-it-all programs you love.
Floppy disk drive	A floppy drive enables you to transfer stuff from one PC to another, or to store data that you don't need on the hard disk all the time. PCs come with at least one of these, so you probably don't have to upgrade this unless yours breaks down.
Power supply	This is the thing that powers it all. After upgrading, you may find that you need more juice to run all your new toys. In that case, you can upgrade the power supply.
Expansion slots	These gizmos enable you to add new junk to your PC such as an internal fax modem, a tape backup, a CD-ROM drive, and so on.

The Motherboard Makes the Right Connections

The motherboard is a circuit board usually located on the floor of your PC (or to one side if it's a "tower" system). Every computer part has access to it, either directly or through a cable.

The motherboard is like a small city. Etched onto its surface are leads (pronounced "leeds") running from the CPU (a computer chip that acts like the brain of your computer) to all the other parts. These leads form an electronic highway called the *bus*. Like commuters at rush hour, computer instructions ride the data bus from memory, the hard disk, or wherever to the CPU and back again. (An instruction must go through the CPU—it can't go from memory directly to the hard disk, for example.) The data bus (or highway) weaves in, out, and around every chip on the motherboard, but at the end it forms a complete circuit—meaning, it closes itself and ends where it started.

Get on the bus.

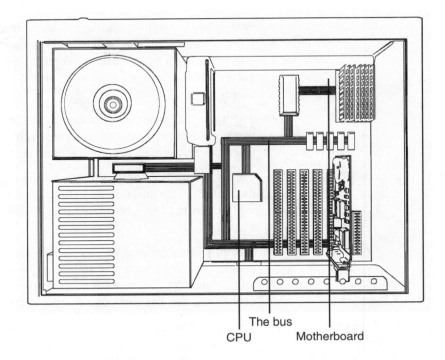

The bus

CPU   Motherboard

Your PC has a second, equally important bus called the *peripheral bus*, which is where all your peripheral devices and the expansion cards plug in. The peripheral bus connects to the data bus (or highway, if you prefer) at the peripheral bus controller (a chip that acts as a traffic signal for data going to one of the expansion boards.) This means that, unlike memory, BIOS, and a few other things such as the system clock, the items on the peripheral bus do not connect directly to the CPU.

Connected to the peripheral bus, and kept separate from the CPU's tiny world of memory, BIOS, and so on, is the rest of the computer universe—the display adapter, modem, printer port, hard drive controller, floppy drive controller, CD-ROM controller, and sound card. The peripheral bus controller serves as a liaison between all the expansion cards and the CPU. Data traveling between the CPU and some device will "transfer" as it were from one bus to another, at the peripheral bus controller chip.

In modern systems, the floppy disk and hard drive controllers are now part of the motherboard. But make no mistake, their hardware is still connected to the peripheral bus, even though their controllers are not located on expansion cards.

16 versus 32

The width of a bus is like the number of lanes on a highway. Most CPUs produced today have 32-bit, if not 64-bit, data busses. The data bus is the electronic highway over which data travels—from the disk drives or from memory—to the CPU.

Generally, however, your PC's peripheral bus is 16 bits wide (32-bit wide standards were tried, but largely failed). The peripheral bus is the electronic highway that connects the expansion slots and the ports on the back of your PC to the data highway. The connection is made at a chip called the peripheral bus controller. Anyway, what's the problem with the data bus being 32 bits, and the peripheral bus being 16-bit or maybe even 8-bit? It means that data being sent *out*—to your video or modem or printer or speakers—has to stop over at a special chip to get chopped in two (from 32 bits to 16), if not four parts, before it can fit onto the narrower bus going to the peripherals. This stopover is the virtual Chicago O'Hare of the computer world; it slows things down, *noticeably*.

One way that PCs get around this problem is to place certain high-intensity tasks (such as calculating and displaying complex graphics onscreen) on their own special highway leading directly to the CPU. This special bus is called a local bus, and every PC sold today has one. With a PCI (Peripheral Component Interconnect) local bus, for example, you don't have to worry that your computerized sales pitch will stop for a five-minute snoozer to gather more video data, giving your victims (uh, clients) time to sneak off. The PCI bus is wider (meaning: it carries more bits than the usual 16-bit peripheral bus), so data doesn't have to be chopped into sushi bits during the crossover from the data bus. (More on PCI later in the chapter.)

Why Upgrade the Motherboard?

First of all, some PCs come with CPUs that you can't remove, so there's no other way to upgrade them. (What's a *CPU*? See the next section.) Also, if you have an old PC (486, 386, and so on), then upgrading the motherboard is the only thing that makes sense. That's because upgrading the CPU alone will not solve a speed problem—data will just get bogged down by the motherboard's slow bus. Plus, for the relatively low price of a motherboard (under $500), you can essentially get yourself a new PC.

Why Not Upgrade the Motherboard?

Replacing the motherboard on a PC may seem like a quick fix for an old PC, and usually it is, but keep in mind that replacing a motherboard creates its own set of problems:

➤ *Everything connects to the motherboard, and if you replace it, you may have to replace a lot of other things as well.* If your PC is pretty old, most of your existing stuff probably won't work with a new motherboard. For example, the memory chips on an old 486 just won't keep up with newer SIMM memory modules. Also, the new motherboard may not be compatible with the type of expansion cards you use. For example, your existing video graphics card may not work with the new motherboard. (See the description of various expansion slot types later in this chapter for more information.) In addition, your hard disk may not be compatible with the new motherboard's on-board disk controller. Also, your various drives (hard disk, floppy, CD-ROM, tape, and so on) may use connectors that are incompatible with the new power supply. This isn't any real big deal, because you can get converters for them, but keep it in mind.

➤ *Where does everything go?* Replacing the motherboard means having to unplug everything and then deciding where each piece fits into the new motherboard—a nasty business at best.

➤ *Does it fit your system?* For most PCs, finding a motherboard that fits your case is easy, but some manufacturers use strange sizes of motherboards to make their PCs smaller—to give them, as they say, a "smaller footprint." You also have to make sure the motherboard you get has holes that match up with the ones in your PC's case. If you can't find a compatible motherboard, you'll have to buy a new case, and that can add to the expense of upgrading.

➤ *A motherboard is easy to break.* Especially if you shove it too hard, or if you're not careful of the leads (the electrical dohickeys) on the bottom.

The Brain of Your PC: The CPU

The CPU is the brain of the PC gang. Like a big brother, the CPU orders around all of its younger siblings: the hard disk, the floppy disk drives, the monitor, and so on, telling them what to do and when to do it.

If the CPU is a slow thinker, then things in PCland don't get done very fast. For example, if you can start your PC, get a cup of coffee, locate the last jelly donut, waste twenty minutes talking to Dan about his car problems, and return to your desk only to find that Windows is still starting up, then you've got a slow CPU.

CPUs have two numbers that help you identify them. The first number is the CPU type, such as 386, 486, Pentium (586), Pentium Pro (686) and Pentium II (786). A 486 is faster than a 386, and so on. Just in case you were thinking this is too easy, some chips have letters such as DX and SX. An SX chip is slower than the same type DX chip. For example, a 486SX CPU is slower than a 486DX CPU.

Don't throw out that old PC!

Intel makes most of the CPUs used in PC-compatibles. In 1989, Intel began making CPUs upgradable. Rather than throw out the whole computer when a faster CPU comes along, people can now take out the old CPU and plug in a new one (or in some cases, leave the old CPU in, and put the new CPU right on top of it, or into a socket alongside the original CPU).

For example, if you own a 486, you can upgrade it to a Pentium and effectively double or triple your processor speed.

Here's the lowdown on the SX/DX business

A 286 is just a 286, no SX or DX, thank you very much. A 386SX is like a 386DX (known to his friends as just 386), except that the 386SX doesn't "talk" as fast to the other PC components. A 486SX is like its cousin the 486DX (or just 486 if you prefer), except that it doesn't do math quite as fast. The DX chip was released first; then later on, the SX chip (such as the 486SX) was released at a lower price.

If you hear about a chip with the letters "DX2," it's a clock-doubled chip. This type of chip has an internal clock that runs at twice the speed of the motherboard clock. For example, a DX2 chip on a 20MHz PC runs at 40MHz. Megahertz, as you'll discover in a moment, is a way of measuring the speed of a CPU chip. Adding a DX2 chip speeds up the PC's processing, but not the speed of the data bus (that electronic highway which shuttles the data to and from the CPU). This lets you put a faster CPU on a slower motherboard *if you want*. Just keep in mind that, with a fast CPU and a slow data bus, your CPU is going to be sitting around twiddlin' its thumbs a bit more than you might like. Of course, because everything at CPU level takes place in milliseconds, you won't notice this slowdown *until* you compare your PC to a similar one with the same CPU, but a faster data bus. So...should you do it? Well, if you plan on keeping your old 486, upgrading the CPU will speed things up nicely, but not as much as a new PC.

A DX4 overdrive chip's internal clock can run at up to three times the speed of the motherboard. These clock-doubled (or -tripled) chips either plug in next to your existing CPU, or they replace it. Some even clamp onto the socket of your existing CPU without actually requiring you to pull out the old CPU first.

You may also hear of a 486SL CPU (L for Laptop), which is similar to the 486SX, except that it's smaller and it includes a feature that allows it to turn parts of itself off when necessary to conserve power. This makes it more expensive, but ideal for a laptop that just loves to run out of power at 20,000 feet when you're flying to a big presentation.

A CPU's second number, measured in megahertz (MHz), tells you how fast the CPU "thinks"—the higher the number, the better. For example, a 100MHz 486 CPU is faster than a 66MHz 486 CPU.

If It Only Had a Brain—the Lowdown on CPU Speed

The MHz does not measure the speed of the CPU's logic, but is a ticker that determines the pace of data shuttling through the CPU. Imagine someone feeding you raisins at the tick of a clock, and you'll get the idea. For example, in a 100MHz CPU, this ticker is counting off 100 million ticks per second, and the data inside is marching to that beat (or rather *grooving* to the beat if you believe the latest Intel ads).

So how much faster is a 100MHz processor than a 66MHz processor? The 100MHz processor is *somewhat* faster, but by how much depends on the application. Some spreadsheet operations take more time than most word processing operations, given the same CPU. How noticeable is the difference? For an accounting program, perhaps not very noticeable at all, whereas a graphics-intensive game may be significantly faster. Remember, all computers do simple math faster than we can blink anyway. So balancing your checkbook might take two thousandths of a second rather than three. But Mighty-Battle-Mega-Tron XII might just be 50 percent faster, if not more, due to a cascade effect in which faster operations (such as high-resolution graphics rendering) reduce the workload on future operations, making them faster in turn.

In summary: If you use your PC for math-intensive tasks such as creating spreadsheets, playing games, or manipulating complex graphics, then a CPU upgrade will improve your disposition more than if you just use a word processor.

Check This Out...

RU my CPU? If you want to know what kind of CPU you have, look at the front of your PC, which probably has a number on it like 4DX2-66, which means that you've got a 486DX2 CPU that runs at 66MHz. You can also open up the PC and look at the chip itself, although some chips don't have the speed marked on them.

Why Upgrade the CPU?

Because the CPU is the brain of your PC, upgrading it can make your PC faster. Also, upgrading a 486 to a Pentium is fairly inexpensive—between $100 and $300.

If you upgrade the CPU and the motherboard together, you can essentially get a new PC for a relatively low price: between $200 and $400.

Why Not Upgrade the CPU?

Upgrading the CPU may sound like the answer to a prayer, but remember that sometimes you may not always want what you ask for:

➤ *Installing the CPU may be a nightmare.* To upgrade, you *may* have to remove the old CPU and replace it with the new chip, or (if the CPU is a surface-mounted CPU and can't be removed) you'll snap the upgrade chip on top of your old chip. Both tasks must be completed without bending a single one of the bazillion tiny "legs" on the chip itself. Count yourself lucky if your PC includes what's known as an OverDrive socket, into which you push your new OverDrive chip—here, you don't touch the original CPU at all. Or, if your PC has a Zif socket, its quick release bar means you'll be able to snap out one CPU and snap in another.

➤ *You must find an upgrade chip that's compatible with your current CPU.* Upgrades for 486 and Pentium chips are readily available, but most are made to replace old Intel or AMD chips, so if your PC uses something different, it may be more difficult to find a compatible CPU upgrade.

➤ *There are limits to what a CPU upgrade can accomplish.* For example, you can upgrade a 486 to a Pentium, but that will not make it as fast as a Pentium PC of the same speed. You see, your CPU sends data back and forth over a data bus—a kind of electronic highway that the PC uses to send data back and forth. The size and speed of this bus limits what even a faster CPU can do in your PC. In other words, your CPU can think fast, but it will still be talking to real slow, real stupid PC parts. Of course, if you upgrade the motherboard as well as the CPU, you eliminate this problem. (But maybe not all your problems, because if all you upgrade is the motherboard and the CPU, you may still be stuck with an old, slow, hard drive, or an old, slow, video card.

➤ *You may experience problems with overheating.* Consider adding an extra fan—there are plenty that snap on top of the CPU itself, cooling it as it works.

➤ *Some systems don't take a clock-doubling upgrade very well, because it throws off the timing of their BIOS.* Clock doubling, you may recall, is where the CPU has an internal clock that runs twice as fast as the motherboard clock. Sometimes this doubling-thing doesn't match up too well with the internal clock, so an upgrade fails. Fortunately, upgrading your clock chip and the BIOS fixes this problem. Unfortunately, you may not be able to upgrade your clock chip or your BIOS (if they're soldered to the motherboard), or are otherwise nonupgradable.

➤ *The new CPU you want might not fit in your existing CPU socket.* At one time, Intel purposefully designed 486DX CPUs to be installed in sockets that were too big for them, for the express purpose of allowing owners to upgrade to the newer, bigger Pentium chip after it was invented. But the sockets that Pentium processors call home are not big enough to support the Pentium Pro. And the Pentium II doesn't even sit in a socket; it rests in a slot perpendicular to the motherboard, almost like a card. What's this mean, in English? Well, you can upgrade a 486 to a Pentium, but not to a Pentium Pro, or a Pentium II. In addition, you can upgrade a Pentium to a Pentium MMX, but not to a Pentium Pro or a Pentium II. Bummer. (For more detail on this bummer-business, read the sidebar coming up.)

The wrenching business of sockets

With regard to upgradable motherboards, there are four types of CPU sockets, all of which were designed by Intel. The earliest upgradable socket, designated Socket 4, is perfectly square and features four rows of *aligned* pins along the outside. A 486DX system with Socket 4 is upgradable, according to Intel, to a 66MHz Pentium OverDrive.

Socket 5 and Socket 7 are identical in appearance to one another, though Socket 7 has a variable voltage requirement. Both are slightly smaller than Socket 4, and sport five rows of *skewed* pins (unaligned) along the outside. These sockets were made for Pentiums, not 486s. But you can upgrade them to any Pentium or Pentium MMX processor that fits the socket. You may need to check with your motherboard manufacturer or with Intel to see if the processor you want is rated for use with your motherboard.

The Pentium Pro (the 686) series uses Socket 8, which is more rectangular than square, and larger than Socket 4. Its pins are bunched up mostly on two opposite sides. Intel claims that existing Pentium Pro systems will be upgradable to future editions of Socket 8-compatible CPUs. But Pentium IIs (786s) don't fit in Socket 8, or for that matter in a socket at all; instead, they sit in a sort of upturned drawer called Slot 1.

Um, Do I Need a Math Coprocessor, Too?

In the old days, hardly any PCs came with a math coprocessor already installed; you usually had to fork out the extra bucks (about $70) for one and put it in yourself. So if you own a PC with a 486SX CPU and you do large spreadsheets, keep giant databases, or play around with complex graphics (which take tons of math calculations to display), then adding a math coprocessor is worth the trouble. (Yes, in case you're wondering, there is a math coprocessor for lowly 8088, 286, and 386 CPUs, but if that's what you've got, you shouldn't bother upgrading the PC at all.)

One piece of good news, though: If your PC has a 486DX (not SX) or a Pentium, Pentium Pro, or Pentium II CPU, you don't have to worry about this math coprocessor business. That's because Intel and the other CPU makers finally got smart and built the math coprocessor function into their CPU chips. The built-in math coprocessor still handles math separately from the main functions of the CPU so it doesn't slow anything down, but you no longer have to buy a separate chip.

Just what coprocessor do I need?

If you're upgrading your 486SX system, then look for a 487SX math coprocessor (now called the DX2/OverDrive chip). Keep in mind that it doesn't do any good if your math coprocessor goes nuts and starts calculating its head off at a speed that's too fast for your CPU. So you'll need to match the speed of your CPU with the speed of your math coprocessor. You can use a faster math coprocessor in a pinch—although I don't know why you'd bother, because the CPU can't take advantage of the fact that the math coprocessor is faster. However, *under no circumstances can you try to use one that's slower.*

By the way, you won't be able to walk into a computer store and just pick up a math coprocessor. Most computer stores don't stock them. So you'll probably have to order it. Just be sure to tell the clerk what CPU you have, and its speed.

Basic Functions Are in the BIOS

BIOS is short for Basic Input/Output System, and it's a set of instructions that tells the computer how to "talk" to its friends: the keyboard, the hard disk, the floppy disk drives, the monitor, the printer, and so on.

The BIOS also plays the PC's butler—performing the lowly tasks that the computer doesn't want to waste its time doing. This includes basic input and output stuff such as paying attention to the keyboard or the mouse, reading and writing files, or displaying information on the monitor. Handling these simple chores gives the CPU time to breathe between calculating the square root of 234,567,483,094 and spell-checking a 200-page document.

The BIOS also handles repetitive tasks, such as the rigmarole the PC goes through to start up each morning. You see, when you start your PC, the BIOS checks everything out to make sure it's all functioning properly. For example, it checks out the keyboard to make sure that it's plugged in, and it checks out memory to make sure a RAM chip hasn't committed suicide in the middle of the night. This part of the BIOS, by the way, is called the POST, or *Power-On Self-Test.*

Name that BIOS Want to know what brand and version of BIOS you have? Just start your PC, and watch for a message onscreen like AMI BIOS (c)1992 American Megatrends.

Another important function of the BIOS is to kick-start the operating system (DOS, Windows 95, or OS/2 Warp to name a few). After the POST, the BIOS loads the operating system into memory and then tells it, "OK, George, I brought 'er in. Now, this baby's yours." From here, the operating system handles the big jobs, sending requests to the CPU. The lowly BIOS continues to run—fetching data, watching for key presses, and scanning for mouse movement.

The BIOS is stored on one or more ROM (read-only memory) chips, located on the motherboard (in newer systems, there is just one ROM chip called *flash BIOS,* because you can upgrade it in a flash, using an update file you might download from the Internet or obtain from the manufacturer). *Read-only* means that the stuff on the chips is meant to be permanent; non-nerds like you and me can't change it, accidentally or otherwise.

Why Upgrade the BIOS?

You don't normally have to upgrade your BIOS because it contains all the information it needs to run the major input and output devices in your system. What it doesn't know, it learns through *device drivers*, special files that supplement its language skills, as it were. For example, if you add a CD-ROM drive to your computer, you need to add a device driver as well, so the BIOS can "talk" to it. Other devices that might cause you to upgrade your BIOS include 3 1/2-inch disk drives, large hard disks (over 528MB), CD-ROM drives, Zip drives, tape backups, and SVGA monitors.

So with device drivers, do you ever need to upgrade your BIOS? Well, if you have an older system, you may notice when you add a fancy new part that its technology is so advanced that the old pokey BIOS just can't keep up, even with the help of a driver. In such a case, you'll need to upgrade the BIOS as well. By the way, since the BIOS is a bunch of chips, how do you upgrade them? Well, lucky for you, it's typically a simple software upgrade (part of the BIOS is stored in those chips, while the other part—the upgradable part—is contained in a file on the hard disk). In the case of newer, flash BIOS, you actually upgrade the chips themselves, using software.

It's not a speed thang

Keep in mind that replacing your old BIOS won't make your PC faster. It just enables it to talk to some new fancy gadget such as a 3 1/2-inch disk drive, large hard disks, IDE anything, SVGA cards, CD-ROM drives, and tape backups. A new set of BIOS chips, by the way, will cost between $30 and $100. A flash BIOS upgrade may not cost you a thing, because you'll probably be able to download it from the manufacturer for free.

Why Not Upgrade the BIOS?

Well, you may not be able to upgrade your BIOS. You see, not all BIOS chips are created equal; for that reason, you might not be able to simply throw a dart at a list of chips, buy the one it lands on, install it, and see daylight. Certain old BIOS chips are only upgradable with certain new ones. The packaging lists the serial numbers of the BIOS chips being replaced; but if you're ordering by phone, make sure you give the order specialist at least the brand name and year of your existing BIOS (from the POST screen you see when you turn your computer on). If there's a discrepancy, you might have to provide the serial number listed on the BIOS chip itself.

Also, keep in mind that some BIOS chips are soldered to the motherboard and are not upgradable (because they can't be removed and replaced).

The PC's Think Tank: RAM

RAM is short for Random Access Memory. RAM is basically the computer's work area. The computer stores data and instructions temporarily in RAM, where they wait until the CPU summons them. For example, when you start a program, your computer places the instructions that make up the program (literally a bunch of numbers) into RAM. The CPU then retrieves or "fetches" these instructions in sequence, as though they were written out on a long scroll or tape. Imagine this tape being fed through a series of virtual spools inside the CPU, with one or more virtual "heads" that read the instructions on this imaginary tape in one or more places, and you get a not-too-unrealistic idea of what goes on inside a CPU with the instructions from RAM.

Besides program instructions, data is also placed in RAM. When you use an application to create something, such as a letter to my editor telling her what a great book you think this is, your computer stores that letter in RAM so the CPU can make your changes to it.

RAM is not a permanent thing, however—that is to say, all the data and instructions that make up the contents of RAM are not permanent. When you "reboot" the computer (when you turn it off and on again using the switch that's on the computer itself), everything in RAM is erased. That means I'll never get to hear your wonderful words of praise unless you save your letter to the hard disk (or at least print it out) before you turn the computer off.

Megabyte
Memory today is measured in megabytes. A *byte* is the amount of memory it takes to store a single character, such as the letter "J." A kilobyte is roughly one thousand bytes, and a megabyte is roughly one million bytes. (Okay, if you've just gotta know, it's really 1,048,576 bytes.)

Now, because RAM is the computer's working area (or its desk, if you will), it places a limit on the amount of things you can ask your computer to do at one time—there's only so much room on that desktop. When you try to run a lot of programs without a lot of memory, Windows will shuffle stuff out of memory to the hard disk, and then back again when it's needed. By doing this, Windows reserves RAM for the stuff on which you currently need to work. This back and forth business really slows things down, believe me, since the hard drive is slower than the RAM. That's why adding more RAM is probably the best thing you can do for a computer. (More on Windows in Part 2, "Upgrading and Repairing Windows.")

The Different Types of RAM Chips

The type of RAM that constitutes the computer's "desktop" is *dynamic RAM*, or DRAM. Information stored in DRAM is made up of electrical charges, which degrade and decay when left to themselves. So, periodically, DRAM has to be dynamically *refreshed (hence, the name)* so all those bits don't literally blow away.

The other type of RAM (referred to scientifically as "The Other Type of RAM") is *static RAM*, or SRAM. Modern computers have a little bit of SRAM tucked away somewhere, in a location referred to as a *cache*. What makes SRAM different from DRAM is that SRAM uses fewer transistors for each bit of storage, so 1) it's denser-packed, and takes up less space; and 2), it doesn't need to have its contents refreshed as long as it's getting power, thus the term "static." SRAM is significantly faster than DRAM, and more expensive.

Why not use all SRAM?

For one, SRAM is too expensive right now to use as your PC's main memory. But more important than that, SRAM can't be mapped the same way as DRAM—meaning, for huge amounts of memory like 32MB, the CPU can't call an address from SRAM the same way as from DRAM. It would not be all that hard to make the CPU able to do that, except for the fact that today's CPU must access RAM the same way as *yesterday*'s CPU for software to remain compatible, so there you go.

Newer PCs use an improved DRAM chip called EDO DRAM, short for *Extended Data Out*. EDO DRAM chips are cheaper than SRAM chips, and yet they really zoom! In a strange sense, EDO is a purposefully *de-evolved* form of DRAM, with certain memory flushing safeguards removed, given that with Pentium CPUs, they are simply not needed. The details of this feature would bore the common sea snail. Suffice it to say that if your computer uses a Pentium and uses EDO DRAM, it cannot use any other type.

If your PC doesn't have EDO memory, it might have Fast Paging Mode. Like EDO, FPM is fast memory; faster because it makes intelligent guesses as to which page of data will most likely be needed next, and loads that into memory. FPM was replaced by the EDO standard.

Faster still than FPM and EDO DRAM is SDRAM or *synchronous DRAM*, a type of memory that synchronizes itself with the clock speed of the CPU (up to 100Mhz). Because clock speeds today are higher than 100MHz, possible replacements for SDRAM technology include RDRAM (Rhombus DRAM) and SLDRAM (SyncLink DRAM).

What's the cache?

Actually, your PC may have a few of these SRAM chips in its *cache*. A cache is a special area where the PC keeps data that it has been using a lot. The idea is that if the PC requests the data several times, chances are it will do it again, so why not keep the data someplace where the CPU can get to it fast? The data in the cache is constantly evaluated so it contains the data that was most recently accessed, under the theory that the data that will be accessed *next* will *most likely* be in the same block. When it isn't, the cache gets loaded with a block of data from the region that is being accessed currently, which does consume some time but not as much as fetching data directly from DRAM each and every time.

Various RAM chips.

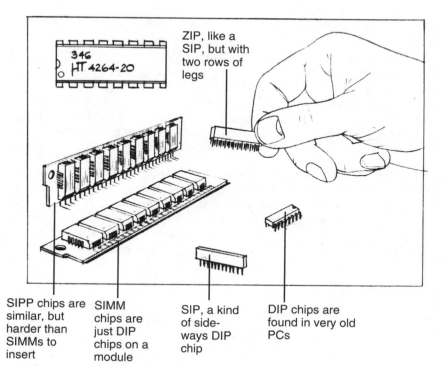

346
HT 4264-20

ZIP, like a SIP, but with two rows of legs

SIPP chips are similar, but harder than SIMMs to insert

SIMM chips are just DIP chips on a module

SIP, a kind of side-ways DIP chip

DIP chips are found in very old PCs

RAM chips are located on the motherboard in rows. If you're lucky, your PC comes with each row of chips prefabricated in one strip, called a *memory module*. There are two kinds of memory modules: SIMM, or *Single In-line Memory Module*, which features a row of surface-mounted DRAM chips on one side. DIMM, or *Dual In-line Memory Module*, features DRAM chips on both sides. If you upgrade your RAM, you can just snap in some modules, and you're done. If your PC doesn't use memory modules, then you're stuck inserting each chip in a row individually. (Ugh.) These single chips are called DIP chips, short for *dual in-line package*.

Memory modules are simpler to insert

DIP chips are bug-like, with tiny legs that have to fit exactly into the corresponding holes on your PC's motherboard. Ironic...this makes them little buggers to insert. The development of the SIMM was in direct protest to this nonsense; the chips are already "installed" on the SIMM, all you have to do is slip the SIMM into its slot. No chance for broken legs here.

There are three varieties of SIMMs: 30-pin with 9 chips, 30-pin with 3 chips (denser memory per chip), and 72-pin with 8 chips. The sizes of DIMM modules are all over the board, the smallest being a 72-pin model that has 32 pins and 8 chips per side, the middle having 144 pins and 16 chips split in two sides the same way, and by far the largest being a 168-pin 16-chip model that's a full 5 1/4 inches long. The 30-pin SIMMs are smaller; you can find these SIMMs in most PCs, except for the Pentiums, which favor the 72-pin variety. By the way, a 30-pin SIMM is mounted on a green circuit board, while a 72-pin SIMM is on a white circuit board, just to make it easier for you to correctly identify them.

There are other chip types as well, although they aren't necessarily popular. One, called a SIP (short for *single in-line package*) looks like a DIP chip on its side, but with only one row of legs. A ZIP (short for *zigzag in-line package*) is like a SIP but with two rows of pins. A SIPP (short for *single in-line pin package*) is kind of like a SIMM—but looks are deceiving. You can *easily* insert a SIMM into a slot, but a SIPP is much more difficult to insert, because it has legs just like a DIP chip which (yes, you guessed it) can easily bend by accident.

More Chips Don't Necessarily Mean More Memory

A series of RAM chips (or a single module with several RAM chips on it) works together to form a single segment of memory. For example, if your PC uses DIP chips, you might insert several 1MB RAM chips into an empty row on your motherboard; you may think that you're updating your PC by several megabytes because you're using so many chips, but instead, you're updating it by *only* 1MB.

It's more likely that your PC uses SIMMs rather than DIPs. Dealing with SIMMs makes it easier to understand this "it takes several 1MB chips to make up 1 MB of memory" nonsense. A SIMM or DIMM looks like a single unit of memory, although if you look at one closely, you can see that a 1MB SIMM really contains an entire row of these 1MB DIP-like chips. The simplicity of using memory modules is that when you insert a 1MB SIMM, for example, you add 1MB in a single step, instead of having to insert each of the separate DIP-like chips. There are a few exceptions to this simplicity, the most notable being some older PS/2 PCs and some newer Pentium systems requiring that SIMMs be installed in pairs; but sometimes, such requirements may actually be found printed on the motherboard itself. (See your user's guide for help.)

So How Much Memory Do I Need?

To run big programs and not have to wait a long time to do it, you need to have lots of memory. How much is enough? Well, some nerds will tell you there's no such thing as "enough" when you're talking about a computer, but for a Windows 95/98 computer, I think a good minimum is 16MB (that is, if you don't mind taking frequent siestas). Me, I run with 32MB.

If you prefer a more scientific method, check out the minimum requirement of the programs you want to run—you're not adding them together, you're just looking for the program that needs the greatest amount of memory. Now, take that number and double it.

How Do I Tell How Much Memory I Have?

To figure out how much memory you already have, watch the screen the next time you start your PC. As your computer gets its stuff together so it can face another workday, the POST (Power-On Self-Test) counts down the amount of memory you've got. Don't expect this information to be too enlightening, however. The number you'll see is usually shown in *kilobytes*, not megabytes, like most people think. To get the amount of megabytes your PC has, divide the number you see by 1024, which is the number of kilobytes in one megabyte. (Some newer PCs do indeed display their memory in megabytes, so be sure to look for the K or the M.)

The difference between RAM and "resources"

If you use Windows 95 or Windows 98, you may from time to time run across something called free "system resources." For instance, one dialog box may tell you that your computer has "32.0MB of RAM. System Resources: 60% free." Does that mean you have just over 19MB free? Of course not; that would make too much sense. In actuality, Windows allocates a portion of memory for the express purpose of remembering where everything else is in the rest of memory. This is the so-called "GDI memory." No matter how much RAM your computer really does have, Windows allocates exactly the same amount of memory for GDI—no more, no less. GDI represents Windows' "system resources." When GDI is full, Windows can't remember any more data blocks, no matter how much *free* memory you really have. Does this mean it might be pointless for you to upgrade your memory beyond a certain amount? Not really, because GDI "remembers" a 1MB graphic image the same way it "remembers" a 6KB icon.

So, for example, when I start my PC, I see the total add up to this number:

32,768

If I divide this by 1,024, I get 32MB. If your PC counts up memory too fast for you to read it, Windows can tell you. In Windows 3.1, open Program Manager's **Help** menu and select **About**. In Windows 95 and Windows 98, right-click **My Computer** and select **Properties**. Your PC's total RAM appears on the **General** tab.

Why Upgrade Memory?

I won't waste much time on this one, because I think I've already covered it pretty well. Basically, if you add more memory, your Windows computer will be able to handle more tasks at one time. Adding memory will make quite a difference in speed. This is the single most important upgrade you can do to improve system performance.

Enough said.

Why Not Upgrade Memory?

Actually, there's no reason not to, unless your computer is simply too old to bother upgrading at all. For example, if you've got a 286, 386, or a slower 486, I would think long and hard about upgrading the thing at all, since nowadays you can get a tremendously more powerful PC, *brand new*, for chicken feed (I've seen them for as little as $700, sans monitor.) Or, if you don't want to start completely over, you can get a new motherboard with a Pentium CPU for $250 or so, and although you may not be able to reuse your current memory chips in the new motherboard (it depends on their type), you will end up using considerably cheaper memory chips.

There's another point to consider, which involves computer capacity versus human capacity: There may be a point at which simply adding memory may be pointless for you. For instance, if your computer is used just for running the average spreadsheets, a 128MB computer probably won't give you any performance gains over a 64MB computer.

So the question here really becomes...

Can I Upgrade Memory?

Funny question. You may be thinking, "If there's a will, there's a way." But it's not always so.

First, you're limited by your CPU's capability. If you have a 286 or a 386SX PC, then your CPU can only handle a maximum of 16MB of RAM—but that's not much of a problem because you shouldn't bother to upgrade such an old PC anyway. As long as you have a 386DX, any type of 486, or Pentium, you can add up to 4GB (gigabytes) of RAM, which is probably way more than you can afford to put in the thing, anyway.

After you find out that your CPU is up to the job, your next problem is where to put the RAM. Memory is arranged on your PC's motherboard in *banks*. Depending on your motherboard, a bank is usually comprised of one, two, or four *rows* of memory chips, each of which is marked with a number, such as 0, 1, 2, or 3. Each bank functions as a *unit* unto itself. This means you can upgrade only in increments *of one bank of memory*.

To find out how much memory you can add, you'll have to open up the PC and see if you have any empty banks open. You might have several slots open, but you can only add as many chips or modules as there are slots in a bank, and no less. In other words, you either fill up the bank or leave it bare. A slot in a bank is comprised either of eight or nine individual chips called DIPs, or posts for memory modules (SIPPs or SIMMs).

RAM chips are found in banks.

Look Ma, no parity!

The nine chips correspond to the nine bits used in parity checking. Some PCs don't bother with parity checking, so they only use eight chips in a row of memory. Some PCs pack these cheaper non-parity checking memory modules, and they even bill it as a feature, "Now, with *no* parity checking!" Now you may think that removing parity checking is a bit of a stretch just to save a buck or two, but actually, it's quite safe. See, CPUs such as the 486 and Pentium contain advanced memory management that practically removes any chance of a parity error occurring anyway. If a problem does occur, the CPU will catch it long before any parity error-checking technique. Just don't try to use the non-parity checking SIMMs in a PC that doesn't have at least a 486 CPU.

Now, suppose your PC has two banks of memory with four rows each, and that it uses the new memory modules (SIMMs). If your PC is a couple of years old, it probably accepts only the 1MB or 4MB 30-pin SIMMs—so assume that's the case here. To upgrade memory, you have to fill a bank, and because your PC has four rows in each bank, you have to buy enough memory to fill those four rows. You can't mix and match the SIMMs you use in a single bank, so you'd have to fill your bank with either four 1MB or four 4MB SIMMs. This gives you either 4MB of memory (if you fill a bank with four 1MB SIMMs) or 16MB (if you use the 4MB SIMMs instead.) It also means that you can't add only 1- or 2MB of RAM to this PC—you have to add at least 4- or 16MB, because your PC only accepts 1- or 4MB SIMMs.

Pentium PCs and some 486s use 72-pin SIMMs, which come in a lot more varieties, including 512KB, 1MB, 2MB, 4MB, 8MB, and 16MB. This means you'll have more flexibility when adding memory to these systems.

Another problem you may run into is a motherboard whose banks are full. At this point, you can decide to replace your RAM chips with higher capacity ones. For example, in our sample system, you could replace the eight rows of 1MB SIMMs with eight rows of 4MB SIMMs, taking you from 8MB of memory to 32MB. You will probably be able to sell your old chips back, and save a bit of money.

You might also run across a situation where certain motherboards only accept certain memory configurations. You'll only be able to figure this out by looking carefully around the edge of the RAM banks for a series of marked posts called *jumpers*. These posts will be clearly marked with memory sizes, such as "8MB," "16MB", and "64MB." If those marked jumper posts are there, then the listed memory sizes are the only memory configurations that your motherboard can work with. The jumper posts are in pairs, with each pair next to a memory number. The pair of posts that is covered up by a small plastic doo-dad called a *shunt* indicates the number that is the current setting for the motherboard. Generally, if the shunt is absent, the motherboard won't work. If there are no jumpers or shunts, however, then the motherboard should be able to accept whatever full banks of chips or modules that are present.

If all else fails, try creating a virtual disk

Although some PCs offer only limited options when it comes to upgrading memory, these old dinosaurs do allow you to create a fake hard disk called a "virtual disk" or "RAM disk" out of what RAM they do have. This can at least speed things up a little. The idea behind a RAM disk is that you can copy files to the RAM disk just like any other drive, and the CPU can read those files quicker because they're already in RAM. The RAM disk is created when you boot up, and it's given a letter, just like any other drive, such as E. You copy data files to this fake drive E and then use those files. You're really using data that's already in memory, so getting to it is faster.

Because RAM is erased when you power down, however, a virtual disk can also be a nightmare. If you use one, make sure you copy your data back onto the real life hard disk before shutting down for the day, or all your stuff on the fake drive E will be lost.

When you don't have a lot of RAM, Windows offers a different option, called a *swap file*. When Windows runs out of memory, it copies data to the hard disk and then back again when needed. This slows down your PC, but it does allow you to work on more things at one time.

Can I Upgrade Memory on My Laptop?

Just as with any desktop PC, you need to check in your laptop's manual to find the limits to its memory upgrades. For example, you may be limited to 16MB right off the bat. Also, a lot of laptops use old CPUs that really don't benefit a lot from added RAM—in other words, they'll still be as slow as molasses. If you decide that you want to add more memory to your laptop, it may cost you more than you think because most laptops use proprietary memory chips designed for that particular brand of computer.

There aren't a lot of options for adding memory to a laptop. Basically, as long as there's a free slot, and you haven't hit the maximum capacity of the machine, you can add memory. The most common type of memory used on modern laptops is the 72-pin DIMM module, because it is so small and so dense. Chances are, if your laptop was manufactured no earlier than 1996, it will use this type of DIMM. The bad news is, many laptop units manufactured earlier than that may require unusual, perhaps proprietary, memory chips, or may not even allow memory upgrades in the first place. You'll need to check with the manual—or, if you don't have access to that, check with the manufacturer—to see just what your options are.

Your PC's Data Highway: Drive Controllers

The drive controller's job is to act as official interpreter between the PC and the hard disk. When the operating system requests a file, the CPU looks to a location at the very top of memory for the contents of that file, as they come in from the hard disk. It's the controller's job to grab (read) data from the drive when the PC needs it, and write that data to that area at the top of memory continually—kind of like an assistant throwing pages at you one at time, as you scan them quickly. The controller retrieves segments of data by moving the head to the requested cylinder, then waiting until it comes around to the next rotation of the disk, then using the read head of the drive to magnetically sense that data once it passes beneath the head.

There are basically four types of drive controllers:

ST-506. This is the oldest type of drive controller, introduced in 1980 by Seagate Technology. Somewhere in every PC is a portion of code that is capable of fooling the BIOS into believing that an ST-506 controller is really present, even if it's not; on many PC motherboards, a real ST-506 controller really does exist for compatibility's sake, even though it's connected to nothing whatsoever. ST-506 controllers are actually used only in very old PCs, such as the original XT. The AT versions of this controller are called WD1002 and WD1003; but the standard here is the same, and so is the connecting cable. (In case you're wondering, the "ST" stands for "Seagate Technology," and the "WD" for "Western Digital.")

ESDI. Short for Enhanced Small Device Interface, Maxtor introduced this type of controller in 1983. ESDI was supposed to replace the ST-506 standard, and to some extent it did, but it's pretty much an antique today. This was the first standard to widen the bandwidth for PC data to 16 bits from ST-506's 8 bits. It was a good standard, but it never had a chance to catch on because IDE (defined next) was mass-produced much sooner.

IDE. Short for Integrated Drive Electronics, because the controller is built into the drive itself. IDE is sometimes referred to as the AT Attachmentor ATA interface. At one time, this was the most popular drive controller sold. However, a new version of IDE, called EIDE (for Extended IDE) is what's featured in most PCs today. EIDE allows you to add larger hard disks than IDE, and more of them (four instead of two). Both IDE and EIDE are capable of controlling CD-ROM drives as well as hard drives, as long as the CD-ROM occupies the last position in the controller's chain— generally called the "slave position." (Okay, a CD-ROM can occupy the master position on the second EIDE controller. But not on the first, because that's the hard drive's position.)

SCSI. Short for Small Computer Systems Interface, a SCSI controller can control several types of SCSI devices at once (up to 7 for standard "narrow SCSI," or 15 for the higher bandwidth "wide SCSI"), including a hard disk, a CD-ROM drive, and a tape drive. The official SCSI standard is on its third edition (SCSI-3), and is working on a fourth. Although SCSI can be a lot faster, for PCs it often isn't thanks to recent EIDE advances; also, a SCSI drive is more expensive than an IDE drive, so upgrading to one doesn't always make sense. On the other hand, SCSI is sometimes more reliable than IDE, so you'll find them often used on big network servers. SCSI was invented for all types of computers, including PCs, Macintosh (where the standard is far more prominent), and UNIX; so a SCSI drive can work on any of these platforms. SCSI drives are often used in large networks because the standard allows the controller to be able to communicate—using a real language—more information about the data and about itself to the controller and to its host; IDE has no such language.

Why Upgrade the Drive Controller?

Because the type of controller your PC uses affects what kind of hard disks you use, you may decide to replace the controller to use a particular drive. For example, if your system uses an IDE controller, you may want to upgrade to an EIDE controller to take advantage of faster EIDE drives, or to have more than two drives in your system (EIDE can handle up to four). Why is an EIDE "controller card" different than an IDE "controller card" even though the cable plug is the same? The presence of one lousy extra bit used by EIDE to identify which drive in the chain is receiving instructions from the CPU is the only difference.

A separate drive controller also controls the floppy disk drives. It is generally not a card (the IBM PS/2 series is one notable exception here). Luckily, there's no alphabet soup here with regard to floppy controllers. You never have to upgrade your floppy controller, because there's literally nothing new to upgrade it to. A PC can control between zero and two floppies, and that's about it. (Some older IBM PS/2s can handle up to three floppies, although why you'd want three, I don't know.)

Why Not Upgrade the Drive Controller?

Because IDE controllers are limited to one or two drives, and EIDE can only handle four, changing your controller to SCSI may seem like a great idea. You could then attach up to seven SCSI devices to it (such as SCSI hard drives, CD-ROMs, IOmega Zip drives, and so on). Even so, you may run into problems because a lot of SCSI devices are incompatible with each other (of course, to solve that problem, you could add more than one SCSI host adapter.) If you stick with just SCSI hard disks on the same controller, however, you should be fine.

Your PC might not actually have a controller card

An IDE controller card is not a controller card. In fact, the controller for an IDE disk drive is on the drive itself. When two IDE drives are chained together (or four drives in the EIDE scheme), the first drive in the chain has what's called the "master controller," and the rest have "slave controllers." So what's the card? That's the interface connection necessary for your master drive in the chain to connect to the motherboard.

So if your motherboard has no IDE controller card although it has IDE drives (a genuine possibility), then the master drive in the chain must be connected directly to the motherboard. For most brands where this is the case, you can still install a so-called "EIDE controller card," and plug your master drive into the card rather than the motherboard.

Save It for the Hard Disk

The hard disk is where you store your permanent data, like programs, and the stuff you create with them, such as letters and things. When you look inside your PC at the hard disk, all you see is a boring metal case about the size of a sandwich. You can't see or touch the hard disk itself; it's protected against the smog, smoke, pollen, and other crud that you and I breathe everyday without even thinking about it.

If you could open up the hard disk, you'd see that it's actually a series of disks (platters) that look like CDs suspended on a central hub. These platters are coated with magnetic particles to form a pattern that, when translated from the ancient Sanskrit (okay, the bits and bytes), forms your data. Read/write heads float between these platters, eagerly waiting to grab this data when you request it.

Read and write Reading is the process of retrieving data off a disk. Writing is the process of saving data onto a disk.

The master hard disk is often connected to the motherboard through a controller card that plugs into one of the expansion slots. Expansion slots are found along one side of the motherboard; you plug a card (a controller card, a modem, a network adapter card, or whatever) into one of these slots to connect it to your computer. (More on expansion slots in a minute.)

Some computers come with removable hard disks—mostly for security reasons. Press a release button, pop out the hard drive, and then hide it with your diamond tiara so no one can snoop through your stuff. By the way, the computer should be off when you're performing all these shenanigans. Also, if your computer has a removable hard drive, it makes upgrading to a larger capacity disk a simple task.

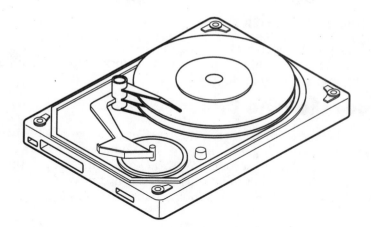

The guts of a hard disk.

Partitioning and formatting your hard disk

How exactly does a computer save data onto a magnetic disk? Glad you asked. First, you have to understand that your computer usually treats the hard disk as one unit, although you can divide the hard disk into smaller units called *partitions*. Each of these partitions is assigned a letter, such as C. For your computer to start using a new hard disk, you have to partition it using a command called FDISK. Basically all you're doing with FDISK is telling the computer the size of each partition, which, like I said earlier, is usually the same as the actual hard disk itself. For example, if you decide to add an 800MB hard disk to your PC, you can treat the whole thing as one drive or partition, or divide it into two partitions (such as C and D).

After you partition a hard drive, you format it. Formatting is a process that divides the platters into cylinders, tracks, and sectors. A track is a circle on which the hard disk actually places the data. Each track is divided into parts called sectors. When the hard disk saves a file, it divides that file into segments that fit into the individual sectors. Now, imagine all the platters of a hard drive stacked atop one another—which is, after all, where they actually are. A cylinder is a cross-section of all the platters at the same track location. The location of a file is kept in something called the FAT, or file allocation table, which is located on the second sector of the hard disk, just after the master boot record which makes the hard drive work in the first place.

Why Upgrade the Hard Disk?

This one's easy: If you need more room for your programs or data, you gotta add a hard disk. You might be thinking of adding a Zip or a Jaz drive instead (or something similar), but a hard disk is the cheapest kind of storage you can buy.

Why Not Upgrade the Hard Disk?

Here again, the question becomes whether or not you *can* add a hard disk. There are several things to look for, depending on whether or not you're adding a drive or replacing your existing one. If you're adding a second drive, you have to find a drive that works well with your first drive. If you don't mind ditching your first drive, you open up more options, but you still have to find one that's compatible with your PC.

Do you really want to do this?

Another factor here is whether or not you feel up to the task of replacing or adding a hard disk to your PC. If you're replacing your old hard drive, you have to take the old drive out, of course. This usually means removing some other stuff so you have enough room to remove the drive.

You then slide the new drive into the empty drive bay and, in a lot of cases, you add an expansion card called a *drive controller* to run the new drive. After you connect the new drive, you have to *set up* the drive. This can get pretty nerdish, so you may want to bribe a guru to help you out here. If you have to brave the depths of CMOS, FDISK, and FORMAT yourself, don't despair—I'll provide the necessary help in Chapter 18, "Hands-On Hard Disk Replacement."

If you want to replace your hard disk, the easiest thing to do is to get the same kind. Here are some tips, based on your current drive type.

If Your Original Drive Is an ST-506 Compatible

First, some ST-506 systems are so old, you may not want to mess with upgrading them at all. But if you have a 486 you want to hang on to, then go for it.

Because finding an ST-506–compatible drive will be difficult if not impossible (and even if you do find one, its capacity will be so small and its speed so slow that you'll wish you hadn't), you should think seriously about replacing the drive controller with something else, such as IDE. Really. Staying with the antiquated ST-506 standard is a waste of time. IDE is cheap, fast, and popular, so you won't run into a problem getting help for the drive when you need it. Unfortunately, this means spending a bit more money, but IDE controllers are fairly inexpensive.

If you decide on IDE, you need to make sure that your new drive will work in your system. As long as you're upgrading at least a 386, you'll be fine.

If you decide you like SCSI, you can go that way, too, but the drive will cost you more. Also, you have to add in the cost of a SCSI controller, which is much more expensive than an IDE controller. However, a new SCSI drive can be a lot faster and perhaps a bit more reliable than an IDE drive. Also, if you haven't already added a CD-ROM drive or a tape drive to your PC, you can buy SCSI versions and gain some speed. It's important to note that SCSI is not a hard drive controller per se, just a device controller that happens to work with hard drives.

If Your Original Drive Is an ESDI

Like ST-506 drives, ESDI drives are hard to find (think: dinosaur), so again, you're better off upgrading to a newer technology such as IDE or SCSI. If you do find an ESDI drive for your system, make sure you get one that's not *too fast* for your existing controller.

If Your Original Drive Is an IDE

If you've got an interface to an IDE drive, either on a so-called controller card (actually an interface card) or on the motherboard itself, get an IDE/EIDE (AT Interface) drive. They're inexpensive and easy to find. If you have one of the newer IDE interfaces (EIDE), you can plug up to four IDE/EIDE drives into it—with an IDE interface, you can have two drives. (With a modern BIOS on your computer, you can, if needed, add a second IDE "controller card" to your system to handle a third and fourth hard disk.)

> **Techno Talk**
>
> **Why can't I find an ST-506 drive?** Drives that work with the ST-506 drive controller are identified by their encoding schemes: FM, MFM, or RLL. You can learn more about those if you want, after you've been given the proper medication.

Check This Out...

IDE or EIDE?

If your PC has an IDE controller, you can use an EIDE drive with it, but it won't be as fast as it should be. Upgrade to an EIDE controller if possible, by removing your old controller, or, if the controller's on the motherboard, by disabling it.

If you decide to buy a SCSI drive for your system for some reason, you'll need a separate controller for it, and you'll probably have to get rid of your IDE drive because the drives will just get into a fight. (Okay, the drives like each other just fine, but the two controllers won't get along too well.) You may be able to get the two to get along if you set up the IDE drive as the boot drive (drive C) and the SCSI as the secondary drive.

If Your Original Drive Is a SCSI

Here, if you're adding another drive, you pretty much have to go with SCSI. SCSI devices connect to each other in what's called a *daisy chain*—kind of like holding hands for a game of whip.

Unfortunately, you can't assume that your existing SCSI controller will work with both your old and your new SCSI drives. Some are just incompatible. That means you may have to buy an additional SCSI controller for the new drive. If you're replacing your old SCSI drive, you shouldn't run into a problem.

If you want to use your SCSI controller with other drives, such as IDE, make sure that it uses WD1002 emulation, which in English means it supports the ST-506 standard. WD1002 was the first hard drive controller that IBM installed in its 16-bit ATs (ST-506 was the first to be installed in its earlier PCs). But even though the WD stands for Western Digital and the ST for Seagate Technologies, the WD1002 is really a 16-bit version of the ST-506.

With a Floppy Disk, You Can Take It with You

Floppy disks (also known as floppy diskettes, or simply *diskettes*) are wonderful little marvels that enable you to copy data onto your PC's hard disk and to copy data back off. You use disks to copy new programs onto your computer's hard disk. You can also use them to copy your own data from the hard disk onto a disk, in case something ugly happens to the originals. When you fix the something ugly, you can then copy your original data back onto the hard disk.

Don't forget to back up!

Data loss is the number one totally rotten thing that can happen to a computer user. To protect yourself, create a *backup*, which basically involves copying the hard disk's data onto something else, such as a series of floppies. If you have a lot of important data (and with today's large hard drives, it's easy to have a lot), you can install a tape backup drive to back it up (see Chapter 23, "Maxi-Infra-Mega Storage Solutions," for information about doing this), or you can use a large capacity removable media drive, such as a Zip or Jaz drive (again, check out Chapter 23 for help). It's a lot easier than using a bunch of disks, believe me.

Basically, disks are small, portable, plastic storage squares. *Disk drives* (or diskette drives) are slots located on the front of your PC; insert a disk into the proper size slot, and the disk drive reads the data on the disk. You can also write data to a disk; this is one way you get data from your PC to somebody else's PC, such as a coworker's.

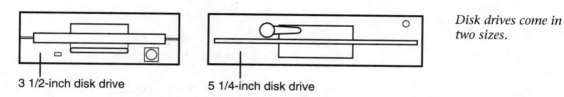

3 1/2-inch disk drive   5 1/4-inch disk drive

Disk drives come in two sizes.

Disks come in two sizes. The larger size, 5 1/4-inch, is not used very much anymore because the smaller size, 3 1/2-inch, actually holds more data (go figure). In addition, the 3 1/2-inch disk is better protected (it doesn't require a paper sleeve). If your PC has only a 5 1/4-inch drive, you can add a second disk drive in the more popular 3 1/2-inch size. A 5 1/4-inch disk is floppy, which means that you can bend it (but of course, don't actually do this, because it ruins your data). This is where the *floppy* in floppy disk comes from. The term "floppy" isn't used much anymore, because the newer and more popular 3 1/2-inch disks are hard. (At least on the outside.)

Disks also come in several *densities*. The denser the disk is, the more data it can hold. That's because the data is more densely (or more closely) packed together on the disk. A *high-density disk* holds more data than a *double-density disk* of the same size. For example, a double-density 3 1/2-inch disk holds 720KB. A high-density 3 1/2-inch disk holds twice that amount, 1.44MB.

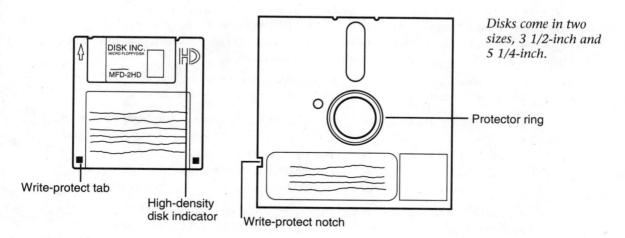

Write-protect tab

High-density disk indicator

Write-protect notch

Protector ring

Disks come in two sizes, 3 1/2-inch and 5 1/4-inch.

Why Upgrade My Floppy Disk Drive?

You pretty much need a 3 1/2-inch drive to survive and to be compatible with the world today—the older 5 1/4-inch disks are getting harder and harder to find. So if your PC only has a 5 1/4-inch drive, you'll probably want to add a 3 1/2-inch drive to it (assuming your PC isn't so old that upgrading it doesn't make any sense). Also, software is sold only in that 3 1/2-inch size (that is, if it's sold on disk at all, and not on a CD-ROM), so upgrading makes sense.

Of course, if your disk drive has gone kaput, replacing it is probably your only option.

I'm your density

How can you tell a double-density disk from its high-density counterpart without sticking it in a drive and doing a directory listing? Well, hopefully, they're marked. If not, on a 3 1/2-inch disk, you can look for the *high-density disk indicator*—a little hole on the opposite side of the write-protect notch. On a 5 1/4-inch disk, it's a little harder to tell. I usually just look at the big hole in the center of the disk. If I see a protector ring (kind of a white edge along the inner part of the hole), then the disk is double-density. If the protector ring is not there, then the disk is high-density.

Why Not Upgrade My Floppy Disk Drive?

Today, there are a lot more options than adding a 3 1/2-inch drive to your PC. For example, you might add a Zip drive instead, and get a larger capacity (100MB) for your removable storage option. (You'll learn about Zip drives later in this lesson.) There are other removable storage options as well, such as LS-120 (120MB) drives, but they're not as popular as Zip drives, so if compatibility is an issue...

But if you still would like to add a 3 1/2-inch drive to your system, you might not be able to, depending on whether or not your computer meets all these conditions:

Does your system have an open drive bay? A drive bay is a slot in the front of your PC's case through which you'll access the new drive. If you have an empty slot, a plastic cover the color of your PC's case is hiding it. If your PC doesn't have an open bay, you can buy a combo drive that contains a 3 1/2-inch and a 5 1/4-inch drive—of course, that means you'll have an old 5 1/4-inch drive that you can no longer use...

Will your DOS version support a 3 1/2-inch drive? Actually, if you have Windows, your DOS is new enough that it will support a 3 1/2-inch drive, so don't sweat it. If you don't use Windows, then check your DOS version by typing **VER** at the DOS prompt and pressing **Enter**. As long as your DOS version is DOS 3.3 or higher, you'll have no problem running the new drive. If your DOS version is lower than 3.3, you'll have to upgrade, because your DOS is so old, it just won't be able to understand the technology behind 3 1/2-inch high-density drives. If you want to use the new extended-density ED 3 1/2-inch drives instead, you're going to need DOS 5.0 or higher.

What's DOS got to do with it?

DOS is short for disk operating system, and for a long time, it was the King Commander of your PC. But now that Windows has inherited the kingdom, whither goest DOS? Well, Windows 3.1 simply placed a prettier picture on DOS—DOS was still the operating system of the PC. But with Windows 95 and Windows 98, DOS is no longer part of the picture—at least, as far as the basic operations of your computer are concerned. You can still access DOS, or at least, a simulation of DOS, through the Windows' DOS prompt, but that simulation is only there for backwards compatibility, in case you need to run some old DOS program.

Will your BIOS support a 3 1/2-inch drive? If your PC is really a dinosaur, you might also have to upgrade its BIOS to accommodate your new drive. The BIOS is a set of chips on the motherboard that handles all the boring input and output tasks. Reading data from a floppy disk falls under its job description. If the BIOS is old, again, it may not know how to deal with the newer 3 1/2-inch drives. One way to get around this problem is to buy a new drive controller with a chip that can handle the drive for the BIOS; however, some very old PCs won't accept help in this manner. Another way is to find a software program called a *driver* that does the same job. Or you can simply update the BIOS itself. To tell whether or not you'll need this kind of upgrade, start with your PC's manual. If it refuses to shed any light, then try the CMOS. What options does it include under floppy drives? If you find out that you have to upgrade the BIOS to support your new drive, see Chapter 16, "Replacing the Motherboard," for help in dealing with the BIOS guy.

What type of connector does your system require? Although this won't stop you from adding a floppy disk drive, it could make it more difficult. Some older systems use pin connectors (they look real similar to the ports on the back of your PC, except they're square), while new floppy drives use edge connectors (with a flat edge and gold leads). However, new drives come with a converter that allow you to connect them to pin connectors.

Are you trying to add a drive to a laptop? I have yet to run across the laptop computer that did not already have a 3 1/2-inch drive installed. You do

What's CMOS?
Pronounced "sea-moss," CMOS contains configuration information about your PC. When your PC starts, CMOS is what tells the computer it has so many disk drives, so many hard drives, so much memory, and so on. CMOS also helps your PC keep track of the current date and time.

43

not need a second disk drive on a laptop; trust me on this one. Should you require a 5 1/4-inch drive, because laptops do not typically have open drive bays and certainly none that big, you'll need to buy an external floppy drive and connect it through a cable to the back of the laptop. Which, of course, you'll have to disconnect when you need to pack up the laptop and take it with you, making the whole thing rather inconvenient to say the least. Rather than adding onto a laptop, you may want to consider adding a drive to your desktop unit (a docking port into which you plug your laptop, effectively converting it into a desktop PC). For one, it's cheaper, and two, you probably use your desktop PC more often anyway.

The Kings of Removable Storage

Besides the usual hard disk drives and floppy disk drives, there is a plethora of storage options for your PC:

Iomega Zip and Jaz drives. By far the most popular option for removable storage today, these drives are easy to install and use. A Zip disk (which looks like a 3 1/2-inch disk, only slightly bigger and fatter) can store up to 100MB of data. A Jaz cartridge stores 100MB or 200MB (depending on which type you buy), or 1–2GB (gigabytes). Disks for a Zip drive cost between $10 and $20 depending on how many you buy, while a 1GB Jaz cartridge costs between $89 and $120, and 2GB cartridges cost $140–$170.

CD-ROM, CD-R, and CD-RW drives. With a CD-ROM drive, you can read CD-ROM discs, which are flat, circular discs similar in size to musical CDs (which, by the way, a CD-ROM drive can also read and play). If you want to record data on a CD-ROM, you need a CD-R (CD-Recordable) or a CD-RW (CD-Rewritable) drive. With CD-R, you can record data one time onto a permanent CD-ROM. You might use such a drive to save documents and files for safe-keeping. With CD-RW, you can resave data over and over again onto a CD-ROM disc. Equipping your PC with a CD-ROM drive nowadays is pretty much a necessity, because most software comes only on CDs. CD-R and CD-RW drives are still fairly expensive, but useful for people who deal with large files on a daily basis, such as graphics files. They are also effective as a backup solution for large hard disks. CD-ROMs, by the way, can store up to 650MB of data.

Tape backups. These drives use cartridges similar in size and shape to musical cassette tapes on which they record your data. Because of their large capacity (from 3–20GB), tape backups provide a perfect solution to the problem of protecting your data. With a tape backup, you can periodically store copies of your data files, and then restore them to your PC when and if they ever become damaged or lost.

Magneto-optical (MO) drives. These drives use a technology that combines the best of CD-ROM and floppy disk drives. MO drives store up to 120MB of data on disks that are similar in size to 3 1/2-inch disks—in fact, they are designed to read 3 1/2-inch disks in addition to MO disks, so you can think of them as a replacement for your existing 3 1/2-inch drive.

DVD-ROM drives. A new guy on the block is the DVD (Digital Video Disk) drive. With one of these puppies, you can play DVD discs, which bring high-quality MPEG video and digital audio to your desktop. And if that wasn't enough, they can read CDs too! For now, DVD-ROM drives are read-only, but a standard for a read-write "DVD-RAM" is coming soon.

Why Add Removable Storage?

With today's large hard disks, it makes sense to have some type of backup storage solution. That way, if something happens to an original file, you can copy it from backup onto your hard disk again. Tape backup drives and CD-R or CD-RW drives are good for this purpose. Jaz drives are useful for making backups as well.

If you need to take data with you (to a client's office, for example), or if you need to share files with your coworkers, then having some type of removable storage is a must. For some people, a common 3 1/2-inch disk drive will do the trick. If, however, you deal with files larger than 1MB, you'll need another solution. Here, Zip drives, Jaz drives, and MO drives fit the bill.

Why Not Add Removable Storage?

When adding any type of drive to your system, you'll run into the same kinds of concerns:

Do you have an open drive bay? If not, most removable storage options come in an external drive version that you can connect to a parallel or SCSI port on the back of your PC.

Do you have an open connector to a controller for the drive? This question is only a factor for tape backups and CD-ROM drives. Some tape drives connect to your floppy disk controller card, so you need to have an open connector to it. Other tape drives connect to a SCSI controller, or to your parallel (printer) port, while still others are equipped with a controller card of their own. CD-ROM drives require an open connector to your IDE/EIDE (hard disk) controller, to whichever IDE drive may be acting as the master (if you haven't designated the CD-ROM as the master), to a SCSI controller card, or to a sound card such as one of the Sound Blaster series that also acts as a SCSI controller.

Do you have an open SCSI port? Zip, Jaz, magneto-optical, and some tape drives all come in a SCSI version that connect to a SCSI port. (These drives also come in a parallel version that connects to a parallel port, sharing the port with your printer, so having an "open" port is not really an issue.) You can have up to seven devices connected to a SCSI port, but most PCs do not come with a SCSI controller, so you'll have to buy one if you go this route. If your system already has a SCSI controller card, you'll need to check to make sure there's an open connector to it.

Are you connecting the drive to a laptop? Devices connect to laptops through their PCMCIA ports. You'll be able to find CD-ROM drives with PCMCIA connectors, but Zip, Jaz, CD-R, CD-RW, tape backups, and magneto-optical drives are not available this way. To connect one of these drives, you buy a SCSI version of the drive, and a SCSI controller that connects to your laptop through one of its PCMCIA ports. These SCSI controllers can run you an extra $100 to $200, but they can run up to three SCSI devices.

Does your power supply have enough juice left for another device? Granted, a power supply is easy enough to replace with one that cranks more voltage. But you shouldn't try installing as big a power drain as a CD-MO drive to have to find that out, because overstressed power supplies have been known to do detrimental things to almost any device hooked up to them at the time.

Techno Talk

PCMCIA what?

PCMCIA is short for Personal Computer Memory Card International Association, and a PCMCIA card (or PC card for short) is used to connect external devices to a laptop computer. A PCMCIA connector is about the size of a credit card, and it fits into a slot on the side of the laptop. The beauty of this single interface is that it's simple to connect any device to a laptop—simply plug it in. The ugly of this single interface is that not a lot of devices come with a PCMCIA connector. Also, most laptops have only one or two PCMCIA slots, limiting their expandability. In addition, there are several standards, Type I, Type II, and Type III (with Type IV on the way), making compatibility with older laptops a big pain.

Expanding Your PC's Capabilities: Expansion Slots

Located at the back of the system unit is a row of slots called *expansion slots*. Expansion slots enable you to expand the capabilities of your computer. Plug something into one of these slots, such as a modem or a sound card, and the computer can use it.

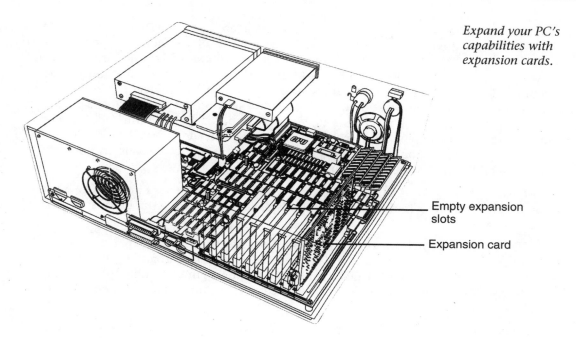

Expand your PC's capabilities with expansion cards.

Empty expansion slots

Expansion card

Of course, nothing in life is that easy. Expansion slots come in several types, and you've got to get a card that fits into the type of slots your computer has. (More on that in a minute.) Also, your computer has only so many of these expansion slots, so when you use them all up, that's it.

What can you find already occupying some of your computer's expansion slots? Well, a video card that controls your monitor, for one. You'll also find one or two disk drive controller cards that control your hard disk and the floppy disk. You may also find an I/O (input and output) card that provides a serial and a parallel port on the back of your PC. Now, it's quite possible on newer, less expensive systems that any or all of these controllers are built into the motherboard. But all of these controllers were designed to be placed on expansion *cards* first, and may have been retrofitted to certain motherboard brands later.

The list of cards that may occupy an expansion slot inside your PC is huge: You may have a card that runs your mouse (or the connector may run directly off the

Expansion cards The things that you plug into expansion slots are called *expansion cards*. Sometimes you'll hear someone call them expansion *boards* or even *adapters* instead of cards.

Any-port-in-a-storm Ports are connectors at the back of your PC. Think of the various ports a ship visits to pick up or deliver cargo—in this case, the "cargo" is data. Through the ports, data enters and leaves the system unit. For example, you connect a printer to a port so you can print data.

motherboard). You may have a modem, a network adapter, or a joystick controller. If you add a CD-ROM drive, you may need something called a SCSI (pronounced "scuzzy") host adapter or an ATAPI IDE controller to run it, or it may run off of a sound card. If you add a scanner, there's a controller card for that (unless you get a scanner that connects to your parallel port). Want to edit your own videos or watch TV onscreen? That's another couple of cards. If you work at home, you can add a telephony card to manage those irritating sales calls. If you're a musician, you may want to add MIDI interface for your digital musical instruments. And believe it or not, you can add an extra fan to cool your system with an extension fan card. Sometimes you can save a few expansion slots by buying a multifunction card that combines several functions in one.

Now, earlier I told you that there are several types of expansion slots in your PC. Again, you have to remember to match up the right size card to fit in the size expansion slot you want to use.

An 8-bit card has a single tab on the bottom which fits into an 8-bit expansion slot. "Eight bits" describes the amount of data that can travel from the card to the CPU in a single clock *cycle*. Eight bits is equal to one *byte*, or the length of a single character. Most PCs today don't use 8-bit slots because they are too slow, but you'll find them on old 286s and 386s.

You can, if needed, insert an older 8-bit card into a 16-bit slot. 8-bit slots, by the way, are known as ISA (Industry Standard Architecture) slots.

*An 8-bit expansion
card and slot.*

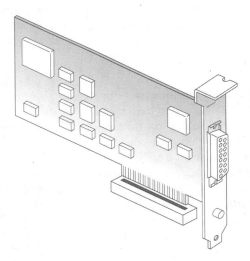

16-bit expansion slots are the most popular today. A 16-bit expansion card has two tabs on the bottom which fit into a 16-bit slot. A 16-bit card is twice as fast as an 8-bit card, because it passes twice as much data to the CPU with each cycle. A 16-bit slot is also known as an ISA (Industry Standard Architecture) slot. You'll find 16-bit ISA slots on 386s, 486s, and Pentiums, Pentium Pros, and Pentium IIs.

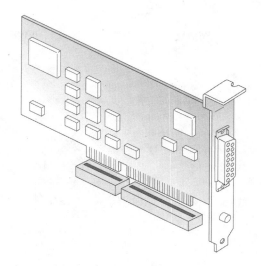

A 16-bit expansion card and slot.

Cycle

Everything happens in a computer within a cycle. For example, if you read a file from the hard disk so you can make changes to it, then the hard disk reads a small amount of the file per cycle, until it reads the entire file. The speed of the computer's CPU determines the number of cycles per second in the computer.

EISA is short for Extended Industry Standard Architecture, and it's not terribly popular. An EISA slot is 32-bit, so it's fast, but not a lot of companies make EISA cards. An EISA card has two tabs on the bottom. You won't find an EISA slot in your typical run-of-the-mill PC, but if you bought a PC from your employer, and it was an expensive one (at least at the time your office bought it), then it may have EISA slots. An EISA slot will support an ISA card, by the way. EISA faded off the radar around 1991 mainly because it was too expensive for manufacturers to implement.

VESA is short for Video Electronics Standards Association, and this type of slot is a direct link to the CPU. VESA local bus (known to his friends as VL-bus) is usually used for video. Updating today's cool graphics onscreen is a boring, time-consuming task, so video is one of the most important things to benefit from this direct link to the CPU. For example, if you're into the new video-in-a-window stuff, this kind of card actually makes the video seem not-too-boringly-slow. Like EISA, it's also a 32-bit expansion slot. VESA cards have four tabs on the bottom. You used to find VL-bus slots in just about every PC sold a few years ago, but nowadays you're more likely to find PCI slots (wait, I'll talk about them in a minute) instead.

An EISA expansion card and slot.

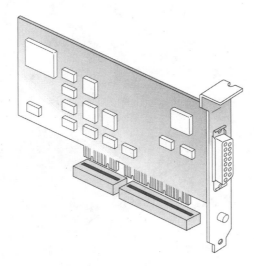

A VESA expansion card and slot.

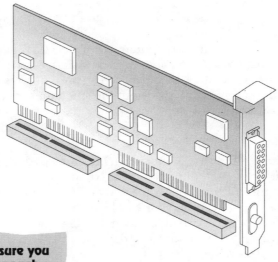

Check This Out...

Make sure you have enough slots Before you start buying things to expand your PC, you need to count the number of open slots and then fill them with the to-die-for items first. That way, you don't run out of slots before you add something you consider critical.

You can find MCA (short for Micro Channel Architecture) slots on older IBM PS/2 computers. Like EISA, MCA slots are also 32-bit. MCA never could catch on, mainly because its creator—IBM—would only license the standard to other manufacturers for a fee, and even then required that they be reimbursed for a percentage of each MCA card sold wholesale. So as even an amateur analyst might expect, not a lot of companies made MCA expansion cards. MCA cards have two tabs on the bottom, but they're different sizes, so they don't fit into anything but an MCA expansion slot. Furthermore, ISA cards do not fit into an MCA slot, unlike EISA.

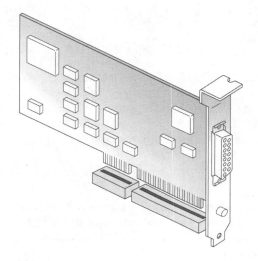

An MCA expansion card and slot.

PCI is short for Peripheral Component Interconnect. You find PCI slots on 486DX4 and nearly all Pentium and Pentium II computers. PCI cards are 32-bit, and they have two tabs on the bottom.

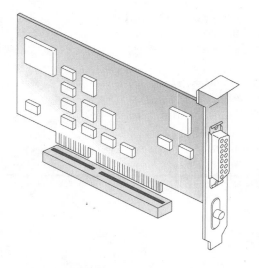

A PCI expansion card and slot.

51

But I have a laptop!

Well, laptops don't come with expansion slots per se, but with PCMCIA slots. These slots make it easy to insert one thing (such as a CD-ROM drive) and later replace it with something else (such as a modem) as your needs change. You insert what is essentially a credit-card–sized expansion board into one of these slots to "install" the device that's attached to it.

There are several PCMCIA standards; laptops usually come with several Type II and Type III slots. Type III are mostly for removable hard disks, and Type II handles everything else. You need to make sure the upgrade item on your list comes in a compatible PCMCIA type to fit the slots your laptop has. The easiest way to do this is to contact the manufacturer of your laptop.

Just in case you don't think all this slot business can get any more confusing, you should know that some cards work with slots other than their own. Confusing? This table helps:

Slot	Kind of PC in Which You Find It	Types of Cards It Takes
ISA	286, 386, and 486 PCs, also Pentiums, Pentium Pros, and Pentium IIs	8-bit or 16-bit cards
EISA	Mostly Power PCs, and some network servers	EISA and 16-bit cards
VESA	Mostly 486 PCs	VESA (VL-bus) and 16-bit cards
MCA	Most Older PS/2s (models 50 and up)	MCA cards only
PCI	Pentium, Pentium Pro, and Pentium II	PCI cards only
PCMCIA	Laptops	PCMCIA cards of the right type

Your PC's Video System

You spend most of your day staring at your PC's monitor (and the other half, staring at the TV), so it makes sense for your PC to have the best video system that you can afford. Your computer's video system may be comprised of these parts: a video graphics controller (graphics card), a graphics accelerator (which may or may not be separate from the main card), a local bus linking the video controller to the CPU, graphics production capability inside the CPU itself (that's what the "MMX" is about in the corner of some of the new Pentium logos), and, of course, a monitor. MMX, by the way, is short for MultiMedia eXtensions. On most PCs built within the last few years or so (486s and Pentiums), you'll see the video local bus—a direct data highway connecting the CPU and the graphics card. This local bus (think of it as the data express) allows graphics data to get processed more quickly, speeding up the time it takes for images to be displayed on your monitor. Until very recently, every video bus has used its own dedicated RAM called VRAM. AGP, a new standard for accelerated graphics, uses your regular memory.

Look out for AGP!

Short for Accelerated Graphics Port, AGP is the newest twist on video technology. In some Pentium II PCs, you may find your old graphics card usurped by a dedicated video bus called AGP. On such a system, your monitor plugs into the usual SVGA port on the back of your PC, which is connected to the AGP. Through it, video signals are shuttled straight from the CPU to the monitor, bypassing the usual graphics card. This speeds up the amount of time it normally takes for graphics to be displayed.

One drawback is that an AGP system does not use dedicated VRAM (video RAM). Instead, AGP uses regular memory to calculate the image to display. So you need to have extra RAM on your PC so this video calculation won't get in the way of the programs you want to run. The plus is that RAM is real cheap, and VRAM is not. So cramming some extra RAM into your system (I'm talking a minimum of 32MB here) won't cost you an arm and a leg, yet you still end up with blazingly fast video graphics. Also, when you deal with VRAM, you run into the limits of the video card—each card is designed to hold only so much VRAM, and that's it. With AGP, you don't have that problem, because there's no real limit on system RAM.

Except for the video bus (if your PC has one, that is), all the components of the video system can be upgraded. Before I can talk to you about what you should upgrade to, let me tell you a bit about the various video standards out there, and what they mean:

MDA, CGA, and EGA. MDA, or monochrome display adapter, is an old monochrome standard that only displays text, not graphics. CGA, or color graphics adapter, was the first color video standard; it displays text in 16 glorious colors, or graphics in two to four colors. Old XTs have CGA monitors, which are like glorified TV sets. EGA, enhanced graphics adapter, came later and improved on CGA somewhat; it can display both text and graphics in 16 colors. The original ATs use EGA monitors, making them the first digital color monitors designed specifically for use with a personal computer.

Hercules Graphics Adapter. The first high-resolution monochrome video standard, HGA, is still in use by a surprisingly large number of systems. In the 1980s, color was expensive, so buyers settled for monochrome—and Hercules was monochrome. In addition, the monochrome standards at the time provided much higher resolutions than color. If you bought a used computer from a bank auction, there's a two-in-three chance it uses Hercules Mono. Hercules is still a major manufacturer of video cards, but unlike the old days, today's Hercules brand card *is not a Hercules Graphics Adapter card*—it's an SVGA card. If you look hard enough, you can find an HGA replacement card for very little money.

VGA (Video Graphics Array). VGA made its first appearance in 1987, increasing the number of available colors to 256. VGA is by far the most common video mode in use today. Monochrome monitors have recently been adapted to use VGA; so a new high-resolution mono monitor needs a VGA card (not necessarily SVGA), and VGA cards are cheap.

8514/A. This is the first very-high-resolution graphics array, although relatively limited in color. If you're using an IBM PS/2, and the pixels (the dots on the screen that make up the images) look really small, then you may be using 8514/A graphics.

XGA (eXtended Graphics Array). IBM's be-all, end-all graphics array that was supposed to put VGA to shame, but it never really got accepted as a standard. Some IBM-brand monitors require an XGA adaptor.

SVGA (Super Video Graphics Array). SVGA takes the more common VGA mode and improves upon it. SVGA gives you the capability to display more colors at higher *resolutions*. SVGA is today's standard; all monitors sold today use it.

One of the more confusing aspects of upgrading video of late concerns the distinction between a "graphics card" and a "graphics accelerator." Due to creative marketing, this distinction is rapidly fading. Many of the more expensive graphics cards tout themselves as accelerators, when at one time the two items were separate entities unto themselves. Suffice it to say that most so-called "accelerator cards" today are also graphics cards in and of themselves, with the acceleration technology built-in.

So what's resolution?

Well, the image you see onscreen is made up of tiny dots called pixels. A screen's resolution is determined by the number of pixels that appear on the screen. Common resolutions include 640×480 (that's 640 pixels across by 480 pixels down), 800×600, 1024×768, and 1280×1024. At lower resolutions, there are fewer pixels to fill the screen, so they're bigger and fatter. At higher resolutions, there are more pixels, which are smaller, so they provide finer detail to an image.

What is this acceleration technology? Basically, it consists of much of the programming and instructions necessary for graphics-intensive programs (read: "games") to render exquisite images, transferred from software onto hardware (namely, ROM chips). This makes rendering such images substantially faster, especially when the manufacturers of such graphics-intensive binary code (read again: "games") agree to commit themselves to this new hardware standard so their programs can benefit. So-called "3D accelerators" contain in hardware much of the programming necessary to render detailed, three-dimensional, moving images.

To make use of accelerator technology, you really need a computer with a modern CPU—namely, a Pentium no slower than 133MHz. In other words, your CPU has to be fast enough itself to be able to drive the accelerator—sort of like, when your automobile has to be going at least 45 MPH for your turbocharger to kick in.

Why Upgrade My Video?

If something breaks, obviously, you'll need to replace it. But unless you're using an SVGA monitor, you should also consider upgrading your video system even if nothing's broken—that is, if you happen to like your eyes and you'd want to be able to continue to *see* out of them.

With a good SVGA monitor, you can get rid of that annoying flicker, stop squinting, and actually *see* what it is you're working on.

Why Not Upgrade My Video?

To get the best image, you need to match up a good video card with a good monitor—meaning, in almost every scenario, you'll most likely need to replace *both* your graphics card *and* your monitor. For example, if you're currently looking at an old EGA or CGA monitor, and you hate it, you'll need to replace both the monitor and your video card because you can't mix and match video standards. For example, you can't buy an SVGA monitor and try to hook it up your old EGA card.

Check This Out...

Update the card, too Keep in mind that VGA and SVGA monitors produce an analog signal, which of course you can't connect to older MDA, CGA, or EGA video cards (which produce digital signals), even though you might want to try. So updating just your monitor and not the card isn't a likely scenario.

If you have a VGA monitor, you can replace your old VGA graphics card with an SVGA (accelerator) card if you need to, and not replace the monitor at all. However, you won't see any improvement in resolution (the monitor controls the upper limits of that). Also, you may only see a small improvement in speed because the card has to step down to VGA mode to work with your monitor; in some situations, you may even experience slower speeds. So again, your best bet here is to upgrade to an SVGA monitor and a good SVGA graphics card.

The Power Supply and Battery

Inside the system unit is a big gray box with lots of wires running out of it, connecting it to, well, basically everything. This gray box is the power supply. Unless you bought your PC off a truck from some guy who talked in a whisper (and who offered to throw in a Rolex for an extra $50), your PC already comes with one of these.

Now, why does the computer have an internal power supply, when you plug it into the wall? Well, the power supply takes your ordinary household current (AC) and "gentlizes" it to the lower voltage current (DC) that your computer's delicate parts prefer.

A typical power supply.

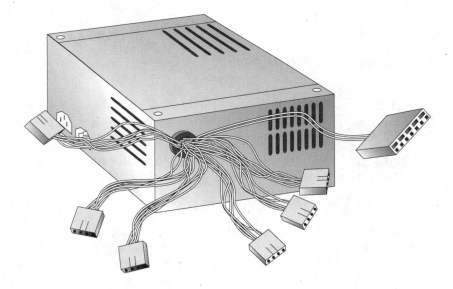

The power supply also contains a fan, which cools down your PC's components. This is very important, especially if your PC has a fast CPU, such as a Pentium.

So why should you concern yourself with the power supply? Simple. If you start adding tons of stuff to your computer, you may need to upgrade the power supply as well. Standard wattage is 180, but if you have a big system, you may need 220 watts or higher.

A shocking fact Don't ever, ever open the power supply box to try to "fix" it. Doing so (even with it unplugged) may fix you dead.

Besides the power supply, there's also a battery in your PC. What for? Well, it powers a tiny chip that helps the PC remember important stuff even after you turn it off, such as the current date and time (and other CMOS stuff). Most batteries last about 10 years before you have to replace them.

How to Tell When You Need to Replace Your Power Supply

Old XTs had a small 135-watt power supply. Older PCs had even less power, more like 63-watts. However, most PCs today have a power supply that puts out 200 to 250 watts. To keep all the PC parts happy, match your computer's needs to the power supply:

PC Part	What It Needs to Stay Happy	Your Totals
3 1/2-inch hard drive	5 to 15 watts	_____
5 1/4-inch hard drive	15 to 30 watts	_____
3 1/2-inch floppy drive	5 watts	_____
5 1/4-inch floppy drive	10 to 15 watts	_____
CD-ROM drive	20 to 25 watts	_____
1MB of memory	5 watts	_____
Average expansion card	5 to 15 watts	_____
Monitor (if powered by the PC)	35 watts and up	_____
Motherboard	20 to 75 watts	_____
286 CPU	20 to 40 watts	_____
386 CPU	25 watts	_____
486 CPU	35 watts	_____
Pentium CPU	35 to 40 watts	_____

Use this table to add up the total number of watts you're currently using. Then, whenever you want to add some new gizmo to your PC, add in the number of watts it needs to determine if you also need to upgrade the power supply. Of course, you can fudge a little, because a lot of devices don't actually suck any power until you use them—this includes things like the floppy drives and CD-ROM drives. A general formula for calculating wattage is voltage times amps.

If you try to start your PC and nothing happens, it may be a power supply problem, but it's hard to tell. One thing to listen for is the fan—if the power supply is working, the fan is on. If you're not sure if you hear the fan or not, hold your hand at the back of the PC to see if you feel any air coming out.

Before you jump to any conclusions, however, test the wall outlet to see if it works. If it passes the test, unplug your PC from its surge suppressor and plug it directly into the wall to see if it works. If it does, the problem's with the surge suppressor. Reset the surge suppressor and try it again.

If your power supply peters out, it may be that it got zapped by a lightning strike. If you don't use a surge suppressor, this can happen. After you replace the power supply, make sure you get a good surge suppressor to protect your PC from damage in the future.

If your PC can't remember what day it is when you power up or if the CMOS settings keep turning up missing, it probably has nothing to do with your power supply—instead, the CMOS battery is going out. Remember that the battery is what helps the PC remember what stuff you've installed and what day it is, even after you turn the power off. The power supply keeps things going once you turn on the PC. If you decide that the battery is the problem and you need to replace it, see Chapter 16 for help in that department. (Keep in mind that some PCs have batteries that are not replaceable; instead, you replace the entire motherboard every 10 years or so—yech.)

If you change the battery and the PC keeps forgetting the date or the CMOS settings, you may have a weak power supply—so weak that it can't keep the battery charged.

If your PC's parts keep burning themselves out, the problem isn't that your power supply is putting out too little power, but *too much*. In any case, it's time to replace the power supply.

The Least You Need to Know

Before you attempt to upgrade a PC, you should know at least a little about how it works, such as:

➤ The motherboard is the "floor" of the system unit, and everything connects to it.

➤ The motherboard uses an electronic transportation system, called a bus, to transfer data back and forth between devices.

➤ The BIOS handles routine tasks such as reading and writing data, updating the monitor display, and monitoring keyboard and mouse activity.

➤ RAM is the working area of the computer. Add more RAM, and the PC can handle larger workloads.

➤ You use the hard disk to store permanent data, which is connected to either an IDE, SCSI, or EIDE controller card.

➤ To take data with you, copy it to a floppy disk. There are other removable storage options you can add to your PC as well, including Zip and Jaz drives, CD-R and CD-RW drives, tape backups, and magneto-optical drives.

➤ Your PC's expansion slots enable you to connect new devices easily.

➤ Your computer's video family contains up to four members: the monitor, the video graphics controller, the video local bus, and VRAM.

➤ The power supply converts ordinary household current into a lower voltage current that the delicate parts of your PC can handle.

Chapter 3

Now, Let's Find Out What Kind of Computer You Have

In This Chapter

➤ What's hanging around behind your computer

➤ Serial and parallel ports revealed

➤ Things you can learn about your PC by just nosing around

➤ Simple ways to get MSD to tell you what it knows about your PC

➤ The secrets Windows keeps

➤ Pulling CMOS (vital system information) from your PC's innards

After months of sweating over the decision, you finally made an investment of your hard-earned money (or at least money you hope to hardly earn) and bought a computer. Now the decision is over, the computer's installed, and you've seen your software actually running for a minute or two. So why not relax, because after all, the hard part's over, right?

Wrong.

I know. I know. You're thinking, why should I worry about what makes the thing work when the sales guy promised that all I had to do was switch the computer on, "point and click" on some corny little picture, and everything would happen automatically?

The problem is that now you have the urge to run some new software and to do that, you'll probably have to install Windows 95, or even Windows 98. So you march down to the local computer store, and, as you're standing in the checkout line, you glance at the System Requirements list on the back of the box, only to discover that your one-year-old computer is now an antique. In other words, your PC is going to need an *upgrade* just so that you can install Windows 95 or Windows 98.

Or maybe you decided to bypass the Windows 95/98 madness, but your mouse starts going on the fritz. Or maybe your boss just told you that you're being transferred to Outer Nowhere, and you're going to have to "telecommute" by modem with your co-workers in the office.

In any case, like it or not, one day you'll realize that the computer store guy lied, and you really do need to know how the dumb PC works because now you have to upgrade it. As much as you might want to, you can't just take it in to some computer store and say, "Upgrade this thing," because at the very least, you'll have to tell the guy *what* to up-grade. Plus, the more you know, the less likely you are to pay $500 for a $50 part. Luckily, learning more about your PC is what this chapter is all about.

Check This Out...

Relax...this is not an SAT

At this stage in the game, don't feel badly if you can't complete this entire list, or even understand what you're supposed to put in most of the blanks. You'll learn more about your computer as you go along. If you want a head start on this list, try locating your PC's original in-voice—it'll help you fill in many of the blanks. Also look at the front of your PC and other devices for model names and numbers. For example, a model number 486SX/ 33 tells you that you have a 486-33MHz CPU. Copy down as much as you can, and then use the tips in this chapter to learn more.

Compiling Your Own Checklist

Before you even start thinking about upgrading your PC, you need to know some things about your computer. For example, you need to know what kind of CPU it has, how much memory it has, and how things are currently set up. This kind of information will help you tell whether you can actually do the kind of upgrade you have in mind on your particular PC. Vital stuff to know *before* you start actually tearing things apart, don't ya think?

After you've done some serious snooping using the tips you find in this chapter, be sure to complete the following list as best you can:

Equipment	My PC
PC brand/model (for example, Dell)	_____
CPU (for example, 486SX/33MHz)	_____
BIOS (for example, AMI, 11/11/92)	_____
Operating system (for example, DOS 3.3)	_____
Total RAM (for example, 4MB)	_____
Type of RAM chips (for example, 120ns DIPs)	_____
Maximum amount of RAM my PC can handle (for example, 16MB)	_____
Hard disk type (for example, Conner IDE)	_____
Hard disk size (for example, 340MB)	_____
Second hard disk type	_____
Second hard disk size	_____
Disk drive A: (for example, 5 1/4-inch)	_____
Disk drive B: (for example, 3 1/2-inch)	_____
Removable media drives (Zip, SyQuest, LS-120, etc.)	_____
Total number of drive bays (for example, 4)	_____
Number of unused drive bays (for example, 2)	_____
CD-ROM type (for example, NEC Multispin6x SCSI)	_____
CD-ROM controller settings (for example, IRQ12)	_____
Monitor type (for example, VGA)	_____
Video card (for example, Hercules Graphics)	_____
Modem type (for example, USRobotics14.4FAX ext.)	_____
Modem settings (for example, COM2 IRQ3)	_____
Number of expansion slots available (and their type: ISA, PCI, etc.)	_____
Network software/version (for example, Novell NetWare 4.01)	_____
Network card settings (for example, DMA 4)	_____

continues

continued

Equipment	My PC
Mouse type (for example, Logitech serial)	_____
Mouse settings (for example, COM1 IRQ4)	_____
Tape backup type (for example, Mountain 350MB)	_____
Tape backup setting (for example, DMA 5)	
Sound card type (for example, Sound Blaster 16)	_____
Sound card settings (for example, IRQ7 DMA 3)	_____
Other (for example, game adapter)	_____

In this list, you probably see many terms you don't understand, including COM, DMA, and IRQ. You'll learn about many terms as you go along, but I will discuss these three right now.

➤ *COM* refers to a COM or serial port. Each COM port is assigned a particular I/O address and IRQ that enables the PC to communicate with the device assigned to that port. Serial devices, such as a modem, mouse, or serial printer, are assigned to these ports. Internal serial devices such as an internal modem also use a COM port. Your PC can have devices assigned to up to four COM ports, although, for the most part, only two can be in use at any one time. So knowing which COM port your various serial devices have been assigned to helps a lot when troubleshooting a problem with a new device.

➤ *DMA* is short for Direct Memory Access channels, and they're the high-speed communications channels your hard disk, floppy disk drives, tape backups, network cards, and sound cards use.

➤ *IRQ* is short for interrupt request. Various devices use IRQs as a kind of tap on the shoulder to the CPU to gain its attention. The system timer, keyboard controller, COM ports, LPT ports, hard disk controller, floppy drive controller, and so on use IRQs. So fighting to get your new device a free IRQ is the number one cause of hair loss. In addition, many devices stake out particular I/O address (a particular area in memory). When you install a new device, you might run into a conflict if that device tries to use an address that some other device calls "home."

For help setting ports, DMAs, IRQs, or I/O addresses, see Chapter 27, "Fiddling with Ports, IRQs, Addresses, and Such."

What You Can Discover by Looking at the Outside

As you learned in Chapter 2, "What Makes Your Computer Tick, and What It Takes to Upgrade Each Component," PCs are named after the CPU (or "brain," if you prefer) they contain. For example, if your PC has a 486 CPU, then it's known as a 486 PC.

A 386 CPU is newer than a 286. A 486 is newer still, and the 586 (otherwise known as the Pentium) is the latest and greatest. As you might expect, newer generally means faster. Sometimes I say the CPU is the "brain" of your computer, which is all well and good, but it's really more correct to say that it's the "engine" of your computer. If you think of the Pentium (or 586) as the computer equivalent of a V8 engine, then that makes your 486 like a V6, your 386 like a four-cylinder, and a 286 like...well, a gas-powered weed-whacker.

By now you're probably wondering what kind of "engine" your PC has. You'll learn the answer to that question later in this chapter, but for now, let's see what you can discover about your PC by simply looking around.

> **Should I upgrade?** For the most part, that question was answered in the last two chapters. But to recap: Always try to repair your PC first. Then, if you have a Pentium or Pentium II, upgrade it to your heart's content. If you have a 486, don't spend more than $400 upgrading it. Instead, just buy another PC. It could cost as little as $700 (without monitor), and it'll save you hundreds of dollars in aspirin.

The Case

A big case called the *system unit* stores your computer's guts. (Some people think that the big box is called the CPU, but the CPU is actually a chip inside the system unit itself. More in a minute.) There are different sizes of system units, and for the most part, you don't really need to care, as long as you get upgrade parts that will fit into your computer's system unit. The big problem with some system units is their small height or *width*, which you'll see in a minute. (By the way, the size of a system unit is described as its *footprint*.)

Older desktop cases, such as the XT and AT cases, are big, about seven or eight inches tall. The floppy disk drives inside are large, too, which explains the need for such a big case. PCs of this type fall into the XT and AT classes, so you shouldn't attempt to upgrade them—it just wouldn't be cost effective, and you wouldn't be satisfied with the results anyway, believe me.

The newer desktop cases are called *slimline* or *small-footprint* cases. About half as tall as the older cases, these don't take up as much room on a desktop. You won't have any problem finding parts to work with these PCs, so don't worry. In addition, some slimlines come with a riser card, which allows full-sized expansion cards to be inserted parallel to the motherboard. One major downside to slimlines: You might find that your slimline case does not contain as much room to expand (empty drive bays and open expansion slots) as you might want.

Some cases are designed to stand upright. These are called *tower systems*, or *mini-towers* (which are half the height of tower systems, and therefore, only half as cool).

System units come in all shapes and sizes.

Slimline or small-footprint PC

Tower PC

A *tower case* is named so because it stands on end (like a tower). This type of case is usually placed under or next to a desk, sometimes on a special stand, which keeps it from falling over. A tower case looks cool and leaves your desktop uncluttered. The big benefits of a tower case are more room for expansion devices and more space for ventilation. (Just in case you were wondering, you should *never* stand a regular desktop PC on end to simulate a tower configuration. It's bad, bad, bad for the hard disk.)

The Power Sockets

At the back of the system unit are one or two power sockets. These connect inside to a *power supply*, which you learned about in Chapter 2. You connect the PC to a wall outlet through one of these power sockets. The second socket isn't used much, because it's for supplying power to the monitor. Not such a hot idea as it turns out because the monitor uses more power than anything else in your PC. Plugging it into the system unit causes a big power drain and might prevent you from installing other devices safely. You plug today's monitors directly into their own wall socket.

Check This Out...

Suppress your surges! Actually, you don't really want to plug your computer directly into a wall socket. That's because, even if the power is off, the PC can get spiked (hit with a sudden surge of electricity) during a thunderstorm, wrecking its delicate innards. So connect your PC and the monitor to a *surge suppressor*, which blows itself up to stop an electrical surge from getting to your computer.

The Video Port

After you plug your monitor into a power source, you still need to connect it to the system unit itself so that it can get a picture from the computer. You do that through a special *port* (uh, connector) called the video port.

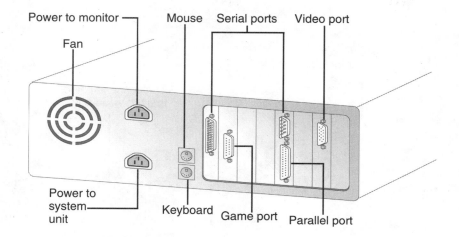

Power to monitor — Mouse Serial ports Video port

Fan

Plug it in, plug it in.

Power to
system — Keyboard Game port Parallel port
unit

You find video ports on your video graphics card or off
the motherboard if your system has on-board video.
Although the graphics card is contained inside your
PC, the video port is located on the outside, for your
plugging convenience. The graphics card controls the
content and quality of what appears on the monitor.
The graphics card and the monitor work hand in hand,
so you have to be sure that the type of monitor you use
works with whatever graphics card you choose. As you
learned in Chapter 2, there are many different kinds of
video cards, of varying quality. Today, all PCs follow
the SVGA standard. If your PC is several years old, it
may follow the VGA standard, but that doesn't mean
it isn't worth upgrading. PCs that use other standards
such as CGA, EGA, and so on, are most likely too old to bother upgrading or repairing.

**A rule of
thumb** All CGA
and EGA video
connectors have 9-
pin male connectors
(pins) at the end of
the cable, whereas VGA connectors have 15-pin male connectors (pins) at the end of the
cable. All video cards have
female connectors (holes).

Check This Out...

If your PC uses VGA or SVGA, your video graphics card has a 15-hole connector. If it uses
an older standard, your video card has a 9-hole connector instead.

By the way, if your PC uses PCI video, it means that the video card is occupying a PCI
slot or is otherwise connected to the PCI bus, a faster data bus inside your PC. PCI video
makes your graphics display faster than it would be if it was connected to the regular
data bus.

Video reality.

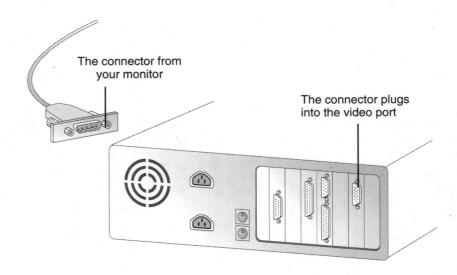

The connector from
your monitor

The connector plugs
into the video port

Check This Out...

Missing a video card?
Some PCs place the video controller on the mother-board instead of on a card. This makes them a pain to upgrade because you have to disable the video controller to add a newer one on a video card. See Chapter 20.

Some Pentium II computers use AGP (accelerated graphics port) to speed up video display. The AGP consists of a set of chips that are hard-wired onto the motherboard and communicate with the CPU through their own dedicated bus, eliminating the need for a graphics card. But because PCs with this type of system have incredibly fast video, it's unlikely you'll want to upgrade it any time soon.

The Keyboard and Mouse Ports

There are usually two special ports (connectors) on the back of the system unit, for the keyboard and the mouse. I say *usually* because sometimes the mouse is connected to a generic port called a *serial port,* which you'll learn about in a minute.

On most computers today, the keyboard and mouse ports are small, round connectors called DIN connectors. (Don't ask me why—okay, it's short for *Deutsche Industrie Norm.* See, I told you not to ask.) Because these keyboard and mouse ports look pretty much the same, little icons such as a small mouse help you identify which is which.

The type of mouse that plugs into these round connectors is called a PS/2-style mouse because IBM introduced this style connector on its PS/2 computers.

The Sound Card

Most computers today come with a sound card and speakers. They provide much better quality sound than you would get through your PC's internal speaker, to say the least. The more expensive sound cards deliver high-quality, stereo sound right on the desktop. Heck, with the addition of a center speaker with subwoofer and a 3D sound card, you can even get surround sound if you want.

Graphics accelerator card

Displaying the pretty pictures that are popular today in Windows, OS/2 Warp, and so on, slows down your computer because it takes time to plot where each dot of color goes. A graphics accelerator card is a special card with unique hardware that helps the CPU make these precise calculations more quickly. People used to have to buy the video card and graphics accelerator cards separately, but now the acceleration function is part of the video card. If your graphics display is slow, you can upgrade to a video card that includes an accelerator. Such a card is often just called a "graphics accelerator," even though it is also a video graphics card.

To tell the big guys from the little guys, you should look for several things:

What number of bits does the card handle? Most sound cards deliver sound using 16 bits of data. The better ones use 64 bits. Suffice it to say, the more bits da betta.

Does it support wave table technology? The term "wave table" refers to a sound technology that allows your PC to re-create sound more accurately. A wave table provides a collection of recorded sounds (*voices*) that, when combined, provide better sound quality than synthesized sound. Some cards allow you to add wave table technology later, with an additional card called a *daughter card* that connects to the main sound card.

How much RAM does it have? Re-creating sound uses up a lot of RAM, so having some on the sound card itself allows the sound card to "package" the sound for the CPU, freeing it up to do other things. The more RAM, the better. You can add RAM to a sound card later as well.

You'll find several ports on the back of the sound card, for connecting various things such as your speakers, a microphone, CD-ROM drive, headphones, and a MIDI instrument (such as an electronic keyboard that supports the Musical Instrument Digital Interface) or joystick.

Networking Connections

If your computer is connected to the company network, you'll see a network interface on the back of your PC. A network interface is an expansion card that handles the sending and receiving of data over the network.

To USB or not to USB?

You might see new computers advertised as having something called a USB port. Short for *Universal Serial Bus*, a USB is designed to handle up to 127 (like you'd need that many) specially adapted peripheral devices through a single port on the back of the computer. You'll learn more about USB in the section, "Any Other Port in a Storm."

You can attach many audio devices to your sound card.

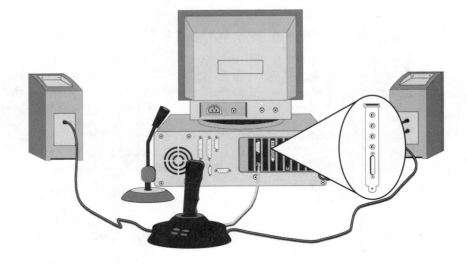

Not on the back? Okay, sometimes you find the keyboard connector on the front or side of the PC instead of in the back. Some computer manufacturers just have to be different, even if it doesn't make sense.

Be sure to line 'em up The plug for your keyboard (and probably your mouse also) is round, so you'll want to make sure that the pins on the plug make contact with the right holes. Make sure that you align the notch on the plug with the notch on the connector. This ensures that you insert the plug correctly.

A network interface is easy to identify because you'll see either a coaxial cable or what looks like a phone line running from the network interface card to the network wall jack.

Any Other Port in a Storm

Your computer comes with at least two generic connectors—the *serial port* and a *parallel port*. These two connectors differ not only in how they look, but also in how they work and in what types of devices you can connect to them.

First of all, think of a port in a shipping area: It's a place to drop off and pick up supplies. In the case of your PC, a port is a place where a device such as a printer or a modem can drop off or pick up data.

A serial port handles data one bit at a time. (Remember that eight bits make up a *byte*, which is equal to one character, such as the letter S.) A serial port is not the fastest port on the block, but it is the most precise. Serial ports are popular because they connect many devices people want to use, such as a mouse, modem, scanner, and so on. So in many cases, computers have two serial ports for people to connect things to.

Fun and games

A game port is typically located on a sound card. There currently are three types of game ports, the most common having 15 holes and supporting most joysticks manufactured since 1995. You plug a joystick or other game device into this kind of port for hours of fun (that is, until you realize that your big presentation is due tomorrow and that, although you still have three aliens to kill, it's not even close to being done).

With a Sound Blaster brand card as well as some others such as Turtle Beach and Roland, you might be able to plug a MIDI device into the game port in place of the joystick, so you can pretend you're Springsteen with a synthesizer.

Serial ports come in two sizes, 9-pin and 25-pin D shell connectors (so called because they look like the letter "D"). Functionally, they are the same; you just need to connect your device to the proper size port. If you need to connect a 9-pin device such as a modem to a 25-pin connector, pop on down to your local Radio Shack for a converter. They're cheap and easy to use.

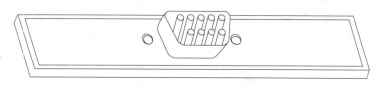

Serial ports come in two varieties.

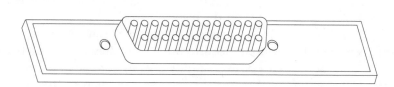

A serial port has a nickname, *COM port*, because these ports are used to communicate with other devices such as a modem or a mouse. Your computer can distinguish up to four COM ports, but many programs, including the first releases of Windows 3.1, recognize only the devices you attach to the first two. This makes serial ports precious, indeed. To add to the confusion, an internal device such as a modem uses up one of these ports without being connected to the outside part of the port. If you then connect two other devices to the serial ports on the outside, you end up with trouble. If you suspect such trickery, turn to Chapter 27 for help.

A parallel port is faster than a serial port because it handles data one whole *byte* at a time, instead of one bit. A parallel port transmits an entire byte each time, so sometimes one bit gets scrambled, causing a "J" to turn into a "P." Extra pins in the parallel port transmit extra information to help the device at the receiving end verify that it gets the right data. If needed, the data is simply re-sent. Parallel devices include printers, tape backup units, and even portable hard drives.

Parallel ports have 25 holes.

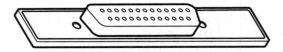

Parallel ports look like inverted serial ports (D shell connectors) because they have holes, not pins. Like serial ports, parallel ports also have a nickname, LPT (Logical Printer) ports. Although MS-DOS is capable of recognizing up to four LPT ports, some computers can use only two. Few people own more than two printers anyway, so this is generally no big deal. However, there are other parallel devices you might own, such as Zip and Jaz drives, as well as some scanners.

In addition to parallel and serial ports, you might hear about these guys as well:

USB port. Short for Universal Serial Bus, a USB port is a new standard for connecting peripheral devices to your PC that is only now being gradually adopted. The plug is square-ish and kinda looks like the connector for your printer or external modem, except that it's about 30 percent the size. USB is much faster than standard serial connections, and because serial technology is much less expensive to implement than parallel technology, USB makes it possible for printers, modems, scanners, joysticks, and other peripherals (up to 127 of them) to be linked to your computer through a simpler, serial connection. For example, you might plug your keyboard into the USB port and then run a cord from the back of the keyboard to your printer, and from your printer to something else. The port makes it simple to connect many things to your PC without hassling with the addressing conflicts that would normally come about in such a daisy-chaining operation (case in point: SCSI). You only need USB on your system if the peripheral you plan to attach supports USB; few do right now.

AGP port. Short for Accelerated Graphics Port, this isn't actually a port you can see. I mean, on a computer that has one of these, you'll see an everyday, ordinary-looking SVGA port for connecting your monitor. The port is actually inside the computer, and it helps get data from the CPU to the monitor for display as quickly as possible. The AGP takes the place of your standard graphics accelerator card. If your computer has AGP, it (supposedly) does not need a graphics adapter or accelerator card, but you still have the SVGA port on the back of the machine.

SCSI port. A SCSI port is attached to a SCSI controller card, or to a sound card such as Sound Blaster, which can act as a SCSI controller, or to an on-board SCSI connector.

The most widely implemented version of SCSI on today's PC can control up to seven SCSI devices, such as a hard drive, CD-ROM, Zip or Jaz drive, tape backup, and so on. A SCSI port usually has 50 holes, which is many more than other connectors, so it's easy to identify.

Firewire (also known as IEEE 1394). This is a special port used for transferring data between two PCs, or between a PC and a data-intensive device such as a digital video camera, VCR, or DVD player. As the name implies, the throughput rate of Firewire approaches speeds that threaten the sound barrier. Consider this: The standard serial port we've all come to know and love transmits data no faster than 9,600 bits per second (bps). USB (defined earlier) transfers data at 12 *megabits* per second (Mbps), which is more than 1,300 times faster. Firewire transfers data at up to 400 Mbps, which is about 43,691 times faster than the maximum throughput rate of everyday serial connections. (Actually, Firewire is evolving to an even faster standard, from 800 Mps to 3.2 Gps—that's *gigabytes per second*.) A digital MPEG-3 video in full stereo would need a connection that fast for a PC to keep up with it in real-time. However, Firewire is not yet widely found on everyday consumer-level PCs.

What Microsoft Diagnostics Can Tell You

After checking your original invoice for information (that is, if you still have it), you might still end up with some blanks on your equipment list. For serious snooping, you need Microsoft Diagnostics, which you can call MSD after you get to know it better. One problem: You'll only find MSD on your PC if you have Windows or DOS version 5.0 or higher.

I don't have it...

If you don't have MSD, you can still find out some more information about your PC. Just restart it and watch the screen. You'll see a message telling you what kind of video card you're using (including video memory and video BIOS version), along with what BIOS you have, and its creation date.

For example, when I boot the system I'm currently upgrading, I see this:

```
AMI BIOS (c)1992 American Megatrends
```

This tells me that the system has the 1992 version of American Megatrends BIOS. In addition, you can use utilities such as Norton Utilities to discover key information about your PC.

MSD digs down into your system and then displays what it finds. Unfortunately, this list includes only the things that the good folks at Microsoft decided you might want to know—so it's not complete. At least it gives you a good start at completing your equipment list. One warning though—the Surgeon General has rated most of this junk hazardous to your sanity, so avoid prolonged exposure whenever possible.

To start Microsoft Diagnostics, exit Windows (or if you use Windows 95/98, restart the PC in DOS mode by shutting down Windows and choosing the DOS mode option in the dialog box that appears). Then, at the DOS prompt, type **CD\DOS** and press **Enter**. Then type **MSD** and press **Enter**.

You see something like this onscreen:

MSD can tell you a lot about your computer.

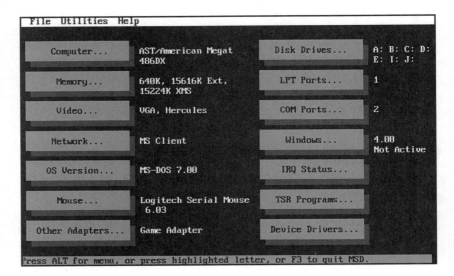

To find out more about a particular component, just click its button. For example, if you want to learn what kind of video you've been using all these years, click the **Video** button. To return to the main screen, click **OK**. When you've learned all you can, open the **File** menu and select **Exit** to return to the DOS prompt.

By the way, if you're curious, the reason the screen tells me I have Windows 4.0 is because I'm using Windows 95. (Jealous? Don't be.) Windows 95 is basically Windows 4.0, if you think about it, because the last version of Windows was 3.x. Anyway, I restarted the PC with DOS, so it's showing as "Not Active." You may see some similar nonsense. Don't worry, because when you restart the PC, Windows 95 will activate itself automatically.

Using My Computer to Explore Your System

If you use Windows 95 or 98, you can use My Computer to uncover more secrets about your PC's configuration. Just right-click on **My Computer** and then select **Properties** from the menu that appears out of nowhere.

On the General tab, you'll see your Windows version, CPU type, and the amount of memory in your computer. Click the Device Manager tab, and you can snoop some more:

Click the plus sign next to an item to see more detail. For example, here I've clicked next to CDROM, and the drive letter of my CD-ROM drive is displayed for all to see.

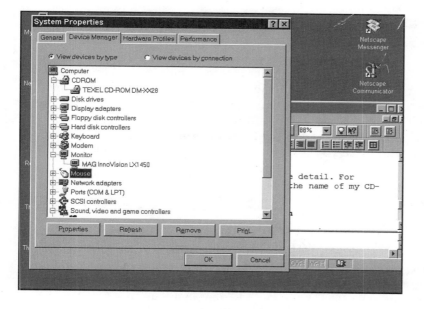

Snooping around with My Computer.

Snooping Around with System Information

If you've installed Microsoft Office 97 on your Windows 95 computer, or if you happen to have Windows 98, you have access to a tool you can use to find out more about your PC, called System Information. To open it, click the **Start** button, select **Programs**, **Accessories**, **System Tools**, and then finally, **System Information**.

Check out this info!

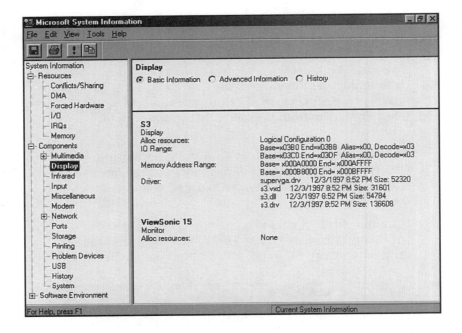

I hope you have your sunglasses, 'cause I don't want you to be blinded by all the information Microsoft jammed into this puppy. Click the plus sign next to **Components**. Then click the item you want to know more about. Here, I clicked **Display** and was treated to some information on my monitor. (Unless you want to overload your brain cells with useless information, make sure that you select the **Basic Information** option.) You can safely ignore most of this stuff; what you want to know is at the bottom of the window: ViewSonic 15, which is my monitor type.

CMOS Remembers Your PC's Basic Configuration

Ever wonder what day it is? Ever wonder how your PC knows, even though you don't? Well, the answer's in the CMOS (pronounced "sea moss").

CMOS is short for *Complementary Metal-Oxide Semiconductor*, and it's a chip inside your PC that stores important information such as the current date and time. After information is typed into the CMOS, it stays there, thanks to a tiny battery that helps it remember, even when you cut off the computer's power supply.

Think of CMOS as a kind of big day planner for your PC, chock-full of important information such as how many disk drives it has and what type they are. CMOS keeps track of other stuff, too, such as the amount of RAM your PC has. But, just like what happens if you lose your own day planner, if your PC loses the information in CMOS (such as when the battery finally dies), it is dead in the water—literally.

Life before CMOS

Some older PCs (museum trash mostly, such as old XT types and the original PCs) don't have a CMOS; instead, these PCs use several DIP switches or jumpers to tell them what kind of hard disk they have and how much memory. A *DIP switch*, by the way, is like a light switch; it only has two settings: on or off. A *jumper* is a couple of tiny metal poles set close together, like goal posts. To turn on a particular jumper, you cover the two posts with a rubber clip (called a *shunt*), which I'll show you how to do in Chapter 27.

By setting a series of these DIP switches or jumpers in a certain pattern of off/on/off/off, or whatever, you actually provide your PC with what today passes for CMOS information in any modern computer.

BIOS and CMOS, why do they sound so similar?

Well, yes, you have a BIOS chip inside your PC. And yes, you also have a CMOS chip. However, they are not the same thing, nor do their purposes overlap.

The BIOS is like a butler, performing all the menial input and output tasks that are beneath the lordly CPU. If a disk needs to be read, for instance, then the CPU dispatches the BIOS to read it, and so on. BIOS (Basic Input/Output System) is, in actuality, a program—more accurately, the first program your computer runs before it knows to go looking for its operating system.

The CMOS, on the other hand, is like a reminder pad to which the CPU can refer whenever it forgets basic information, such as how large the hard disk is, or how much memory there is. (CMOS actually refers more to the chip's own construction than to anything having to do with the computer.)

So, while your CMOS is still in good health, copy down the information it contains. That way, when the battery supporting the CMOS dies, and your PC ends up with amnesia, you can re-create the CMOS data by typing it back in. Just turn to Chapter 16, "Replacing the Motherboard," for information about replacing the battery. Then jump to Chapter 27 to learn how you can restore your PC's "memory" (CMOS).

Check This Out...

Still no CMOS If you try all these things and still no CMOS, look in your owner's manual for help.

How you get to the stuff CMOS contains depends on your PC, but it's probably one of these three ways:

➤ Reboot your computer and press **Ctrl+Alt+Escape** or **Ctrl+Alt+S**. You can also try **Ctrl+Alt+Enter** or **Ctrl+Alt+Insert**.

➤ Reboot your computer and watch the screen for a message telling you what key to press for **Setup**. Then press it. (It may tell you to press **F1** or **F2** or even **Delete**.)

➤ Restart your computer with a Setup disk in drive A. (This is usually what you need to do for an AT-type 286 PC or a PS/2.)

➤ Uh, remember that an XT or earlier type PC doesn't have a CMOS program. Instead, CMOS is set up by moving a bunch of jumpers on the motherboard.

After you get the CMOS open, copy down the information it contains. Don't worry if you don't understand what it all means; your PC does. Just make sure that you copy down the information correctly. Or, if you have a printer, turn it on and press **PrintScrn** to print it.

Device	CMOS Setting				
Hard disk C type	_____				
Hard disk C settings	Cyls___	Hds__	WPcom__	LZ__	Sec__
Hard disk D type					
Hard disk D settings	Cyls___	Hds__	WPcom__	LZ__	Sec__
Disk drive A type	_____				
Disk drive B type	_____				
Base memory	_____				
Board memory	_____				
Extended memory	_____				
Display type	_____				
Other stuff:	*Setting:*				
_____	_____				
_____	_____				
_____	_____				
_____	_____				
_____	_____				

Follow the onscreen instructions for getting out of CMOS. You're probably safe with just pressing **Esc**, as long as you don't actually change anything.

While we're on the subject, if you add a new disk drive to your PC, add more RAM, replace the motherboard, or change any other basic component, you have to run your PC's Setup program to tell CMOS about it. Don't worry—you'll learn how to do that in Part 5: "Getting Your PC to Figure Out What You've Done."

The Least You Need to Know

Before you attempt to upgrade or repair a PC, you should know a little about how it works. In this chapter, you found out some mighty interesting facts, such as:

➤ The CPU is the PC's brain (or engine, if you prefer). This is where the processing takes place. Upgrade this, and your PC can think faster.

➤ You shouldn't bother to upgrade anything older than a 486 PC.

➤ A tower case is vertically oriented, whereas a desktop case is horizontally oriented.

➤ Video cards and your monitor work together. Most likely, when you upgrade one, you upgrade the other.

➤ Your PC has only a few serial and parallel ports, so you should be picky about what you decide to connect them to.

➤ To learn more about the stuff your computer has, look at your original invoice for information.

➤ A great way to find out a lot of information about your PC is to use Microsoft Diagnostics. Just type **MSD** at the DOS prompt.

➤ CMOS is a special chip that keeps track of some of your PC's basic "ingredients," such as the number of disk drives, the size of the hard disk, and the amount of memory.

➤ If your PC's battery goes dead, your CMOS information is lost forever, so make a copy of your CMOS information before disaster strikes.

Chapter 4

What You Need to Know Before You Open Your PC

In This Chapter

➤ Preparing for the fifth disaster of the day

➤ Backing up important stuff

➤ Getting ready for the big moment

➤ Uncovering your PC's innards

I'm not really much of a mechanic, but given enough time, I can usually take something apart and put it back together with only a few miscellaneous parts left over. For me, opening up a PC and playing around with its guts is about as much fun as getting my teeth cleaned. But when I absolutely have to, I perform upgrades to my PC, and even if you're not much of a mechanic either, you can, too.

If you've upgraded a few things on your PC already, you probably started the same way I did—with some of the easy upgrades such as replacing your keyboard, mouse, or printer. If you want to upgrade anything else, the chances are pretty high that you'll need to actually open up your PC, and that can be real scary.

In this chapter, you'll learn how to do just that without frying either your PC or your nerves.

Don't Leave Home Without Your Emergency Disk

Before you upgrade anything on your PC (or install a new program, for that matter), you should update your emergency disk. With an emergency disk, you'll be able to restart your PC should something (such as a bungled upgrade) prevent you from doing so. If something happens to prevent your PC from starting normally, just slip the emergency disk into drive A and restart your PC from it.

What do I put on it?

An emergency disk contains a copy of your operating system (DOS or Windows), the Autoexec.bat file, and the Config.sys file. When your PC first starts, it checks drive A for a copy of the operating system and the configuration files. If there isn't a disk in drive A, then your PC boots with the copy of the operating system and configuration files that it finds on the hard disk. You see, the fact that you've copied the core of your operating system onto the disk is what makes it *bootable* (it's what makes the PC start from the disk, instead of using the hard drive). If something you do during your upgrade (such as changing the configuration files) accidentally causes the hard disk not to work, you can put your emergency disk in drive A and start the computer that way.

Some newer PCs like to check both drive A and B for a copy of the operating system before going onto the hard disk. (How rude!) However, this is extremely rare. In any case, your emergency disk (made for drive A) will work on these PCs, too.

How to Create Your Emergency Disk

To create an emergency disk in Windows 3.1, start File Manager. Grab a disk that fits drive A. Then open the **Disk** menu and select **Format Disk**. Select the **Make System Disk** option and click **OK**.

After you format the disk, copy the configuration files onto it (you'll find them lurking in the root directory of C):

```
AUTOEXEC.BAT
CONFIG.SYS
```

Copy the Windows system files as well (they're hiding in the Windows directory):

```
WIN.INI
SYSTEM.INI
```

If you've compressed your hard disk using DriveSpace, use this command to copy that file onto the disk as well. (If you use Windows 95 or 98, you'll find this file lurking in the \WINDOWS\COMMAND directory instead.):

```
COPY C:\DOS\DRVSPACE.BIN A:
```

If you used DoubleSpace (the older version of the drive compression program) instead, well, use *this* command:

```
COPY C:\DOS\DBLSPACE.BIN A:
```

You'll probably want these additional files as well, which you'll find in the DOS directory, or, if you use Windows 95 or 98, in the \WINDOWS\COMMAND directory:

```
FDISK.EXE
FORMAT.COM
MEM.EXE
SCANDISK.*
MSD.*
RESTORE.EXE
UNDELETE.EXE:
SYS.COM
MSAV.EXE
```

If you replace your hard disk at any time, you'll need the FDISK and FORMAT commands to finish the job. The MEM command helps you check RAM, and SCANDISK helps you check the hard disk. MSD you already know; it's a diagnostic tool. RESTORE and UNDELETE can help you if an important file gets trashed, and SYS can restore your system should your hard disk become corrupted. The MSAV command helps you check for viruses when you suspect that they may be the reason your PC won't boot correctly.

Having two disks is OK If you run out of space on your emergency disk, you can put the last set of files on another disk. You don't have to update these files ever, so having them on a separate disk won't hurt.

If you use Windows 95 or Windows 98, there's an easier way around this mess. To create an emergency disk: Open the Control Panel and double-click **Add/Remove Programs**. Click the **Start Disk** tab, and click **Start**. The disk won't have all the files on it that you need, so be sure to copy WIN.INI and SYSTEM.INI onto it as well. In addition, copy these files from the Windows directory:

```
SYSTEM.DAT
USER.DAT
```

Keep your emergency disk in some handy place, where you can get to it quickly when you need it. No, not on top of your computer—it'll just get warped by the heat. And not next to the telephone, where there's a small chance the magnet inside might mess with the data. Put it in your top desk drawer, or in your file cabinet.

Time Out! Check Your Config Files

Check your configuration files before you copy them to your emergency disk. Use Notepad to view the contents of the Autoexec.bat and Config.sys files. Make sure that all the programs, drivers, and files use a complete path, with a *drive letter* and *directory name*. For example, if you have this command in your Autoexec.bat:

```
MOUSE
```

and you boot your PC from drive A, DOS wouldn't be able to find the mouse driver because it assumes that the driver is located on the disk (that is in drive A). The driver is actually hiding out in the root directory of the C drive. To fix all this confusion, you add the complete path (with the drive letter and the directory) to the MOUSE command, like this:

```
C:\MOUSE
```

By adding a complete path to all the programs and drivers in the AUTOEXEC.BAT and CONFIG.SYS files, DOS will be able to find all of them when you boot from drive A.

The other way to help your computer find all your drivers when you boot from drive A is to copy the necessary driver files to your emergency disk in the first place. It's a bit more trouble than simply editing AUTOEXEC.BAT and CONFIG.SYS, but at least if your hard drive goes completely down, you may be able to restore some parts of your system (such as your mouse). On the other hand, most of those drivers are of no use to you if the hard drive's down anyway, so you may not want to bother copying them to the emergency disk. I copy the drivers to the disk as long as I have the room.

Check This Out...

Zip that lip! Don't compress (zip) the files to make them fit onto one disk. You can't use compressed files unless you unzip them, which you won't be able to do if your hard disk is damaged and you're trying to use your emergency disk to get out of your mess.

The Ins and Outs of Using Your Emergency Disk

To be useful, you have to keep *updating* your emergency disk. For example, when you install something new, such as a new CD-ROM drive or a new program, it'll probably make changes to your configuration files. So, this is what you do:

➤ *Before* you install a new program or a new toy, update your emergency disk by copying the AUTOEXEC.BAT, CONFIG.SYS, DRVSPACE.BIN, WIN.INI, and SYSTEM.INI files onto it.

➤ Now that you have an updated emergency disk, install your new toy and then run its setup program. The setup will probably make changes to the configuration files to add a driver program, for example. After the setup program is done, you should restart the PC so any changes it might have made to the configuration files will be activated.

➤ If the changes caused by the setup program end up wrecking your life (and your PC), then undo them by copying your good, older versions of the configuration files from your emergency disk back onto the hard disk. If you can't get Windows to start, use these commands from the DOS prompt:

```
COPY A:\AUTOEXEC.BAT C:\
COPY A:\CONFIG.SYS C:\

COPY A:\DRVSPACE.BIN C:\DOS or
COPY A:\DRVSPACE.BIN C:\WINDOWS\COMMAND

COPY A:\WIN.INI C:\WINDOWS
COPY A:\SYSTEM.INI C:\WINDOWS
```

➤ If, on the other hand, the changes made by the setup program seem to work fine (your new toy is happy, you can still run all your programs) then repeat these commands to copy your updated CONFIG.SYS, AUTOEXEC.BAT, DRVSPACE.BIN, WIN.INI, and SYSTEM.INI onto your disk. Just change the drive letters to copy stuff from your hard disk to drive A, as in

```
COPY C:\AUTOEXEC.BAT A:
COPY C:\CONFIG.SYS A:

COPY C:\DOS\DRVSPACE.BIN A: or
COPY C:\WINDOWS\COMMAND\DRVSPACE.BIN A:

COPY C:\WINDOWS\WIN.INI A:
COPY C:\WINDOWS\SYSTEM.INI A:
```

Go back and get the CMOS

If you skipped over Chapter 3, "Now, Let's Find Out What Kind of Computer You Have," go back and print out a copy of your CMOS information—you know, the stuff that tells your computer where and what your hard drive is—and so much more—before you continue. Not having this could literally cripple your computer if the CMOS ever gets lost.

Steppin' out

If you have at least DOS 6.0, or Windows 95 or 98, you can step through the commands in your configuration files, and bypass the one that may be messing things up. To do that, press and hold the **F8** key as the computer is starting up, and you'll see a menu. (On Windows 98 PCs, press and hold the **Ctrl** key when starting up.) Press **Shift+F5** to step through each of the configuration commands. Press **Enter** or **Y** to accept a command, or **N** to bypass one.

Now, Back Up Your Data

Making a backup of your data is like wearing a seat belt when you drive. It's uncomfortable, and sometimes you can get by without one, but if you ever slam into a wall at 60 mph, you'll be glad you took the time to buckle up.

So, before you perform any surgery on your system, make sure you've got backup copies of your important data, such as important reports, letters to your lawyer, tax filings, and so on. That way, if the patient dies on the table, you can always restore the important parts after you get the body working again.

Backing Up with DOS

If you don't use Windows, you'll have to use DOS to back up your data. If you're using a DOS version prior to DOS 6 (such as DOS 3.3, 4.0, or 5.0), first, I have to ask you why. Then I'll tell you to type this at the prompt (if you're not sure what DOS version you have, type **VER** and press **Enter** at the DOS prompt):

```
BACKUP C:\*.* A: /S /L
```

and press **Enter**. You see a prompt to insert a disk into drive A. Do that and press **Enter** again. Eventually, DOS asks you for another disk, and so on. Make sure you actually insert a different disk; if you keep the same one in the drive, DOS will write over the top of its data and ruin the whole backup. While DOS is doing its thing, amuse yourself by labeling each disk as you go along.

Bummer

Make sure that you have enough disks to finish the job. Even though DOS will format disks for you as it goes along, this adds an enormous amount of time to an already tedious task. So get your disks ready by formatting them before you start.

How many will you need? That depends on how large your hard disk is, and on how many of its files you're planning on backing up. But if you're using high-density disks, they'll hold about a megabyte or so.

If you have at least DOS 6.0, then there's an easier way to go about this. At the prompt, type **MSBACKUP** and press **Enter**. If you've never done a backup before (shame, shame), MS Backup will perform some tests; get yourself two disks of the same size and density as the ones you'll be using for the big backup. Just do whatever it says, and, when it's done, you end up at the main screen. Click **Backup**.

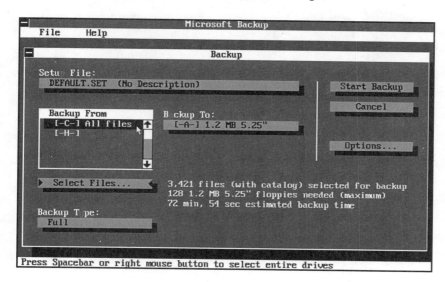

MS Backup makes it easy to select what you want to back up.

From here, you can select what you want to back up and skip over things you already have copies of, such as your programs (which you still have on installation disks). Start by clicking on drive C in the **Backup From** box. Select the drive you want to back up to (such as drive A) in the **Backup To** drop-down list box. If you don't want to back up certain directories, just click the **Select Files** button and then click the files you don't want to back up. (A check mark indicates the ones you will back up.) Click **OK** to return to the Backup screen and then click **Start Backup**. You do the disk shuffle with MS Backup, too—just pop in disks when it asks for them.

Backing Up with Windows 95

If you use Windows 95, open the **Start** menu, select **Programs, Accessories, System Tools**, and then finally, **Backup**. (If you didn't install Backup when you installed Windows 95, then hang your head and go install it. Then come back here to do your backup.) Again, if this is the first time you've done a backup, you'll have to get past a bunch of rigmarole (just do what the screen tells you to do) before you finally get here:

To back up everything, open the **File** menu and select **Open File Set**. Then select the **Full System Backup Set** and click **Open**.

Using MS Backup with Windows 95.

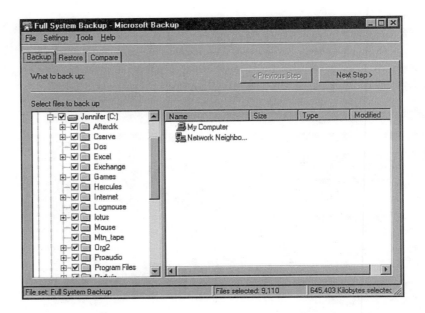

If you don't want to waste time backing up silly program files, double-click the check box in front of the drive you want to back up. This takes a while; Windows has to go through and put a check mark in front of all the files. You can tell Windows which files to ignore by clicking them one at a time to remove the check mark.

When you're done selecting files, click **Next Step**. Click the drive you want to back up to (such as drive A or, if you're lucky, your tape drive) and click **Start Backup**. If it asks, type in a name for your backup set, such as **Important Files Only**, and click **OK** to finally get the backup under way. Every so often, while you're backing up to disks, MS Backup will ask you to switch disks in the drive; each time you do, you don't have to hit Enter, just let it go. Of course, if you're backing up to tape, then you won't have to switch disks. When it's done (in a year or two), click **OK**.

Backing Up with Windows 98

Backing up your files with Windows 98 is a little different than with Windows 95, although it begins the same: click **Start**, select **Programs**, select **Accessories**, select **System Tools**, then select **Backup**.

A welcome screen appears with a cup of coffee. Take a big gulp and then select **Create a new backup job** and click **OK**. Select **Back up My Computer** (to back up the whole shebang) or **Backup selected files, folders, and drives**. Click **Next**.

If you chose **Backup my selected files, folders, and drives**, then click the items you want backed up (selected files appear with a check mark), then click **Next**:

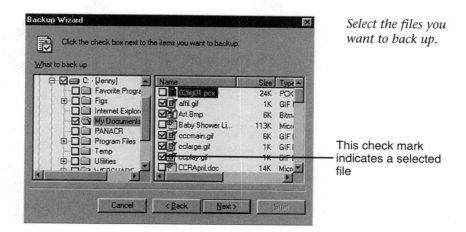

Select the files you want to back up.

This check mark indicates a selected file

Tell Microsoft Backup whether you want to back up **All selected files** (which copies all the files you selected, regardless of when they were last backed up) or **New and changed files** (which backs up *only* the selected files that have been created or changed since the last backup). Click **Next**. Select the drive and folder to which you want the backup copied, such as drive A, then click **Next**. Select any additional options you want, then click **Next**.

Give your backup job a moniker, such as Full Backup. You can later reuse this job to complete the same type of backup procedure. Click **Start** and the backup process finally begins. When the backup is complete, you'll see a message telling you so. Click **OK**. If you want to see a summary, click **Report**. Click **OK** when you're through.

The Tools of the Trade

Before you attempt an upgrade, you'll need to gather some tools together so you can successfully get your PC apart. You'll need a small flathead screwdriver as well as small and medium Phillips screwdrivers.

If you don't mind looking a little nerdy, get yourself a set of cool computer tools. You can find them at any computer store. They include extra tools for removing chips and retrieving dropped screws—and, at about $20, they won't break your wallet. They generally include those strange foreign "nuthead" screwdrivers (yes, that's what they're really called) that look like a combination screwdriver and mini-socket wrench. For some PC tower cases, you may need a nuthead screwdriver to take the cover off. Make sure your tools have nonconducting handles made of hard plastic, PVC, or ceramic.

Get yourself a set of cool tools.

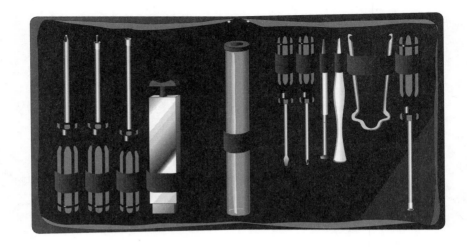

A few more handy tips to keep in mind:

➤ Grab a couple of empty pill bottles, 35mm film cans, or even an old egg carton; any of these containers makes a great gathering place for the various screws you'll encounter.

➤ You may also want to grab a flashlight (it gets pretty dark in there), a box (for storing spare computer parts), and a can of compressed air or dust remover. (Hey, while it's open, you might as well do some cleaning.)

➤ Two things you'll find pretty indispensable are paper and a pencil. You can write down the switch and jumper settings of any card you remove in case your fingers fumble at some point and accidentally change one of them. A switch, by the way, is like a tiny light switch, and a jumper is a set of pins connected by a removable gizmo called a shunt. You'll learn how to set switches and jumpers in Chapter 27, "Fiddling with Ports, IRQs, Addresses, and Such." Paper's also handy for writing down part numbers, cable orientation and placement, or any other info you find important. (I've saved some space along the margins here for you...)

Check This Out...

Call me indispensable
If the idea of opening up your PC gives you the shivers, invest in a bit of insurance in the form of a grounding strap. This neat gizmo straps around your wrist and prevents you from accidentally zapping your expensive toy. Well worth the money, in my opinion.

➤ A Sharpie (or other indelible pen) makes a handy gadget for marking cables and such so you can get them back where they belong after disconnecting them during the installation of some new toy.

Opening Pandora's Box Without Frying Yourself or Your PC

Opening your PC's system unit for the first time is a bit like digging up Al Capone's vaults. There's a lot of anticipation, maybe a little fear, and just when you begin to think you should put on something bulletproof, you find out there's nothing in there that can kill you. All this fuss over nothing may ruin your image among friends; that can happen—just ask Geraldo. You'll soon learn that being a bit scared (and therefore, a bit more careful) is better in the long run than tons of confidence.

To open up your PC successfully, all you really need are a few screwdrivers and a bit of common sense.

The 12 Steps to Success

1. *Prepare for disaster.* Before you do anything, I mean anything, you should back up your data and update your emergency disk. Remember, anything you don't save, you should be prepared to *lose*. Also, make sure you have a copy of your PC's CMOS data. See Chapter 3 for help.

2. *Read the instructions that came with your new part.* The documentation may actually give you some real information, such as how to get your exact brand of PC to talk to your new part. If it tells you to check out a text file on an enclosed disk, then do it. Type **TYPE A:README.TXT | MORE** at the DOS prompt to read the file. (The TYPE command tells DOS to display the contents of the README.TXT file, and MORE tells it to pause when a screen is full so you can actually read it. The | character (alias: "pipe") is located on the same key as \. Press **Enter** to move to the next page of the file.) If this command fails to display anything onscreen, it could be that the file is called something else, such as READ.ME, README.1ST, or something similar.

3. *Turn off your PC and unplug it.* No, it's not enough to just turn the darn thing off. Unplugging the PC from the wall ensures that there's absolutely no possible way that you could plug something into the computer while it's on. And believe me, you really don't want to do that.

   Also, remove any other plugs, such as the one that connects your monitor, modem, or printer to the PC. (You'll probably have to unscrew it first.)

You can print it If you'd rather print out the README.TXT file, type this at the DOS prompt instead: **TYPE A:README.TXT > PRN.**

4. *Clear the area.* All those parts have to go somewhere, so make room on your desk for them before you find yourself struggling to keep your hold on a 20-pound monitor. Use all the magic at your disposal to remove excess electricity from your workplace: Stand on a static free tile or linoleum floor, use a wooden desktop to work on, touch

a doorknob to remove your own static, and so on. Also, place both your PC and yourself on some surface that doesn't conduct static electricity, such as wood, Formica, concrete, plastic, or linoleum. Don't stand (or put the PC) on carpet!

5. *Unscrew the cover.* You probably need a screwdriver for this, and your film cans, egg carton, or whatever other clever device you plan on using to corral the screws. Be sure to undo only the screws holding the cover on. Don't do as I did one time and accidentally unscrew the power supply. Just stick to the screws along the outer edge of the cover. This figure helps:

Make sure you undo the right screws.

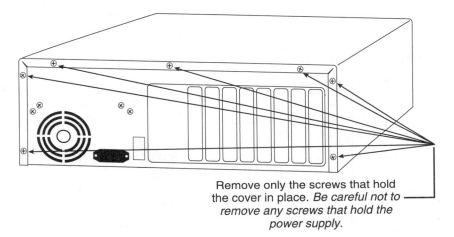

Remove only the screws that hold the cover in place. *Be careful not to remove any screws that hold the power supply.*

Check This Out...

Check for hatch releases or locks A hatch release secures some covers; you press this hatch release to remove the cover. Some systems have more than one release. Keys lock other covers; you have to turn the key to the "unlock" symbol (which looks kinda like an open padlock) to remove the cover.

6. *Remove the cover.* You may want to check through the PC's manual for this one. To pull off most desktop unit covers, you slide the cover backwards and then lift it straight up. With some other PCs, you may have to do the exact opposite—slide the cover forward and then lift it up. For some of the older IBM-brand PCs, there may be hinges so the cover doesn't actually come off but instead lifts up. On a tower unit, either one side comes off, or the entire "n" shaped cover lifts straight off. On some units, the front panel or bezel comes off as well. You may have to tug a little, but be careful not to pull any cords loose while you're tugging. Put the case somewhere where you won't trip over it. There may be a plastic back panel on your tower PC that you can pull off first—there are no screws to it, so it should just snap right off.

7. *Ground yourself.* Touch something metal, such as your PC's cover, to discharge static electricity. Don't dance (or otherwise move your feet) while you're working. *Don't touch anything inside the PC until you're sure that you're grounded.* After you discharge yourself, no matter how nervous you get, don't scratch your head or shuffle your feet. It takes a minimal amount of static to zap just about any part of your PC—I'm talking less static than it takes to zap a friend—so don't move when working on a PC, or, just before touching something inside the PC, discharge any static by touching a file cabinet, a coworker, or whatever.

> **Sure-fire static protection**
> Again, it's really worth the money to invest in what some computer stores call a "grounding strap" that you place over your wrist to prevent you from building up any static while you work. You can also buy an antistatic mat that does the same thing; you just stand on it to avoid static buildup.

8. *Get that dust outta there.* Big, flaky, dusty things in your expansion ports can literally short them out if you plug something new in and push them deep into the connector pins. Don't use furniture polish or anything you ordinarily use to dust your candelabra and other valuables. Don't use a cloth either. Instead, go to your local computer store and pick up a can of dust-blasting spray. It has one of those thin straws like on a WD-40 can; but rather than squirting lubricant, this straw blasts a powerful spray of air that literally eats (blows away) dust without touching it. It's not terribly expensive, but replacing your motherboard is.

   You may also want to clean the edge connector of any new expansion card you want to install. Use some rubbing alcohol and a Q-tip.

9. *Out with the old, in with the new.* To remove an expansion card, unplug any cables attaching it to the motherboard or to any of your peripherals. Unscrew the retaining screw and put the little guy somewhere where he can't roll away. (Nuthead screwdrivers take off retaining screws in a flash.) Grip the card at the top with both hands and pull straight up. Avoid the metal leads sticking out of the back of the expansion card—they just love to cut fingers.

   To install a new expansion card, find an open slot that's of the proper type. (Confused about expansion slots? See Chapter 2, "What Makes Your Computer Tick, and What It Takes to Upgrade Each Component.") Unscrew the retaining screw holding the slot cover in place. Again, put the screw somewhere where you won't lose it. Remove the slot cover and hang it as a decoration in your cubicle. (Don't throw it away; if you ever take the card back out, you will need it again.) Hold the card at the top with both hands and gently position the edge connectors on the bottom of the card over their slots. Gently rock the card until it slips into place. You may have to apply just the right amount of downward pressure to insert it.

If you're installing a chip instead, such as a RAM chip, make sure the little guy's legs are straight, and not bent. Then position the chip's legs over the corresponding holes on its holder. Gently press the chip into place, but don't force it—you could break one of its legs.

Push the expansion card gently into place.

Retaining screw

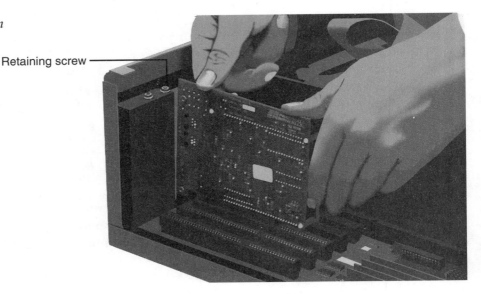

10. *With the cover still off, plug the PC back in, turn it on, and check to see if your new toy works.* Yes, with the cover *off*, you should test to see if you properly connected the new part, so you can quickly correct it if it isn't, *before you put the cover back on.* If something's wrong, you'll usually hear a few beeps. If that happens, turn the PC off, unplug it again, reconnect things, and then fire it back up to test your adjustments.

11. *Close up the box.* Repeat step 6, only backwards. After Humpty Dumpty's back together again, plug everything back in and start up the PC.

12. *Introduce the computer and your new toy to each other.* With most new parts, you'll have to run some kind of setup program which comes on some disk. You might also need your original Windows 95 or Windows 98 installation CD-ROM, in case Windows needs to install a few new files of its own to accommodate the new part. The setup will make changes to the configuration files so your computer can talk to the new part. See Chapter 26, "Getting Windows to Recognize Your New Toy," for help.

What Could Go Wrong

Here's a quick checklist of things to watch out for:

➤ Before you begin work, remove potential disasters from your work area such as cups of coffee or cans of soda.

➤ Unplug your PC and ground yourself before you touch anything.

➤ Unlike a mattress tag, no one's going to arrest you if you remove tags on any chips that you find, but if you do, you may lose some irreplaceable bit of information. Also, some tags are actually put there to *protect* a chip from damage.

➤ Even if you bought your new CD-ROM and sound card together, you should only try to install one thing and get it to work before you attempt to install something else.

➤ Don't attempt to repair a broken power unit or monitor—you can easily end up electrocuting yourself and having a really bad hair day. Replace it instead.

➤ Don't push, shove, bend, spindle, or mutilate any piece that you're trying to get into your computer. If it doesn't fit, don't try to force it. Be especially careful of the pins on tiny chips, which break pretty easily when you force them into the wrong slots, or cards, which tend to bend when you push them the wrong way.

➤ Use your pencil and paper to make a note of the order in which you remove parts— in most cases, you'll have to put them back in the reverse order. Also, make note of the orientation of any cables, and any switch settings you encounter.

➤ Mail in your registration now, while you still know where it is. Also, keep your manuals in one place. Hang onto any big boxes in case you need to ship something back if it stops working after only a week.

The Least You Need to Know

Upgrading your PC may be a bit scary at first, but not if you remember these things:

➤ Create an emergency disk and update it.

➤ Back up any data you don't want to lose.

➤ Copy down your CMOS settings.

➤ Get a flathead screwdriver and several Phillips screwdrivers together, or purchase a computer toolkit.

➤ You may also want to get something to keep loose screws in, along with a small flashlight, and a pencil and paper.

➤ Make sure you unplug the PC before beginning any work.

➤ Keep yourself grounded as you work, so you don't accidentally discharge any static electricity.

Part 2
Upgrading and Repairing Windows

You might not think you need to repair an operating system, but even Windows can use some help now and then. So, after your computer is locked up for the third time in one day, you can look to this part for some honest, down-to-earth help.

Wanna make Windows faster? Wanna make it sing? Or do you just wanna make it work? Never fear, the answer's here.

And to top off this part, you'll find the help you've been looking for on how to get connected to the Internet, and leave Windows far, far, behind you.

Chapter 5

Fixing Common PC Problems— Windows Style

Your computer's acting strangely. Before you panic, it's important to realize that this doesn't always mean that you'll have to replace something. More than likely, there might be a problem with Windows that you can fix quickly and easily with the tricks you'll find in this chapter. There are several simple solutions you can try, including shutting down some programs to free up some badly needed memory, or even turning off the darn thing and grabbing a quick cup of coffee. With Windows, restarting the PC solves hundreds of weirdness problems, believe me.

After you return from your java break, turn the PC back on and see whether it's still acting strangely. If it is, you'll find some additional solutions in this chapter that you can try. If they don't fix the problem, try the more specific Windows-related solutions in Chapters 6, 7, 8, and 9. They are guaranteed to make Windows behave (well, at least better than it has been). If you decide you need to replace a part, it just so happens that the rest of this book covers that very thing.

What to Do When You're Not Sure What the Problem Is

It's hard to define weird. Computers, after all, are pretty strange creatures, even when they're well. If your PC is making strange noises, flipping strange little zigzags across the screen, or generally acting uncooperatively, then try some of these things:

➤ The first thing to check is the cables, to make sure that none are loose. If you find a guilty party, plug it back in and then get a screwdriver to stick it in place permanently. If you have one of those cases where two cables are supposed to plug in right next to each other, but the engineers didn't leave enough room for both cable ends to coexist, consider a trick that the pros use: Attach an extension cable to one of the ends, even if you have enough cable anyway. For some reason, the connectors on extension cables are thinner than the connectors on standard cables. Just make sure that you don't get a long extension cable—say more than 15 feet or so. Long cables cause their own problems with signal degradation.

➤ Next, try shutting down Windows, turning off the PC, waiting 15 to 20 seconds, and then turning it back on again. This forces the computer to clear all the gook out of its memory (RAM). It's amazing how often this can make the Windows weirdos go away—especially if you usually never turn off the computer.

➤ If you've shut down Windows improperly sometime lately (by turning off the PC instead of following the normal exit procedure), then Windows was not able to clear out the temporary files from its Temp folder. Delete them yourself and restart Windows.

➤ If the computer is still acting strangely, then turn it off again. With the computer turned off, remove all your cables and inspect the little pins—whether they're in the cable end or the connector end. Are any of them bent over to one side? If so, take a pair of needle-nose pliers and carefully bend the pin back in place. Don't yank, though; it's only wire and, therefore, very cheap and easily broken.

➤ Are you working at home? If so, do you have a big-screen, color TV, big monitor, or a high-wattage stereo set? If so, don't just turn off your computer but unplug it also. Sometimes high-power receiving equipment generates what geeks who love the alphabet like to call "RF interference," which cuts right into the electronic signals going on in your computer's bus. (Sound unlikely? Actually, your PC is more likely to catch RF interference than a computer virus.)

➤ Is your surge protector making noise? If it is, its fuse may be about to burn out. No big deal here, just replace the burned-out fuse. (Of course, if the surge protector only cost you $20 or less, then toss it and get a new one instead.) You see, burning out fuses is exactly what surge protectors are designed to do, before something burns out your computer. (Uh, you do have a surge protector, don't you?)

➤ Do you keep anything large and magnetic close to your monitor, like, say, a magnet? You're not using your monitor as a catch-all for old sticky notes clamped together with a magnetic clip, are you? In any case, put anything the least bit magnetic out of the way of your monitor and system unit.

➤ Is the weirdness centered on the mouse? If so, try giving it a spring cleaning. Flip the mouse over and open the latch that holds the trackball. Use something dry and nonmetallic like a toothpick to scrape all the gook off the rollers. Don't use your fingernails; your fingers deposit oils that cause the type of grime that makes it easy for the mouse ball rollers to pick up gunk off your desktop or mouse pad. To keep the mouse clean, refrain from letting your kid roll it on the carpet (where it will pick up lint) or eat at your desk (where tiny crumbs can fall on the mouse pad and be picked up by the roller). If this doesn't fix the problem, try borrowing a mouse that's the same brand and see whether the problem goes away. If your friend's mouse works, then you will know that there's nothing wrong with your PC, but there is something wrong with your mouse. See Chapter 11, "Easy Repairs for Peripherals," for more help.

➤ Try using an antivirus utility to check the hard disk for viruses. A virus is a program that can wreak havoc on your PC, destroying files and rendering your computer useless. A mild virus might only display an annoying message. A virus can get on your computer through an infected disk, or an infected file downloaded from an online service or bulletin board. Don't panic—most computer weirdness has nothing to do with viruses, but you should at least eliminate that possibility. If the utility does find a virus, it can usually remove the bugger with no problems. (If you haven't updated your antivirus utility for a while, it's worth the time to download the latest virus signature file from the manufacturer's Web site. The best brands update their signature files every month.)

➤ If you try all these things and the PC refuses to act normally, you might want to call for help. Before you do, however, make sure that you can help your helper by giving him this information:

   ➤ *Can you duplicate the problem?* Does the weirdness happen when you attempt a particular task, or is it a one-time thing? Is the weirdness related to a particular program? If so, try backing up your program's data and reinstalling the program—this usually fixes the problem.

   ➤ *What have you changed lately?* If you just installed a new part, there are probably some additional things you need to do before you can use it. (See Part 5: "Getting Your PC to Figure Out What You've Done.") These "additional things" involve making changes to the configuration files, CONFIG.SYS and AUTOEXEC.BAT. Also, if you've just installed a new program, it's likely that the program itself also made changes to your files.

101

➤ If you suspect that the setup program for your new application or your new part has made changes to the configuration files that are causing your computer's weirdness, use your emergency disk to copy the original versions of your files back onto the hard disk and restart the PC. After you get your PC back, try making the changes to your configuration files one at a time, so you can isolate the one that caused the weirdness.

➤ Still crazy after all these years? If you've tried all the preceding tricks and Windows is still acting a bit crazy, try defragging your hard disk (as explained in Chapter 8). If you're running Windows 95, you might want to download Service Pack 1 to upgrade your software, or you might prefer to jump on over to Windows 98. See Chapter 9 for help.

When Your PC Won't Start

Although this one is pretty scary, try to not panic—it doesn't necessarily mean that you've killed the PC. Check these things:

➤ First, start with the cables. If you find one trying to escape, guide the loose cable back to its plug. Then screw it in place to prevent another episode.

➤ Next, make sure that the PC is getting power. Take a lamp or other convenient appliance and stick it into the socket you normally use for your computer's plug. Does it work? (Some outlets are *switched*, by the way, meaning that you have to flip a light switch on to turn on the power to that outlet.)

➤ If you use a surge protector with your PC, it might have gone off. If necessary, reset the surge protector by pressing its **Reset** button. An inexpensive surge protector doesn't usually have one, which means that it just burns itself out to save your PC. Give it a nice burial and buy a new one.

➤ If you've plugged in the computer, and the power is on, the next thing to check is the monitor. Is it getting power? If so, are you turning it on? If you have a power saver monitor, its power light will blink yellow if the monitor is turned on while it's properly connected to a computer that has switched itself to low-power mode. Usually, typing one character or jiggling the mouse should jog the computer out of low-power mode. If the monitor is on, fiddle with the brightness and contrast knobs for a while. Some newer monitors, especially those made by Mag Innovision, display TV-station-like color test patterns if they're turned *on* and working properly but not receiving a signal from the computer. Perhaps the data cable is unplugged, or the computer is turned off or not getting power. If you have a new monitor, you're not seeing a blinking yellow light near the power button, and you're not getting the test pattern, your problem may be in the monitor, not the computer.

➤ If you use your emergency disk (see Chapter 4), can you get the PC to start? If so, there may be a problem with the hard disk. See the next section for help.

➤ Do you hear beeping when the computer starts up? If so, there might be a problem with the motherboard or a RAM chip (count the number of both long and short beeps; this will enable a technician to tell you the exact problem). The problem might be your keyboard (make sure that nothing is pressing down on it) or the monitor (make sure that it's plugged in), or you might have left a disk in drive A (if so, remove the disk and restart the PC).

➤ Are you seeing a message such as `Non-system disk or disk error`? If so, remove the disk you accidentally left in drive A, take two steps back, and restart the computer. Does the message say, `CMOS RAM error`? If so, the information in CMOS is wrong, or your battery is going out, or something dinked with CMOS. You can easily reset defaults; see Chapter 27. See Chapter 16 for help with the battery. Does the message say `Bad or missing command interpreter`? If so, then you've accidentally deleted an important file called COMMAND.COM. Use your emergency disk to start your PC; then copy the file back to the root directory from the disk.

➤ If you use Windows 95 or 98, then something might have happened to Windows that's preventing it from starting. You should, at the very least, be able to start Windows in Safe Mode, which means that it loads a minimum of drivers to get you up and running but not working perfectly. When you start your computer, you might see a numbered menu rather than your usual startup screen. Type **5** to start up Windows in Safe Mode. You might notice that the CD-ROM is disabled, for instance, during Safe Mode. While in Safe Mode, check to make sure that your hard drive's directories are where you expect them to be, test your mouse, and then exit Windows the normal way and restart. If you *don't* see that numbered menu a second time and instead you see your normal startup screen, whatever strange thing that might have gone wrong might have been eradicated by some other strange thing in Safe Mode that you didn't even see.

➤ If you exited to DOS from Windows 95 or 98 and you can't get back to Windows, the problem is with the startup files that Windows generates for DOS mode. Using the EDIT program from DOS, open CONFIG.SYS from the root directory of drive C and look for a line at or near the top that reads `DOS=SINGLE`. Delete that entire line. Save the file; then open up AUTOEXEC.BAT. Look for a line at the end that refers to `win` and ends with `/wx`. Delete that entire line, save the file, and exit the editor. You should now be able to start Windows by rebooting your PC.

When Your PC's Locked Up

If you're working away at the computer and you suddenly realize that the PC's no longer paying attention, it might be locked up. Here are some things you can do to get its attention.

➤ First, press **Esc**. This is the universal get-me-out-of-here key, and it might just awaken your Sleeping Beauty.

➤ Next, press **Ctrl+C** (or **Ctrl+Break**).

➤ If you're working in Windows 3.1, press **Ctrl+Esc** to display the Task List. Select the rotten program (the program you were using when the PC decided to freeze up) from the list and click **Delete** to end it.

➤ If you're using Windows 95 or Windows 98, try to get back to the taskbar. (You might have to minimize a window or press **Ctrl+Esc** to get back to it.) When the taskbar is visible, right-click the problem program and select **Close** from the pop-up menu. This terminates the darn thing.

➤ If everything else fails, you might have to restart your PC to get its attention. Do this by pressing **Ctrl+Alt+Delete**. But be warned! Restarting your PC this way causes you to lose any work you haven't already saved. Sorry, but that's the way it goes. Also, keep in mind that restarting your PC this way causes its own set of problems: Specifically, Windows won't delete your temp files. Delete them yourself after you have everything back in order: You'll find them in the Windows Temp directory.

➤ If you're using Windows 3.1, you see a message asking you whether you want to terminate the program that's gone to sleep on you. Click **Yes**. Windows terminates only the one program, so your other work should be okay. If you're using Windows 95/98, the **End Program** list appears when you press **Ctrl+Alt+Delete**. Select the bad program—look for anything listed as (Not Responding)—and click **End Task** to terminate it. You might see a message telling you that the program is not responding. (Duh.) Click **End Task** again to end the thing. Again, this should not affect your other programs. If you're shutting down a major application such as Microsoft Word, you might need to *repeat* this process from the beginning. Why? Because such applications run in *two* pieces, so if you launch Word again, it will see its other part already running and come to the conclusion that some *other* user is operating it. So any of the files that application was running when you tried to shut it down the first time will be inaccessible, until you close that application. So press **Ctrl+Alt+Delete** again and look for the bad program a second time. If you don't see it, click **Cancel**; otherwise, choose the application again, click **End Task**, and then click **End Task** again at the dialog box. (Annoyances such as this are the price of progress.)

➤ As a last resort, turn off your PC (or press the Reset button), wait a bit (usually 15 to 20 seconds), and turn it back on. This certainly gets the PC's attention, but it also causes the computer to close everything down. Keep in mind that if you had been working on something and you hadn't saved it yet, it will be lost when you turn off your PC.

Keep in mind that turning your PC off and on a lot doesn't do much for its delicate parts, which will heat up, cool down, and then heat up again when you turn it back on. Better to leave the PC on all day until you go home, except in cases like this, where you have to turn off the thing just to get its attention.

Save early, save often! At one time or another, no matter how careful you are, your PC is going to lock up on you, and anything you haven't saved will be lost. So be sure to save your work often. Most programs offer an automatic save feature, which saves your work at timed intervals, such as every ten minutes. In some cases, you need to turn on this feature for it to work. Check the program's manual for help.

When a Program Has Problems

If one of your programs has gone off the deep end, try these things:

➤ If you use Windows and the program has simply stopped responding, try exiting it. If you can't exit it properly, Windows can shut down the dumb thing for you. Just press **Ctrl+Alt+Delete** to display the Close Programs list. Select the program from those listed and click **End Task**. Depending on how well behaved the program is, you might see an additional dialog box telling you that the program is not responding to Window's nicely phrased request to shut down. Click **End Task** again.

➤ If you try restarting the program with no luck, you might have to restart Windows as well. Just make sure that you close down any other programs you're running before doing so.

➤ If you can't get a new program to start at all, you might not have enough resources for it. Typically, the problem is not enough memory—fixing this problem might mean an upgrade. However, if you're trying to run a game from DOS on a Windows PC, you probably have enough memory, but dumb old DOS just doesn't know it.

What happened to my work? Needless to say, if you exit a program improperly, it will not get a chance to save your open files. So you might lose some work. How to avoid this problem? Well, first off, save your files periodically *while you're working on them*. Luckily, most programs today will do this for you automatically. But for the few that don't, you'll need to click that Save button and click it often.

To fix the problem, edit your CONFIG.SYS (or, if you use Windows 95/98, the CONFIG.DOS) to add the following commands:

```
DEVICE=C:\WINDOWS\HIMEM.SYS
DEVICE=C:\WINDOWS\EMM386.EXE NOEMS
DOS=UMB
```

Add the commands, in this order, in front of all the other commands. The NOEMS part of the EMM386.EXE command is optional, but it prevents some of your RAM from being used for something useless called expanded memory.

I've got tons of RAM; why doesn't DOS know?

Back when DOS was a baby, the thought of 1MB of RAM was almost unthinkable, it was sooooo big! So that was the upper limit placed on DOS. When it became evident that 1MB of RAM wasn't enough, clever programmers figured out a way to fool DOS into working with more. Sparing you the boring details, suffice it to say that DOS needs help in being able to access any memory above the 1MB mark. This help comes in the form of a device driver called EMM386.EXE and its friend HIMEM.SYS. Load these two files through your CONFIG.SYS, and DOS will wake up counting multiple megabytes of RAM.

➤ When you can't fix a program any other way, try reinstalling it. Back up your data files first; then remove the program and reinstall it. To remove a program from Windows 3.1, make sure that you've backed up any of your own data files that might happen to be in that program's directory; then delete that directory. To remove a program from Windows 95/98, use Add/Remove Programs in the Control Panel.

Keeping Your Desktop Organized

One of the neat things about Windows is that it duplicates the way you work, with its desktop analogy that mimics your own desktop. Actually, one of the yuckiest things about Windows is that it uses a desktop analogy, enabling you to keep your Windows desktop as unorganized as your real desktop.

Been having trouble with your desktop lately—like, you can't find it when you need it? Wondering how to organize it well enough to live with comfortably? Try these tips:

➤ With the Windows 3.1 Program Manager, try organizing your icons into groups that make sense *to you*. Just because the program manufacturer likes to dump its icons into a folder it creates, such as Lotus or Microsoft, that doesn't mean you like it that way. Try dragging the program icons you use every day into one folder, such as Applications, or some another folder you create. (To create a folder, open Program Manager's **File** menu and select **New**. Then select **Program Group**.)

➤ With Windows 95/98, organize the Start menu so that it suits the way you work. Click **Start**, select **Settings**, and then select **Taskbar** (or **Taskbar & Start Menu**). Click the **Start Menu Programs** tab and then click **Advanced**. Here, you're using Explorer, so you use the same techniques to organize programs as you would to organize files. To create a new folder, use the **File/New** command; to move programs, just drag them to their new folder.

➤ Save yourself some hassle and dump your favorite programs into the StartUp folder, which will tell Windows to start the programs automatically for you every day.

➤ By the way, you don't have to place programs within folders on the Start menu. If you use your spreadsheet program a lot (but not enough to start it every day by using the StartUp folder), then place its command on the main Start menu rather than under the Program menu.

➤ Remove the icons you don't use from the desktop, such as My Briefcase, Network Neighborhood (if you're not connected to a network), The Microsoft Network, The Internet or Internet Explorer (which you might not use if you use Netscape instead), Online Services, and the Inbox or Outlook Express (if you use some other email program). Then place icons you do use on the desktop, by simply opening Explorer, right-clicking a program's start file, and dragging it to the desktop. When the pop-up menu appears, give it a wink and select **Create Shortcut(s) Here.**

➤ Simplify, simplify, simplify. Instead of using a graphic background in Windows, why not go back to a simple, single color? Using a color rather than a graphic will use less memory, help Windows run faster, and make your desktop appear less cluttered. In Windows 3.1, you use the Color icon in the Control Panel to change colors. In Windows 95/98, right-click the desktop and select **Properties**. On the **Background** tab, make sure that you've selected **None** under both **Pattern** and **Wallpaper**. Then click the **Appearance** tab and select **Desktop** from the **Item** list. Select the color you like from the **Color** list.

➤ In Windows 95 or 98, to make your desktop less messy, arrange your icons in neat rows. Right-click the desktop and select **Arrange Icons,** or just drag the icons where you want them on your desktop, perhaps in two columns, one on either side of the screen.

➤ If your screen is cluttered, you probably have trouble locating an icon on the desktop when needed. If you have Windows 98, or if you've upgraded your Windows 95 system (see Chapter 9), you can use the Windows toolbars to help you find your desktop even when your screen is filled with windows. For example, if you display the Quick Launch toolbar on the taskbar (by right-clicking the taskbar, selecting **Toolbars**, and selecting **Quick Launch**), then you can click the View Desktop icon at any time to minimize all your open windows and display the desktop, lickety-split. You can also display the Desktop toolbar, which contains the icons for all the programs on the desktop. Then, as long as you can see the taskbar, you can start any desktop program you need by simply clicking its button on the Desktop toolbar.

➤ Is your Windows 95 or 98 taskbar full of program buttons and active resource indicators (those little pesky icons in the lower-right corner next to the clock)? Try this: Move your mouse pointer to the upper boundary between the taskbar and the desktop, so that it becomes a black up-and-down arrow. Click and hold down the mouse button and then drag the pointer up, so that the shadow emerging from the taskbar is two taskbars tall. Release the mouse button, and you'll have a taskbar with twice as much space as before. The resource icons at right will scoot to the right into a taller, though thinner, compartment. You'll also have two rows of wider, easier-to-read program buttons.

The Least You Need to Know

If there's one lesson for you to learn in this chapter, it's that it's never over 'til it's over. In other words, don't jump to the conclusion that something's broken when it's not. Here are some other tidbits to remember:

➤ If your PC starts acting funny, check the simple things first, such as making sure that it's plugged in and powered up and that all cables are properly connected.

➤ Remember that some useful utility programs can help in times like these. My favorites include Norton Utilities and other utilities packages from McAfee (Network Associates) and MicroHelp.

➤ Your best insurance against total disaster is a good backup. Your second best insurance against disaster is to save your work often.

➤ Sometimes the easiest way to get something to work again is to turn your computer off and then back on again.

➤ Before real trouble strikes, make sure that you create an emergency disk and keep it current. See Chapter 4 for help.

Chapter 6

Repairing Your Operating System

In This Chapter

➤ Which upgrades make Windows 95 or 98 the happiest

➤ Oh, yeah, there's stuff about Windows 3.1, too

➤ Some ways to make Windows run faster without upgrading your hardware

---

Windows 95 is a pumped-up version of Windows 3.1, which means that it's faster, easier to use, and contains less than half the fat. Windows 98 is Windows 95 and Internet Explorer run together through a blender.

Unfortunately (or fortunately, depending on your point of view), neither Windows 95 nor Windows 98 looks very much like Windows 3.1. And they can't always run on a computer that can run Windows 3.1.

Whoa. Take two steps back.

Yep, that's right; even though your old PC is currently running Windows 3.1, that doesn't guarantee that it can run Windows 95 or Windows 98. Before you get all bummed out, jump over to Chapter 9, "Replacing Your Operating System," and take a look at Windows 95 and Windows 98 and see if either one is even something you need right now. If not, come back to the second half of this chapter to learn ways you can push old Windows 3.1 to its limits.

Meanwhile, if you've got Windows 95 or Windows 98 and you'd like to get the most out of it, read the first sections in this chapter.

Ways to Get the Most Out of Windows 95/98

If you're migrating from Windows 3.1 to Windows 95, or from there on to Windows 98, you'll be taking advantage of the full 32-bit capabilities of your 486 or higher CPU. Gone are those nasty problems like GPFs (General Protection Faults) and swap file overloads. In their place are some new, fresh, nasty problems. Don't get the wrong idea here; you are improving your computer in the long run. But just like when NASA upgraded its manned space rockets from the Titan II to the Saturn V, the number of potential headaches increased along with the benefits. Here, you'll learn some tricks for making some of those headaches go away.

Cleaning Up the Registry

The Registry acts as a notebook for Windows 95 and 98, remembering key details about your computer and its setup. For example, in the Registry you'll find your desktop preferences, device settings, and software configurations. It's so important, that if something were to happen to the Registry, you might not be able to even start Windows! With a faulty Registry, at best, you'd be able to boot your computer into command prompt mode (which looks just like DOS did back in the Ice Age of Computing).

Back up your Registry

Your Registry is important, so before you attempt to make any changes to it, you should make a backup copy. This backup is typically stored on the hard disk, because the file is too large for a floppy. However, if your PC has larger removable storage such as a Zip drive, you should use it instead.

To back up your Registry, you use RegEdit. Click the **Start** button and select **Run**. Type the command, **C:\WINDOWS\REGEDIT** and click **OK**. Open the **Registry** menu and select **Export Registry File**. Type a filename, select **All** in the Export area, and click **Save**. (Be sure to make a note of the directory in which the copy is saved, should you need it later.)

One problem with the Registry is that, because it holds so much information about Windows, it tends to get pretty cluttered, especially with old data (such as software you've removed or devices you've upgraded). Because the Registry is so large, if you can remove some of the unneeded data, not only will you get more room on your hard disk, but your system will run faster.

To streamline your Registry, you use a program called RegClean, conveniently provided for you by Microsoft, and downloadable online via `http://www.iconshareware.com/software/util/sysutil/msregclean41_download.html`. Why the program isn't shipped along with Windows is a mystery. Still, the program is a breeze to use. You basically just tell it to go, wait while it does its thing, and instruct it to commit the corrections to whatever errors it may have found (it tells you there are errors even when there are none, which is a bit odd). Then RegClean backs up the Registry for you, makes its changes, and advises you to reboot Windows. There's nothing more to the program than that, and it is indeed a lifesaver. If for some reason RegClean does *cause* an error, you can easily undo the changes made to your Registry by double-clicking the undo file that RegClean generated automatically during the cleanup process.

Streamlining Your Startup

One negative about using Windows is that it takes so long to start! Anything you can do to improve the process is a blessing for sure. Some ideas for improving the process:

➤ *Ignore your startup programs.* You may have many programs in your Startup folder. For example, you might have an electronic day planner, your Web browser, and your word processor all loading automatically. Microsoft Exchange, Outlook, and Outlook Express (which are all email clients) take about a year and a half to load. To prevent the programs in the Startup folder from loading, press **Ctrl** while starting Windows. If you need one of your startup programs later on, however, you'll need to start it manually. To permanently disable automatic startup of any or all programs, delete their icons from the \Windows\Startup folder; these are just shortcut icons, not the actual programs.

➤ *Why waste time restarting your computer when all you really want to do is restart Windows?* First, restart your PC in the usual manner: click **Start**, select **Restart the computer**, then hold the **Shift** key while clicking **Yes**. This is not a smart way to restart the PC if it has been on for several days. Instead, power down the PC, then power it back up.

Check This Out...

Don't mess with the Registry Using RegClean to clean up the Registry is fine, because basically the work is done for you. You should not, however, try to mess with the entries in the Registry yourself. Doing so can seriously damage Windows.

Check This Out...

Create a quick Restart icon If you often reboot Windows (and not the PC), create a restart Windows icon for your desktop. First, start Notepad and create a file called RESTART.BAT that contains this one line:

`@EXIT`

Drag the file from Explorer to the desktop to create a shortcut. Then right-click the shortcut and choose **Properties**. On the **Program** tab, select **Close on exit**. When you want to reboot Windows without restarting your PC, double-click the shortcut.

➤ *Speed up startup.* You can speed up the Windows startup process by removing any boot delay and skipping the Windows logo banner. Here's how: Using Notepad, edit the file MSDOS.SYS, which you'll find in the root directory. In the [Options] section, add the line, **BootDelay=0**. To refrain from advertising Windows during startup, get rid of the banner by adding the line, **Logo=0**.

No Windows banner here! Another way to bypass the Windows banner at startup is to press Esc as the computer is booting.

➤ *Bypass Windows login.* If you're tired of logging into your PC, especially if no one else has access to it anyway, then set up Windows so you can bypass the login procedure. Double-click the **Passwords** icon in the Control Panel. On the **User Profiles** tab select **All users of this PC use the same preferences and desktop settings**. On the **Change Passwords** tab, click the **Change Windows Password** button. Change the password to nothing. Now, at this point, Windows won't be able to remember the password to log you onto the Internet; but if it's not a problem for you to remember it yourself and type it in each time, you can disable all passwords in this way.

Avoiding Crashes

When I find myself in the middle of some big project and maybe I haven't saved my file in a while and suddenly my keyboard freezes up and the computer refuses to respond, I start to feel like one of those old cartoon characters—you know the guy, you'll catch him chasing after a fast desert bird and after smashing into a cliff, bouncing off a ledge, and crashing through some trees, he ends up falling into a lake. All we see are his fingers, as he counts down "One, two, three," finally disappearing completely under the water.

I hate it when a program crashes.

Why does it happen? Basically, Windows gets so confused with all the things it's supposed to be doing that it loses track of some program, gives up on it, and blanks out. Or, it may be the program's fault; some programs don't know how to behave.

What can you do to avoid crashes? Well, you can stop running programs, but that's hardly practical. Instead, why not try some of these tips:

➤ *Restart your computer periodically.* Some people like to keep their computers running all the time, never shutting down at the end of each day. If you're one of those, you may want to rethink your game plan and shut down every couple of days or so. This gives Windows a chance to completely clear up memory, and reallocate its resources.

➤ *Update your programs when you can.* At least in theory, having the latest and greatest versions of your software should eliminate some bugs (it may just trade one set of problems for another, however).

➤ *Upgrade to Windows 95/98 versions.* Windows 3.1 and DOS programs usually run okay under Windows 95/98, but if you can upgrade to the version that is *supposed* to run with your operating system, you'll get improved performance.

➤ *Tame that old Windows 3.1 program.* If you've got a Windows 3.1 program that's been giving you pains, you might be able to tweak it just enough to solve the problem. To do this, you use a program called MKCOMPAT. Click the **Start** button, select **Run**, and type **MKCOMPAT** in the Open text box. Open the **File** menu and select **Choose Program**. Select your program from those listed and click **Open**. Try any of the options listed—it's hard to say which ones may fool your Windows 3.1 program enough to get it to behave. The idea is to make it feel "at home" under Windows 95/98. After making your selections, open the **File** menu and select **Save**.

➤ *Use two hard disk drives.* Huh? You read right. Install your main applications on your C drive, then keep your personal data on your D drive. This is easy to do with IDE drives; just make your D drive the slave to the C drive master. This way, should an application failure, an installation glitch, or (worst case scenario) an operating system failure take out your C drive, all your personal data on your D drive is safe even if you have to reformat C. This measure does not eliminate the need for you to back up your personal data; but as long as you keep the installation discs for your applications and your operating system close at hand, even a drive C failure should not become a complete disaster for you, because reinstallation of these things is simple and only a waste of a day or so of your time. Also, having all your data on one hard disk makes it easy for you to always keep it backed up properly.

> **Be prepared!** Make sure you always have a current backup of the Registry and your data in case a simple crash turns into something less fun.

Removing Duplicate DLLs

Windows applications have a tendency to use certain files, called *libraries* or *DLLs*, that are supposed to be shared with other applications. However, because their installers place these files only in the application's native directory rather than a directory where other applications may actually share them, several copies of the same DLL may inhabit your hard drive at any one time.

Rather than spend a year hunting down duplicate filenames and deleting all those names that aren't in the \System subdirectory, consider downloading a shareware utility from http://www.fineware.com called Space Hound. There, you'll find separate 16-bit (Windows 3.1) and 32-bit (Windows 95, NT) versions. What this program does, among other things, is plow through all your directories and take note of the locations of duplicate DLLs. You can then instruct Space Hound to delete these duplicates safely, leaving one copy intact and in a share-worthy location, so all your other applications continue to work properly.

Other Things to Try

Here's a list of other things you can try to improve your system's performance under Windows 95/98:

➤ *Minimize the Backup program.* When performing a backup, be sure to minimize the window. Believe it or not, backup will run almost 25 percent faster if you do.

➤ *Delete those darn temp files.* Temp files are files that programs create, use temporarily, and then delete. As long as the program doesn't crash on you, it should clean up after itself and delete its temp files. If you have to reboot the computer or reboot Windows, or restart a crashed program, you'll end up with files in your TEMP directory that will never be deleted. To avoid this problem, delete your temp files each time you restart your PC by adding the following line to your AUTOEXEC.BAT:

```
Echo Y¦If Exist C:\Windows\Temp\*.* Del C:\Windows\Temp\*.* >Nul
```

➤ *Where's that darn desktop?* Do you sometimes find yourself minimizing a bunch of windows just so you can get to something on the desktop? Well, no more: Instead, click the **Start** button, select **Run**, and type . (dot). Click **OK**. The desktop will appear.

➤ *Get rid of your unused fonts and save yourself some hard disk space.* Click **Start**, select **Settings**, and then select **Control Panel**. Double-click the **Fonts** icon. Select the fonts you want to bump off, open the **File** menu, and select **Delete**. A warning appears. Click **Yes**, and Windows 95/98 zaps the files. If you accidentally delete a font you wanted to keep, put on your "I'm sorry" face and restore the files from the Recycle Bin. Just open the Recycle Bin, select the font you want back, then open the **File** menu and select **Restore**.

➤ *Reduce the amount of space your programs take up.* This not only frees up hard drive space, but it often makes the program start faster as well. Simply uninstall your programs, then reinstall them, this time using the **Minimum** or **Typical** option. Be sure, of course, to back up all your data first.

The best thing you can do for your system

Just about the best thing you can do for your PC (if you use Windows 95, that is) is to update it with Service Pack 1. Included in the service pack are system updates, bug fixes, system administration tools, and updated drivers. You can download the service pack from Microsoft's Web site:

www.microsoft.com/windows95/info/service-packs.htm

Installing the service pack will update your Windows version number from 4.00.950 to 4.00.95A, if it isn't there already. Further revisions to Windows 95 are available for download from:

www.microsoft.com/windows/pr/win95osr.htm

These multiple enhancements collectively bring your 4.00.950A edition of Windows 95 to what is called "OSR2" (OEM Service Release 2) status. That means your Windows 95 should, after all those OSR2 files are downloaded and installed, work just as well with just as much functionality as a brand new computer sold retail.

Determined Not to Switch to Windows 95 or 98? Repairs That Could Make Windows 3.1 Happy

Just because you can't afford to upgrade, that won't stop you from wanting your PC to run just a little bit better. In the rest of this chapter, you'll learn some tricks you can try to stretch your existing resources and keep your money from the upgrade man just a little longer.

Upgrade DOS

If you use Windows 3.1, you can do a lot of things to improve the performance of your PC without actually upgrading to Windows 95 or 98. However, you need the latest version of DOS.

The latest (and last) standalone version of MS-DOS is 6.22. If you wanted to compress your hard disk, for example (double the number of files it can hold), you will need at least version 6.21 to use DriveSpace to compress your hard drive. If you have version 6.0 or 6.2, you can use DoubleSpace instead.

After you've purchased the latest version of DOS, exit Windows and insert the first disk into drive A. Then type:

    A:SETUP

and press **Enter**. Follow the instructions onscreen to complete the installation.

Techno Talk

How can I tell what DOS version I have?

Well, if you have Windows 95 or Windows 98, you have DOS 7.x, so you won't need to update anything. Other than that, you can't be too sure, because Windows 3.1 will run on anything that's at least DOS 3.1. To tell what DOS version you have, type **VER** at the DOS prompt and press **Enter**.

Check This Out...

This goes for Windows 95/ 98, too You should clean up your StartUp folder as well. Only place in the folder the programs you use every day.

Use Your Startup Group Wisely

For starters, make sure that Windows automatically starts up only those programs that you *truly* use every day. If you're in doubt about the usefulness of something, take it out of the Startup group. I used to have my Web browser in my Startup group, but I didn't always use the thing every day. So instead of waiting for Windows to load it on days when I might not use it, I just removed it from the Startup group and then started it manually when I wanted to run it.

If you use the same documents every day, put the documents in the Startup group, instead of the program you used to create them. For example, if you have a sales spreadsheet that you use every day, put it into the Startup group, and not Excel or Lotus 1-2-3. Windows then opens Excel or Lotus 1-2-3 for you during startup and loads your spreadsheet automatically.

Get Rid of Unused Fonts

Get rid of fonts you don't use. Practically every program comes with loads and loads of fonts, most of which you probably don't use. A list of the names of all these fonts is in the WIN.INI (a Windows configuration file). Windows reads this list every time you start it, which, if it's full of the names of lots of fonts, can take a long time. In addition, the font files themselves sit on the hard disk, taking up room. Getting the extra fonts out of there saves time in starting Windows, in addition to making room on the hard disk.

Now, if you're nervous about removing a particular font, copy it to a disk first. You can reinstall it later if you decide that this was all some cruel mistake. To get rid of a font in Windows 3.1, open up the **Control Panel** and double-click the **Fonts** icon. Highlight the fonts you want to murder and click **Remove**. You see a warning; to remove the font from the WIN.INI and from the hard disk, click the **Delete Font File from Disk** option. Click **Yes**, or if you're committing mass-murder, click **Yes to All**. Click **Close** to return to the Control Panel.

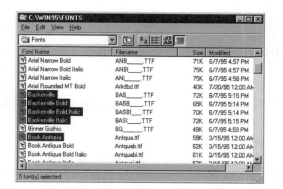

Murdering fonts in Windows 3.1.

Create a Permanent Swap File

If you use Windows 3.1, one of the simplest ways to speed the darn thing up is to switch to a permanent swap file. (If you upgrade to Windows 95/98, you don't have to worry about the swap file—it's already as fast as it's gonna get. See the box for more details.)

The Windows 95/98 swap file

Windows 95/98 combines the "best" of the temporary swap file and permanent swap file business in Windows 3.1. The swap file in Windows 95/98 is *dynamic,* which is a fancy way of saying that it changes its size as needed. Also, the Windows 95/98 swap file works in a noncontiguous (broken up) space (just like the old temporary swap file in Windows 3.1), but unlike Windows 3.1, there's no penalty in performance.

So you get the benefit of a temporary swap file (you don't have to permanently allocate hard disk space when the swap file may never use it) and the benefit of a permanent swap file (speed, baby, speed). Also, Windows 95 can place its swap file on a compressed drive, such as drive C, so chances are, it can be larger than the one you used under Windows 3.1.

And if this is almost too good to be true, there's more: Windows 95/98 sets up its permatemp swap file without any help from you. The only thing you may ever want to do is change the hard drive it uses (which is drive C), but even that is rare.

You see, when you run Windows and you start up all your programs, it can quickly run out of memory (RAM). Even though Windows can juggle multiple programs at once, you are only one person, and for the most part, you can only work on one thing at a time.

So when you start a program, open a few files, and then switch away from the program, Windows takes the stuff you're not currently working on and "swaps it out" of memory by copying it to the hard disk temporarily, to a place called the *swap file*.

When you installed Windows 3.1, it created a temporary swap file, which means that it staked out some space on the hard disk each time you started Windows and then removed itself when you exited. If you don't have a lot of space on the hard disk, then the temporary swap file ends up being pretty tiny and pretty worthless. In addition, it takes Windows longer to access a temporary swap file because the file itself is broken into tiny bits and scattered all over the hard disk.

If you do have some room on the hard disk, it's worth the trouble to create a permanent swap file, because it lets Windows stake out a permanent area on the hard disk for swapping things out of memory. A permanent swap file provides faster access because the file is *contiguous*, which for a big word, simply means that all its parts are together on the hard disk, making it easier for Windows to get data out of it.

Reorganize your disk first Before you switch to a permanent swap file, you should reorganize your hard disk. See the section, "Reorganizing the Hard Disk," located in Chapter 8, "Fixing Hard Disk Hassles."

The only negative here is that you need to have room on a *noncompressed drive* to create your permanent swap file. This noncompressed drive is usually drive H. If you find that you have some room on drive H, then here's what you do to create a permanent swap file under Windows 3.1: In Windows, exit all your programs, open up the **Control Panel** and double-click the **386 Enhanced** icon. Then click the **Virtual Memory** button to see the Virtual Memory dialog box. Click the **Change** button and the dialog box expands faster than your stomach after a Thanksgiving dinner.

Now, open the **Type** list and select **Permanent**. If you see an option to **Use 32-bit Disk Access**, select it (well, read the box coming up first, then decide if you want to try this option). That's it—click **OK**. Windows asks if you really, really want to create a permanent swap file. Click **Yes**. You need to restart Windows, so click **Restart Windows**.

Other Things to Try

Still stuck with Windows 3.1? Here are some other things you can do to speed things up:

➤ *Put your affairs in order.* With a little utility called DEFRAG, you can reorganize the files on your hard disk so it doesn't take Windows so long to open the files when you need them. See Chapter 8 for more information.

➤ *Give your existing memory a boost.* Using another utility called SMARTDrive, you can help Windows make the best use of the RAM your PC has. See Chapter 8 for the how-tos.

➤ *Stretch your limits.* Windows 3.1 will be a lot happier if you give it more memory—which makes this the single best upgrade for your computer. Adding just 4MB of RAM will make a huge difference! See Chapter 19 for help.

➤ *Double the hard disk, double your fun.* If the only problem you have right now is that you're running out of space for new programs, then why not double the hard disk? It's easy with DoubleSpace or DriveSpace (see Chapter 8).

Big drive? Read this

Some of the really huge hard disk drives (a gigabyte or more) don't work with the 32-bit Disk Access feature of Windows 3.1. If you have one of these gargantuan drives, and you chose the 32-bit option, restarted Windows, and saw nothing but the dead of night, then go find the manual that came with your hard drive (hopefully your dealer gave it to you).

You may have to install a special driver to make your hard disk work with 32-bit disk access; the most common one is called Disk Manager (Western Digital and some other brands provide it with their drives). The manual tells you for sure. Next, find the disk that contains this driver and use the automatic setup procedure that runs from DOS to install it.

If you can't find a driver and you need to use Windows now, then you can undo the 32-bit access thing, with a little work. Type **CD\WINDOWS** and press **Enter**. Then type **EDIT WIN.INI** and press **Enter**. Use the down arrow to go through the file until you find the line: 32BitDiskAccess=Off. Change the Off to **On**, save the file, and exit EDIT. You can now use Windows again.

Memory is even faster

Even though a permanent swap file is faster than a temporary one, it's a turtle compared to the real speed demon—your computer's memory. Memory is a lot faster to access than anything on the hard disk. So if you can afford to upgrade anything, memory is the best way to spend your bucks, especially if you plan on using Windows. See Chapter 19, "Make Mine More Memory," for help.

RAM Doubler

You can almost double the amount of memory that Windows 3.1 perceives as your RAM with a software program called Connectix RAM Doubler for Windows 3.1. Of course, it doesn't actually increase the physical amount of RAM that you have, but it does manage it better than Windows can.

RAM Doubler shuffles things in and out of memory as needed, saving them temporarily on the hard disk until they're called for again. The reason that RAM Doubler can squeeze more memory space out of RAM is that it also compresses (shrinks) the information in RAM, kinda like DriveSpace does for the hard disk.

Similar utility programs—such as Connectix Agent 95 and Quarterdeck MagnaRAM—are available for Windows 95, though professional tests not only show significant performance *degradation* using these programs, but an annoying tendency for all that "doubled" RAM to be absorbed twice as readily as before.

The Least You Need to Know

Regardless of which operating system you decide to use, you can always get just a little bit more out of it:

➤ The best upgrade you can make for either version of Windows is to add memory.

➤ If you use Windows 95/98, you should clean up the Registry periodically to remove any unneeded entries and reduce its size.

➤ If you use Windows 95/98, speed up your start process with the tricks listed in the section, "Streamlining Your Startup."

➤ If you use Windows 95/98, remove duplicate DLL files when possible.

➤ If you use Windows 3.1, you can speed it up by creating a permanent swap file. If you use Windows 95, the swap file is already as fast as it's gonna get.

➤ Also, if you use Windows 3.1 or Windows 95/98, you can speed things up by using your Startup group wisely. In addition, delete any fonts that you never use to add a little extra speed.

Chapter 7

Running Low on Memory? Unjam Your RAM

In This Chapter

➤ Get more use out of your RAM with MemMaker

➤ Setting up something permanent with Windows 3.1

➤ Swapping ideas and swap files

RAM is one of your PC's most precious resources because it's the area in which your PC works. When you want to work on something at your desk, you get it out of a drawer (or off the floor) and place it on your desktop. DOS does basically the same thing; it retrieves files off the hard disk (or disk or CD-ROM) and then places the files on its "desktop," which is called RAM. After the files are in RAM, DOS can begin processing them.

All programs need memory to run—some programs need a lot of memory. Not having enough memory affects the way your programs work and can even prevent some programs from starting. So it's just good sense to make the most of the RAM you have.

But I have plenty of memory!

So you might think. But if you're running with just DOS, or DOS with Windows 3.1, programs can only run in the first 640KB of memory—that's how the first computers were designed. Above 640KB and below 1MB is an area of memory reserved for the computer's use. To access memory above 1MB, the computer needs help, which comes in the form of a memory driver. Just as your PC uses a mouse driver to communicate with the mouse, it uses a memory driver to manage this upper area of memory. The area of memory above 1MB is typically referred to as *extended memory* because it's an extension of the regular 640KB processing memory. Some of this memory can be converted into *expanded memory*, which is basically the same memory, it's just handled differently, by an expanded memory driver. Hardly any programs today use expanded memory; all abide by the extended memory standard, including Windows. DOS programs and Windows 16-bit programs (designed for 3.1) continue to work under these limitations in Windows 95 and 98, but the operating system carves out an exclusive chunk of system RAM for each of these programs. So each program has a *virtual machine* all to itself, at least from its own perspective.

Making the Most Out of Memory with MemMaker

MemMaker is a program that you can use to optimize your PC's memory use (if only it could help you remember where you left your keys). You see, your PC can't really access any memory over 1MB, at least, not without help. This obvious shortcoming dates back to the early days of DOS, when the powers that be decided that 1MB of memory was more than any computer would ever need. These people were also, by some weird coincidence, the same ones who thought no one could ever need more than one car, TV, or telephone.

What's a device driver?

A *device driver* is a file that helps your computer "talk" to peripheral devices, such as a CD-ROM, mouse, sound card, and so on. Device drivers set up a pro-tocol between your CPU and your peripherals' own processors.

Since the advent of Windows 95, Windows manages memory operations, not DOS. Windows 95, Windows 98, and all versions of Windows NT perceive your computer's RAM as one contiguous block of memory, rather than a 640KB base with a heck of a long tail hanging out. But some peripherals continue to rely on DOS to run their device drivers, and, of course, there are DOS applications that you and others still love to run. Whenever DOS is brought back into the picture, the old memory problems rear their ugly heads once again.

So the problem still remains: how to get the computer to access memory above the 1MB limit? The solution is simple, as it turns out: all you need to do is to load the proper device drivers.

But to get the most out of memory, you have to load not only these memory device drivers but also any other device drivers you have in the most effective order. The order depends on the size of the device drivers your system uses. Trying to figure out the exact placement of all these drivers is like putting together a puzzle with no edge pieces. So give yourself a break and let MemMaker do all the work for you.

How to Use MemMaker If You Have One of the DOS 6-Somethings

If you have one of the DOS 6-somethings (DOS 6, 6.2, 6.21, or 6.22), then you can use a utility called MemMaker to *optimize* (improve) your system's use of memory automatically, making it "be all that it can be."

To begin to optimize your system, exit all programs; then type **CD\DOS** and press **Enter**. Type **MEMMAKER** and press **Enter**. A message appears, asking you to choose between Express (for real people like us) and Custom optimization (for geeks). To use Express, just press **Enter**. Then you're asked whether you use any programs that require expanded memory. If you're not sure, choose **No** because you can always rerun MemMaker and change it later.

A message appears, asking you to press **Enter** so that MemMaker can restart your PC. Do it, and MemMaker analyzes your system and makes changes to your AUTOEXEC.BAT and CONFIG.SYS files. Press **Enter**, and MemMaker tests your new configuration.

MemMaker will then ask whether your new configuration is **OK**. Basically, if your PC didn't blow up during reboot, then your new configuration is okay. Press **Enter** for Yes if the computer restarted okay, or press the **Spacebar** and then **Enter** to answer No (and continue testing different configurations).

Finally, MemMaker shows you all the fine work it's done and takes a bow. Press **Enter** to exit MemMaker.

What to Do If You Have Windows

If you're using Windows 3.1, no problema, as long as you also have one of the DOS 6-somethings (DOS 6, 6.2, 6.21, or 6.22). Just exit Windows 3.1 before you do your MemMaker stuff.

If you're using Windows 95 or Windows 98, then you have essentially DOS 7, and you can also join in on the MemMaker merriment. Restart your PC with DOS and then run MemMaker. Just click the **Start** button,

> **Check This Out...**
>
> **MemMaker and Windows 95/ 98** If you use Windows 95 or 98, you don't really need to use MemMaker for Windows' own purposes because Windows is good at managing memory on its own. However, if you run DOS programs (such as games), you'll get better performance (but not necessarily higher scores) if you run MemMaker.

select **Shut down**, and then select **Restart** the computer with DOS. After you get the friendly prompt, follow the MemMaker steps given earlier.

Creating a Permanent Swap File in Windows 3.1

What's a swap file? A *swap file* is a temporary storage area that Windows uses for data. When memory gets full, Windows swaps data out of memory to the hard disk, where it sits, mumbling and grumbling, until it's needed again by some program. At that point, the data is swapped back into memory.

Earlier, you learned many ways to speed up Windows 3.1. One way is to switch from a temporary swap file to a permanent one. A permanent swap file provides faster access because the file is *contiguous*, which for a big word simply means that all its parts are together on the hard disk, making it easier for Windows to get data out of it.

The only negative here is that you need to have room on a *noncompressed drive* to create your permanent swap file. This noncompressed drive is usually drive H. If you have some room on drive H, then here's what you do to create a permanent swap file under Windows 3.1: In Windows, exit all your programs; open up the **Control Panel** and double-click the **386 Enhanced** icon; click the **Virtual Memory** button to see the Virtual Memory dialog box; click the **Change** button; and the dialog box expands faster than your stomach after Thanksgiving dinner.

The Virtual Memory dialog box expands so that you can create a permanent swap file.

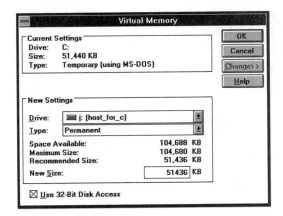

Reorganize your disk, first

Before you switch to a permanent swap file, reorganize your hard disk first. See the section, "Reorganize the Hard Disk," located in Chapter 8, "Fixing Hard Disk Hassles."

Now, open the **Type** list and select **Permanent**. If you see an option to **Use 32-bit Disk Access**, select it (well, read the box first and then decide whether you want to try this option). That's it—click **OK**. Windows asks whether you really want to create a permanent swap file. Click **Yes**. You need to restart Windows, so click **Restart Windows**.

Big drive? Read this

Some of the really huge hard disk drives (a gigabyte or more) don't work with the 32-bit Disk Access feature of Windows 3.1. If you have one of these gargantuan drives and you chose the 32-bit option, restarted Windows, and saw a smaller hard drive than you know you actually have, then go find the manual that came with your hard drive (hopefully your dealer gave it to you).

You might have to install a special driver to make your hard disk work with 32-bit disk access; the most common one is Disk Manager (Western Digital and some other brands provide it with their drives). The manual tells you for sure. Next, find the disk that contains this driver and use the automatic setup procedure that runs from DOS to install it.

If you can't find a driver and you need to use Windows now, then you can undo the 32-bit access thing, with a little work. Type **CD\WINDOWS** and press **Enter**. Then type **EDIT WIN.INI** and press **Enter**. Use the down arrow to go through the file until you find the line: `32BitDiskAccess=Off`. Change the Off to **On**, save the file, and exit EDIT. You can now use Windows again.

The Least You Need to Know

Memory is one of your computer's most important assets. To make sure that your PC uses RAM wisely, remember these things:

➤ Your PC needs help to access memory above 1MB. This help comes in the form of a device driver.

➤ To load your device drivers into memory in the most effective order, cheat and use MemMaker.

➤ MemMaker comes with DOS versions 6 and over. (Windows 95 and 98 come with DOS 7.)

➤ Run MemMaker with Windows 95/98 only if you plan to run DOS programs, also. Otherwise, it's unnecessary.

➤ If you use Windows 3.1, you'll improve your PC's performance immensely if you create a permanent swap file.

➤ To create a permanent swap file, you must have enough room on your hard disk. A 5 to 10MB swap file is usually a good size, but it all depends on the size of your hard disk.

Chapter 8

Fixing Hard Disk Hassles

In This Chapter

➤ What to do when your hard disk doesn't respond

➤ Spring cleaning your files

➤ Make your hard disk smarter with SMARTDrive

➤ Double your PC's hard disk space with DriveSpace or DoubleSpace

➤ Reorganize your files with DEFRAG

Because you store all your important files on your hard disk, it isn't hard to understand why its health becomes important so quickly. In this chapter, you'll learn ways you can deal with a malfunctioning hard disk (short of replacing it, that is) and tricks you can perform to keep your hard disk running well.

What to Do When Your Hard Disk Plays Hide and Seek

If your PC won't start normally, but it starts when you use your emergency disk, then something is probably wrong with the hard disk. Try investigating these possibilities:

➤ *First of all, did you (or some new program you tried to install) make changes to the configuration files, CONFIG.SYS or AUTOEXEC.BAT, recently?* You'll probably know if some program made changes, because they typically tell you so before doing it, although boorish programs make changes without your permission. If so, a *device driver* file, which the PC uses to access data on the hard disk, may have been accidentally deleted. For example, if you compressed your hard disk as explained later in this chapter, then you may have deleted the device driver file which starts DoubleSpace or DriveSpace (the disk compression program). Or, if you have a large hard drive and you use a DOS version earlier than DOS 4.0, you may have deleted the device driver file that your DOS uses to access large disks.

In any case, if you suspect that you (or some installation program) changed the contents of your configuration files, then copy them back to drive C from your emergency disk and restart the computer.

Your insurance agent Your best insurance against disaster is a backup of your important data files. See Chapter 4, "What You Need to Know Before You Open Your PC," for how-tos.

➤ *If you use Windows 95 or Windows 98, have some changes been made to your \WINDOWS\SYSTEM subdirectory?* You see, you may not even have a CONFIG.SYS or AUTOEXEC.BAT file in the root directory of your main hard disk, because Windows 95/98 doesn't need them. But Windows 95 and Windows 98 do use device driver files—Windows tries, for the most part, to select those drivers for itself, in a process called *Plug and Play* (PnP). In this case, the drivers that Windows expects to see are often kept in the \WINDOWS\SYSTEM subdirectory, and accidentally deleting one of these files from that directory is as potentially dangerous as deleting a driver file that CONFIG.SYS would need. To see if you have a missing PnP driver, go into your **Control Panel** and pull up **System**. In the dialog box, click the **Device Manager** tab, and look for any listing whose icon contains a yellow-and-black exclamation point. If you see one, then something has been reported wrong with that device, perhaps having to do with a missing PnP driver.

What are the AUTOEXEC.BAT and CONFIG.SYS?

The AUTOEXEC.BAT and CONFIG.SYS are two of your PC's configuration files. At startup, the AUTOEXEC.BAT will execute (carry out) any commands it contains, such as automatically starting a program for you. For Windows 95 and Windows 98 systems, AUTOEXEC.BAT is run by DOS, not Windows (yes, you read right); so any programs that you want AUTOEXEC.BAT to run for you should be DOS programs. What qualifies? Generally, driver programs for your hardware, especially the kind of hardware that Windows' Plug and Play doesn't recognize.

CONFIG.SYS contains information that's used to modify the basic setup of your computer. Here, you'll find things such as the PATH command, which tells DOS the directories to search when looking for a file, and the DEVICE command, which is often used to load your memory device drivers (the programs that allow DOS to access memory over 1MB). Both files, by the way, are located in the root directory of your boot drive (drive C:).

If you use Windows 95 or 98, you may or may not have these configuration files, because they're only necessary if the setup of your computer requires the help of DOS, not Windows. But when you "Exit to DOS mode," a file in your \WINDOWS subdirectory called DOSSTART.BAT is copied over into the AUTOEXEC.BAT file that is run at the beginning of your DOS session. That AUTOEXEC.BAT file then goes away when you restart Windows.

➤ *Your CMOS may be damaged or incorrect.* CMOS, you may remember, is a chip inside your PC that stores important information such as how large your hard disk is. If you've recently changed your computer's battery, or if you've added some other major part, such as a new floppy disk or more RAM, then you may need to update the CMOS info. See Chapter 27, "Fiddling with Ports, IRQs, Addresses, and Such," for help.

➤ *Think back. Has your hard drive been giving you trouble for the past few months?* Has it had trouble reading files, or saving them? If so, you may have a real problem. To figure out what might be wrong, check the hard disk first with a good utility program such as Norton Utilities or McAfee PC Medic. When you buy an emergency toolkit utility program, you should take the time while your hard disk is *well* to make an emergency disk from that program's CD-ROM. If it's too late to do that, stick with Norton's emergency disk that comes in the box along with its CD-ROM. If you decide to get some more personal help, be sure to tell your rescuer what's been going on.

Check This Out...

Protecting your interests

If your PC has any communication with the outside world—through borrowed disks, the Internet, or some online service—then there's a chance a virus might invade your system and wreak havoc on your files, and possibly prevent you from even being able to start your PC!

So, before disaster strikes, protect your files with a good antivirus program such as Norton AntiVirus or CyberMedia AntiVirus. Such a program can keep a lookout for the types of changes viruses like to make, and then alert you to trouble. The program can also help you get rid of the virus and repair the damage.

To help your antivirus program repair your system, you should create an emergency disk that will help you start your system when it won't start on its own (the antivirus program will help you create an emergency disk). In addition, you should perform backups of your vital data often. A backup enables you to restore any file that the antivirus program couldn't fix.

Cleaning Up the Hard Disk

There are many reasons why you might want to take the time to periodically go through your hard disk and get rid of unused files. For one, you'll gain some hard disk space. And two, your hard disk will run more efficiently—not a bad bargain.

Cleaning up your hard disk isn't difficult, but it will take some time, because you have to first identify the files you can get rid of. Here are some obvious places to look:

➤ *Your TEMP directory.* Files copied to your TEMP directory are supposed to be just that, *temporary*. But, if you exit a program improperly, or restart your computer while programs are still running or while you're still connected to the Internet, these temporary files are never deleted. Your TEMP directory is typically located in the Windows directory, although you can place it anywhere.

➤ *Your Internet browser's cache.* When you visit a Web page, its contents are downloaded to your system for display: all its text, graphics, Java apps, and so on. Several separate files make up the average Web page, all of which are stored by your Web browser in its cache, for quick retrieval the next time you visit that same page. With most modern Web browsers, this cache is periodically monitored, and the oldest files in the cache are frequently cleared. But older Web browsers (by "older," I mean *weeks and weeks* older than the newest edition) do not automatically clear their caches. You can clear the cache yourself if you like, and reacquire some hard disk space. To clear the cache in Netscape Communicator, open the **Edit** menu and select **Preferences**. Then click the plus sign in front of **Advanced** in the Category list. Click the **Clear Disk Cache** button, and click **OK** to continue. To clear the cache in Internet Explorer 4.0, open the **View** menu and select **Internet Options**. Then, on the **General** tab, click the **Delete Files** button.

➤ *The Recycle Bin.* If you use Windows 95 or Windows 98, then your deleted files are not really deleted, but simply moved to the Recycle Bin. This means you can easily recover any file you've deleted by accident. It also means that your unwanted files, like some clingy relative, never go away until you push them out the door (by emptying the Recycle Bin). To empty the Recycle Bin, right-click it and select **Empty Recycle Bin** from the shortcut menu that appears.

➤ *Downloaded files.* Sure, the Internet is cool and full of really neat things like graphics and sound files and movies and all sorts of great stuff. It's easy to fall into the trap of downloading the neat things you see, to show your friends, if for no other reason. Well, months have passed, and the sound file of Cuba Gooding, Jr., saying "Show me the money!" is getting a bit thin. Hopefully, you're in the habit of storing the files you download in the same directory, which will make it easier to delete them.

➤ *Old data files.* Sure, you needed that sales report last month, and you referred to it every day during the annual budget conference. But you haven't looked at it in months, so it's time to store the file on disk or Zip disk, or tape, and remove it from your hard disk. You should repeat this process for any other similar files.

➤ *Delete old .BAK files.* Some installation programs make a backup copy of your configuration files prior to making any changes to them. After you install a program and you've checked that your computer is functioning well, you may want to delete these unneeded backups. These files may end in .BAK, .OLD, or .001, .002, and so on. Use File Manager or Explorer to help you locate and delete them.

When they're gone, they're gone!

Be careful; when you empty the Recycle Bin, the files you deleted are gone for good—which means that you won't be able to restore them if you later decide that you made a mistake deleting them in the first place. You can look over the file list prior to emptying the bin; just double-click the **Recycle Bin** icon, scan the list, then open the **File** menu and select **Empty Recycle Bin** when you're ready to let go.

For your protection

For safety's sake, you should download all your files into the same directory, or better yet, the same disk (such as a Zip disk). That way, you can easily check the files for possible viruses *before* they wreak any havoc. You should also invest in a good antivirus program and *use* it. The program can tell you when a virus is active—a good thing to know, don't ya think?

131

➤ *Delete automatic document backups.* Many applications such as Microsoft Office 97 give you the option of keeping the next-most-recent version of your current documents as backup files, generally ending with .WBK. When your documents are no longer in the editing stage, and are completely finished, use File Manager or Explorer to delete the .WBK files, because your applications won't perform that job for you.

➤ *Dusty old programs.* Sure, that tax program helped you out of a jam last April. But do you still need it taking up room on the hard disk now that it's October? If not, consider removing it. In Windows 3.1, use the program's uninstall utility (if there is one), or simply delete the program's directory, and remove its icon from Program Manager. In Windows 95/98, double-click the **Add/Remove Programs** icon you'll find in the Control Panel. Then select the program you want to remove and click **Add/Remove**. If you don't see your program in the list, try looking for an uninstaller called UNINSTAL.EXE or UNWISE.EXE (really, that's what it's often called) in your program's main directory. If you don't find such a beast there, you might look for a SETUP.EXE in your program's main directory, and check for an uninstall option from one of the dialog boxes that comes up.

➤ *Old email.* Email messages are saved in folders on your hard disk, and they can quickly add up. To save hard disk space and make your email program run more efficiently, delete your old email messages periodically, or at least "archive your archives"—a silly term which refers to the capability some email clients give you to compress the contents of your directory of older messages, so they consume less space although you can still read them.

➤ *Remove junk files that ScanDisk created.* Delete any files in your root directory (or directories, if you have more than one hard drive) named FILE0001.CHK, FILE0002.CHK, and so on. Believe me, you do not need them. A program called ScanDisk (which I'll talk about later in this chapter) is responsible for creating these files. ScanDisk converts this rubbish into files supposedly in case there's anything inside of them you want to save for some reason. Unless you really do know how to use the Norton Disk Editor (hands up, all of you who do..., I don't see any hands), then just go ahead and delete these little aftermaths.

Check This Out...

Save time and delete your files, too! Windows 98 comes with a neat utility called Disk Cleanup, which removes unwanted files simply and easily. You'll find it by choosing **Programs**, then **Accessories**, and then **System Tools**.

For Windows 3.1 and DOS: Pump Up the Hard Disk with SMARTDrive!

The hard disk in your computer subscribes to the "turtle principle": It figures that nobody's going to remember how slow it is if it still finishes the race and coughs up a file.

But if you're using DOS or Windows 3.1, and you'd rather fly than crawl, you can make your hard disk faster by making it *smarter*. All you need is a bit of RAM and a little fella called SMARTDrive. Don't lose any sleep wondering how it works—it just does.

If you use Windows 95 or Windows 98, it handles SMARTDrive internally, without the help of the AUTOEXEC.BAT, so skip this section and don't worry about it anymore.

Anyway, chances are that you may not have to actually *install* SMARTDrive, because it is probably installed for you, if you have Windows 3.1.

If you don't use Windows but you have at least DOS 6, again, SMARTDrive is probably installed for you, so you can just sit back and relax. If you want to be sure, type **SMARTDRV /S** at the DOS prompt and press **Enter**. If SMARTDrive is installed, you see a message telling you so, followed by some parameters and settings.

If it's not installed, then type **EDIT C:\AUTOEXEC.BAT** at the DOS prompt and press **Enter**. The contents of the AUTOEXEC.BAT file appear onscreen, for all to see.

Press **Ctrl+End** to move to the end of the file, press **Enter** to create a new line, then type:

> C:\DOS\SMARTDRV.EXE.

Save your work by opening the **File** menu and clicking **Save**. Now you can get out of here. Just open the **File** menu and click **Exit**.

Now you need to add something to your CONFIG.SYS file as well. Type **EDIT C:\CONFIG.SYS** and press **Enter**. Look for the line, C:\DOS\HIMEM.SYS, at the beginning of the file. If you don't see it, press **Enter** to create a blank line, use the up-arrow key to back up to it, and add the darn thing— **C:\DOS\HIMEM.SYS**—yourself.

> **Bad command or filename?** If you get the error message: Bad command or filename, type **PATH=C:\DOS**, press **Enter**, and try it again.

Save the file and exit as before. After you see the C:\> prompt, restart your system by pressing **Ctrl+Alt+Delete** to make SMARTDrive active.

Double Your Hard Disk

If you're running out of space on your PC's hard disk, but you can't afford to add an additional hard disk right now, there may be a way for you to live with the situation a while longer—by doubling your disk.

With disk doubling, a *disk compression* program "shrinks" your files using a kind of "computer shorthand" that enables it to store those same files in less space than dumb ol' DOS and even Windows—actually, a little more than half the space. Which is why compressing your hard disk is called *doubling*, because you end up with almost twice as much space for files! After you compress the hard disk, you can still open, save, copy, and delete files just like you did before—your hard disk handles the compression process invisibly, so you don't have to worry about how it works—it just does.

The only potentially bad news here is that you have to have at least DOS version 6.0 to get disk compression for free. If you have DOS 6.0 or 6.2, then you get a program called DoubleSpace with which you can compress your hard disk. If you have DOS 6.21 or 6.22 or Windows 95/98 (which has essentially DOS 7), then you get DriveSpace instead.

Check before you run a new utility

After you compress the hard disk, you can safely use any of the utilities that come with DOS (such as SMARTDrive or DEFRAG) without any problems at all. But if you want to use some other utility such as a disk repair utility, a memory manager, or an antivirus program on your compressed drive, make sure that it's compatible with DoubleSpace or DriveSpace first.

Compressing a Hard Disk Under Windows 3.1 and DOS

Regardless of whether you use DoubleSpace or DriveSpace, follow these steps to compress your hard disk—but remember, you have to have at least DOS 6-something to do this. (If you use Windows 95 or Windows 98, skip ahead to the appropriate section.)

First, exit all programs, including Windows. Then come to a screeching halt as you stop to do a complete system backup. If something goes wrong here, you'll have to get back your data. So *do a backup now*. In addition, it's a good idea to defrag your hard disk before compressing. See "Reorganizing the Hard Disk" for the necessary how-tos.

Finally, at the C:\> prompt, type **CD\DOS** and press **Enter**. Now, type **DBLSPACE** or **DRVSPACE** and then press **Enter**. You see a message touting all the benefits of compressing a drive. Choose **Express setup**.

Now, keep in mind that some portion of your drive remains undoubled (uncompressed); the operating system recognizes this portion as if it were a new drive and assigns it a brand new letter. If you want this uncompressed not-really-a-disk-drive to be called anything other than drive H:, type a different drive letter now. Press **Enter**.

This compression stuff takes about one minute per megabyte to compress, regardless of how fast your computer is. Click **Continue** (which completes the compression process) or press **Esc** to exit (which stops it). After the disk compression is complete, a summary displays, showing information about the compressed drive. Press **Enter**, and your system restarts with the compressed drive active and ready to use.

Compressing a Hard Disk Under Windows 95 or Windows 98

If you use Windows 95 or Windows 98 and you haven't compressed your hard disk yet, this section shows you how to do it. (Uh, if you have a really large hard disk, DriveSpace may force you to divide it into smaller portions such as drives C, D, E, and so on. Before you start, see the sidebar coming up for info on a Plus! pack that can help.)

> **Can't do that!** If you use Windows 95 or 98 and its FAT 32 file system (it's an option: you may not have it), then you won't be able to double your hard disk using a compression utility. Sorry.

You should defrag your hard disk before compressing it. See "Reorganizing the Hard Disk" for info. Then, click the **Start** menu. Select **Programs**, select **System Tools**, and then select **DriveSpace**. Whew!

Now, select the drive you want to compress from the list. I'm guessing that it's probably drive C. Open the **Drive** menu and select **Compress**. Okay, so far.

Click **Start**. You see a message telling you to do a backup. If you haven't done a backup lately, it's a good idea to do one now, so click **Back Up Files**. Just do as it says, and no one will get hurt. (Have a pile of disks handy.)

After you complete the backup, you end up back where you started (well, practically). Click **Compress Now**. Keep in mind that this compression stuff takes about one minute per megabyte to do, so go get a cup of coffee and a good magazine.

At some point, DriveSpace tries to restart your computer. If it needs help, click **Yes** when you see a prompt asking you if you want to restart the computer.

Converting a DoubleSpaced Drive to DriveSpace

If you've recently upgraded to DOS 6.21 or 6.22 and you compressed your hard disk with DoubleSpace, you can leave it as it is, or convert it to DriveSpace compression. Why bother? Well, the conversion doesn't take very long, and your hard disk will run better with DriveSpace. (If you're using Windows 95, you don't have to convert your hard disk at all; it can use either DoubleSpace or DriveSpace compression. But if you want to convert the drive, just start the DriveSpace utility by selecting it from the **System Tools** menu—select **Programs**, **Accessories** to see the System Tools menu option—and then follow the onscreen prompts.)

Make way for DriveSpace!

DriveSpace needs some elbow space in which to work. Make sure that you have at least .6MB free on drive H: (the uncompressed drive) and around 4MB free on drive C: (the compressed drive). If you don't have enough free space, remove some not-often-used files to make room and then convert the drive.

Back up your files first; then, in case something goes wrong, you can at least get your data back. Then when you're ready, type **DRVSPACE** at the DOS prompt and press **Enter**. You see a message warning you to do a backup. Because you've already done one, just laugh and press **Enter** to continue.

DriveSpace runs a scan to check your disk, and then it starts converting the drive. When DriveSpace is done, press **Enter** to restart your system with a DriveSpace drive.

Use your newly converted DriveSpace drive as you did before; there aren't many differences between DoubleSpace and DriveSpace, certainly none that you can see.

Reorganizing the Hard Disk

DOS is not a very good housekeeper; in fact, it's pretty sloppy when it comes to organizing files on the hard disk. (And even if you use Windows 95 or Windows 98, you can't escape its lousy file system, because it's based on DOS—unless of course, you're using the FAT 32 file system.) When you (or some program you're running) tell DOS to save or copy a file to the hard disk, DOS begins saving the file at the first unused portion of the disk that it finds. More often than not, DOS finds out in mid-save that the unused portion is smaller than the file it's trying to save; so DOS breaks that file up into tiny bite-size pieces which it then scatters all over the hard disk, in whatever spots seem the most convenient.

Although all these goofy antics may make DOS seem all the more endearing, this sloppiness makes your PC work harder to locate the files you need. It can also mean that although it appears that you have several megabytes of free space, you can't save a 150KB file because DOS's hard disk space is in too many tiny pieces. So if you've been noticing that it seems to take a long time (in PC-time, meaning more than a couple of seconds) for your PC to open documents for you, you can speed up things a bit by reorganizing the hard disk. In any case, you should probably defrag once a month, if you use your PC every day.

If you're using one of the DOS 6-somethings (you know, DOS 6.0, 6.2, 6.21, or 6.22) or if you have Windows 95/98, then you're in luck because they come with a handy tool called DEFRAG, which you can use to *defragment* (nerd word for reorganize) your hard

136

disk. If you don't have one of the DOS 6-somethings, then you can upgrade your DOS version (you'll find help earlier in this chapter), or you can buy a set of utilities such as Norton Utilities.

Defragmenting a Noncompressed Disk

A compressed hard disk holds about twice as much data as its noncompressed brother. If you have a compressed disk, then the way you reorganize its files (defrag) is a bit different. Skip to the next section for help. (If you use Windows 95 or Windows 98, skip to the appropriate section.)

Defragging takes a while for your PC to complete, so you may want to start this at the end of the workday and let it run overnight. *Just follow these steps if you use Windows 3.1 or DOS*: Exit all programs, including Windows; at the C:\> prompt, type **DEFRAG**, press the **Spacebar**, and type the letter of the drive you want to defrag, followed by a colon (for example, type C:).

> **Error!** If you get the error message Bad command or filename, take two steps back, type **PATH=C:\DOS** and press **Enter**. Now, try again.

The whole thing now looks something like this:

```
DEFRAG C:
```

Now, press **Enter**.

DEFRAG takes a look at your hard disk and then comes up with a recommendation for the best way to reorganize it. If it tells you that your hard disk is pretty well organized already, then just press **Esc** to skip the whole thing. If it recommends optimization, then get on with it by clicking **Optimize**.

DEFRAG does its thing and beeps at you when it's done, telling you, "Optimization complete—go home now." If you want to defrag another hard disk, click **Another Drive**. Otherwise, just click **Exit DEFRAG**. After you land back at the prompt, press **Ctrl+Alt+Delete** to restart the PC. This makes sure that the picture of your hard disk that's kept in memory (namely, the contents of the FAT file table) is current.

Defragmenting a Compressed Disk

If you read the first part of this chapter, you already know that a compressed disk stores more files in the same space than a noncompressed disk because it's smarter. What makes the disk smarter? Well, a compression utility such as DoubleSpace or DriveSpace takes over the file management from DOS, using a kind of "shorthand" that enables it to squeeze the same data into a smaller space. Because disk compression uses this special shorthand business, you need to follow these steps to reorganize its files (to defrag the disk).

May I recommend red wine with your DEFRAG?

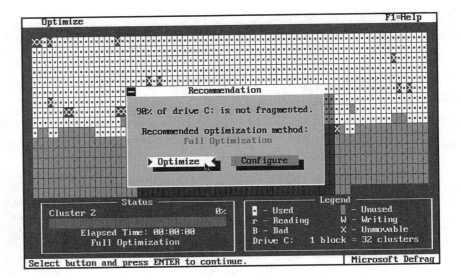

Now, Microsoft is going to warn you that defragging a compressed drive may not be worth the trouble. That's because a compressed drive organizes its files differently from the way a normal noncompressed drive does. All you usually get with defragging is a compressed drive with a bit more room on it—but it isn't any faster. All this will lead you to believe that defragging your compressed disk is not worth the bother. *Au contraire*—if you don't defrag your disk every once in a while, it will eventually get so disorganized that even DOS won't want to deal with it. So eat your vegetables and defrag every month or two.

When you're ready to defrag, follow these steps if you're using Windows 3.1 or DOS (if you're using Windows 95/98, again, skip to the next section). Just keep in mind that the defragging thing takes a while to complete, so don't start this in the middle of the day unless you're looking for a way to go home early.

This doesn't work for Stacker-compressed drives

If you compressed your hard disk using some other utility such as Stacker or SuperStor, then you need to follow its directions to reorganize your files. The steps here are only for DoubleSpace or DriveSpace users.

Exit all your programs, including Windows. Then type **DRVSPACE** or **DBLSPACE** and press **Enter**. Choose the drive you want to defrag; hint: This is probably drive C. Now, open the **Tools** menu and select **Defragment**.

138

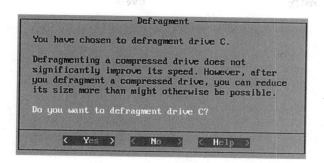

You see a warning similar to the one in the figure, telling you that this may not be worth doing. We've already determined that you're stubborn, so ignore all the warnings by clicking **Yes**. If you've changed your mind, press **Esc** instead.

This takes a while, as defragging reorganizes your files and restarts the PC a couple of times. When it's finally done, the Optimization menu is left open for you. Just select **Exit**, and you're through.

Why do it?

If there's not a lot of benefit in defragging a compressed drive, why is there an option for it? Well, although the compressed drive isn't faster, you may gain a little more room on the drive by reorganizing it. Also, as I discussed earlier, DOS will have an easier time finding a file on an organized compressed disk, rather than a disorganized one. (This means it'll be faster.)

Defragmenting a Disk with Windows 95/98

With Windows 95 and Windows 98, it doesn't matter whether you're trying to defrag a compressed or noncompressed disk; Windows 95 handles both the same way. Also, in Windows 95/98, you can keep working while you defragment your hard disk (but your boss doesn't have to know that).

Just click the **Start** menu and choose **Programs**. Select **Accessories** and then select **System Tools**. Now, after ten minutes of seemingly endless menus, you can finally choose **Disk Defragmenter**.

To defrag or not to defrag?

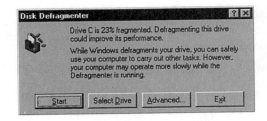

Select the drive you want to defrag and then click **OK**. The Disk Torturer (okay, Defragmenter) takes a look at your hard disk and gives you a recommendation for the best way to reorganize it. If it says that your hard disk is pretty well organized, just click **Exit** to forget the whole thing. If it says that you need to organize things, then get on with it by clicking **Start**.

Now, although you can keep on working while Disk Defragmenter does its thing, you may not want to. For one thing, if you ever save something to the hard disk while you're defragmenting, the entire defrag process will start over from block one. That might not be so bad every so often, but if you're defragmenting the hard drive where your \TEMP directory is located, the defrag process could restart itself every thirty seconds or so. So unless you like having your computer perform pointless yet technical operations in the background, you should probably schedule your defragmentation for a time when your computer isn't busy working for you.

If you want to pause the Disk Defragmenter while it's running, just click the **Pause** button.

When it's done, you see a message telling you basically, "Defragmentation complete—go away now." If you want to defrag another hard disk, click **No** (I Don't Want to Go Away). Otherwise, just click **Yes**. That's it.

Check This Out...

Relax, you're running Windows 98 Windows 98 comes with a task scheduler that you can use to schedule system maintenance tasks such as defragging a drive to occur at regular intervals, while you take a snooze.

Check This Out...

Wait a minute! After you select the drive you want to defrag and click **OK**, the Windows 98 Defragmenter will start defragging it without asking please. If you want to stop, click **Stop**, then exit the program.

Converting to FAT32

If you use the latest version of Windows 95, or Windows 98, you can convert your hard disk to the FAT32 file management system, and save hard disk space. In addition, your computer will be able to grab files quicker. Also, you will be able to create disk partitions that are greater than 2G (a partition being a logical compartment of a drive that is assigned its own drive letter, such as C:). Just like anything that might sound too good to be true, this is. Keep these things in mind if you decide you want to convert to FAT32:

➤ FAT32 and disk compression (uh, DriveSpace) *do not mix*.

➤ After you convert, you won't be able to uninstall Windows 98 if you ever want to.

➤ Some of your disk utilities, such as sector editors (Norton Disk Editor), undeleters, and data deletion programs, won't work with FAT32.

➤ You won't be able to dual boot with FAT32. By dual boot, I mean one day you might start Windows 98, work with it for a while, then restart and use Windows 3.1.

➤ After converted, your hard disk can never go back to FAT16, the file system used by Windows 95 and Windows 3.1. However, this shouldn't affect your ability to run your old programs or to read your old files.

If after all this, you still feel like converting your hard disk, then make sure you do a complete backup first. You won't be able to use the backup if your system is converted, but if something goes wrong, you could reformat, reload the backup, and you'd be okay.

When you're ready, click the **Start** button, select **Programs**, select **Accessories**, and select **System Tools**. Then select **Drive Converter (FAT32)**. Follow the steps in the wizard.

If you have a new PC that's running OSR2 version of Windows 95, your hard disk may be using FAT32 right now. But, if you later installed OSR2 on an existing system, you can "convert" your hard disk to FAT32—by reformatting your hard drive, that is. You can *convert* your hard disk from the old FAT (FAT16) to FAT32 if you switch to Windows 98 first.

Create More Space on Your Hard Disk with ScanDisk and CHKDSK

When DOS deletes a file, it does a pretty sloppy job of it, leaving bits of old deleted files sitting around in the DOS junkyard, trading stories and hubcaps. (Windows 95/98 have this same problem, because their file system is based on DOS.) If you want to know why DOS is so sloppy, read the sidebar coming up. Anyway, these little unused bits of old files that were never actually deleted are called *lost clusters* or *lost chains*. There are several commands that come with DOS to help you get rid of these old files and free up otherwise-unused disk space. Which one of these commands you use depends on your DOS version.

The truth behind why DOS is a slob

When you delete a file, DOS doesn't really delete it. Instead, it erases the *reference* to that file and marks the spaces it used to occupy as "available." The next time you save a file to disk, DOS may place it in one of these available spots, overwriting the deleted file and reclaiming the space for use.

Sometimes DOS erases the reference to the file, but forgets to mark all the spaces that the file was using as "available." That results in little parts of old file spaces not being reused because DOS goofed. These dusty parts of old files are called *lost clusters* or *lost chains*.

If You've Got DOS 6.2 or Higher

If you've got an earlier DOS, such as DOS 6.0, DOS 5.0, or DOS 3.3, then skip to the next section for help. Now, before you use ScanDisk, you must exit out of any programs, such as Windows. Type **SCANDISK C:** and press **Enter**.

Network users, beware! Do not use ScanDisk on a network drive, such as drive F. If you do, your network administrator may hang you up by your keyboard, and believe me, it's not a pretty sight.

ScanDisk entertains you with a magnificent display of check marks as it looks for problems. If ScanDisk uncovers a problem, an error message appears. Should ScanDisk uncover lost data, press **Enter** to save the lost data in a file, or press **L** to delete it (which is what I normally do, because it's usually data from some old deleted file I don't even want anymore). If you're asked to create an Undo disk, you can stick a blank disk in drive A and press **Enter**. An Undo disk allows you to change your mind and undo what ScanDisk does. But take it from me, Undo disks are risky, like jumping off the tightrope in hopes there's a net below. You can skip Undo by pressing **S**.

ScanDisk also checks out your hard disk for physical problems with a surface scan (you should probably do one of these about once a month or so). This is a bit noisy, so if you decide to do it, don't get too worried when it starts crankin'. Just press **Enter** when prompted, or press **N** to bypass this step. Logical problems with your files are rarely the result of a physical defect in your disk; however, if the problems you're having don't seem logical (okay, what problem ever does?), a surface scan may be in order. If you find out you have a physical problem with your hard disk, you should think about replacing it. See Chapter 18, "Hands-On Hard Disk Replacement," for help. In the meantime, don't let a day go by without backing up your files.

After the scan is complete, you can view a log of the results by pressing **V**. Press **X** anytime to exit.

If You've Got DOS 6.0 or Below

If you have a DOS version earlier than DOS 6.2 (such as DOS 6, DOS 5, or DOS 4), you don't have a SCANDISK command. Instead, you'll use CHKDSK to clear away all those lost clusters and lost chains.

A couple of warnings first: Exit all programs before you use CHKDSK, including Windows. Also, *don't try to use CHKDSK on a network drive, such as drive F*. Okay, now type **CHKDSK C: /F** and press **Enter**.

What's that /F thing for?

If you forget the /F switch, CHKDSK will pretend that it's fixing the problem, but when you run CHKDSK again, the problem will still be there. The /F switch tells DOS to write the changes to the disk. If you get a message like this

```
Errors found, F parameter not specified
Corrections will not be written to disk
```

then you have forgotten to type /F. Retype the command and be sure to include the /F switch.

If CHKDSK finds an unused part of a deleted file, it displays something like this:

```
2 lost allocation units found in 1 chains.
8192 bytes disk space would be freed.
```

You have lost clusters or chains, so press **Y** to convert them to usable space. DOS creates a file to contain the data that was in each lost cluster. The data is probably unusable because it's part of an old file. To delete the files, type **DEL C:\FILE????.CHK** and press **Enter**.

Running ScanDisk with Windows 95/98

Unlike running ScanDisk under DOS, you don't have to exit any programs to run ScanDisk in Windows 95/98. To run ScanDisk in Windows 95/98, click the **Start** button, select **Programs**, select **Accessories**, select **System Tools**, and then finally, select **ScanDisk**.

Under **Type of Text**, click **Standard**. The other option, Thorough, actually tests the hard disk itself, and that's a bit much for today, thank you (you may want to run the test some other time, however). Click **Automatically fix errors**.

Click **Start.** ScanDisk does its thing, cleaning up after little lost clusters. When it's done, it proudly displays the results. Click **Close.**

Picking up after the crash

For Windows 95/98 users, if your computer ever does crash, or if you hit the reset button before formally shutting down your computer, then when your computer powers on again, by default it will automatically run ScanDisk in an automated mode. If you do absolutely nothing, ScanDisk will check all your hard disks for errors (except for the surface scan part); and if you don't respond to any of the prompts, ScanDisk will assume you consent to it fixing any problems it finds, even if those problems are unrelated to the reason why your computer crashed in the first place.

The Least You Need to Know

Upgrading is no fun. There's the money for the parts, and of course, the time it takes to install each part after you get it. Never mind the terror some upgrades instill. So if you can avoid upgrading your hard disk while maintaining your sanity and your productivity, so much the better. Here are some ways to do just that:

➤ Clean off old files periodically to make more room on the hard disk for new stuff.

➤ Double the space on your hard disk with either DoubleSpace or DriveSpace. If you're using DOS version 6.0 or 6.2, then you use DoubleSpace to compress your disk. If you're using DOS version 6.21 or 6.22, you use DriveSpace instead.

➤ You can make your hard disk faster with SMARTDrive. SMARTDrive creates a disk cache out of memory for storing your most-often-used data. A cache keeps frequently requested data close at hand—in memory. Because memory is faster than the hard disk, SMARTDrive helps your computer reach the files it needs more quickly.

➤ Because your operating system splits files into bits and places them on the hard disk willy-nilly, occasionally you need to get them back in some kind of order so your computer can run faster.

➤ You can reorganize the files on your hard disk with DEFRAG.

Chapter 9

Replacing Your Operating System

Windows 95 is faster and easier to use than Windows 3.1. Windows 98 is even leaner than Windows 95 and also has a Web browser. Windows 95 and 98 can't always run on a computer that runs Windows 3.1.

Before you get all bummed out, take a look at Windows 95 and 98 and see if either one is even something you need right now. If you decide to upgrade to either Windows 95 or Windows 98, you'll find step-by-step instructions, along with a listing that tells you exactly what your PC will need.

What's Windows 95?

The first thing you'll probably notice about Windows 95 is that its windows, including Program Manager, seem to be missing.

So where are the windows?

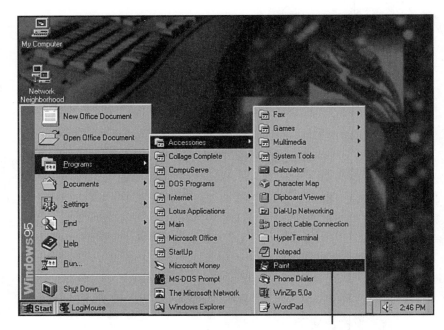

Start a program by selecting it from a menu

Well, after you start a program, the window frame that normally surrounds it is still there, but the group windows—those little boxes such as "Main" and "Applications" that grouped various icons together—are gone. Instead of starting a program by opening several group windows to find its icon and then double-clicking it, you open several menus and then select the program's name from a list. Easier? I dunno. It took me a while to figure out where everything was, but I got used to it quickly enough. However, if you like clicking icons, you still can. Just click the program file and drag it onto the desktop to create a shortcut icon.

The next thing you notice about Windows 95 is that it's sporting a whole new look.

My Computer   Network Neighborhood   Explorer window

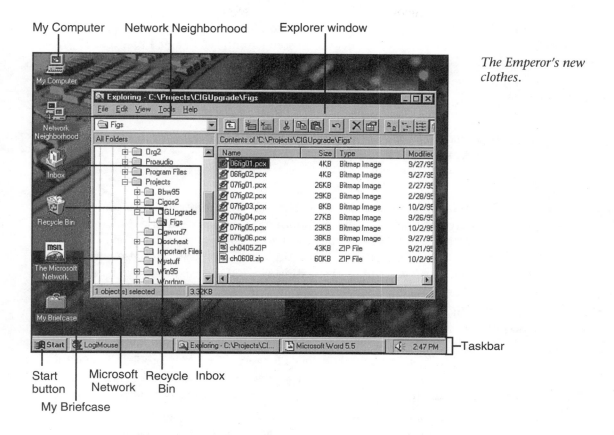

The Emperor's new clothes.

Start | Microsoft Recycle Inbox
button | Network Bin
My Briefcase

Here's what's behind the new duds:

➤ *Taskbar.* It's the gray strip at the bottom of the screen, and you use it like you used to use the Task List—to jump from one program to another. Because the taskbar stays visible (unless you choose to hide it, of course), you don't have to fumble for the Ctrl and Esc keys like you do to view the Task List.

➤ *Start button.* This one's easy to spot because it has the number one seat on the taskbar. Click here to view endless menus.

➤ *Explorer.* Bye-bye, File Manager. In its place is a retooled version called Explorer. Easier to use? Maybe—but it takes some getting used to because it works a bit differently than its papa. But at least you can give a file a decent name, such as "Sales Figures for 1st Quarter" instead of some dumb DOS name like SALES95.WK4.

➤ *My Computer*. Think of this as your PC's attic—you won't come up here very often. But if you do, you can learn lots of things about your computer—that is, if you can find anything at all, what with the silly way My Computer works, compared to Explorer.

➤ *Network Neighborhood*. You won't find Mr. Rogers here. Instead, you find a listing of all the computers, printers, and whatnots connected to your office network. (If you're working at home and aren't connected to a network, you won't see this icon.)

➤ *Inbox*. The Inbox is your local "post office," only instead of *receiving snail mail* (uh, letters delivered by your friendly neighborhood postman), you use the Inbox to send and receive mail through your network's email system and whatever online service you use (such as CompuServe or America Online). You can also connect to Microsoft Fax, if you want to send a fax instead. (Of course, to send or receive a fax or to use an online service, you'll need a modem.)

➤ *Recycle Bin*. In the old Windows, if you deleted a file, it was pretty much gone. Oh, you might have been able to get it back if you had the Undelete tool installed on your computer, and you used it quickly enough. The Recycle Bin definitely makes getting back files you accidentally delete a lot easier. The only problem is that the Recycle Bin doesn't empty its own trash: you've got to do that job on its behalf when you're ready to say a permanent good-bye to your recently deleted files.

➤ *The Microsoft Network*. "Hey, here's an idea," thought Microsoft, "Just in case our customers don't already have an online service, why don't we make it super-easy for them to sign up for ours?" Which you can do, by the way, just by double-clicking the MSN icon—that is, assuming you have a modem. MSN is similar to other online services such as CompuServe and America Online.

➤ *My Briefcase*. Who said you can't take it with you? Well, if you have a laptop and you transfer files between it and your desktop PC all the time, this little gadget makes it easy to keep the files in sync.

What Makes Windows 98 Different?

Windows 98 is the marriage of the Windows 95 interface with the functions of a Web browser, such as Internet Explorer. By seamlessly blending these two functions, Windows

98 allows you to access information from the Internet quickly and easily, while making routine computer tasks such as creating a report, or copying and deleting data files much easier.

Here's what makes Windows 98 different:

➤ *Active Desktop*. The Active Desktop places up-to-date Web content at your fingertips, such as current news, weather, and stock market reports.

➤ *Web Style (single click) option*. With this option turned on, you can work within the desktop the same way in which you work in a Web browser, by single-clicking to open a file or a folder, just as you might open a sound file on a Web page by single-clicking it. This option affects the icons on the desktop and also the icons within My Computer and Explorer.

Push technology

By the way, this business of receiving information from the Web automatically is called *push technology* (because the information appears to be pushed at you, rather than pulled by you). The Channel bar provides its information to your desktop via push technology—the only problem being that it's way too easy to sign up for all this information, and way too hard to digest it all. So don't let the glamour of a new technology blind you too the wear and tear on your Windows resources, not to mention your already short attention span.

➤ *Channel bar*. Subscribe to any of over 100 channels, and you can have their custom Web content delivered to your desktop daily, without having to lift a finger. Best of all, it's free (at least, for now…).

➤ *Windows toolbars*. Why should your programs have all the fun? Windows 98 comes with its own set of toolbars you can use to start frequently used programs, access the desktop, and visit Web pages.

➤ *Explore your files*. If you like, in My Computer or Explorer, files can be displayed within their own Web-like pages, making it easier for you to access information the way you want to.

➤ *Easy maintenance*. Tired of trying to remember to pay all your bills on time, keep all your appointments, *and* maintain your PC at its peak efficiency? Well, with the Maintenance Wizard, at least one of your problems is solved—with it, you can schedule maintenance tasks such as defragging your drive, removing unwanted files, and scanning the hard disk for errors.

➤ *Connection Wizard*. Need help getting connected to the Internet? How about a Wizard that steps you through the whole nasty process?

➤ *Keep Windows up-to-date*. As long as you have a connection to the Internet, updating your version of Windows has never been easier—as simple as selecting the Windows Update command from the Start menu.

➤ *Let's do lunch*. With Microsoft NetMeeting, you can easily conduct online conferences, sharing your thoughts, ideas, and files with your colleagues worldwide.

What You'll Need to Move to Windows 95

There is a good chance that if your PC can run Windows 3.1 now, it can probably run Windows 95. Trouble is, it may not be able to do anything else. In other words, you may be able to get Windows 95 installed on your old PC, but you won't be able to get much done, because your PC will be a lot slower.

So what do you really need to run Windows 95? Well, use this table to tell:

What Microsoft Says You Need	What Works Even Better
386DX CPU	Windows 95 is basically a snail on slow computers. So get yourself a 486SX, 486DX, or a Pentium, Pentium Plus, or Pentium II CPU.
4MB of memory (RAM)	No way do you want to run Windows 95 with anything less than 8MB—it'll just be tooooo slooooow. If you want nirvana, try *at least* 16MB.
40MB of free hard disk space	I really have no idea where Microsoft got this number. My Windows 95 directory takes up 116MB, but of course, I installed *everything*. If you're picky about what Windows 95 features you install (yes, you can pick and choose what features to include during installation), you may be able to get away with 85MB.

What Microsoft Says You Need	What Works Even Better
VGA monitor	Yes, you can still make a long-distance call from a rotary phone, but why would you want to? So instead of viewing all those cute icons and great graphics with a simple VGA monitor, get a Super VGA. For speed, add an accelerator card.
What else?	Other things you may want to think about getting include a CD-ROM drive, a tape backup (to protect all that data), a modem (the better to dial up the Internet with, my dear), and a sound card (for listening to all the new Windows sound effects).

So how much will all this stuff cost you? Well, let's look at our shopping list:

Item	What It'll Cost Ya
Faster CPU	$150–$650
Extra hard disk	$160–$180 for about 2GB
More memory	$50–$200 for 16MB
SVGA monitor	$230–$380 for a 15-inch monitor
Video card with accelerator	$120–$200
CD-ROM drive	$90
Tape backup	$190 for 5GB
Fax modem	$100–$150 for 56.6bps
Sound card	$50
Total bill	**$1,190–$2,090**

Of course, if your PC actually needs this much work, pitch it and get a new one; it will cost about the same. A better strategy is to add what you need now, such as more memory, a larger hard disk, and a faster CPU. In any case, after you decide what you can afford to add, check out the individual chapters for step-by-steps.

Upgrading Your Programs

If you upgrade to Windows 95, do you have to upgrade all your programs to their new Windows 95 versions? Well, no. Most Windows 3.1 applications run just fine—in fact, better—under Windows 95. But there are some 3.1 applications that, like some cats, just don't take well to new surroundings. If you need to make sure that your program will run okay under Windows 95, contact the program's manufacturer.

16 bit versus 32 bit

You may be wondering about the difference between 16-bit and 32-bit applications, and whether that affects your decision to upgrade to Windows 95 or 98. Well, Windows 3.1 applications are 16-bit, because Windows 3.1 is a 16-bit operating system. What this means is that data is shuffled in and out of RAM 16 bits at a time.

Windows 95 and 98 double the width of one memory address to 32 bits, effectively increasing the speed with which these operating systems do business. If you buy a Windows 95 or 98 program, you can take advantage of this technology. If you insist on using your old Windows 3.1 programs, however, they won't run any faster under Windows 95/98, but they might run better, given the fact that they'll run under an improved modified 16-bit *kernel*—a type of "subsystem" that is, in many respects, Windows 3.1 running under Windows 95 or 98.

Also, keep in mind that you can't save documents with longer filenames in Windows 95 with a 3.1 application unless you upgrade your program—because the 3.1 application won't let you. If you try to use a 3.1 application to open a file that was given a long name in Windows 95, you will see that the file's name has been given a different, abbreviated name that fits the old naming conventions. For example, a file called REALLY BIG FILENAME.DOC will appear as REALLY~1.DOC to a Windows 3.1 application. The file will still work, but you may have to do some guessing to figure out which file is which. When you're running from a DOS prompt in Windows, the DIR command will show you *both* filenames—the old "eight-dot-three" version in the left column, and the new, long form in the right column. But a file selector dialog box in a program built for Windows 3.1 (16-bit) will only show you the "eight-dot-three" version.

So what do you get for your upgrade dollar? Well, Windows 95 applications are obviously designed to run specifically with Windows 95. So, unlike Windows 3.1 programs, they can take advantage of all the speed Windows 95 has to offer.

Of course, you can still run DOS programs under Windows 95, although I'm not at all sure why you'd want to, because it's like using a Ferrari to navigate rush hour traffic. But if you must, you'll be glad to know that DOS programs run better under Windows 95. In fact, incredibly better—if you can give such praise to a DOS program.

Plug and Play

One thing you probably hear about every time Windows 95 is mentioned is something called *Plug and Play*. So what does it mean? Well, it's basically a newer technology that allows devices (such as your modem) to identify themselves to your computer, so your computer knows exactly how to talk to them. Does this mean that you have to run out and get specially marked Plug-and-Play devices to work with Windows 95? Nope. Windows 95 is perfectly capable of identifying most common devices, regardless of whether they are Plug and Play (PnP). But if you decide to add a new device, you may want to make sure that it's Plug and Play or Windows 95-compatible.

Upgrade your utilities Before you upgrade to Windows 95, make sure you upgrade your utilities as well, such as your backup program, antivirus program, uninstallers, and rescue utilities. Do not use a Windows 3.1 utility under Windows 95, unless you like playing Russian Roulette with your data.

Plug and Play with Windows 3.1

If you buy a Plug-and-Play device and you don't upgrade to Windows 95, that's okay. The device will work perfectly well under Windows 3.1. Just don't expect the system to automatically install the device for you. Don't worry—I cover all the details in Chapter 26, "Getting Windows to Recognize Your New Toy."

Plug and pray

The truth behind the Plug and Play hoopla is rather dismaying. To get PnP to work, you have to have three elements working together: a PnP operating system (that's Windows 95), a PnP device (such as a CD-ROM drive, a modem, or whatever else you want to add to your PC), and a PnP-compliant BIOS. The BIOS is a chip (or a bunch of chips) on the motherboard that control the basic input and output of your PC. Unless you bought your PC yesterday (okay, in the last two years), you don't have a PnP-compliant BIOS. To get one, you gotta upgrade the BIOS (that is, if an upgrade is available). See Chapter 16, "Replacing the Motherboard" for help in that department.

So what do you get with Windows 95 on a non-PnP PC? Well, a pretty nice operating system that's still better at identifying new devices than Windows 3.1 ever was. A little wonder called the New Hardware Wizard tries hard to identify whatever device you throw at it. You might still run into trouble, but if you need help prodding Windows 95 to install your new device, see Chapter 26.

How DirectX and Gaming Can Affect the Rest of Your PC

If you use your computer to run games (and who doesn't from time to time), *and* you use a game that uses DirectX, you may notice some funny things if you decide to upgrade to Windows 95. "What funny things, you ask?" Well, you may notice your fonts will be sized differently. You might notice that some screens or some windows update themselves with a bit more snap. You might also notice that the way some other Windows programs update their windows after DirectX is installed, is by a whole new method of *not* updating their windows; so when you click the scrollbar, the old window contents never leave before the new contents arrive. This, you have probably guessed, is bad. But this does not have to be the case, especially if your graphics card happens to be one of the "leading" brands (ATI, Diamond, Hercules)—users of these brands have reported fewer problems.

What else can go wrong, however? DirectX changes the way user input is processed, from *all* your devices—joystick, mouse, *and* keyboard. So you may one day start typing "G" and get "GGGGGGGGG"; itt, aas tthey saay, caann haappenn.

So, if you decide to upgrade to Windows 95, *and* you encounter these problems with your game, uninstall the game, and DirectX itself, and the problem will go away. Although DirectX is generally installed automatically with your game, you'll have to uninstall it manually through the Add/Remove Programs portion of Control Panel. Your other alternative is to upgrade to a leading graphics card, such as those listed earlier. Want to know in advance if you're going to have a problem if you install your game under Windows 95? Check online to see if others who have your brand of computer, graphics card, fancy keyboard, and other devices have reported problems. If not, you may be safe. When DirectX works, it is glorious. When it doesn't, it makes the U.S. Congress look like, well, the U.S. Congress.

Upgrading to Windows 95: Step by Step

Before you install Windows 95, do the following:

➤ Make sure that you update your emergency startup disk (see Chapter 4, "What You Need to Know Before You Open Your PC").

➤ Perform a backup of your data files.

➤ Clean off any files you no longer need.

➤ Defrag your drive (Chapter 8, "Fixing Hard Disk Hassles," can help you with these last three).

In addition, you should clean up your AUTOEXEC.BAT and CONFIG.SYS files, using Notepad. Type REM in front of any TSRs you may be using, such as memory managers like QEMM, and virus protection programs. Replace your memory manager with these two lines, located at the very beginning of the CONFIG.SYS file:

```
DEVICE=C:\WINDOWS\HIMEM.SYS
DEVICE=C:\WINDOWS\EMM386.EXE
```

If you have access to the Internet, check online at www.microsoft.com for any known incompatibilities with your hardware. You can also check with your manufacturers' Web sites. While you're there, you might as well download the latest drivers for your peripherals and install them.

Lastly, you need to decide if you want to keep DOS/Windows 3.1 on your system (a process called dual booting). This takes up a lot more hard drive space, and it's hardly ever necessary, unless you have a finicky game or other application that won't run under Windows 95's version of DOS. Oh, and dual booting does let you remove Windows 95 easily, if you think you'll need that as an option.

If you decide you want to dual boot, all you have to do is install Windows 95 into a new directory, instead of into the Windows directory. However, this also means that you'll need to reinstall any application you want to run under Windows 95, and remove it from Windows 3.1 (if you no longer need it there, that is.) If you install Windows 95 with the dual boot option, then when you want to boot to your old system and not Windows 95, just press **F4** when starting your computer.

Right. Ready to go? Follow these steps:

1. Insert the first disk into its drive, open File Manager, and double-click the **SETUP** file.

2. Read the license agreement and click **Next**.

3. Select the directory you want to use; Windows is the default. (You should select the same directory that contains Windows 3.1, unless you're going for the dual boot thing, in which case, you need to specify a new directory, such as WIN95.) Click **Next**.

4. You're asked if you want to save your Windows 3.1 and DOS system files. Click **Yes** and click **Next**.

5. Select **Typical** install, unless you're short of hard disk space, then you can go with **Compact**.

Select the type of install you want.

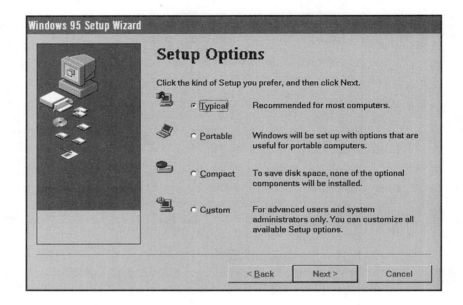

6. Enter your name and company and click **Next**. If asked, supply the CD key.

7. Next, you're asked to select which hardware devices your computer has installed, but Windows 95 has not yet detected. (Don't worry if this list appears incomplete.) Make your selections and click **Next**.

8. Select the Windows communications tools you desire, such as MSN, Microsoft Mail, and Microsoft Fax. Click **Next**.

9. Double-check the components you want installed, then click **Next.**

10. You're prompted to create a startup disk. Get out a disk for drive A, click **Yes**, and let Setup do its thing.

11. Setup finally begins copying its files to your hard disk. This will take a while, so go get a cup of coffee. You only need to stick around if you're installing with disks, and not a CD-ROM.

12. After copying your files, Setup reboots your computer. If this does not appear to work after a few minutes, reboot the PC yourself.

13. Setup continues by setting up the Control Panel among other things. You may be asked to complete the setup of Microsoft Exchange, if you selected the Microsoft Fax or Microsoft Mail options. Then you're done!

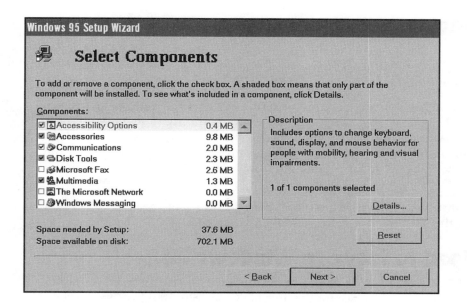

Windows à la carte.

Upgrading Windows 95?

Yes, there are upgrades to Windows 95 that you might want to install. And yes, you don't have them on your PC, even if you bought your copy of Windows 95 yesterday. That's because it's the original version—the only one sold to the public (yech).

There is something called Microsoft Plus! which includes some fun stuff you can't run on a 386 PC. So as long as you've got a 486 or a Pentium, you might as well join the party. What do you get? Well, an Internet Connection Wizard (to help you establish your Internet connection with a minimum of fuss), special theme wallpaper, icons, and sounds for your desktop, System Agent (an automated disk maintenance program), DriveSpace 3, Windows Messaging (which replaces Microsoft Exchange), and various display enhancements.

> **Check This Out...**
>
> **Missing something?** If one of your computer's hardware devices is not working when you start up Windows 95 for the first time, you can setup the device yourself; see Chapter 26 for help.

In addition to Microsoft Plus!, there's another enhancement to Windows 95 called OSR2. Trouble is, you can't buy it; it only comes on newer computers with Windows 95 installed. You can, however, download most of the updates that constitute the differences between the first Windows 95 and OSR2, from Microsoft's own Web site, and install them yourself. They are located at `http://www.microsoft.com/windows95/info/updates.htm`. Good luck!

Upgrading Mistakes to Avoid

If you run into any problems trying to start your computer after installing Windows 95, you can always uninstall it (using the startup disk you created in step 10, and the UNINSTAL program it contains). You could then try reinstalling Windows 95 again.

Don't try to run SCANDISK or any other disk-altering utility in the midst of an installation operation that's gone wrong. You might have an opportunity to get back on track, because Windows 95 and Windows 98 Setup are capable of picking up where they left off if they happen to crash, or even if the computer gets turned off accidentally. If you run a disk-altering utility, this catch-up capability goes away.

If your system crashes in the middle of setup, don't reformat your hard drive just yet. Use your emergency disk to boot up with a prompt, then just run Setup again. It will figure out for itself that the last time it was run, things didn't go well.

What You Need to Move to Windows 98

If you're running Windows 95 now, you can run Windows 98, no problem—your only concern will be having enough space for the upgrade (from 120–200MB of *free* hard disk space). If you're upgrading from Windows 3.1, make sure your PC meets these minimum requirements:

What Microsoft Says You Need	What Works Even Better
486DX/66 CPU	If you've got a slower PC and you think Windows 95 is a turtle on it, you should see Windows 98. You really should have a Pentium CPU to run Windows 98.
16MB of memory (RAM)	Try 32MB if you want to avoid pulling out your hair.
120–350MB of free hard disk space	You might be able to get away with using only 120MB, but you'll find yourself using 200MB *easy*.
VGA monitor	Here again, you really should upgrade to an SVGA monitor, if you haven't already. And here, an accelerator card is probably more important than with Windows 95.

What Microsoft Says You Need	What Works Even Better
CD-ROM drive	Right now, there don't seem to be any plans to release Windows 98 on disk, so you'll pretty much need to get a CD-ROM drive.
What else?	Again, a tape backup or high-capacity removable storage (Zip, SyQuest) makes sense, as does a modem (so you can take advantage of all that Active Desktop stuff), and a sound card, of course.

Other Upgrading Concerns

After your computer passes the Windows 98 muster, you're probably wondering about other issues as well:

Upgrading your programs. You can run DOS, Windows 3.1, Windows 95, and Windows 98 programs under Windows 98. The only thing you need to be careful of here is utility programs, such as antivirus programs, disk optimizers, rescue utilities, uninstallers, and so on. If you have at least Windows 95 versions of these programs, you should be fine—as long as you're not using the FAT32 option under Windows 98.

Upgrading your drivers. Whenever possible, try to upgrade to the Windows 98 versions of your hardware drivers, such as your CD-ROM driver. The Windows 98 CD-ROM contains a plethora of drivers, along with a categorized list of those drivers, yet there's still the possibility that a driver for your specific hardware may be missing. Check online with the manufacturer, or give 'em a ring.

Whither Navigator? If you use Netscape Navigator and you prefer it over Internet Explorer (IE), you probably won't like what you'll find in Windows 98. IE4 is highly integrated into the operating system, so much so that it's hard to get rid of. Both My Computer and Explorer use it, and so does the Active Desktop. Navigator and its container application, Netscape Communicator, will *run*; but what IE tries to do is be so much *in your face* that you might even forget to use Navigator once or twice. And indeed, you may encounter problems (unintentional, I'm sure, eh, Billy?) when trying to use Navigator as your Web browser of choice.

FAT32

FAT32 is a new file management system available under Windows 98, and the OSR2 version of Windows 95—it is especially designed for the larger hard disks in use today. If you use Windows 98 to convert your hard disk to FAT32, your existing files will take up less room, and hard disk access is much faster. In addition, a FAT32 drive uses less of your precious Windows resources. However, FAT32 is not compatible with FAT16, the (retroactively named) file management system in use under DOS, Windows 3.1, and Windows 95. This won't present any real problem to your programs, except your disk utilities, including DriveSpace, the Windows disk compression program.

Plug and Play. Like Windows 95, Windows 98 supports PnP devices. In fact, it does an even better job of it, making the process of adding a new device to your system even easier than it was before. At least, for the most part: Some devices prefer to leave their address with the standard BIOS, and let Windows 98 contact them there whenever it's good and ready. These devices are more difficult for you to set up under Windows 98; on the other hand, you may be more likely to set them up *correctly*.

Forget Windows 3.1. Unlike Windows 95, you cannot set up Windows 98 to run from a different directory, so Windows 3.1 can be run alternately (called the *dual-boot option*, introduced earlier).

Upgrading to Windows 98: Step by Step

Currently, you can only upgrade to Windows 98 from Windows 95, although Microsoft does plan on releasing a special upgrade program for Windows 3.1 users (how nice of them). Meanwhile, to upgrade from Windows 95 to Windows 98, follow these steps:

1. Insert the Windows 98 CD-ROM. You'll see a message asking if you would like to update your system. Click **Yes.**

2. A Welcome screen appears. Click **Continue**.

3. Read the license agreement, then click **I accept the Agreement**. Click **Next**.

4. The setup program checks your system for problems, available disk space, and existing Windows components. Enter the Windows 98 product identification number when prompted, and click **Next**.

5. You're asked if you want to save your original system files. Click **Yes**, then click **Next**.

6. Select your country from the Establishing Your Location list and click **Next**.

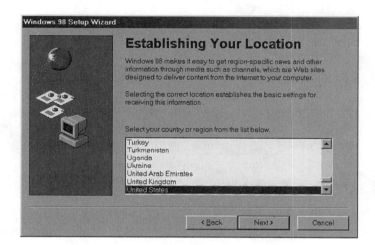

You are here.

7. You're prompted to create an emergency startup disk. Click **Next**.

8. Insert a disk in drive A and click **OK**. Insert another disk when prompted and click **OK**.

9. Remove the last disk when prompted and click **OK**.

10. The setup program is ready to start copying files. Click **Next**.

11. The Windows files are copied to your system. This process will take a while. Eventually, your system is restarted automatically and the Welcome to Windows 98 dialog box appears. Type your **User name** and **Password** and click **OK**.

12. Windows completes its setup. You can select **Registration Now** to register your copy of Windows 98. Of course, you'll need a modem to complete this task. When you're through, you can select **Connect to the Internet** to create your Internet connection, or **Discover Windows 98** to learn more about this exciting operating system. Finally, select **Maintain Your Computer** to schedule regular tune-up tasks that keep your system running at peak performance.

*Hi, I'm Jennifer, your
Windows' tour guide.*

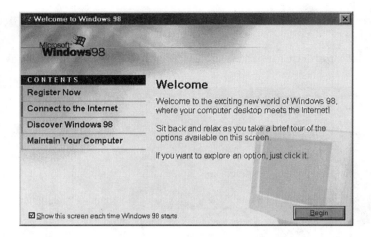

Upgrading Mistakes to Avoid

Actually, the installation of Windows 98 is fairly easy. If something goes wrong, you can always start your PC with your emergency disk and attempt to install the thing again—really, it doesn't mind.

In addition, you may want to double-check that you have the most current driver for any device that continues to give you trouble. The Internet is the easiest place to locate and download such drivers, from the manufacturer's own Web site. Any drivers that you do download separately will have to be *installed* separately. So don't install these drivers until *after* you've installed Windows 98, because the Windows 98 setup process could undo your work.

The Least You Need to Know

There's a lot you need to know before you decide to switch to Windows 95 or Windows 98. Here's a quick rundown:

➤ Yep, when you upgrade to Windows 95, you don't see Program Manager or File Manager anymore.

➤ Windows 95 replaces the Program Manager with the taskbar, a Start button, and tons of menus. Explorer replaces the File Manager.

➤ You can really use long filenames in Windows 95 (up to 255 characters, in fact).

➤ If you delete files in Windows 95, they aren't destroyed. Instead, they get *recycled*—so you can get them back later if you need them.

➤ To switch to Windows 95, your PC should have at least 8MB of RAM and about 85MB of free hard disk space. You might also want to add a CD-ROM drive, fax modem, tape backup, and sound card while you're at it.

➤ Windows 98 has everything Windows 95 has, plus more: Active Desktop, single-clicking, Channel bar, its own toolbars, and easier functionality.

➤ To switch to Windows 98, you'll need a faster CPU (486DX minimum), more memory (16MB), a larger hard disk, and a CD-ROM drive.

Getting on the Information Highway

The Internet is a collection of interconnected networks, located worldwide in government offices, businesses, universities, research facilities, and so on. You connect to the Internet through an Internet service provider (ISP), then navigate your way to the particular server-computer that contains a file you want to view or download. That file is then displayed on your monitor or copied to your system. When the Internet was young, you accomplished this rigmarole using a text-based command system called UNIX (and you thought DOS was scary). Nowadays, you use a Web browser (such as Netscape Navigator or Internet Explorer) to explore the Internet instead. Of course, this brings up another question: *What exactly is the Web, anyway?*

Wanna know more? If you'd like to learn more about the Internet, the World Wide Web, and other nifty things, check out *The Big Basics Book of the Internet* published by Que.

Where do I get a Web browser? You can purchase a Web browser program at your local computer store or download one from the Internet. Some ISPs will provide a browser for you to get you up and running quickly.

The Web (World Wide Web) is *not* the Internet. Nope. It's just a part of it (albeit the most popular part). To make the Internet (which is based on text-driven UNIX) more friendly, a language called HTML (Hypertext Markup Language) was developed. With HTML, data can be displayed graphically, and commands can be issued with a mouse. In addition, HTML can be used to link related documents (Web pages) together, making it easier to find the information you need. The Web did for the Internet what Windows did for DOS—it made it friendly, easy to access, and very, very popular. To view the HTML documents that make up the Web, you use a Web browser. Your Web browser, by the way, is not just for use on the Web. You can use it to download files, and visit just about any site on the Internet, including FTP (file downloading) sites, Gopher sites, and Usenet (newsgroup) sites. You can even use your Web browser to send and receive email.

Shopping for an Internet Service Provider

To crash the Internet party, you go through your *host*. Your host in this case is an Internet service provider (ISP), whose server (which is connected to the Internet directly) acts as your gateway to the Internet itself.

ISPs come in three different flavors:

➤ Indirect-access through an online service such as CompuServe, The Microsoft Network, or America Online. Here, you become a member by paying a monthly fee. For that, you get access to exclusive content such as discount shopping, travel assistance, games, children play areas, and so on. You also get access to the Internet; however, because you're going through an online service to connect, your Internet access is slower than it would be with the other two methods described here. On the other hand, online services offer special screens and menus that help you search for information, locate the best places on the Internet, and basically have fun.

➤ Dial-up access is made through a modem, where you dial into an ISP's computer, and through it, access the Internet. You can locate any number of local ISPs by checking your Yellow Pages, the newspaper, or simply asking your neighbors and friends. You pay a fee here, too, but unlike an online service, an ISP typically does not provide you with anything beyond email and Internet access—this means you won't get any help finding what you need out on the Internet (at least, not through your ISP). However, you will get a much faster connection than you would have with an online service.

➤ Persistent connection is usually made through your company's network, which is in turn connected directly to the Internet. You don't dial up here, you just log onto the network, and then access the Internet whenever you want.

What's an intranet?

An intranet is an *internal* Internet, whose access is typically restricted to company employees only. Many intranets span the globe, making it a cost-effective way to share company information. An *extranet* can be formed, if needed, by joining several companies' intranets into one interconnected network. This enables companies that work closely together to share information.

After establishing an intranet, a company converts its documents and other information to HTML format, then places them on the company's intranet server(s). To view these documents, employees use their Web browsers, just as they might use a Web browser to view a document out on the Web.

What you should know about 56Kb modems

If you want a fast connection (and who doesn't?), you may be considering a 56Kb modem, or you may already have one. One thing you need to know is that, until recently, there hasn't been a standard in 56Kb transmissions. Silly as it seems, two different methods for transmitting at 56,000 baud were proposed, and modems using each of the two methods (known to their friends as X2 and K56flex) were sold. So if you have a 56Kb modem sold prior to February of 1998, it supports one of these two standards.

The winning standard in the 56Kb fight was...neither one. The International Telecommunications Union adopted its new V.90 standard for 56Kb telecommunications based on a little of this and a little of that, plus some ideas of its own. Many modem manufacturers, including Hayes, are offering upgrades to existing 56Kb modem users, to make their modems compliant with the new V.90 standard. These upgrades are generally in the form of software that can be downloaded from the manufacturers' Web sites, and can perform the flash ROM upgrades automatically, painlessly, and for free.

Unless you're lucky enough to already have a persistent connection through your company's network, you're gonna have to pay for the ISP service you choose. You'll typically pay more for an online service, but they offer more frills. Local ISPs are usually cheaper than national ISPs, because you don't usually have to pay for long-distance connection charges, although some offer toll-free numbers. Beyond price, the key, really, is whether you can get connected *quickly and easily whenever you want.*

Some additional things to consider when choosing an ISP:

➤ Do they provide detailed instructions and phone support during the setup process?

➤ What modem speeds do they support? For example, if you're going to use a 56Kb modem, you'll want to know if they support the type you currently have, or if they're making the switch to V.90.

➤ What type of phone lines do they have (ISDN, T1, and so on). What's the ratio of phone lines to customers? (You don't want to get busy signals when trying to connect to your ISP.)

➤ What type of connection to the Internet does the ISP have? In other words, are they just running a standard Internet server, or do they have their own routers? One way you might be able to tell without asking: Look at the domain name at the end of their own Web site's home page. If it ends in .net, then they do have routers that actually run part of the Internet, rather than simply feed off of it. That's a very good thing, because it means this ISP has a very fast connection.

➤ What type of Web browsers do they support, and what versions? For example, if you plan on using Netscape Communicator, it would be nice to know that the ISP's support people are familiar with it.

Check This Out...

Help is on the way As I mentioned in the previous section, one criterion you should use when selecting a good ISP is how much they will help you in the process of getting connected to them, and through them, to the Internet. Most will help you some, but the better ones will stay on the phone until you're up and running, no matter how long it takes. Because getting connected to the Internet is not an easy process, having a good technical support person available to you is invaluable. (Of course, so is this book!)

➤ There's a lot to know when comparing prices. For example, are you limited to a particular number of minutes per month, or is there simply a set fee with no time limits? Is there a local or toll-free number you can use? How many email accounts you can set up without incurring an extra charge?

➤ Is there a charge for setting up your own Web page? Are you limited to a single page, or can you have several? Are there any other limits involved?

How Do I Get Connected?

To make your connection, you need to install TCP/IP software. TCP/IP (Transmission Control Protocol/Internet Protocol) controls the transmission of data throughout the Internet. With your TCP/IP program, you'll be able to "talk" the language of the Internet.

After TCP/IP is installed, you'll need to set up the connection to your particular ISP. After you're properly set up, you'll initiate the connection process, fire up your Web browser, and you're ready to go.

If you use Windows 3.1, your TCP/IP program is called Winsock. If you use Windows 95 or Windows 98, you'll use a program called Dial-Up Connection instead.

Details are coming up, but before doing anything, give your ISP a ring and have him tell you the following:

➤ What kind of account you use, SLIP or PPP

➤ IP address, DNS address, and gateway address to which you'll connect

➤ The name of your ISP's server

➤ The phone number of your service provider

➤ Your host and domain names (these will probably be your name, and your server's name, as in jfulton@mcp.com)

➤ Your username and password

While you're at it, you might as well have your ISP give you your email address and password, the name of the mail servers (incoming and outgoing), and the name of the newsgroup server.

> **Connecting through your company's network?** If you're planning to connect to the Internet through your company's network, you don't have to do a thing except log on to your network in the usual way and start your Web browser. Any setup that's involved should be completed by your network's system administrator.

> **Using an online service?** If you've decided to use CompuServe, AOL, or MSN as your ISP, you won't need to do anything to connect other than install their software. Then follow their directions for connecting to the service and initiating your Internet connection.

Getting Connected with Windows 3.1

You can probably get a copy of Trumpet Winsock from your ISP, either on a disk, or by downloading it from their server. To download a file, you'll need to use Terminal, which you'll find in the Accessories group. Start Terminal, then open the **Settings** menu and select **Phone Number**. Enter the ISP's phone number and click **OK**. Next, open the **Settings** menu again and select **Terminal Emulation**. Select the type of emulation your ISP suggests, such as TTY. Click **OK**. Open the **Settings** menu once again and select **Communications**. Select your modem speed (baud rate), and the data bits, stop bits, and parity your ISP told you to use. Then click **OK** again.

Gotta configure.

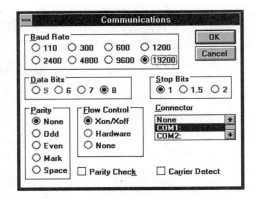

Terminal is finally ready, believe it or not. Open the **Phone** menu and select **Dial**. You're connected. Log in to the ISP server using the password they gave you, then follow their instructions to navigate the menu system until you get to the download area where you can download your files. If you're given a choice of transfer protocols, choose XMODEM. Then open the **Settings** menu and select **Binary Transfers**. Choose **Xmodem/CRC** and click **OK**. Using the ISP's menus, select the file(s) you want to download. When it says it's ready, open up the **Transfers** menu and select **Receive Binary File**. Type a filename and select a directory for the file, then click **OK**. You can watch the progress of the download at the bottom of the Terminal screen. When you're done, choose exit from the ISP server's menus, open the **Phone** menu and select **Hangup**, then exit Terminal.

To install Trumpet Winsock, copy its files into a directory you create, such as, \WINSOCK. Then edit your AUTOEXEC.BAT and add the WINSOCK directory to the end of the PATH command, like this:

```
PATH=C:\DOS;C:\WINDOWS;C:\WINSOCK
```

Start Trumpet Winsock and enter all the basic configuration info you were given. Click **OK** to save everything. In the Trumpet Winsock program, open the **File** menu and select **Exit**.

To connect to the Internet, double-click the **Trumpet Winsock** icon. Then open the **Dialler** menu and select **Login**. Type the phone number of your ISP and click **OK**. Enter your **username** and click **OK**. Enter your password and click **OK**. That's it! Start whatever Internet program you want, such as your Web browser.

When you want to log off, return to the Trumpet Winsock program and open the **Dialler** menu and select **Bye**.

Getting Connected with Windows 95

First, configure TCP/IP: open the Control Panel and double-click the **Network** icon. Select **TCP/IP** and click **Properties**. Click the **IP Address** tab, and select either **Obtain an IP address automatically** (if your ISP told you that you don't have an address assigned to you), or **Specify an IP address** (and then fill in the address).

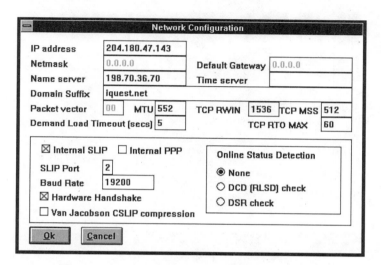

Configuring Winsock.

Next, click the **DNS Configuration** tab and select **Enable DNS**. Enter your Host and Domain names (such as jfulton and indy.net), then type the DNS server address and click **Add**.

Click the **Gateway** tab, and type in the gateway address. Click **Add**. Click **OK** twice to get out of there.

Still with me? OK. Click **Start**, select **Programs**, select **Accessories**, then choose **Dial-Up Networking**. Double-click the **Make New Connection** icon. Give your connection a name, like Indy Net, then click **Next**. Type your phone number and click **Next**. Click **Finish**, and you're done.

Well, kinda. Right-click your new icon, and select **Properties**. Now, if you need to display a terminal window (think: logging in manually), then click **Configure**, and on the **Options** tab, select the **Bring up terminal window after dialog** option. Click **OK**.

Got OSR/2? If you've got the OSR/2 version of Windows 95, then you also have the Connection Wizard, a nifty gadget you can use to create your Internet connection. See the next section for help.

Get that DNS.

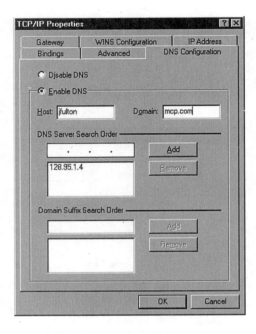

Gateway to the Internet.

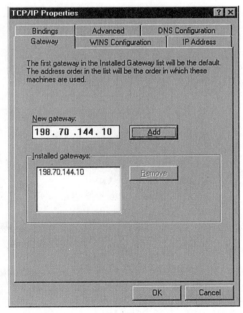

Next, click the **Server Type** button. Choose your server type (PPP, SLIP, or CSLIP) from the **Type of Dial-Up Server** list. Then click **OK**.

To connect to the Internet, double-click the icon you created. Enter your username and password. (Click the **Save password** box if you want.) Click **Connect**. If you use a terminal window to log in, then after it appears, type your login name and password, then click **Continue**. (If you're using a SLIP or CSLIP connection, you'll need to make note of the IP address that's assigned to you after connecting. Scroll to the right, and jot it down. *Then* click **Continue**, and type the IP number in the dialog box that appears next.)

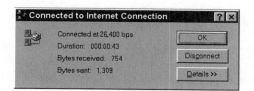

Logging in to your ISP.

Start your Web browser or other Internet program. When you're tired of it all, double-click the Dial-Up Networking icon you'll find on the right-hand side of the taskbar (it looks like a couple of PCs, one behind the other).

Getting Connected with Windows 98

Windows 98, comes with something called the Connection Wizard which you can use to establish your Internet connection.

Begin by clicking the **Start** button, selecting **Programs**, selecting **Internet Explorer**, then selecting **Connection Wizard**. The Get Connected dialog box pops up. Click **Next** to get started.

You're faced with some options. Click **I want to set up a new connection on this computer to my existing Internet account using my phone line or local area network (LAN)** and click **Next**. Select **Connect using my phone line** and **Next**. Click **Create a new dial-up connection** and then click **Next**.

Type in your **Area code** and **Telephone number** and click **Next**. Then type in your username and password and click **Next**. This next screen you can probably skip, unless your ISP told you that you need to set up a SLIP connection, log on manually, use a login script, and/or enter a specific IP and DNS address. If you do, click **Yes**, do what it says, and no one will get hurt. Otherwise, click **No**.

No TCP/IP? If you don't have TCP/IP installed, open the **Network** icon in the Control Panel, click **Add**, click **Protocol**, then click **Add** again. Select **Microsoft** in the Manufacturers list, and select **TCP/IP** from the Network Protocols list. Then select **Dial-Up Adapter** from the configuration list, and click **Properties**. On the **Bindings** tab, select **TCP/IP**. Click **OK**. Click **OK** again to close the Network dialog box.

Wanna find an ISP? The Connection Wizard can help you find an ISP, if you don't already have an Internet account set up with someone. The listings are all for national ISPs; if you prefer to work with someone local, check the Yellow Pages instead.

173

Type a **Connection Name**, such as the name of your ISP, then click **Next**. The rest of the wizard concerns setting up an email account and your newsgroup reader. Just follow the prompts. Click the **Finish** button, and you're done.

Connecting to the Internet with Windows 98 is the same as with Windows 95: double-click the Dial-Up Networking icon you created. Type your **username** and password and click **Connect**. After you're connected, start your Web browser. When you're done, double-click the Dial-Up Networking icon you'll find on the right-hand side of the taskbar.

Upgrading Mistakes to Avoid

The most important mistake to avoid is choosing a lousy ISP. If you follow the tips given earlier, you should avoid most of the clunkers. If you begin to feel like they just don't care about your business, leave 'em for somebody else. Remember, there are many national ISPs you can choose from, or you can always go with an online service.

You can avoid most errors by watching your typing. Enter your server addresses, phone number, username, and password correctly. If you're not sure, go back and double-check.

Sometimes when you try to connect to your ISP, it will not work, but it may be because all the phone lines going into the ISP are temporarily busy. In this case, just try again, and then avoid peak periods if you can, such as 6 to 9 p.m. on weeknights.

The Least You Need to Know

Upgrading to an Internet connection is not as hard as it seems, if you remember these things:

➤ If you connect through your company's network, it's called a persistent connection. To connect to the Internet, all you need to do is to connect to your network.

➤ Online services are friendly, helpful, and they offer lots of neat perks, besides an Internet connection. And besides, getting your connection configured is *easy*.

➤ If you connect to the Internet through a modem, then you'll use a *dial-up connection*. A dial-up connection is faster than using an online service, but it is harder to set up initially.

➤ To create a dial-up connection with Windows 3.1, you have to install and configure Trumpet Winsock, which is the leading connection product for that platform.

➤ With Windows 95 and Windows 98, you use Dial-Up Networking to create your Internet connection. With Windows 98, you use the Connection Wizard.

Part 3
Easy Upgrades and Repairs

Got a klunky keyboard, a malfunctioning mouse, or a pain-in-the-neck printer? Well, in this section, you'll learn some quick fixes for what ails 'em, as well as easy repair solutions for other peripherals such as your monitor, floppy drive, CD-ROM, sound card, and modem.

If kicking, punching, and pleading didn't work, you can always toss the darn things out and replace them with something that does. Even if you've never attempted to upgrade or replace anything on your PC before, you'll find the upgrades I cover in this section (replacing your keyboard, mouse, or printer) the easiest to try.

Easy Repairs for Peripherals

Don't assume that you have to replace *any* computer part just because it's acting funny. The problem may be that you accidentally knocked a cord loose, or something equally as silly. In this chapter, we'll look at common maladies, and how to cure them.

Keyboard Calamities

Keyboards don't usually die, but they can wear out. When a keyboard is on its last legs, the keys stick, you type G and get GGGGGGGGGGGGG, and theSpacebardoesn'twork anymore. But even so, there are other things that can go wrong with a keyboard without it necessarily meaning it's time for a replacement. In this section, we'll explore the problems that can lead to keyboard calamities.

When the Keyboard Goes Beep! Beep! Beep!

If your keyboard beeps at you every time you press a key, the problem is not with the keyboard, but with the PC. What's happened is that your computer's gone into a tizzy over something, and it's locked itself up. Every key you press at this point goes unheard (technically speaking, the keyboard buffer is full), which is why you're hearing the beeps. Restart your PC and everything should be all right again. (Keep in mind that when you restart your PC, you lose any work you haven't already saved.)

Check This Out...

Sound familiar?

If you use Windows (and who doesn't anymore?), this problem may sound a bit familiar. That's because it's sometimes easy for Windows to get a bit confused, and to freeze or lock up. (Actually, it's the program you're using that's confusing Windows...) So if this problem happens to you more times than you'd like to think, then check out the special Windows section for more help in taming that Windows monster: Part 2, "Upgrading and Repairing Windows."

Little Lost Keyboard

If you start your PC one day and get this message: Keyboard not found. Press F1 to continue, don't assume that your keyboard's still out on an all-nighter with your mouse. This message is telling you that the PC can't communicate with the keyboard, and that's probably because the keyboard cable is loose. So return the wayward plug back to its socket (uh, after turning the PC back OFF again), and restart the PC. By the way, make sure you use the right socket; a lot of computers have a mouse and a keyboard port right next to each other, and darn if they don't look real similar. However, they are usually marked with cute symbols (such as a small rodent) that helps you to tell them apart.

You might also get this error if you held down some key while booting. Remove your cat from the keyboard and try restarting the PC. If you still encounter a problem, try using a different keyboard. If it checks out okay, try yours again. If yours doesn't work, replace it.

If you just bought a new keyboard, make sure it's set up right; most have a key on the bottom that controls whether they are being used on an XT (286) system, or an AT (everyone else) system. Set the switch to AT and try rebooting the computer.

Spilled Coffee and Other Common Disasters

If you spill something on your keyboard, don't panic—there may still be a chance to save the patient. Turn off the PC and use a dry cloth to wipe up what you can. Flip the keyboard over to let it drain for about a day. You can dry the keyboard with a hair dryer if you want (low heat setting, of course), but I'd still wait about a day before you try to use the keyboard. After a day or so, plug the keyboard back in, cross your fingers, and turn on the PC.

If that doesn't work, you can do a more thorough job of cleaning by removing the keys with a small flat-head screwdriver. Using the screwdriver as a kind of lever, gently pry up along the bottom edge of each key to remove it. Just make sure you make a note of where each key was located before you actually remove the darn thing. After you get the keys off, use a dry cloth to clean as much as you can. You can spray cleaner on the cloth, *but don't spray anything (besides compressed air) into the keyboard itself.* Some keys, such as the Spacebar and the Enter key, are real buggers to get back on, so don't bother to remove them. Clean up what you can and try the keyboard again.

What to Do About Sticky Keys

Perhaps you didn't spill anything on it, but your keyboard has developed a few sticky keys anyway. First, make sure that it's not the repeat rate that's causing the trouble—the repeat rate controls how hard you must press to get a key to repeat. If the rate's too sensitive, then keys will repeat when you don't want them to. In Windows, you just go to the Control Panel, and double-click the **Keyboard** icon. There, you can adjust lots of settings, including the repeat rate.

If that doesn't work, try cleaning some of the sticky keys and see if that helps. Gently pry off the gummy key using a small flat-head screwdriver. If the key is located in the middle or top of the keyboard, feel free to pry off a few extra keys from the lower rows so you can easily get to the gummy key. After you have the key off, clean its socket with a dry cloth sprayed with some type of cleanser. *Do not spray anything on the keyboard itself.* Replace the key and test it to see if it acts a little better. Don't forget where the keys belong; you'll really fool yourself later if you forget.

The truth about H2O If the spill is really bad, you can douse your keyboard in water—it won't ruin anything as long as you unplug the keyboard before you douse it. Use distilled water, though, because it's free of minerals that can gunk up the keyboard's components. And, of course, make sure the entire keyboard is dry, dry, dry before you try to plug it back in again.

Absolutely, positively, completely, overwhelmingly, *do not use WD-40 on your keyboard,* or any other part of your computer. Sure, it greases things up fine, but it also conducts electricity! Believe me, WD-40, 4-in-1 Oil, or any other such type of industrial lubrication can do worse damage to your machinery than the strongest cup of coffee.

Check This Out...

Other ways to bust the dust You can clear a lot of dust bunnies out of your keyboard with a can of compressed air with dust-eating cleaner added or a computer vacuum. The can of air runs about $10, while the vacuum costs about $30—either one is a good investment. This is the only can of anything whatsoever that it is absolutely safe for you to spray into your keyboard.

When You Can't Tell What the Keys Are For

If some of the letters on your keyboard are worn off, it's no big deal—unless you're a hunt-and-peck typist. Now, if you're like me, then you probably hate to spend hard-earned bucks replacing something that still works at least 75 percent…okay, 60 percent of the time. If you can get your hands on a used keyboard somewhere, you can pry the keys off that you need and use them on your keyboard. Some mail order shops sell replacement keycaps—get a copy of *Computer Shopper*, and you can locate hundreds of mail-order sources for all sorts of items, not just keycaps. Before you go overboard about a few missing letters, keep in mind that if you have to, replacing a keyboard is easy, and it only costs between $20 and $70, or as much as $150 if you're into things like chrome.

What to Do When Your Puppy Attacks the Keyboard Cable

You may also encounter a problem with the keyboard cable wearing out. Usually the trouble is pretty easy to spot—the keyboard stops working or every key you press results in an error. Although you can replace the keyboard cable, it's not a good idea to try because you can only take the keyboard apart so far before you are literally showered with springs, clips, and keycaps. If you're careful, you can do it, but if you accidentally loosen the wrong screw, blammo! So in a case like this, just replace the keyboard rather than spending your life putting it back together.

Mouse Miseries

A mouse is a fun, simple tool you can use to avoid getting your hands dirty using the keyboard. But when your mouse refuses to cooperate, you may soon wish you could jump back in time when all you had to deal with was brushing all the eraser shavings off the company books. Well, don't panic—most mouse problems are easy to solve, as you'll soon see.

When Your Mouse Has Gone to Disneyland

If you've suddenly lost the use of your mouse, or it's acting funny, try some of these tricks:

➤ *Has your mouse gotten loose?* Its tail (the cable) needs to be connected to the back of the PC. If you're not sure where to plug it in, check out Chapter 3, "Now, Let's Find Out What Kind of Computer You Have." After you plug it back in, you need to restart the PC for the mouse to start working again. Of course, before you restart your PC, use keyboard commands to save your open data file (if any) and exit the program. You remember them, don't you? To open a menu for example, you press **Alt** plus the menu's first letter. So to save a file, press **Alt+F** to open the File menu and then **S** to choose Save.

➤ *Is the mouse cable all twisted and torn?* Check the mouse "tail" for damage; if you see some, the mouse is probably beyond repair. This damage might be caused by a run-in with a vacuum cleaner or, heaven forbid, a mouse of the *other* variety. Try testing your system with a similar mouse, to see if it works.

➤ *Are you using a program that supports a mouse?* In other words, are you expecting to see a mouse pointer where one doesn't belong, such as at the DOS prompt? Try going into a program that you know for sure supports a mouse. Windows is a good example. Do you see the mouse pointer?

➤ *Is the mouse playing hide and seek with you?* It's easy to hide a mouse pointer at the edges of your screen. So move the mouse around and see if its pointer pops out of its hiding place.

➤ *Have you cleaned your mouse lately?* If not, it probably needs it. See the next section for help.

➤ *Is the mouse driver installed?* If, after starting your PC, you end up with a missing mouse, then the driver (the program that enables the PC to talk to the mouse) isn't loaded. Someone (or some setup program) was probably fiddling with your AUTOEXEC.BAT file. Use EDIT to open the AUTOEXEC.BAT file and add the command, which is usually something like: C:\DOS\MOUSE, to get the mouse working. If you use Windows 95 or 98, use the **Add New Hardware** icon in the Control Panel to reinstall the mouse driver.

➤ *Is your mouse pointer jumping all around, or moving in only one direction?* First, give it a good cleaning. Then, if needed, check your AUTOEXEC.BAT and CONFIG.SYS to make sure that only one mouse driver is being loaded. (With Windows 95/98, check the Mouse icon in the Control Panel.) Also, make sure you have the latest mouse driver installed. You should also check for device conflicts; see Chapter 27, "Fiddling with Ports, IRQs, Addresses, and Such," for help. Oh, and if you're using Windows 3.1, and you have the latest mouse driver, and so on, then the problem could be an old BIOS. Upgrade it, and the mouse should stop jumping around.

➤ *Have you installed a new device lately, such as a modem?* If so, it may be conflicting with your mouse. See Chapter 27 for help.

➤ *Are you trying to use a converter to plug a PS/2 mouse into a serial port, or vice versa?* If so, it may not work. The electronics of the two different types of mice are different. Some mice will work, because they contain both types of electronics—they are called combo mice. However, you can't usually tell whether a mouse is a combo mouse, because they usually aren't marked, and the manual typically doesn't say. Just about the only way you'll know that you've got a combo mouse is when you notice that it comes with a converter in the box.

➤ *Does your PC insist that you load the Microsoft Mouse driver after you install a Microsoft program?* You may encounter this problem if you just installed a Microsoft program, and it replaces your mouse driver with the Microsoft driver, and you happen to use a different brand of mouse (and driver) than Microsoft. Make a quick edit of the AUTOEXEC.BAT file to return it to its previous state (and to load the previous mouse driver) to fix the problem. Normally, I'd tell you to make a backup of your AUTOEXEC.BAT before you make any changes to it, but if your mouse isn't working then you don't want to keep this AUTOEXEC.BAT file anyway. However, you should have made a backup copy *prior* to installing your new program, and if that's the case, copy it back on top of your newly changed AUTOEXEC.BAT (that is, if the mouse driver was the only thing the program's installation changed).

Maybe it was something I did?

Has your serial mouse been working fine up to now, but suddenly it stops working right after you install some kind of serial device such as a modem, joystick, scanner, or serial printer? The problem is that the new device and your mouse duked it out over a COM port, and the mouse lost.

You see, all serial devices communicate with the PC through a COM (communications) port. Each serial device needs its own COM port, or it gets mucked up and doesn't work. So if your mouse and some new serial device are messing with each other over the same COM port, you have to switch one of them to a different port. See Chapter 27 for more help.

➤ *Are you having trouble seeing your mouse on a laptop?* If you use Windows 95/98, then turn on mouse trails: double-click the **Mouse** icon in the Control panel, then click the **Motion** tab. Select **Show Pointer Trails**. With the **Pointers** tab, you can increase the size of the pointer as well.

➤ *Does the mouse feel funny, or is it too hard to double-click properly?* If so, you can adjust the mouse sensitivity using the **Mouse** icon in the Control Panel. For example, you can switch to a left-handed mouse, adjust the double-click speed, and make the pointer bigger or slower.

➤ *Does your mouse work only in Windows, but not in DOS?* If your mouse works only in Windows 95/98, but not when you reboot to DOS, then you do not have a DOS driver loading, and you need one. Edit your DOSSTART.BAT (located in the Windows directory) and load a DOS mouse driver, after installing it from your mouse disk.

Cleaning a Mouse

If you've had your mouse for a while and it suddenly starts acting weird, chances are that all you need to do is clean it. You see, there's a roller ball on the underside of the mouse that just loves to grab dust, dirt, hair, and any other disgusting thing on which it can get its, uh, hands.

First, exit all programs and turn off the PC so it doesn't go nuts with all the screwy signals it'll receive during the cleaning process. Flip your mouse over on its back and open the hatch that holds the trackball in place. (You see an arrow telling you which way to twist or push the hatch to get it to open.)

Remove the trackball. Now, take a toothpick and gently scrape the gook off of the two or three rollers you find inside the mouse. You can dip the toothpick in rubbing alcohol if you like, but not anything that's oily (like acetone) because this does more harm than good. Someone may tell you to use a Q-Tip for this, but Q-Tips leave their own fuzz behind as well, so I don't recommend using them.

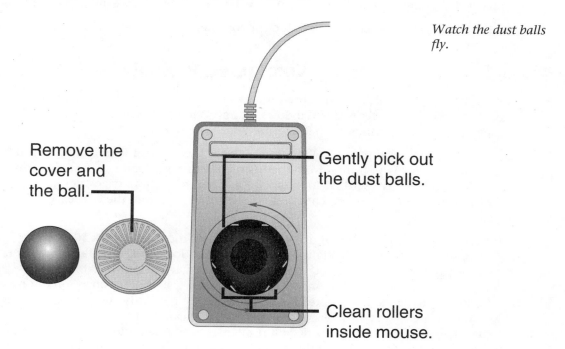

Watch the dust balls fly.

Remove the cover and the ball.

Gently pick out the dust balls.

Clean rollers inside mouse.

Use a lint-free cloth or warm soap and water to clean the trackball, too. Don't use rubbing alcohol on the rubber—it'll mess it up. When you finish cleaning, put the whole thing back together and try it out.

Fixing a Cordless Mouse

If your cordless mouse starts acting strange, it may be low on batteries. The batteries go either in the mouse itself, or in the receiving thingie (the box that's attached to the PC, which receives the mouse signals from the cordless wonder).

Your cordless mouse works just like the remote to the VCR. If you've got tons of tapes piled up in front of the VCR, the remote doesn't work; same thing with your cordless mouse—if it keeps cutting out, it's probably because you've got tons of junk piled up in front of the receiving unit. Just move the junk, and your mouse should be fine. If you're still having trouble, the problem may be your monitor—it may put out too much RF interference and hamper reception.

When Your Printer Makes You Feel Powerless

It's not hard for a printer to make you feel powerless: Just a few minutes of gently trying to coax some paper through, resetting the printer two or three times, and trying to reprint a document over and over can turn even a fullback into a weeping maniac.

Well, no more. In this section, you'll find the solutions to the most common printer problems.

Make Sure Your Printer Is Configured Properly

If your new printer is acting goofy, the easiest solution is to check its configuration. (Steps on how to install a printer under Windows 3.1 and Windows 95 and 98 are covered in Chapter 26, "Getting Windows to Recognize Your New Toy.")

To check a printer's setup under Windows 3.1, open the **Control Panel** and select the **Printer** icon. Select your printer from the **Installed Printer** list, and click **Setup**. Here you can change the printer's settings for memory, graphics resolution, page orientation, and the like. To set the printer port, choose the **Connect** button from the Printers dialog box instead.

To check a printer's properties under Windows 95 or Windows 98, click **Start**, select **Settings**, then select **Printers**. Right-click your printer's icon and select **Properties**. On the **General** tab, you can print a test page if you want. On the **Details** tab, you can change the printer port and the printer driver. (Capturing a printer port is something you might do on a network; it's like stealing a printer for your exclusive use.) If you want to share your printer with coworkers on the network, you can do it with the **Sharing** tab. On the **Paper** tab, you can set the default printer size and orientation. On the **Graphics** tab, you can adjust the quality of the graphics you print. The higher the quality, the more time it'll take to print them. On the **Fonts** tab, you can install new fonts, and on the **Device Options** tab, you can set the printer's memory.

Saving an Old, Slow Printer

If your printer is a turtle, you can easily speed it up without replacing it. A printer by nature is slower than your computer, which means that the PC can easily send data to the printer faster than the printer can print it. What happens in most cases is a bottleneck: The stuff you send to the printer creates a logjam back at the computer end, waiting for the printer to catch up.

While your computer waits around feeding your printer a page to print every so often, you wait in frustration for your PC to start paying more attention to you. To solve this problem, get yourself a print spooler program. When you print something, the computer tosses it over to the print spooler and gets on with its life. The print spooler then takes over the boringly slow job of feeding the printer.

If you have Windows 3.1 or Windows 95/98, then you already have a print spooler because it's built-in (in Windows 3.1, the print spooler is called Print Manager; in Windows 95/98, the spooler doesn't have a name, but it's accessible through the printer icon on your desktop, or through what Windows unceremoniously calls the Printers Folder). But if you're just using DOS, adding a print spooler program really makes a difference. Getting a DOS-based print spooler is quite a pickle, because most people carry only a limited amount of DOS programs (everything's Windows, don't ya know). If you insist on using DOS, it's worth your time to locate a good DOS utilities package such as Norton Utilities or Mace Utilities, which includes a terrific DOS-based print spooler.

Another way to speed up a slow printer is to add a print buffer. A print buffer acts as a holding spot for stuff you send to the printer, just like the print spooler. But unlike a spooler (which is a program), a buffer is a series of RAM chips, which means that it's faster. If you have a laser printer, then it has a print buffer built-in. There's a good chance, however, that the amount of RAM your printer comes with is minimal—such as 512KB (also known as printer memory). Don't get sad; you can usually increase the speed of your printer by adding more buffer RAM to it. Also, some printer sharing devices (commonly called A/B switches) come with their own print buffers. So if you're stuck sharing a printer with someone, get an A/B switch with lots of buffer RAM built-in; it's worth the extra investment.

My Printer Doesn't Print!

If your printer doesn't print at all, make sure it's on, and that it's online ("online" here means that its communication channel to the computer is open). To put a printer online, press its **On Line** button or switch.

If the printer's on but not responding, check for paper jams. Also, make sure that it's not out of paper. If your cheap boss is making you share your printer with a coworker through one of those A/B switch boxes, make sure that the switch is set to your PC. If everything else checks out, you should try printing with another program. If that works, then the first program is set up with the wrong printer. Use the **File**, **Print** or **File**, **Printer Setup** command to change the designated printer.

My Printer Keeps Jamming!

One last thing
Sometimes when your printer won't print, the villain is the printer cable. It's sad, but occasionally your cable will just go bad. So before you chuck your printer, consider replacing the cable instead. Or better yet, borrow a cable from a friend and see if your printer works with it.

If you're having problems with paper jams, there are several possible explanations. If your dot-matrix printer jams, you might be using paper that's too thick. If you're using regular tractor-feed paper, the problem could be that you've got the paper too taut (or too loose). Tractor-feed paper guides are those two rubber things with the pins that look like tank treads and hold on to your paper. If possible, readjust the position of the guides so your paper doesn't appear to have any warps or buckles in it, and so the paper is aligned correctly. Another possible problem with tractor-feed is that the paper guides may be gumming up. Be careful here: household oil such as 4-In-1 fixes the gumming up problem, but it can oil up your paper if you use too much, and if you get a drop in the wrong place, disaster can strike in a form not seen since the opening of the movie, Commando.

A Problem That Looks Like a Paper Jam but Might Not Be

Now, if the document you sent to the printer prints on one line so an entire page looks like one long very, very black stripe, you may think you have a paper jam when you don't. You see, when a dot-matrix printer reaches the end of a line, it waits for a signal telling it to drop down to the next line. The techies call this "line feed at carriage return," or CR/LF for short. The CR/LF signal can come from the printer, or from the computer, depending on how both devices are set up. If that signal doesn't come at all, then the dumb printer keeps printing over the same line. Likewise, if it comes from both the computer and the printer, then you get double-spaced print when you don't want it.

To solve the problem, adjust the line feed settings, both for your printer and for the program you're using. Your printer may have a line feed switch marked "CR/LF," or it may have a series of DIP switches (generally either in the back of the printer or below the print carriage). A DIP switch looks like a tiny light switch; push it up for on, or down for off. Look for help with the DIPs in Chapter 27. In any case, after you change the line feed setting, you need to turn off your printer and then wake it back up again before it'll realize that you've changed anything. Now don't change the line feed unless you're sure you have a problem, because, well, your nice printer may start suddenly printing weird. If the printer only prints goofy in one program, then the printer setup in that program is probably the guilty party.

It's overwhelming!

If you're printing to a network printer, it can easily become overwhelmed with the huge number of jobs it needs to print. No problem; it'll just print one job at a time until it's done. However, it may mean that you'll become overwhelmed waiting so long for your document to print. If you want to see where you stand in the long line to the printer, double-click the **Printer** icon on the Windows 95/98 taskbar (or on the desktop in Windows 3.1), and the print queue appears. If your network administrator has granted you special permissions (more accurately, if your administrator has ignored the network printer setup, and left it just like it was when it was installed), you can move your document to the top of the list by dragging it there. (Just don't tell anyone I told you…)

Laser or Inkjet Printer Jams

If you're having printer jams on a laser or inkjet printer, then again, the problem might be that the paper is too thick. If you're trying to use copier paper, don't. Laser paper is specially treated so the printer can grip it properly. When buying reams of paper, look for thirty-pound bond (written "30# bond") or greater.

Also, there's a right way and a wrong way to load laser paper into your printer. When paper is pressed at the factory, it goes through hot rollers in one direction; the best path for that paper through the printer is the same direction. Check the package end for the arrow that tells you which direction you should load your paper. In addition, keep your laser paper in a dry, cool place—not in your damp basement.

I'm Having Trouble Printing My Envelopes and Labels!

If you're trying to print an envelope through your laser printer, read the manual. There's usually some short paper path you can use so your envelope doesn't come out looking like your dog chewed it. This paper path may be located above the regular path, or you may have to throw some switch to turn the regular path into a shortened one. Also, if you're trying to print labels on your laser printer, make sure that you get a style of blank labels that's specifically designed for laser printing, or else the labels will peel off and stick inside your printer. Also, just like envelopes, use the shorter print path for your labels.

The dog ate it Some cheaper envelopes, if loaded wrong, will melt (well, their glue will melt) when you run them through your laser. This could gum up your printer, so be sure to check your manual for the proper loading procedure.

You may also be wondering "which way is up"—in other words, should you put the envelope in face up, or face down? Well, the answer to that quandary is in your owner's manual. If it helps, my laser printer makes me put envelopes face up along the left-hand side of the paper feed. You can also load a test page to check out your printer's orientation: Take an 8 1/2- by 11-inch sheet of paper, write the word "Top" on it, then run it through, making a note of the way it comes out of the printer.

The Printout Is Garbled!

If your printout looks as illegible as a doctor's prescription, the problem may be the cable. First of all, you want to be sure to place your printer only a short distance from your PC. Longer distances (and longer cables) tend to garble up the data unless that data's boosted by a printer-helper (otherwise known as a parallel line extender).

If your printer cable's loose, remove it. Check all the pins; if one of them is bent, gently bend it back. Then replace the cable and try printing again.

Another thing you might want to check when the printout is goofy is whether or not you selected the correct printer within your program. In most programs, you can get to the printer selection screen through the **Print** or **Printer Setup** command on the **File** menu. Just change the printer to the exact brand you're using and then try printing again. In Windows 3.1, you can change the default printer though the **Printer** icon in the **Control Panel**. In Windows 95/98, open the **Start** menu, select **Settings**, and then select **Printers**. To add a new printer, double-click the **Add Printer** icon. To make an existing printer the default one, right-click the printer's icon and select **Set As Default**.

If you have a PostScript laser printer, disregard anything you've ever read that told you that there's only one PostScript version. There are actually well over 12,000 or so versions. If your program has both a listing for your particular brand of printer and another listing for "PostScript printer," by all means choose your particular brand for your printer driver. Don't choose the latest and greatest PostScript driver on hand because you think it will improve your PostScript printing. In other words, only choose the HP LaserJet 4 driver if you own a LaserJet 4; if you own an old Apple LaserWriter Plus, don't install the HP drivers.

If the only choice your program gives you is "PostScript," and your sparkling new PostScript laser printer is goofing up pages, you may need to check whether your printer has a "step-down" emulation mode for an older edition of PostScript. If that's the case, set it into emulation mode and choose the appropriate driver. For example, if your printer emulates an HP LaserJet III, then set it in emulation mode and choose the HP driver. Of course, if you've invested big bucks in a fancy schmancy page printer, you won't want to step it down to a lower mode just to get the thing to print. Solution: Get the right PostScript driver for your printer from the manufacturer, an online service, a BBS, or the Internet.

I Can Hardly Read My Printout!

If your printout is getting light, it may be time to change the printer's ribbon, inkjet, or toner cartridge. You can try increasing the print density setting in your program or printer driver before you replace your ribbon or other ink source. This makes your printouts darker, but if it's really time to change the ribbon, inkjet, or toner cartridge, then you won't see much improvement.

On the other hand, if even the lightest subject matter prints too dark, try decreasing the print density setting. If it's down to almost nothing and things are still dark, the problem may be that your program isn't properly creating gray-scale graphics for your printer. Word processors are especially prone to this problem whenever there is a graphic on the page. Make sure your program is properly configured to handle gray-scales. (If you're printing with PostScript, you should not have this problem under any circumstance, unless something's really, really wrong—like a toner leak.)

> *Check This Out...*
>
> **Not yet!** If you just can't stand having to change the toner in your laser printer all the time, you might get a bit more out of each one by removing the toner and gently shaking it, and then reinstalling it.

After you change the toner cartridge on a laser printer as explained later in this chapter (this is best done, by the way, in the dark, to avoid damaging the developer drum unit), use a dry, soft toothbrush or similar instrument to sweep off any loose toner from the components. In any event, your documents will be streaked for a while—this is just spilled toner dust working its way out. (Be careful when changing the toner cartridge, and make sure you don't get any on you—it just won't come out, no matter what super duper cleaner you use on it.) It's always a good idea to have the printer run a couple of test pattern pages to get the streaks out of the system. If your printouts are streaked after you've had the toner in for a long while, there may be a problem with the toner. Check to see if your cartridge is the type that you can reseal, and if it is, then try resealing the cartridge and changing it again. If that doesn't make a dent in the problem, your print drum may be going out, and you'll need to take your printer in to a registered service center for the necessary surgery.

My Printout Is Only Half There!

If your non-PostScript laser printer only prints part of your document, then you may be asking it to do too much. You see, for a laser printer to print a page, it first has to cram the image for that entire page into its memory. The imaging system has to have access to the whole page, otherwise nothing works. For most plain text pages, you only use a trickle of the printer's memory when you print these pages because the image is not complex. Add a few fancy fonts, and it gets harder. Add a couple of fancy graphics, and it gets harder still.

Your only fix here is to either simplify your document by using less graphics and only one or two fonts, or by adding more memory to the printer. For some printers, this is about as fun as at-home ulcer surgery, so have your registered service representative take care of it for you.

If your PostScript laser printer only prints part of your document, then your problem may not be in your computer or your printer, but rather in the document itself. Try ejecting the page manually. If the page is incomplete, or the text is in 1200-point type rather than 12-point, then as a test, try printing out something else—anything other than the same document again. If that something else prints just fine, your problem may be with the PostScript instructions that your program is sending to your printer for that one document. This is a good time to see if there are any other types of PostScript drivers that work with your brand of printer.

Replacing a Ribbon in a Dot-Matrix Printer

If you need to replace the ribbon in your dot-matrix printer, first trot down to the computer store and buy one. Be sure to get the exact type that matches your printer. There are lots of differences here, so double-check the box before you buy. Don't take the old ribbon with you, because it's pretty messy and not really necessary as long as you know which brand of printer you have. Just jot down the ribbon's part number on a piece of paper and ask for that specific part number. If the store doesn't have your printer's own brand of ribbon, you can perhaps use another brand that's listed as a replacement for that specific part number.

The way you should replace your ribbon varies a bit from printer to printer, but here are the basic steps:

Printer ribbon types vary...

Really old printers, such as a Star NX-10, don't have self-contained ribbon cartridges like modern printers. Instead, the ribbon is a simple spool; in fact, it's the same spool that's used in an IBM Selectric I *typewriter*. You thread one of these printer ribbons like you would thread a reel-to-reel tape recorder.

Old printers aren't the only ones with ribbon installation instructions that vary from the following general directions. For example, the newer Epson Stylus uses an ink cartridge/print head combo kinda like an inkjet cartridge. To remove it, you flip a little lever which pops the whole gizmo out. You then replace it with another ink cartridge/print head combo, so you get a new print head every time you replace the cartridge.

1. First, lay out a couple of pieces of paper, roll up your sleeves, remove your tie, and what the hey, change into old clothes. Now, rip open the plastic bag and take the new ribbon out. Lay your new ribbon on the paper and save the bag for later.

2. Next, turn off the printer. You may be tempted to move the print head out of the way, but don't. Moving the print head manually can cause big, expensive problems—just check your printer's manual before you try it.

3. If there's a ribbon-release lever, flip it. Then press and hold the funny clips on either side of the ribbon and lift the ribbon out of the printer. Some models, such as certain Okidata printers, have a cartridge that is bolted down with three screws. Anyway, unlock the ribbon and take it out. Put the old inky thing into the bag you saved from the new ribbon.

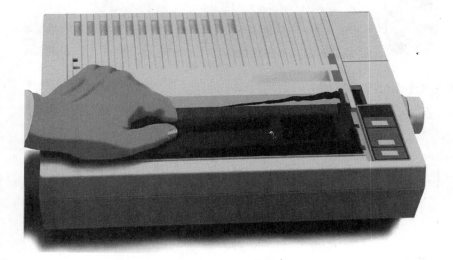

Press the retaining clips and remove the old ribbon.

4. Position your new ribbon in place, but don't lock it in just yet. Thread the ribbon between the print head and the print shield.

5. Push down to lock the ribbon cartridge in place. If there are any retaining clips, make sure they snap in place, too. Now, turn on the printer and test it out. If it doesn't work, take the ribbon out and start over. If it does work, go wash your hands; you've probably got lots of ink on them.

Make sure you insert the ribbon between the print head and the shield.

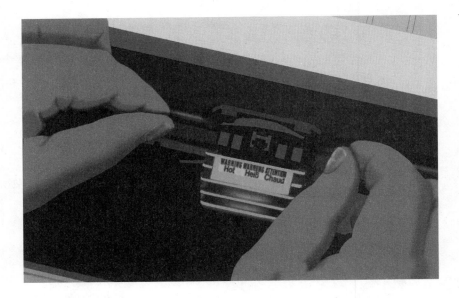

Replacing an Inkjet Cartridge

Replacing an inkjet cartridge is not as messy as it sounds:

1. To replace the cartridge on your inkjet printer, you need to first unpack the cartridge itself. Then remove the seal that covers the bronze print head.

2. Lay out a piece of paper. Remove the old cartridge by pulling backwards at the top of the cartridge, away from the green dot on the cartridge holder. It should snap loose. Put the old inky cartridge on the paper for now.

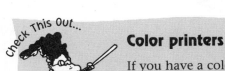

Color printers

If you have a color inkjet printer, its cartridges are contained in a single unit. Press the release clips and pop the cover, and you can replace individual cartridges as needed. You'll find that the black ink goes out more quickly than the other colors. Keep in mind that you don't have to replace all the colors each time (at least, not with most printers); just replace empty cartridges as needed.

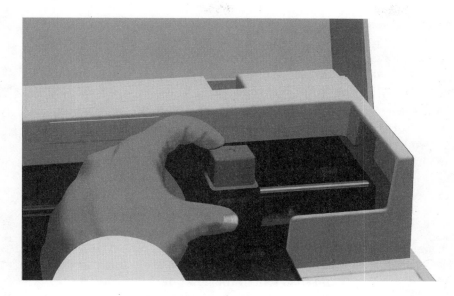

Remove the old cartridge by pulling from the top.

3. Take the new cartridge and position it so the arrow points forward, toward the green dot on the holder.

4. Slide the cartridge into the holder and use your thumb to snap it into place.

5. Throw away your old cartridge.

Replacing the Toner Cartridge in Your Laser Printer

Most every laser printer manufactured today uses toner cartridges, rather than the old toner reservoirs the owner had to fill manually through a bottle and a straw. Installing a toner cartridge is kinda messy, but fairly simple.

1. Turn the printer off, and let it cool down. While you're waiting, lay out a few pieces of paper, roll up your sleeves, throw away your tie, put a drop cloth down and change into your painter's duds. Open the front or top of the printer. (Check in your printer's manual for the exact steps for opening your printer—there's usually some kind of "hood release" button.)

2. Grab the tab on the old cartridge and lift it up and out. Put the old icky cartridge on the paper for now. Take this opportunity to clean any dust you see inside the printer with a clean cloth and a bit of rubbing alcohol. Most manufacturers recommend cleaning the corona wire each time you change the toner—that's the wire that heats or "sets" the toner onto the paper as it comes out of the printer. Some

193

manufacturers even give you a special brush that's kept on a conspicuous clip inside the printer just for that purpose. Also, some manufacturers expect you to change other parts near the toner, such as a felt filter. Check in the manual for how-tos, because this procedure varies a lot. Also, while you're working in there, don't touch anything that's still hot—if you're not sure what's okay to touch, check the manual.

3. The old, charred, burned-out toner powder is generally collected in a little bottle or reservoir. With newer toner cartridges, this reservoir is part of the cartridge itself; but with older printer models, the bottle actually rests in its own, separate cradle. If that's the case, lift out the bottle now, carefully. There should be a cap clipped to the side of the bottle. Peel off this cap and use it to close the bottle. Throw the bottle away and replace it with a new one from your toner cartridge kit.

Is it really dead? Before you replace your old toner cartridge, you may want to gently shake it, replace it, and test it out. You might be able to get a few more "pages" of life out of it—who knows?

4. Now for the truly yucky part. Open the foil wrapper holding your new toner cartridge. Some manufacturers make you reuse the distributor unit, so you may have to unsnap yours from the old toner cartridge and snap it onto the new one. After you get the whole rigmarole together, continue with the next step.

5. Hold your toner cartridge at either end and gently rock the cartridge back and forth to distribute the toner gunk. Don't turn the thing upside down unless you don't mind wasting some toner to create a permanent designer floor pattern.

6. Remove the seal that holds the toner in place. Slide the cartridge into the printer until it snaps into place. If there's a retaining thumb screw, twist until it's snug but not too tight. Close the panel. Turn your printer on and print a few test pages. Don't be surprised if you see some streaking; if you spilled a bit of toner earlier, it'll take a while to work itself out. Printing a few test pages usually takes care of the problem.

Adding More Memory to Your Laser Printer

Adding more memory to your laser printer keeps it from choking on the big complex graphics and fancy fonts in your documents. To add more memory to your laser printer, you first have to figure out whether it will fit. In other words, do you have an empty memory slot into which you can put more RAM? For example, my laser can take up to 4MB of RAM, but it only has one more slot to put it in. So if I try to upgrade from my current 2MB, I can either upgrade to a total of 3MB by buying the 1MB upgrade board, or to 4MB by buying the 2MB board instead. I can't buy 1MB now and another 1MB when I can afford it. Ugh.

Slide the new cartridge in place.

The second thing you need to figure out is how to insert the RAM. Some laser RAM comes in nice, easy-to-insert SIMMs, while others come in funky hard-to-deal-with DRAM chips. Others come on *daughter cards* that connect to the main memory card. And some (I'm not kidding here) actually come on boards that you need to *solder* to the printer's motherboard. Ugh.

So you better buy the exact RAM upgrade kit for the brand of printer you own, or you'll be stuck with a bunch of junk you can't do anything with. Don't try to steal RAM out of your PC to use in your printer—it just won't work.

The method for inserting your new printer RAM obviously varies by printer, but you'll find general information on inserting various RAM chips in Chapter 19, "Make Mine More Memory."

Uh, There's Something Wrong with My Monitor

Before you decide to throw everything out and invest in a new video system for your PC, here are some things you should check:

➤ If you see a faint after-image of some program on the screen, it could be that you left that image onscreen for too long, without any movement going on. When that happens, the unchanged image starts to burn itself into the screen. If that's happened, there's not a lot you can do now. To prevent burn-in in the future, get yourself a good screen-saver program.

➤ If your once-quiet monitor suddenly starts making a loud humming noise, it may be that the old guy is going out, and you'll have to replace it soon. If the monitor only squeaks while you're in a particular program, it could be that the program is trying to make the monitor display stuff that it's not capable of. If you can switch the program to plain VGA mode, chances are your monitor (unless it's a dinosaur) can take it.

➤ If your monitor starts displaying funny colors or no color at all, check the cable to ensure you plugged it in all the way. Also, look at the video plug for any bent pins. If you find some, bend them back (gently, gently). If the funky colors appear only when you're using a particular program, check its setup to see if you can change the *palette* (a fancy word for color wardrobe).

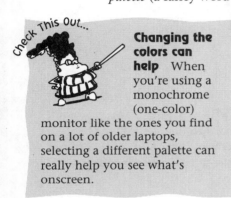

Changing the colors can help When you're using a monochrome (one-color) monitor like the ones you find on a lot of older laptops, selecting a different palette can really help you see what's onscreen.

➤ If you're having trouble reading what's onscreen, another thing you might try is playing around with the contrast and brightness knobs. The contrast knob is marked with a half white, half black circle; the brightness knob is marked with a little sun symbol. You could also change the screen resolution. A higher resolution (such as 1280×1024) allows your monitor to display complex graphics more clearly. They will, however, appear smaller onscreen. So changing to a lower resolution (such as 640×480) may be more to your liking, because objects will appear larger.

Fixing a Drive That's Floppin'

Some of the problems that occur with floppy disk drives have more to do with "operator error" than something that's actually broken, so you might be able to fix whatever's wrong without replacing the drive. For example, you might start up your PC one day and see this nonsense:

```
Non-system disk or disk error. Replace and strike any key when ready.
```

Nothing's wrong with your disk drive, or the hard disk itself. In fact, nothing much is wrong at all; you simply left a disk in drive A when you booted (started) your system. Take the silly thing out and reboot your PC by pressing **Ctrl+Alt+Delete**. Do not strike a key like the message tells you to—doing that can infect your PC if the disk that was left in the drive has any viruses.

The PC Won't Read My Disk!

If you insert a disk with the hope that your PC can read its data and it can't, check a couple of things first before you chuck the disk (or the drive). First, remove the disk and tap it in your palm a few times. This aligns the magnetic material inside. Reinsert the disk and see if your PC can read it now. Be sure to close the door on a 5 1/4-inch drive—if you didn't before, that may be the reason why your PC can't read the disk. If you're trying to read the data on a 3 1/2-inch disk, remove it and check the metal cover. Slide it back and forth a few times to loosen it up, and then retry the disk. You can also run CHKDSK and ScanDisk to make sure there's nothing wrong with the disk.

New drive? If you just installed a new floppy drive, and you're having trouble getting it to read disks, you need to check your installation—specifically, the data and power cables. See Chapter 21, "Replacing a Floppy Drive," for help.

Next, you may want to try using the disk in somebody else's computer. If it works there, that can mean that your drive's having some problems. Try another disk in your drive. Same trouble? Well, before you call 911, try cleaning the drive. Then check CMOS to see if the drive is set up properly (see Chapter 27 for help). You can also open up the PC and make sure that the drive's data and power cables haven't come loose or something else equally as silly. You might also want to check your system for viruses. If the drive light does not come on at all, and you immediately get an error, then the floppy drive controller may be bad. Yech.

If the disk doesn't work in your friend's drive, then something may be wrong with the disk. Did you format the disk properly? If you copied data to the disk, the disk was formatted, but it may not have been formatted correctly.

If you're trying to copy something to the disk and you can't, the problem may be that the disk is *write-protected*, which somebody did to keep the data on the disk from being overwritten. Remove the tab from your 5 1/4-inch floppy (it looks like a piece of tape) or flip the tab back down on your 3 1/2-inch floppy. (On a 3 1/2-inch floppy, the write protect tab is located in the upper left-hand corner when the disk is flipped on its back.) If the disk doesn't have a tab, it's probably been removed because the originator really, really wanted to make sure that you never deleted its data. If you still want to, you can; just get a piece of tape, and cover up the write-protect hole. After you do this, you can use the disk again.

Look out for ED disks!

There's a new kind of disk out there that you should be aware of because it looks like a 3 1/2-inch disk, but it isn't. If your disk is tattooed with the letters "ED," then it's an extended-capacity disk. Look closely, because the "HD" on a "High Density" disk looks like an "ED" from a distance. Mr. ED can hold a lot more data (2.88MB) than his similarly sized friend, but he only works in an extended-density drive. Don't worry about running into many of these guys soon—they're fairly expensive, so most people don't use them.

If the drive still can't read the disk, check its capacity. Are you trying to read a high-density disk in a low-density drive? If so, it won't work. If you're sure that the disk is the right capacity for your drive, and the disk came from a coworker, then it may be that his drive, or your drive, is out of alignment. If the problem keeps cropping up with other disks, you should check out the guilty drive—just keep in mind that repairing the drive may cost more than replacing it.

A Mac disk won't work

If you borrowed a friend's Macintosh disk, it probably won't work in your PC, unless it came from a Power PC. That's because most Mac disks are formatted funny, at least from a PC's point of view. (Unfortunately, this will sound pretty strange when you discover that your friend's Mac can probably read your PC's disks, but I can't help that.)

If you get an error message while trying to use your disk (like Sector not found), you should try to copy whatever you can off the disk. If the drive won't let you copy anything but you need to save an important file, you'll have to use a disk recovery utility like the ones you'll find in Norton Utilities or CyberMedia First Aid. Uh, good luck.

Lastly, if you keep getting problems with your drive not being able to read disks, then the drive itself may be going out. But first, *clean the drive*. Then test to see what types of disks the drive is having trouble reading. Can it read disks if it formats them, but not others? If so, then the drive might be misaligned, and needs to be replaced. You might want to open up the PC and check the data and power cables to make sure they didn't accidentally come loose after you drop-kicked the PC when it lost your marketing campaign.

I Can't Format This Disk!

If you try to format a disk and you get some bogus message about invalid media or something, you probably tried to format a disk to the wrong capacity. For example, if you insert a low-density disk into a high-density drive and type this:

FORMAT A:

You get an error message because the drive tries to format it as if it is a high-density disk. If it is of the 3 1/2-inch variety, then try something like this:

FORMAT A: /F:720

If it's a 5 1/4-inch disk, try this instead:

FORMAT A: /F:360

Another way you can tell you're trying to format a disk to the wrong capacity is that the formatting will take a long time, and you'll end up with a bunch of bad sectors on the disk after it's through. Again, format the disk to its native capacity. You can also get this problem with cheap disks, so make sure you buy name-brand ones whenever possible.

If you still have any of those DOS-based "skew-sector formatting" utilities that were popular back in the Ice Age, get rid of them. They don't work with most modern disk drives; and even if one works on yours, the disk that your machine may read will probably be illegible on 95% of the other disk drives in the world. It's just not worth it for 10 extra KB of storage.

> **Which drive is which?** If you can't format your disk because you're having trouble figuring out which drive is A and which is B, type DIR A: and look to see which drive light comes on. The drive that lights up is A. If you get an error message telling you: Not ready reading drive A. Abort, Retry, Fail?, press A for Abort.

My Disk's Stuck or Broken!

If the disk is stuck in the drive, turn the computer off, and using a small flat knife or screwdriver, gently pry the disk out. Be careful not to damage the drive, however.

If you have a 3 1/2-inch disk that's got a bent metal cover, take the darn thing completely off. The disk will work fine without it. However, copy the contents of the disk onto a new disk as soon as you can; without the cover, the data on the disk is not protected.

CD-ROM Catastrophes

Not a lot typically happens to a CD-ROM drive after it's installed properly, but sometimes a few funky things might occur.

I Can't Hear My CD!

If you can't hear your musical CD after sticking it in your CD-ROM drive, don't panic—this doesn't mean you've wrecked your only copy of the Hansons' CD. Check these things:

> ➤ *First, does your PC have a sound card?* If not, you won't be able to play musical CD-ROMs except through the headphone attachment on the CD-ROM drive itself. See Chapter 24, "Sensational Stereophonic Sound," for help in adding a sound card to your computer. If your system does have a sound card, then make sure that your CD-ROM drive is connected to the sound card with a cable. Also, make sure it's connected to the correct connector—some sound cards come with several CD-ROM connectors, designed for each of the major CD-ROM drive manufacturers, such as Panasonic, Sony, and so on.

➤ *Try another CD.* Does it work? If so, then the problem's with the particular CD you were trying to play. You might be able to just keep replacing that faulty CD until your driver recognizes it.

➤ *Make sure that your speakers are plugged in, and that they are turned on.* Also, check the volume knob on the speakers if they have one.

➤ *If you use Windows 3.1, have you installed the MCI audio driver?* Use the **Drivers** icon in the Control Panel to add it.

➤ *In Windows 95/98, check the volume control.* Double-click the horn icon on the status bar. Then make sure the **Mute All** option is *not selected* under Volume Control. To listen to your CD through the speakers, make sure the **Select** option under Audio CD is checked. If you want to listen only through your headphones, and not through the speakers, then turn *off* the **Select** option.

➤ *You may not have the CD Player program installed on your Windows 95/98 system, so there's nothing to respond to your CD when you insert it.* With your Windows 95/98 CD-ROM in the drive, under Control Panel, go to **Add/Remove Programs**, then click the **Windows Setup** tab. Choose **Multimedia** in the list, then click the **Details** button. In the second list that comes up, **CD Player** should have a check mark next to it. If it doesn't, click it so it does, then click **OK**, then click the other **OK**. Windows will go through the motions of installing the CD Player program from the CD-ROM.

➤ *You may want to check the CD-ROM driver to make sure that it is properly installed.* In Windows 95/98, use the **Add/Remove Hardware** icon in the Control Panel. In Windows 3.1, use the **Drivers** icon in the Control Panel instead. Also, check for hardware conflicts, especially if you've just installed some other new piece of hardware. See Chapter 27 for help.

➤ *Can you play programs through the CD-ROM?* If not, the problem is with the drive, and your audio CDs won't work any better. You should attempt to reinstall the CD-ROM driver; see Chapter 22, "Adding a CD-ROM or DVD-ROM Drive," for help.

➤ *Did you insert the CD correctly?* The label should be facing up.

➤ *Is the CD making noise?* If you have a high speed drive, then the reason for the noise might be the CD-ROM disc itself. If the paint on the label side of the disc is uneven, then it will spin in the drive like an out-of-balance washing machine. You can't do much about this one, but to see if that's the problem, try out another disc, and see if the noise goes away.

In addition to these things, you should check out the solutions listed in the section, "Sound Card Problems," coming up.

Why Don't the Speakers Shut Off When I Use My Headphones?

Trying to play a little rock n' roll at work? Well, that's okay—as long at the boss doesn't find out, I guess. Of course, that means you'll have to shut off your speakers so the sound comes only through your headphones.

In Windows 95/98, check the volume control: Double-click the horn icon on the status bar. To listen to your musical CD-ROM only through your headphones, and not through the speakers, make sure the **Select** option under Audio CD is *not* checked.

Windows 3.1 does not support CD audio through the operating system; any "jukebox" or other audio software is generally provided by the software that accompanied your sound card.

My CD-ROM Drive Just Doesn't Work!

If you're having trouble getting your CD-ROM drive to read a CD, try these things:

➤ *Do other CDs work okay?* If so, then the trouble is obviously with this particular CD. Try cleaning its surface with a soft cloth.

➤ *Is the disc loaded properly?* Typically, the label side is up, the clear (non-printed) side is down. On some drives, however, the exact opposite is true.

➤ *Is this a CD-R disc?* If so, whoever made it may not have done a real good job. Some CD-Rs are sloppily made, making it difficult if not impossible for other drives (other than the originating one) to read them. Try reinserting the disc, or cleaning its surface. Some drives may not be able to read CD-R or CD-RW discs at all, and yours may be one of them. Try different discs to see if this is the problem. Is the CD-R disc a standard, 74-minute disc, or is it one with extra capacity? If so, your drive may not be able to read it.

➤ *If the problem isn't the discs, it's the drive.* Try cleaning the drive first, then check its power and data cables to make sure they have not come loose for some silly reason. Check the CD-ROM driver, and download an update if possible.

Sound Card Problems

The whole point, it seems, in having a sound card in the first place is to get, um, *sound*. So if you've turned to this section because you're *not getting any sound*, take a few aspirin, a walk around the block, and then read on.

Where's the Sound?

Not hearing anything from your million dollar megablaster speakers? Check out these things:

➤ Did you recently install some new piece of hardware? If so, it may be causing a conflict with your sound card. See Chapter 27 for tips on what to do.

➤ Make sure everything's plugged in (and into the correct jacks), and that the speakers are turned on, and receiving power.

➤ Check the volume knob on the sound card (if there is one, it would be in the back of your computer where all your cards' plugs are located). Make sure this master volume knob is set to at least medium volume. Sometimes, there's so little space on the back of a sound card that there's no way to mark the knob; so "medium" would be halfway in-between as far as the knob can go one way and as far as the knob can go the other. In Windows 95/98, this volume knob is augmented by the Volume Control, so Windows' idea of "loud" is no louder than your sound card's current volume setting. Make sure that Windows' own master volume on the mixer control is set correctly, and that the Mute All option is not selected.

➤ One way to make sure that your speakers are working is to plug your headphones into the sound card. If they work, you have a problem with your speakers. If you have headphone jacks on your speakers themselves, try plugging your headphones in there. If you hear good sound from both sides, the problem may be in the cord that connects one speaker to the other. Make certain that cord is secure and undamaged. It's easy to replace the cord; your nearest Radio Shack should have one.

➤ If you can't hear sound while playing a particular program, you will need to check its setup program to make sure that the correct sound card is selected.

➤ If you can hear sound, but it is unclear or garbled, some other device may be conflicting with your sound card. See Chapter 27 for help. If the problem only occurs with certain sound files, it could be that they were not recorded well.

➤ If you're having trouble hearing sound from just one of the speakers, then most likely, that speaker is turned off or not receiving power. You can also check the volume balance in the Volume Control panel in Windows 95/98 by double-clicking the horn icon on the status bar. In addition, you can rerun the sound card's installation program and make sure you select stereo output (and not mono).

➤ If you're getting interference through your speakers, try switching to shorter cables. Long cables, especially with amplified speakers, are particularly susceptible to interference. Try moving the speakers and see if that helps. As a last-ditch effort, try an electronics store; they should carry products that help overcome RF interference.

➤ Is your sound card the same card as your modem? To find out, check to see if your incoming phone line plugs into the same card as your speakers. If they're on the same card, you may not be able to hear good sound while you're online. The solution to this problem in the short term is to wait until you've logged off to play your CD; in the long term, it's to replace both your sound card and your modem. (Believe me, you'll be happier.)

Don't try this at home

Don't try to use your home stereo speakers with your PC. For one, they won't work. The signal coming from your PC's sound card is too weak to power most stereo speakers, because your sound card does not have an amplifier. (PC speakers have little amplifiers in them.) Even if they did work, or if you were able to rig an amplifier between the PC and your stereo speakers, unless those speakers are shielded, they may interfere with the performance of your monitor.

➤ After trying everything else, in Windows 95/98 you can always reinstall the sound card driver using the Add/Remove Hardware Wizard, which you'll find in the Control Panel. See Chapter 26 for more help. With Windows 3.1, run the sound card installation program again if you like. Check the card's manual to see what changes should have been made, then after running the installation program, check the WIN.INI and SYSTEM.INI files to see if they've been changed correctly (you'll find them in the Windows directory).

My Headphones Aren't Working

Darn. And you were going to jam to the Stones today. Well, try these things:

➤ In Windows 95/98, double-click the horn icon on the status bar. Then make sure the **Select** option under Audio CD is *not* checked.

➤ Are you trying to listen to some sound being generated by the sound card, and not the CD-ROM drive? If so, you must plug your headphones into the sound card, and not the CD-ROM drive.

➤ Do your headphones include a separate volume control? So *that's* what that strange looking sliding bar does.

➤ You should also check the volume control knob on your CD-ROM drive, and see if it has accidentally been turned down all the way. (Because most people don't use these volume knobs, it's easy to forget they're there.)

My Microphone Won't Record Anything

Darn, and you were going to record your every thought. Try these things:

➤ Make sure your microphone is plugged into the correct jack on your sound card, and turn the microphone ON if it has its own switch.

➤ With a Sound Blaster card under Windows 3.1, you can run the SB16 Mixer utility, and turn up the Mic setting.

➤ In Windows 95/98, use the Volume Control to turn on the microphone: double-click the horn icon on the status bar. Then open the **Options** menu and select **Properties**. Select **Recording**, make sure the microphone control is turned on, then click **OK**. In the Volume Control dialog box, make sure that the Microphone item is selected.

➤ Stop playing your CD. Sometimes a microphone's input channel and the CD's output channel are the same channel.

Adjusting the microphone control in Windows 95/98.

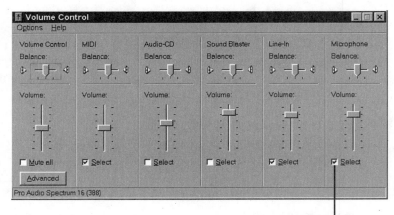

Make sure this box is checked.

When Your Modem's on the Fritz

When your modem refuses to cooperate (communicate), try some of these tricks:

➤ First, dumb questions: Is the modem on, and is it plugged in? Also, is there a phone line running from the modem to a phone jack?

➤ Have you ever used this particular phone jack before? To test a phone jack, plug a regular phone (not one of those digital read-out things) into it and see if it works.

➤ Can you hear a dial tone, and then, the modem dialing? If not, first check the preferences in your communications program to see if it's turning off your modem's internal speaker, or at least turning it down so low that you can't hear it. If that's not the problem, the computer may be having trouble locating the modem. This usually happens when you select the wrong communications (COM) port during setup. Select a different one and retry the modem.

➤ Does the modem have a COM switch? Older modems have a switch that sets the COM port, and this switch must match the setting you choose during setup. Check the modem's manual for help. Also, the communications program you want to use needs to use the same COM port the modem is on, or they won't find each other.

➤ Does the modem answer at the other end? If you're not sure that the number you're trying to use is a valid one, dial it using a regular phone. Be sure that the modem is dialing a "9" if it's needed to get an outside line. For most modems, you can add that 9 to the number you're dialing by separating it with a comma, as in "9,5551212"—this tells the modem to pause a second to access the outside line.

➤ Do you have call waiting installed? If so, you need to disable it before using your modem, or the modem will disconnect you if another call comes in. The best solution is to have separate phone and modem lines. In the meantime, add * 70 in front of the phone number you want to call, like this: ***70,555-9089**. If you use an old-fashioned rotary (pulse) system, then add **1170** instead, like this: **1170,555-9089**.

➤ If you get connected and *then* the modem acts funny, the settings (parity, bits, and so on) may be off. If you're seeing garbage onscreen, make sure the speed (baud rate) you're using is set *equal to* or *lower than* the modem you're calling. For example, if the modem you're calling is set to 2400 baud, don't dial in at 9600 baud or higher. Also, make sure the terminal emulation is set to the same thing that the receiving modem is set to.

➤ If you're typing a message and you can't see what you're typing onscreen, then turn on local echo. There may be some menu command for this, or you can type **ATE1** and press **Enter**.

➤ If you're seeing double (two of everything you type), then change to full duplex and turn off local echo.

➤ If you can't get the modem to hang up, try typing the command **ATH** and pressing **Enter**. If that doesn't work, try pressing **Ctrl+H** (for hang up) and then **Ctrl+X** (to exit). Next, try exiting your communications program, and turning off an external modem. As a final resort, reboot your PC.

➤ Try unplugging your telephone from the extension plug (marked "Phone") of your modem. Sometimes a faulty phone can cause a feedback that affects the modem.

The Least You Need to Know

If there's one lesson for you to learn in this chapter, it's that it's never over 'til it's over. In other words, don't jump to the conclusion that something's broken when it's not. Here are some other tidbits to remember:

Beware of digital phone line jacks If only a digital phone works in the jack, then don't try to use that particular phone line for your modem, because it carries extra digital gook that can interfere with modem communications. (Normal phone lines are analog, not digital.)

➤ If something starts acting funny, such as the printer, the monitor, or your mouse, check the simple things first, such as making sure the item is plugged in and powered up.

➤ Remember that there are some useful utility programs that can help in times like these. My favorites include Norton Utilities, and if you can find an old copy of it, Mace Utilities for DOS (alas, Mace Utilities is no longer sold since its distributor was bought out).

➤ Your best insurance against total disaster is a good backup. Your second best insurance against disaster is to save your work often.

➤ Sometimes the easiest way to get something to work again is to turn it off and then back on again.

➤ Before real trouble strikes, make sure that you create an emergency disk and keep it current. See Chapter 4, "What You Need to Know Before You Open Your PC," for help.

➤ Before you replace your mouse or your keyboard, clean it well and see if that doesn't perk it up.

➤ If your printer isn't printing, make sure that it's on and online. Check for printer jams and make sure that the printer's not out of paper.

➤ If your floppy disk drive is not reading your disk, make sure that you can read the disk in some other drive. Also, try reformatting the disk.

➤ If your CD-ROM or sound card is not working properly, check that it's installed correctly, with the right drivers, and that there isn't a conflict with some other device.

➤ Test your modem by plugging a telephone into the wall jack to check the line. Listen for the modem dialing. Then check your communications parameters and make sure they are set correctly.

Replacing a Funky Keyboard

The keyboard is the part of the computer that news photographers or made-for-TV movies show up close when they want to show off someone using the *computer*.

However, PC keyboards are no big deal today. They get sticky keys, have their springs or connections worn out too soon, or have a bad run-in with something as benign as a Pepsi. If your keyboard's showing these symptoms or something even worse, it's probably time to replace it. Lucky for you, replacing a keyboard is a simple and relatively inexpensive thing to do (from $20 to $70, with most keyboards costing $50).

Don't give up just yet!
Before you replace your keyboard, you may want to see if the problem can be solved by a simple cleaning or some other easy trick. See Chapter 11, "Easy Repairs for Peripherals," for how-tos.

Shopping for a New Keyboard

After you decide to replace your old keyboard, you'll have to make quite a few choices. For the most part, your choice of keyboard is one of personal preference, and this section describes your various options.

First, Make Sure You Buy the Right Connector Type

One part of your decision that you can't control is the type of connector your keyboard uses. There are only two types: the larger, "AT" five-pin DIN connector, or the smaller, "PS/2" six-pin DIN connector.

The right connections.

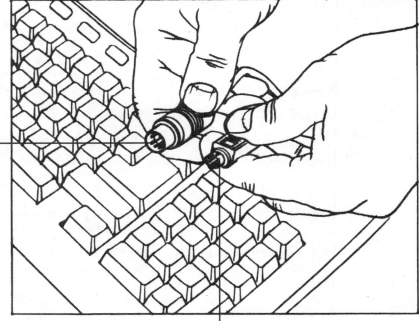

The larger five-pin DIN connector

The smaller six-pin DIN connector

How Does Your Keyboard Talk?

After you learn which keyboard type and connector to use with your PC, you'll still find yourself with a lot of choices. Another part of your choice that you can't control is the *type* of keyboard your PC uses. By type, I don't mean something that you can see. Instead, I'm talking about the way in which your keyboard communicates with your PC. From a mechanical perspective, there are only two keyboard types: the XT-style and the AT-style. You can't really tell one type from the other just by looking, because the difference doesn't depend on the number of keys, but rather on the internal electronics. But the original XT keyboards have only 83 keys, and they are missing the fancy running lights of modern keyboards.

So how will you know which keyboard type to buy? Well, all modern keyboards are AT-style, so it shouldn't be an issue unless your PC was built prior to 1981—in which case, my question to you is, why are you bothering to upgrade it? (Of course, the decision is up to you...) If you do buy the wrong keyboard type, some keyboards come with a switch on the bottom for changing from AT-style to XT-style, so you can just flip the switch to make the keyboard compatible with your PC. If you're in doubt about the age of your computer, make sure the replacement keyboard you buy has this switch, so the type isn't a problem.

> **You can get an adapter...**
> There's not a lot of difference between these two connectors, except their size. In fact, you can use an adapter to convert one type of connector to the other. That is, if you can find someone who carries the adapter. In most cases, you're better off getting a keyboard with the right kind of connector for your PC.

The granddaddy of them all, the old XT keyboard.

The original AT keyboard has 84 keys. The extra key is the Sys Req key, put there by some evil mainframe programmer at IBM who was out to protect his job by stopping the PC revolution in its tracks with a key that confuses people.

Again, you probably won't find an old AT keyboard anywhere except in a museum. That's because they're not sold today, although they are electronically compatible with modern PCs. (Well, kinda. You can connect an AT keyboard to your PC, but it may or may not be able to talk to a modern PC, depending on the PC's BIOS.) You'll notice that besides the extra key, the layout is quite different from the original XT keyboard. The AT keyboard accommodated users who wanted a friendlier keyboard, with a larger Enter key, a separate Numeric keypad, and indicator lights for the Num Lock, Caps Lock, and Scroll Lock status.

The AT keyboard added one whole key.

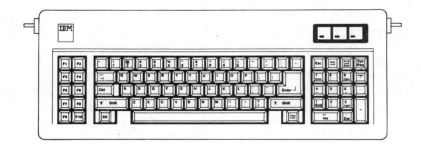

The most popular keyboard today is the Enhanced 101-key keyboard. Notice that there are two more function keys, and that they're lined up at the top of the keyboard. The Enter key is smaller, though, but the backslash key is in a more convenient spot. A few keyboard manufacturers from some other planet put the backslash key to the left of the Spacebar. Some manufacturers have added a few more keys around the Spacebar, bringing the total to 104, and on some, 107. These extra keys are great if you plan on using the keyboard more than the mouse to control Windows 95/98.

The Enhanced keyboard.

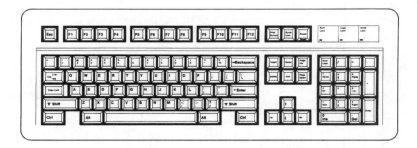

Other manufacturers restored the larger Enter key from the old AT keyboard to their version of the Enhanced keyboard. You lose the convenient placement of the backslash key, but hey, if you don't use DOS, who cares? In any case, you should be able to use an enhanced-style keyboard on just about any PC, unless it is really old (built prior to 1981).

Can You Say Er-go-nom-ic?

A popular version of the Enhanced keyboard is the *ergonomic* keyboard. The premise of ergonomic keyboards is that they are supposed to be gentle on your hands; *ergo,* it reduces the stress normally placed on the hands when they try to twist themselves into position to type on a regular keyboard. The design enables your wrists to stay level with the floor as you type, thereby avoiding *repetitive stress injuries* such as carpal tunnel syndrome. Ergonomic keyboards arrange the keys into two sets, dividing the middle by a blank space, and angled outward to fit the natural twist of your wrists. Some models enable you to adjust the degree of this space. The better models (including Microsoft's version) position each key at the medically prescribed inclination for each finger and at the proper angle for your wrist. In addition, the Spacebar is sometimes (but not always) hacked in two, giving you one Spacebar for each set of keys. Don't fall for a cheap keyboard—make sure that the design fits the way you work by typing on it before you buy it.

Microsoft's version of an ergonomic keyboard.

Other Cool Features to Look For

Another feature you may find on your keyboard is *mapping*, which enables the keyboard to mix up the purpose of the keys. For example, you can make the F1 key act like the Escape key if you want. I find this feature incredibly annoying, because it is ever so easy to accidentally map a key when you don't want to. I once mapped the Tab key on my Gateway keyboard when a book fell on it. To get out of the mess, I had to press this bizarre key combination: **Ctrl+Alt+Suspend Macro**, which told the keyboard to return to its original nonconfused state. If this ever happens to you, check out your computer manual for help in getting the keyboard back to normal.

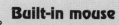

Built-in mouse

Another feature to look for is a built-in mouse, which may take the form of a button or trackball, or a flexible key which you can bend in the direction you want the mouse pointer to move. Some keyboards even come with a touchpad with which you control the mouse pointer by tracing your finger over its surface. There are many ways to marry a mouse to the keyboard, and frankly, I find most of them too funky to use. Try them out and judge for yourself.

If you use Windows 95 or 98, you might like a feature found in most keyboards today: the "Windows" key. This key is marked with the Windows logo, and you typically find it hiding next to the Ctrl and Alt keys. When you press the Windows key, the Start menu appears, making it easier for you to start a new program or perform some Start menu task without taking your lovely hands off the keyboard. You may find an additional Windows key as well, which opens a shortcut menu for you—cool, if you dislike using the mouse.

If you look hard enough, you can find just about any type of keyboard, including a multicolored one designed for kids, a collapsible one for those of us who work in a closet, and a sound keyboard for musician-wannabees that includes speakers, a microphone, and a volume control. Regardless of which keyboard you choose, remember that you're going to live with this decision for a while. The main thing you do with a keyboard is type, so why not test out the typing on the same keyboard you plan to buy? Spend a little time trying out your new friend before you decide to take it home. What you're looking for here is a keyboard that feels comfortable, which usually means that its keys are not too smooshy and not too hard. If there's a mouse or trackball included with the keyboard, try it out, too, although the sensitivity of the mouse can be adjusted through Windows.

Let's Go Shopping

Here's what to look for when buying a new keyboard:

➤ Look for one that is the same type (XT or AT) as the keyboard you're using now, or look for a keyboard with the XT-AT switch on the bottom.

➤ Make sure you get a keyboard with the same type of connector as the one you currently own. If you decide to use a DIN adapter, keep in mind that some keyboards with special functions may not work with an adapter.

➤ Test out your keyboard by typing a long passage and making sure you like the way the keys feel. I personally like the Keytronic keyboards for durability. I also liked the Microsoft Natural (ergonomic) keyboard, after I finally got used to using it.

➤ Check out the size of the Enter key, keeping in mind that a larger Enter key causes the backslash key to turn up in inconvenient places. In addition, look at the position of the Ctrl, Alt, and Esc keys and see if they are located in the places in which you're used to finding them.

➤ Consider an ergonomic keyboard if you type a lot, or if your wrists hurt.

➤ If you need to replace your mouse, look for a keyboard that includes one or a mouse substitute, such as a built-in trackball or a touchpad. Just keep in mind that such a keyboard also entails installing the second device correctly—in this case, you'll need to install the trackball or touchpad device into a serial or mouse port.

➤ You may want to see if your keyboard supports *mapping*, and, if it does, make sure the key that maps the other keys is located in a hard-to-bump-when-you-don't-really-want-to mess-up-your-keyboard kind of place.

Replacing the Keyboard (Uh, Anybody Could Do This)

After you purchase your keyboard, it's pretty simple to connect it. Start by exiting all programs and turning your PC off. You should never plug or unplug anything from your PC while it's on. If you do, something bad can happen—for example, the nerd police might show up at your door.

Disconnect your old keyboard. Keep the thing in a box labeled "Spare PC Parts," for the time when your new keyboard's keys, cable, or whatever starts wearing out. My box of spare parts has helped me more times (and saved me more moola) than you can imagine.

Reconnect the new keyboard. Don't worry—the plug only fits one way, with the little dent on the top of the connector facing up. If you accidentally bought a keyboard with the wrong connector, you can exchange it or buy a converter.

Help for heavy-duty typists If you're concerned about carpal tunnel syndrome, make sure you buy a wrist rest with your ergonomic keyboard. A wrist rest is a soft pad that sits in front of the keyboard, on which you can rest your wrists. A mouse rest is nice, too. For ergonomic keyboard designs that have a curved bottom edge, you probably won't need a wrist rest, because the curved edge acts as a wrist-rest substitute.

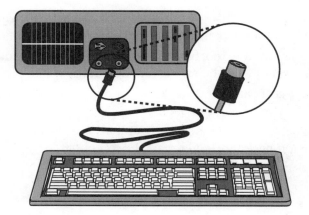

Connecting a new keyboard is easy.

Turn the PC back on. The computer wakes up and searches for the keyboard. If something's wrong, you see an error message. Check out the next section for help. Otherwise, you're home free.

Upgrading Mistakes to Avoid

If you get an error message when you try out your new keyboard, turn the PC off and check the cable again. Turn the PC back on. If the problem doesn't go away, try these things:

➤ You may be trying to use an AT-type keyboard on an XT-type PC. If your new keyboard has an XT-AT switch, flip it to XT and try the keyboard again.

➤ You may have accidentally bent one of the pins in the connector when you plugged it in. If so, try to *gently* bend it back and then try the keyboard again.

If neither of these tricks coaxes your new keyboard into working, you may want to return it. If the new one has the same problem, then take your PC in for a checkup; there may be something wrong with the keyboard controller chip.

The Least You Need to Know

Replacing a keyboard is just about one of the easiest upgrades anyone can do. When shopping for a new keyboard and installing it, remember these things:

➤ Before purchasing a new keyboard, make sure that you test it out first to see if you like the feel of the keys.

➤ If you're concerned about carpal tunnel syndrome and you spend a lot of time on your PC, you may want to consider an ergonomic keyboard or a wrist rest.

➤ If you need a new mouse, too, or lack the space to operate a mouse, you may want to look at a keyboard with the mouse function built in.

➤ To replace your keyboard, turn the PC off, unplug your old keyboard, plug your new keyboard in, and turn the PC back on.

➤ If you have trouble with your new keyboard, it's usually a loose cable. So check the cable, replace it if necessary, and restart the computer.

Chapter 13

Replacing a Mangled Mouse

In This Chapter

➤ Replacing your old mouse with a new one

➤ Adding a mouse to a mouseless system

➤ Installing your new mouse without pain

A *mouse* is a piece of plastic about the size of a bar of soap that attaches to your PC by its "tail," or cord. Underneath, the mouse contains a trackball that helps it sense the direction in which you move the mouse. You point to objects onscreen by shoving the mouse in the correct direction. Cute idea, but if you push your mouse around and nothing happens, you've got a problem. In this chapter, you'll learn how to replace your ailing mouse with something that works.

No problem?
Before you replace your mouse, check out Chapter 11, "Easy Repairs for Peripherals," which provides tips you can use to possibly revive it.

Choices, Choices, Choices

A new mouse costs between $10 and $140, depending on how picky you are. My mouse, a Logitech MouseMan Plus, costs about $60. A Microsoft Mouse costs between $55 and $80. However, you can find many generic mice for around $10 to $30. Mitsumi makes a very inexpensive (as low as $15), surprisingly durable replacement mouse that it sells exclusively to computer manufacturers—which explains why it doesn't come in a box. But you might be able to find it for sale anyway wrapped in bubble wrap at your local computer store. You might want to try it outside of the bubble wrap first, to make sure it's not *used*; but this more-than-adequate substitute outperforms many a Microsoft-brand mouse.

While shopping for a new mouse, you may also want to invest in a new mouse pad if yours is trashed—look for one with a built-in wrist rest. (If you're new to this mouse business, a mouse pad is a small foam or plastic pad where a mouse hangs out, rather than running around on your desktop and picking up all the crud you keep there.)

Before you run out to get your new mouse, keep in mind that they come with one of three connectors: bus, serial, or PS/2. Look at your old mouse, and get the same type of connector for your new mouse. If you're *adding* a mouse to your system, make sure you get one that fits an open connector. For example, if your PC comes with a PS/2 mouse port, then by all means, get a PS/2 style mouse. Otherwise, get a serial mouse—however, if you don't have an open serial port, then you'll need to get an I/O card, too, which will add both a serial and a parallel port to your PC. Bus type mice are difficult to find, so if you're adding a mouse where none has gone before, don't bother with them.

The following picture shows a serial connector and a PS/2 connector. (Bus connectors vary by manufacturer. However, a lot of them look suspiciously like PS/2 connectors, only skinnier.)

Bus Mouse

It's unlikely that you'll add a bus mouse to a mouseless system, because they're kinda hard to find, and they are much more expensive. If your PC already uses a bus mouse and you need to replace it, however, you'll find it easier to get another bus mouse (provided you can find one). How can you tell if you have one of these critters? Well, a bus mouse connects to a special card in your PC, which takes up one of the expansion slots. Unlike a serial mouse, a bus mouse doesn't communicate with the PC through a COM port; instead, it uses the expansion bus just like any other expansion card. This means that if you use a bus mouse, you may still have conflicts with other devices through the IRQ setting, but you won't run into the problem of not having a free serial (COM) port into which to plug the mouse. If your computer is one of the slower models, you may notice the bus mouse is somewhat faster than a serial mouse; however, you won't notice any difference at all with modern computers.

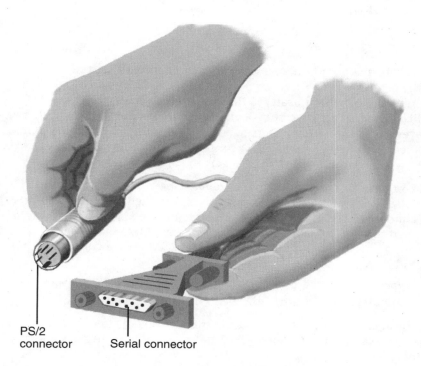

Choose a replacement that matches your old mouse type.

PS/2 connector   Serial connector

The bus mouse connects to the PC through the plug on the bus card; the type of plug varies by manufacturer, so be sure to get the same kind you were using. A bus mouse is rare, so you may run into a problem locating the exact brand and model of mouse you had before. Take it with you to your local computer store to see if they can help you order a replacement mouse.

Serial Mouse

A serial mouse plugs into one of the serial (COM) ports on the back of your PC. There's usually two, so using one for your mouse may or may not be a problem, depending on what other things you're trying to connect. Other serial devices include modems, serial printers (which are kinda rare), joysticks, and scanners, among others. A serial mouse is the most common type of mouse available, but it usually comes with a connector that fits a nine-pin serial port. If you're going to connect your serial mouse to a fat 25-pin port, be sure to buy a 9-to-25-pin adapter if your new mouse doesn't come with one.

> **Check This Out...**
>
> **Serial ports** Your mouse plugs right into the serial port—at least, most of the time. (If you have a bus or a PS/2 mouse, it'll plug into its own connector.) A serial port at the back of your PC is easy to identify because it has pins; the connector at the end of the mouse cord has an equal number of holes. Serial ports come in two sizes, 9- or 25-pin. Mouse connectors come in only one size—with only nine holes.

What's an IRQ?

To get somebody's attention, you wave your hand, whistle, or yell, "Hey, you!" The devices you connect to your PC can't whistle or yell, but they do need some way to communicate, so they use an IRQ, or *interrupt request*. An IRQ is like a special "message box"—when a device needs to get the CPU's attention, it leaves an urgent message in its own IRQ. For example, when you punch the keyboard, it leaves a message in IRQ 1. The interrupt controller constantly checks the IRQs, so it makes sure that the CPU gets the message right away.

Most PCs have 16 IRQs, but many of them have already been assigned to normal devices, such as the keyboard, hard disk, floppy drives, and the COM and LPT ports. If you connect a mouse to your PC, you have to assign an available IRQ to it. A serial mouse is connected through a COM port, so it uses the same IRQ that the COM port uses. If you choose a bus or a PS/2 mouse, you'll save a COM port (a connector), but you'll use up another IRQ.

The only type of "PC" that does not use IRQs is the IBM PS/2 (Models 50 and higher), or any computers that have the so-called MicroChannel bus.

This whole IRQ business can get nasty; if you run into a problem after installing your new mouse, you can turn to Chapter 27, "Fiddling with Ports, IRQs, Addresses and Such," for help.

PS/2 Mouse

A PS/2 mouse connects to your PC through a special PS/2-style mouse port. Even if you don't own an IBM PS/2, your PC may have one of these ports; they're usually marked with a cute mouse icon. One warning: Be careful not to plug a bus mouse into one of these ports; the silly thing could damage the motherboard. You must plug a bus mouse into its own bus (expansion) card.

Choosing a Brand and Model

Even though you now know the type of mouse connector you need to shop for, you are still faced with a truckload of choices. Logitech, Microsoft, and Mouse Systems are among the leading mouse manufacturers; you'll find that they and scores of smaller companies offer lots of variety.

Mice come in all shapes and colors. They even come in lefty and righty varieties. Before you get overwhelmed by all the special mouse features, remember that one of the most important factors is how the mouse *feels*. If possible, try out your new mouse before you buy it and see if it fits comfortably in your hand. Also, check its weight. Some of the cheaper brands are just that—cheaply made, lightweight, and flimsy.

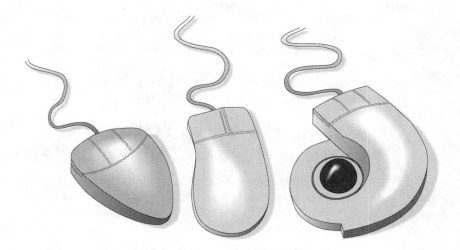

Nice mice.

Some mice have three buttons—some programs ask you to use that third (middle) button for something. Most of the time, you'll use the left and right buttons, so don't jump for a third button unless you know that you have a program that requires it for something. (Even so, most of these programs let you get away with using a two-button mouse if you don't opt for three.) Logitech mice (the most popular of which have at least three buttons) come complete with a nifty setup that enables you to program the middle button for your

choice of things, such as Help, automatic click-and-hold, or single-click double-clicking. The newest Logitech mouse has a fourth button for the thumb, and my husband's Logitech was done over in a black marble treatment that looks like a '60s leisure suit. Even though I use a Logitech mouse, I still end up ignoring the middle button most of the time. Not that there's anything wrong with having extra buttons—the Prohance PowerMouse/70 comes with 17 buttons that you can program for common functions like cut, copy, and paste.

Microsoft's newest mouse, IntelliMouse, incorporates a wheel on its middle button. With it, you can quickly scroll and zoom through your Microsoft Office documents, Internet Explorer Web pages, and other applications that support its use. Logitech offers a similar feature that it calls "Plus" as in First Mouse Plus or Mouseman Plus.

If you're tired of moving your mouse around, or if you're limited on space, you might want to consider a stationary mouse, otherwise known to its friends as the *trackball*. A trackball is kind of like an upside-down mouse—the ball is on top. With a trackball, the mouse stays still; you move the mouse pointer by moving the trackball itself. Buttons on the trackball enable you to click, double-click, and drag.

A New Year's resolution Mice come in different resolutions, from 200 to 400 dpi (dots per inch). The higher the resolution, the more sensitive the mouse can be. You can change the active mouse *sensitivity* in Windows, but some mice have the capacity to be more sensitive than others, by virtue of their resolutions. For example, when you move a mouse set at 400 dpi a certain amount, the mouse pointer moves *half the distance onscreen* as a mouse moved the same amount, but set at 200 dpi. The more expensive mice feature drivers that allow you to set their "mouse resolution" in dots-per-inch; everyday mice that we peons use have no such features.

A cordless mouse is a good choice if you do a lot of multi-media presentations with your PC, or if you hate it when the mouse cord gets tangled on all the junk on your desk. The receiving unit plugs into your PC's serial or PS/2 port; you wiggle the hand-held mouse in your palm or on a not-too-far-away desktop to move the mouse pointer.

Installing the Thing (Okay, So You Might Have to Think a Little)

Before you install your mouse, get a small flathead screwdriver. Unless you're installing a PS/2 style mouse, you need the screwdriver to screw the mouse connector in place. But I'm ahead of myself.

First, turn off your computer and remove your old mouse. Next, if you're replacing your old mouse with a mouse of the same type, plug your new mouse into the old mouse's connector. If you're adding a mouse, or replacing your old mouse with a new type, then plug your new mouse into the appropriate connector. For example, plug a serial mouse into an available serial connector.

The Nitty-Gritty About Connectors

Now, a couple of comments about mouse connectors:

Serial ports. Your PC probably has two of these; your mouse can use either one. A serial port is easy to identify; it's the one with *pins*. If the free port has nine pins, fine. Your mouse connector plugs right in.

If the free port has 25 pins, plug your 9-to-25-pin adapter into the mouse connector and then plug the whole contraption into the free serial port. Sometimes these adapter things are called DB25 to DB9 connectors—but whatever the name, you won't have any trouble finding one at your local computer store.

PS/2 ports. A PS/2 port (usually called the "mouse port") is small, round, and has six small holes. The mouse connector has pins arranged in a small ring that fits right into the PS/2 mouse port, which is typically marked with a small mouse symbol, so it won't be confused with the keyboard port, which may be similar in size.

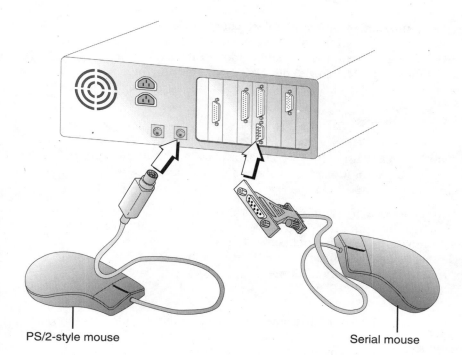

Plug your mouse into the appropriate connector.

PS/2-style mouse

Serial mouse

Bus ports. The bus port is located on the bus card. If you're adding a bus card to your PC, you have to open up the system unit. Before you do, read the instructions in Chapter 4, "What You Need to Know Before You Open Your PC," to avoid messing something up.

After you connect your mouse, use your screwdriver to lock it in place. Some mouse connectors use thumb screws instead (which you can screw in with your thumb), and some have no screws at all.

Announcing the New Guest

> **Check This Out...**
>
> **Be careful where you plug that in!** If you're connecting a PS/2 style mouse to your PC, be extra careful that you use the port marked with a mouse, and not the port intended for the keyboard. Plugging your keyboard and your mouse into the wrong ports can damage your computer considerably, possibly rendering it inoperable.

Now, before you can use your new mouse, you need to tell your PC how to communicate with it. This involves running the mouse's Setup program to install a *mouse driver*. A mouse driver is a computer program that tells your PC exactly how to talk with your particular brand of mouse. Think of it as a kind of translator specializing in mouse-speak.

You should run the Setup program even if you replace your old mouse with a similar brand; it updates your mouse driver to the latest and greatest. If you plan on using the mouse with Windows, you need to run the special Windows Setup, too. Check out Chapter 26, "Getting Windows to Recognize Your New Toy," for more help.

No open ports

If you need to add a new serial port because your computer has only one and you're already using it, get yourself a so-called "multifunction" I/O (input/output) card. It only costs about $30, and you get an extra parallel port in the bargain.

If your PC has two serial ports and you're using both, you need to get a bus mouse because you've reached the limit on serial ports, partner. (Unless you have Windows 95, version OSR2, or Windows 98, in which case, you have four serial ports.) (Here's hoping your PC has a free expansion slot to put it in.) The bus card provides the port into which you can plug your new mouse.

Don't forget that emergency disk! Be sure to update your emergency disk *before you run any Setup program.* See Chapter 4 for help.

The Setup program asks you a lot of questions, including what COM port your mouse is using. If you're using a bus or PS/2 mouse, you won't be asked this because, uh, it doesn't use a COM port. If you use a serial mouse, and you used the larger 25-pin port built into your PC, then it's probably using COM2. If you plugged the mouse into the smaller 9-pin port, then it's probably using COM1. Don't ask how I know—it's a real science. After the Setup program's done, you need to restart the PC to bring your new mouse to life.

Upgrading Mistakes to Avoid

If your PC uses several serial devices, such as a mouse, scanner, modem, or joystick, and your mouse isn't working after you try to install it, the problem may be that two of your serial devices are trying to talk over the same COM (serial) port. You see, even though your PC can handle up to four COM ports, only two can be active at any one time. This is pretty head-grinding stuff; so jump to Chapter 27 for help in sorting it out.

If your mouse works in DOS programs but not in Windows, it's probably because you didn't run the Windows Setup for your Windows mouse driver. See Chapter 26 for help in that department. If your mouse works in Windows but not in DOS, you still need to see Chapter 26. (Remember, even though your mouse works in DOS, it won't work in Windows until you install some kind of Windows mouse driver.)

If you're having trouble using your mouse in a particular program, then you may have to check the program's configuration to make sure that you selected the right mouse. You won't have to do this with any Windows program, because Windows handles the mouse's talking. In addition, a lot of DOS programs don't require you to choose a particular mouse, because they just let device drivers do the talking. But there are a handful of DOS programs that require you to pick your mouse brand from some kind of setup list (WordPerfect 5.1 is one of them). If you don't find your brand listed, then choose Microsoft Mouse (it's the most generic kind of mouse driver, and it probably works with whatever kind of mouse you own).

Installing a cordless mouse

The procedure here is pretty much the same, except that you connect the receiver to the PC instead of the mouse's cord. Make sure you have a clear path to the receiver, so the mouse signal can get through. Also, most cordless mice will operate to a maximum of five feet from the receiver, so keep your distance.

In addition, the setup program may make a change to your Autoexec.bat, adding the line, `MODE COM1:96,N,8,1,P`. If you have problems with your mouse, it may be because Windows has assigned a different baud rate (other than 9600 baud used in the MODE statement) to COM1. To change the baud rate in Windows 3.1, use the **Ports** icon in the **Control Panel**. Use the **Settings** command to see the baud rate. In Windows 95/98, use the **System** icon instead. Then go to the **Device Manager** tab, select **COM1**, and click **Properties** to see the baud rate.

If you run into any other problems, the mouse may be encountering interference from a radio-like device, such as a cordless telephone.

If you're trying to install a touchpad, keep in mind that your mouse driver may still be active, so response time will be slow. You can uninstall the mouse driver, and continue on your merry way. Just don't uninstall the mouse before you install the touchpad, or you'll be using your keyboard to do it. Yech.

The Least You Need to Know

Installing a new mouse is not usually difficult, but there are some things you should remember:

➤ Before you replace your mouse, clean it well and see if that doesn't perk it up.

➤ There are lots of mice you can choose from. You have your choice in shape, color, number of buttons, and left-handed or right-handed.

➤ Your new mouse has one of three possible connectors: bus, serial, or PS/2. Get a replacement mouse with the same type of connector that your old mouse used.

➤ To install a mouse, turn your PC off and then plug the new mouse in. Turn the PC back on and run the mouse's Setup program. Run the Windows Setup program if you plan on using the mouse under Windows.

➤ If you run into problems with your new mouse, more than likely there's some kind of COM port/IRQ conflict. See Chapter 27 for the mind-numbing explanation on what to do.

Chapter 14

Choosing and Installing a Painless Printer

In This Chapter

➤ Shopping for a printer

➤ Printing in glorious technicolor

➤ The latest in photo printing

➤ Installing your new printer

Printers are handy little fellows. After you work hard all day creating the perfect letter, presentation, worksheet, or graphic, your printer enables you to create a handy hard copy so you can bother people far and wide with your creativity. That is, when your printer works. If your printer is kaput, there's good news in this chapter. Here, you'll learn what you should look for in a replacement, and how to install your new printer after you've found one you like.

Printers: 101

There are basically three different types of printers you can buy: dot-matrix, inkjet, or laser. These printers vary not only in the method they use to toss ink onto paper, but also in their quality. In the upcoming sections, you'll learn exactly what you can expect from each printer type.

Most printers print only in black and white, but color versions of all three types are available. In addition, high-quality color photo printers are now competitively priced for the consumer market.

Printers come in three basic types.

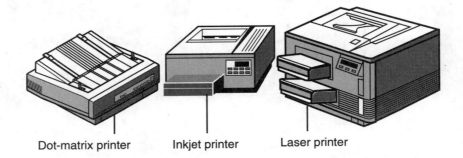

Dot-matrix printer   Inkjet printer   Laser printer

Shopping for a Dot-Matrix Printer

A dot-matrix prints by firing a series of pins against a ribbon, which in turn deposits tiny dots of ink on paper. These dots form images of letters, numbers, or graphics. The quality of the output of a dot-matrix printer depends on the number of pins it uses. The more pins, the closer the dots, and the better the image. Although dot-matrix printers are still available, they are no longer the bargain they once were, for many reasons:

➤ 24-pin dot matrix printers (the highest quality) cost between $190 and $700. For the same price range, you can get a color inkjet or a laser printer, both of which offer better quality, especially when printing graphics.

➤ You'll have difficulty printing on ordinary stationery with a dot-matrix printer, which typically requires form-feed paper (with tiny holes along each side that fit onto rollers which feed the paper through the printer).

➤ With the availability of paper, ribbons, and parts becoming more scarce, dot-matrix printers are not as inexpensive or as easy to operate as they once were.

About the only thing a dot-matrix printer might be useful for is printing multipart forms.

Shopping for an Inkjet Printer

An inkjet printer prints by spraying ink through a series of jets, forming tiny dots of ink on paper. Like a dot-matrix printer, these dots form printed characters or graphics.

Inkjet (also known as bubblejet or deskjet) printers offer printout quality that's only slightly less classy than that of a laser printer, but for a few hundred dollars less. (Inkjets cost anywhere from $150 to $350.) They're also generally whisper-quiet. On the downside, they are slow and expensive to use—especially the brands that require you to buy specially coated paper.

The quality of the output of an inkjet printer is measured in dpi, or *dots per inch*. All inkjet printers nowadays will print in both black and white, and in color, but at different resolutions. When printing in black-and-white, the resolution ranges from 600 to 720 dpi, depending on the brand you buy. When printing color, the resolution typically goes down to around 300 dpi. The speed of an inkjet printer ranges from slow to slower: 1 ppm (*page per minute*) to 9 ppm, depending on whether you're printing in black and white or color (color typically takes longer to print). By comparison, laser printers print from 6 ppm to 24 ppm.

Some inkjet printers can even scan in images, with an optional upgrade kit. If you're into digital imaging, you may want to get a inkjet printer specifically designed for printing photos—it's a bit more expensive, but the quality is fantastic.

When shopping for an inkjet printer, keep in mind that some inkjet printers, like laser printers, come with built-in fonts. The advantage here is that when you use a built-in font, your PC doesn't have to download it to the printer. This saves time and allows your printer to handle more fonts and graphics on the same page without running out of memory. Of course, having built-in fonts does not prevent you from using the regular fonts on your computer. Using these fonts will cause the printer to print more slowly, however.

> **Check This Out...**
>
> **How much memory does it come with?**
> When shopping for an inkjet printer, be sure to check out the amount of memory (RAM) it comes with. Just like a laser printer, an inkjet printer will print faster if it has more on-board memory. An inkjet, however, needs less memory than a laser printer, say 512KB. Another handy option to consider is a sheet feeder that handles envelopes.

Shopping for a Laser Printer

A laser printer prints an entire page at a time. First, the printer assembles the page in memory and then uses its laser to "burn" an image of that page onto a drum. The drum rotates into the toner, picking up ink in the pattern of the image. The drum then brushes against the paper, transferring the inked image onto it. The paper passes near a heated wire on its way out, drying the ink and making the image permanent.

Sounds like science fiction, right? Well, expect to pay a bit more for all that technology. Still, noncolor lasers are surprisingly affordable (from $250 to $2,500, with most averaging around $400 to $700).

Printer languages

Some laser printers come with *PostScript* capability; others are *HP-PCL–compatible*. PostScript is a printer language that translates a page into a series of math equations much harder than the ones that stumped you in high school. This enables PostScript printers to print scalable fonts and cool graphics without breaking a sweat.

HP-PCL is a printer control language created by Hewlett-Packard, the leader in laser printers. Although not nearly as complex as PostScript, nor as adaptable to heavy-duty graphics, PCL's advantage is its speed. Also, if you use WordPerfect and you deal with a lot of PCL-based forms, then having PCL is a plus for you. If you get an HP-PCL printer, you can sometimes add PostScript capability (if you need it) through a special expansion card, or through software. Some more expensive laser printers come with the capability to use both PCL and PostScript—and because the two printer languages do not intrude on each other's territory, it makes sense to get a printer that handles both.

Software-based PostScript interpreters such as GhostScript (available via the Internet) may substitute for a PostScript interpreter in your printer, giving you much nicer print quality and greater graphics capability. The downside of these interpreters is that they are separate applications, not just drivers; so you have to pretty much lead them by the hand all the way through the print process. Don't let this turn you off, however; GhostScript and its kin can actually be faster on the newer Pentiums, given the processor speed of a typical PostScript printer.

Like inkjet printers, the quality of a laser printout is measured in dpi, or *dots per inch*. Laser quality ranges from 600 to 1200 dpi. Laser printers have inkjet printers beat not only in quality but also in speed, which, like inkjet printers, is measured in ppm, or *pages per minute*. Laser print speed ranges from 6 ppm to 24 ppm.

If you want color, you might want to consider your proximity to a printing shop before you start shopping for a laser printer. That's because only big shots can afford color laser printers. However, some of the latest models can be had for between $3,200 and $4,000, which is not as bad as the $10,000 price tag of the first color laser printers. Still, if you're looking for good quality color printing, I'd check out photo quality inkjets.

Like inkjet printers, laser printers also come with built-in fonts. You see, when you use a built-in font, the PC doesn't have to waste time downloading it from your PC. Also, using built-in fonts allows your printer to handle more fonts and graphics on the same page without running out of memory.

By the way, laser printers come in two types: parallel and serial, which describe not only how they transmit data to the PC, but also the kind of port to which you should connect them. Most printers use a parallel port, so you probably have one free—this makes a parallel printer your best choice. If you fall in love with a serial printer, just make sure you have a serial port open so you can connect the printer after you get it home.

Installing Your New Printer

First, disconnect your old printer. Start by turning it off and removing any paper. Disconnect the cable and the power cord. Next, remove your new printer from its box. Be sure to look inside the printer and remove any shipping materials such as those silly foam peanuts—sometimes they're placed there to keep delicate parts from moving during shipping. But if you don't remove them all and you turn on the printer...well, you get the ugly picture.

Follow the steps given in Chapter 11, "Easy Repairs for Peripherals," for inserting the ribbon, inkjet, or toner cartridge. Follow the manufacturer's directions for inserting any other miscellaneous parts. For example, when I got my new laser, I had to insert the drum unit (yech). (Again, if you need help inserting the toner cartridge, see Chapter 11.)

Connect the printer cable to the back of the printer. Connect the other end to your PC, to the port with 25 holes in it (the parallel port). If your printer has a serial cable, connect the printer to the port with 25 pins at the back of your PC. With an adapter, you can connect it to a 9-pin serial port instead.

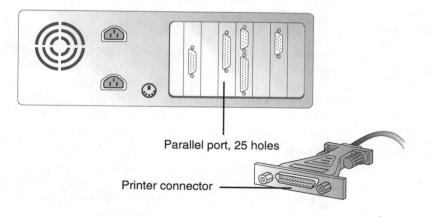

Connect the printer to your PC.

Parallel port, 25 holes

Printer connector

Some setup stuff

If you have a laser printer with a serial port (rather than the parallel port), then you'll probably have to push lots of buttons on its control panel to set nasty things like the baud rate, data bits, and parity. You'll find the control panel on the front of the printer.

In any case, you'll need to make sure that Windows knows the COM port (serial port) into which you plugged your printer. See Chapter 27, "Fiddling with Ports, IRQs, Addresses, and Such," for help. Also, if you plan on using your printer with DOS programs, you'll have to add the following two commands to one of your PC's configuration files, something called the AUTOEXEC.BAT:

```
MODE baud, parity, data bits, stop bit, PMODE LPT1=com port
```

For example, if your printer prints at 9600 baud, with 8 data bits, 1 stop bit, and no parity on COM2, then your two commands would look like this:

```
MODE 9600,N,8,1,PMODE LPT1=COM2
```

For help in dealing with the AUTOEXEC.BAT, see Chapter 26, "Getting Windows to Recognize Your New Toy."

Plug the power cord in. Add paper and turn your printer on. Use the self-test mechanism to test your printer (that is, if it has one). This usually involves pressing several buttons on the printer's control panel at the same time. What you'll get is a page full of numbers and letters. If your printer doesn't have a self-test mode, don't fret; all it does is test whether the printer works at *all*, not whether it's set up to work with your computer. That'll come in a minute.

Emergency disk alert! Get your emergency disk in order before you run any setup program. See Chapter 4, "What You Need to Know Before You Open Your PC," for help.

After you connect your printer, you'll need to run its Setup program to install the printer *driver*. A driver, you may remember, is a program that helps your PC talk to a specific part, such as the printer. Run the Setup program even if you have the same kind of printer you had before; it'll update your printer driver to the latest version. In addition, print a test page if given that option.

If you use any DOS programs and you've changed printer models, you'll need to change the printer selection in those programs to print from them correctly. In most cases, you can change the printer selection with the **File**, **Print** or **File**, **Printer Setup** command. Some programs make you rerun their setup to install a new printer, so check the manual for the program if you run into problems. If you plan on using the printer in Windows, you'll need to run the Windows Setup, too. Turn to Chapter 26 for help. After you set up your printer, be sure to open one of your programs and print something as a test.

Upgrading Mistakes to Avoid

If the printer doesn't print at all, don't forget to turn it on and hit the **On Line** button. You can do a test print by pressing the **Print/Reset** button.

If your printer prints garbage, you may have it cabled incorrectly. If you're connecting the printer to the parallel port on the back of your PC (the 25-hole female port), then you must connect the other end of the cable to the parallel port on the printer. This port will also have 25 holes, but it may have two tiny wires like wings at each end. This is a Centronics port, and you have to buy a special cable with a Centronics connector at one end to use it.

Some printers that come with two ports on the back require that you throw a switch to indicate which port you are going to use. Check your printer documentation, and then set the switch to the port you connected your printer cable to.

Your PC may have more than one parallel port, and you may have connected your printer to the wrong one. One of these ports is known as LPT1, and the other is LPT2. When you ran the printer's setup program, you chose one of these ports, and that's the port that Windows (or DOS) will attempt to send printer data to. If your printer's connected to the other port, the print data was sent to a house where no one lives. Try switching your printer cable to the other parallel port.

If the printer chokes on your printouts from one program but not another, then you forgot to select the correct printer in the program with which you're having printing problems. Open the **File** menu and choose **Print** or **Print Setup** to select the right printer this time.

If you're trying to print something under Windows 95 or Windows 98, you must have 2MB of free hard disk space. Try clearing old files off the hard disk if needed, to make room.

One last thing to check: Is your printer driver the most current one? If you're using Windows 95 for example, you may need to get a Windows 95-compatible driver from the manufacturer of your printer, especially if there wasn't a driver for your printer on the Windows CD-ROM. (You can usually download the latest driver for your printer from the manufacturer's Internet site.)

The Least You Need to Know

When your printer starts giving you problems, you don't always need to replace it. Instead, try these fixes:

➤ If your printer isn't printing, make sure that it's on and on line. Check for printer jams and make sure that the printer's not out of paper.

➤ If your printer refuses to print a document, or only prints part of it and then chokes, it may be that you're running out of printer memory. Add more memory to your printer if you can, or make the document simpler by removing excess fonts, using the fonts built into your printer (if there are any), or removing large graphics.

➤ Don't invest in a dot-matrix printer unless you absolutely need to print multipart forms.

➤ When looking for an inkjet printer, compare ppm (pages per minute) and dpi (dots per inch) resolution. These numbers will vary depending on whether the printer is printing in black and white or color.

➤ For high-quality color printing, consider a photo-quality inkjet printer.

➤ If you need high-quality black and white printing, get a laser.

➤ When comparing lasers, consider ppm (pages per minute), dpi (dots per inch) resolution, and the amount of memory it comes with (also consider the amount of memory you can add later). You might also want to make a note as to whether the printer supports PCL and/or PostScript.

Part 4
Revving Up Your PC with More Skillful Upgrades

In Part 3, you got your feet wet with some easy upgrades—things that don't require you to actually open up the PC. In this part, I'll lead you through what is otherwise the scary process of checking out what lurks below your PC's cover.

The pain will be worth it though, because in this part I'll show you how to rev up your PC with a new CPU, a brand new motherboard, a powered-up power supply, a bigger hard disk, more memory, better video, another floppy drive, a new CD-ROM, DVD-ROM, Zip, or Jaz drive, a slick tape backup, a great sound system, and a fast fax modem. Along the way, I'll show you the tricks that will keep you from frying yourself or your PC in the process.

Chapter 15

Getting Your PC to Go Fast with a New CPU

In This Chapter

➤ Shopping for a new CPU

➤ Replacing your PC's brain

➤ Adding a math "nerd" to your PC

Sometimes the only thing wrong with an old PC is its speed. Well, the speed of a PC is largely controlled by its "brain" or CPU. So by upgrading the CPU, you can make your PC "think" faster. Do not, however, expect a CPU upgrade to perform miracles; as discussed in Chapter 2, "What Makes Your Computer Tick, and What It Takes to Upgrade Each Component," your fast CPU is always limited by the speed of the data bus (the electronic highway over which data travels to and from the CPU). So sometimes, what you really need to do is upgrade both the CPU and the motherboard *together*.

In this chapter, you'll learn how to do just that, along with another "mind-boggling" operation: adding a math coprocessor.

Shopping for a New Brain

Back in Chapter 2, you learned about the various types of CPUs and how fast they don't go. Here's a recap:

CPU	Comment
8088, 8086	These two chips are so old, they're practically dead.
80286	Found in old AT-type PCs.
80386	Found in second-generation AT-type PCs, dating from 1985 to 1991.
80386DX	A true 386.
80386SX	Slower version of a 386, built for AT motherboards.
80386SL	386 designed for laptops.
80486	Found in third-generation AT-type PCs, dating from 1989 to present.
80486DX	A true 486. *This is what we have*
80486SX	Slower version of a 486.
80486DX2	Clock doubler; doubles the speed of equivalent 486. If sold as an upgrade, Intel calls it an OverDrive chip. *This is what we have.*
80486DX4	Three times the speed of equivalent 486.
80486SL	486 designed for a laptop.
80586	Intel calls its version of this chip the Pentium. Introduced in 1993.
5X86	Compatible with Intel's Pentium, but built by Cyrix.
K5	Compatible with Intel's Pentium, but built by Advanced Micro Devices.
Pentium OverDrive	Upgrades a 486 to a Pentium (586).
Pentium Pro	Equivalent to 80686 (formerly called P6).
6x86	Compatible with Intel's Pentium Pro, but built by Cyrix or IBM.
K6	Compatible with Intel's Pentium Pro, but built by Advanced Micro Devices.

CPU	Comment
Pentium MMX	Any version of a Pentium with extra graphics technology.
Pentium II	Essentially the 80786. Pentium II MMX is the same chip; all Pentium IIs as it turns out, have MMX.
K7	AMD's clone of the Pentium II.

Your computer might have any of the CPUs listed here, but *unless it has at least a 486*, it won't be worthwhile trying to upgrade it. Why? Because unless you upgrade your motherboard, too, it'll be like driving a twelve-lane highway with a one-lane toll booth every five miles—in other words, your upgraded CPU will get nowhere fast on your slow motherboard.

Popular makers of upgrade CPUs include Intel, DFI, Cyrix, IBM, Evergreen, Kingston, Trinity Works, and Improv Technologies. You can get upgrades for your 486SX, 486DX, Pentium, and Pentium Pro. The kind of upgrade chip you can get is limited by the original chip with which you're starting, and the socket configuration of your motherboard. That's because the replacement chip needs to fit in the same slot, or in a special upgrade socket and work with the parts already in your PC. So you need to shop for a replacement chip specifically rated for your original CPU. For example, the chip you need to upgrade from a 486DX 33MHz is different than the one you need to upgrade from a 486SX 33MHz.

> **Check This Out...**
>
> **What's the cost?** A new CPU costs anywhere from $100 to $290. Most cost about $100.

Here's the lowdown: Got a 486? You can make it a Pentium/586. Got a Pentium? You can make it faster and add MMX, but you *cannot* make it a Pentium Pro. Nor can you make a Pentium Pro a Pentium II; the sockets are simply incompatible. Can you upgrade a Pentium II to a faster Pentium II? Not yet, but soon, I bet.

You should find out the brand of CPU your PC is currently using, because upgrade chips are designed to replace specific brands, such as Intel or AMD. So before you go shopping, you must know *exactly* what kind of CPU your PC actually has: its brand (such as Intel), its type (such as 486), and its speed (such as 20MHz).

> **Techno Talk**
>
> **What's a 586?** Chip manufacturers other than Intel aren't allowed to use its registered "Pentium" trademark, so their "fifth-generation" upgrade chips are instead called 586 chips. A 686, by the way, is equivalent to a Pentium Pro, and a 786 is the equal (more or less) of a Pentium II.

So open up your computer and take a real long look at the CPU (see Chapter 4, "What You Need to Know Before You Open Your PC," if you need help getting it open). It's usually the largest chip on the motherboard, marked with something like 80486 across the top. Intel-brand CPUs have the big lowercase "i," if not the word "intel" written on them. If you need help locating the thing, pull out your good old manual. It should show you the CPU's exact location. Write down the chip's name and manufacturer. You also need to make a note of the chip's speed, such as 33MHz. (The chip label won't have the little "MHz," but the speed is generally the last few digits of the chip title.)

While the PC's still open, make a note about how the CPU is mounted. Some CPUs are mounted (kinda glued) to the motherboard. This makes upgrading difficult, if not impossible—don't give up hope, because there are a limited number of upgrade chips designed to clip onto surface-mounted CPUs. Thankfully, most CPUs have tiny pins on the bottom that fit exactly into tiny holes in a black square holder-thing on the motherboard. To upgrade these babies, you just pull them out and replace them with a chip that fits. By the way, do you see two extra rows of holes around your CPU? If so, then your 486 CPU is fitted with a socket for a Pentium chip. This is good to know. If you don't see the extra rows of holes, do you see an empty blue socket nearby? That's an OverDrive socket, designed for an OverDrive upgrade chip. Even if you don't have one, however, you might still be able to upgrade with the OverDrive brand of chips, because the newer OverDrive chips are designed to fit over top of your existing CPU.

Ask your manufacturer! Call the manufacturer of your PC to find out what kind of upgrade chip you should get. If you decide to get an OverDrive chip, find out if you need an interposer, a flat chip that fits underneath the OverDrive chip, between it and the socket. You'll need an interposer if your PC does not support the OverDrive's write-back cache (an internal CPU cache that writes its data back into memory when the cache itself is cleared—the purpose of which is to speed up write tasks to disk).

Armed with your CPU's brand name (Intel), type (486), and speed (33MHz), you're ready to go to the computer store to get your upgrade chip. Make the salesperson swear a thousand times that you've got the right chip. Then go find somebody else and make them swear, too.

Performing Brain Surgery (Replacing the CPU)

Replacing the CPU in your PC is relatively easy, that is, if you try not to think about all the things that can go wrong. First of all, make sure that you buy the right chip! Using the wrong upgrade chip can damage your PC.

When you have the right chip, follow the steps in Chapter 4 for opening your PC. *Follow all the steps,* such as backing up your data, copying down your CMOS information, and updating your emergency disk. Remove any parts that stand in the way of the CPU. Make a note of what you remove and where the cables go, so you can get everything back together again. A perfectly safe thing to do is mark on the ribbon cables with a magic marker—something simple like "HD" and an arrow pointing to the hard drive—before you unplug any cables.

Uh, my CPU seems to be glued in place

While you have the computer apart, check the CPU carefully. If it is soldered permanently to the motherboard, or if it's surface-mounted so all you see is chip and no socket, you probably can't upgrade it. True, Evergreen Technologies does offer a few chips designed to clip onto a surface-mounted CPU, so there's hope. But in a lot of cases, your best bet is to see whether you can get a replacement motherboard that will fit your PC's case and work with all your other parts. Actually, replacing the motherboard isn't hard, but it's also not a lot of fun because you have to take all the things off it and then reconnect them to the new motherboard—feel free to have someone at a service center replace the motherboard for you if you're feeling at all uneasy about doing it. If you're game to try it yourself, I give you how-tos in the next chapter.

Put it in OverDrive!

Keep in mind that some 486 and Pentium PCs come with a blue OverDrive socket that sits next to the CPU. If that's the case, you won't have to worry about actually *removing* the old CPU. Just leave it there; the new CPU will override it electronically—at least, some OverDrive chips are designed this way. Newer OverDrives require you to remove the old CPU— check the instructions that come with the chip.

Also, some other chips are designed to plug into the top of your existing surface-mounted chip, thereby overriding (deactivating) it. The instructions that come with these kinds of chips will provide additional details on how to clip it onto your existing chip.

Now, before you touch your old CPU, *make sure you discharge any static electricity!* Touch your coworker, a metal table, or whatever, then stand still so you don't build up any more static. Or, better yet, invest in a grounding strap that you wear on your wrist—it's worth the money! Keep in mind that, even though your PC may be completely unplugged from the wall, its power supply can still retain enough electricity to send a spike through your body (if you're not properly grounded), which can literally bounce off you and onto another part of your PC, thus frying it. (My husband, who's normally very careful, has lost a floppy drive this way.) Before you begin to remove the CPU, take a minute to look at it. You'll see a notch or a dot at one corner. Use your pencil and paper to make a note of the orientation of this notch. You'll see why in a minute.

Careful... Don't touch the CPU's legs (connector pins) because that can damage the chip, and if you ever needed to reuse the CPU someday, you wouldn't be able to.

239

If your PC comes with a ZIF (zero insertion force) socket, thank your lucky stars, because all you have to do to get the old chip out is to pull the lever back.

With a ZIF socket, removing a CPU is easy.

Lift out the old chip ———

Pull the lever back ———

If your PC doesn't have a ZIF socket, then it'll take a little more work to get the old CPU out. Your upgrade kit probably came with a tool, called a chip remover, for prying the CPU out. If your kit didn't come with a chip remover, then use a small flat-head non-magnetic screwdriver. With your tool, gently pry up *each side* of the CPU *just a tiny bit.*

Techno Talk

It's wired! If your CPU uses an LCC socket (Leadless Chip Carrier—you know, for CPUs that don't use pins but instead have tiny gold leads on the bottom), then you'll find two funny wires holding it in place. Remove one wire at a time by placing one hand at each end and gently pushing the wire to the closest edge. Remove the second wire the same way, and you can lift the chip right out.

Don't try to remove the socket, which is flat against the motherboard; just remove the CPU, which sits inside the socket. Repeat this process several times, lifting the CPU just a little bit higher with each pass. Eventually, you'll be able to lift the CPU out of its socket. Don't be tempted to rush this process; doing so will damage the CPU and possibly the socket.

After you remove your old CPU, it's time to put in the new one. First, take a good look at the empty socket. One corner of the socket will be notched or beveled in some way to indicate the location of pin 1—the chip will be marked with a dot as well. You have to match the notch or bevel on the replacement chip with the notch on the socket. In addition, the corner with pin 1 in it is often marked with a dot.

A big fan

If you upgrade to a Pentium, you should add a fan to the CPU (if it doesn't already have one, that is). It'll only cost you about $20, and it's easy to install—just make sure you get the right size fan for your CPU. Most clip onto the top of the CPU. Some clip to the top and bottom of the CPU, like a sandwich. In any case, add the fan prior to installing the new CPU, then connect its cable to your power supply. (OverDrive CPUs typically come with their own fans, which get their power from the CPU socket.) If you do not have enough power connectors and you must split power from a device, split it with the floppy disk drive.

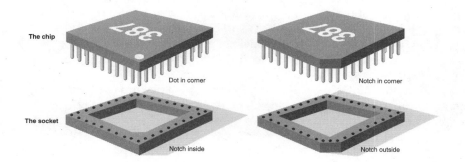

The chip

The socket

Dot in corner   Notch in corner

Notch inside   Notch outside

Match up the notch on the socket with the one on your CPU.

After you correctly align the chip, make sure you line up all the pins with all the holes. Press down on the chip carefully. If your PC has a ZIF socket, the chip should fit in pretty easily; just make sure that the bar is still up. If you have a regular socket, then you'll have to press down pretty hard to get the chip in, but be careful not to bend your motherboard—you could break it. Put something like a magazine or a stack of newspaper under the motherboard to absorb some of the shock if needed. (That's right, there's actually some space between the bottom of the motherboard and the bottom of the PC case. Just slip a few sheets of newspaper in there to "stiffen" the motherboard so it won't bend down if you press too hard to get the CPU in.) As an alternative, you can remove the motherboard from the system unit, place it on newspaper or some static-free surface, insert the CPU, and then place the motherboard back. (If you feel like you're pressing too hard and that you might break the motherboard, you can always stop and take the thing into a service center for somebody else to finish.)

If you have a ZIF socket, be sure to swing the lever back into its original position. Next, set any jumper settings as needed. Some motherboards are designed for multiple CPU types; you set the jumpers for the particular type of CPU you are using. Check your manual for more details, or check the motherboard, near the CPU socket—some motherboards have the jumper settings printed right on them. See Chapter 27, "Fiddling with Ports, IRQs, Addresses, and Such," if you need help setting jumpers. Typically, to turn a jumper on, you place a flat tube of plastic called a shunt over the top of two pins aligned side by side. To turn the jumper off, you move the shunt so it covers only one of the pins.

After you've set the jumpers (if needed), it's time to plug your PC back in and test the new CPU by powering up your computer.

The end of the socket is near!

The newest Intel Pentium II motherboards feature CPUs that are not bare chips with prongs underneath. Instead, the new CPU device is a relatively large plastic *cartridge* about the size of an audio cassette or small pocket camera. It's "installed" onto the motherboard by sliding the cartridge into the space between the motherboard's two big, black, perpendicular posts until the cartridge locks in place—a process no more difficult than loading film. Removing the CPU is about as easy. Within the next two years, it is conceivable that this kind of device—which Intel calls "Slot 1"—will render obsolete the bare chip configuration altogether, and ordinary everyday people will be remembering to change their CPU once its expiration date comes up. This is not a joke.

Upgrading Mistakes to Avoid

If your new CPU doesn't work, turn the PC off and check for any stray legs hanging out of the socket or folded up underneath. If so, remove the CPU, gently bend the leg back, and try inserting it again. Also, check to make sure that the CPU is aligned properly, with pin 1 in the pin 1 hole on the socket. In addition, check carefully to make sure that the CPU is inserted fully into the socket (this may be hard to tell if a fan is in the way).

Upgrade software Some chips come with upgrade software that you must run to make the chip work. Your PC should boot fine, but then you'll need to run the software to test the chip and upgrade your system. Follow the steps in the upgrade packet, and you should be okay.

Next, recheck any jumper settings. (Some motherboards require that you change settings when inserting a faster CPU.) Also, if you are dealing with a non-Intel CPU, check with the manufacturer to make sure there are no conflicts with the hardware in your PC, such as the video card.

If the PC starts with a boot disk, but you've lost your hard drive (in other words, you can't switch to C:), you'll have to re-enter your CMOS info. See Chapter 27 for help. Also, double-check any jumper settings you might have changed.

When you're sure you've got everything right, put your PC back together and get back to your life.

Helping Your PC Cheat at Math (Adding a Math Coprocessor)

As I mentioned in Chapter 2, you do not need to add a math coprocessor unless you do a lot of math-intensive tasks, such as spreadsheets, CAD, or high-end graphics work. Also, unless you have a 486SX (not DX), or lower, you don't need to add a math coprocessor, because it's built into newer CPUs.

Now, compared with replacing your CPU, adding a math coprocessor is relatively easy. First, make sure you get the right coprocessor for your system. If you need to, open up your PC and check out the exact type of CPU that you have and then get the math coprocessor that matches that model. You do have a choice of brands here, but not of types; there's only one that works with your installed CPU. For example, if you have 486SX, then get a 487SX math coprocessor.

> **Not needed?** If your PC has a 486DX, Pentium, or Pentium II, then the math coprocessor is built in. So don't worry; be happy!

When you're ready, open up your PC, following all the steps in Chapter 4. Be sure to back up your data, update your emergency disk, and so on.

Look around and locate the empty socket for the math coprocessor. It is probably the only empty socket on the board. You may find other empty sockets—in pairs—for extra ROM chips. Ignore these impostors. You're looking for a single empty socket, usually very close to the CPU.

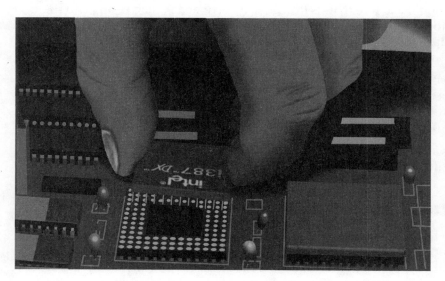

Line up the chip's pins over the holes correctly.

Controlling the heat

Many CPU chips have protruding clips on top called heat sinks. They dissipate the heat generated by fast chips so they don't overheat, by radiating the heat through a forest, if you will, of tall, aluminum pillars. Other CPUs feature a miniature fan clipped right to the top, with a spinning propeller blade under a plastic screen so your fingers don't accidentally get cut off. You may need to attach a heat sink or a fan clip to your new upgrade chip, that is, if the manufacturer recommends it. In other cases, you may want to get a fan card (an expansion card that's basically a fan) to help with the heat problem—here, I'm assuming you've got an open expansion slot to spare. When you order your CPU upgrade, just ask what the dealer recommends.

If you have to remove a thing or two to clear a path to the coprocessor socket, go ahead. If you need help removing something, check out the appropriate chapter in this book. As you whack your way through the PC forest, take a second to make a note about what you're removing and where it goes. Also note any switch settings on the part before you remove it, in case you accidentally knock the switches out of position.

Now, before you touch the coprocessor, discharge any static you might have built up by touching a door knob, a file cabinet, or a coworker. Don't touch the computer—that's not where you want the static to go.

Examine the chip and make sure that its little legs are bent at a 90-degree angle to the chip. If you need to, gently realign any lazy legs. An easy way to do this is to gently press one side of the chip against the top of your desk, or to use a small flat-head screwdriver. Flip the chip over and repeat.

Line up the notch or blunt corner on the chip with the same notch, corner, or dot on the processor socket. Some sockets have an extra row of holes that run all the way around the chip. Just make sure the chip doesn't go in so that two rows end up on one side of the chip. Now, gently press the chip into its socket.

Check the chip to make sure that none of its legs are hanging out. If so, remove the chip, bend the leg back in place, and replace it. When you've got the chip in right, turn your PC back on.

Upgrading Mistakes to Avoid

The easiest way to tell whether your new math coprocessor is working okay is to run MSD (Microsoft System Diagnostics). At the DOS prompt, type **MSD** and press **Enter**. If you don't have MSD on your system, or for some reason it doesn't run when you type MSD, you'll find it on the Windows 95 or Windows 98 installation CD-ROM, in the \OTHER subdirectory.

Click the **Computer** button and check the math coprocessor status. If MSD doesn't think you have a math coprocessor, then you'll have to check a bit further.

If your new coprocessor came with software, you'll have to run it to upgrade your system. If not, you'll probably need to flip some switch somewhere or change your CMOS to tell your PC all about the new math coprocessor. See Chapter 27 for help. When you're set, put your PC back together and go math-crazy.

The Least You Need to Know

Before you begin upgrading the thinking parts of your PC, consider these things:

➤ To replace your old CPU, you have to get a *compatible* upgrade chip.

➤ Keep in mind that your faster CPU has to work with all your old, slow components, especially the old, slow data bus on the motherboard.

➤ You only need a math coprocessor if you use programs that do a lot of math, such as CAD (Computer-Aided Design) programs, huge spreadsheets, or large databases. A math coprocessor also speeds up some graphics-intensive programs.

➤ Your new math coprocessor needs to match the type of CPU you use.

➤ A math coprocessor is built into 486DX, Pentium, and Pentium II chips.

Chapter 16

Replacing the Motherboard

In This Chapter

➤ Giving your computer a new mother

➤ Jump-starting a dead battery

➤ Updating your old BIOS

If your computer is old (say a 486SX), rather than replacing just the CPU, you might want to consider chucking the whole thing and replacing the motherboard instead. Why? Well, for one thing, you'll end up with a matched set: a fast CPU and a fast data bus to match it. If your CPU is fast, but your data bus is not, then the CPU sits around half the time, twiddling its thumbs while data is fetched.

In this chapter, you'll learn how to change out your motherboard for something newer. You'll also learn how to replace your computer's battery, and to update its BIOS (Basic Input/Output System).

Shopping for a New Motherboard

Here are some pointers to keep in mind when shopping for a replacement motherboard:

➤ Make sure the motherboard will fit your PC's case (see the next section on form factors for more information). Also, make sure the holes in the motherboard align with the same holes in the case. In addition, check that your new motherboard is compatible with your existing power supply (make sure it supports the same power connector).

➤ If the ports on the back of your PC fit into their own special openings (as opposed to fitting into the expansion card openings), then you will need to replace the case as well. In any event, consider buying a new case with the motherboard as a matched set.

➤ Some motherboards come with CPUs; this may save you some money. It will certainly save you some time and trouble.

➤ Make sure the motherboard will accommodate the memory chips you plan on reusing, if any.

➤ Check what type of CPU your motherboard is designed to carry; you want to match the CPU with the motherboard (and the motherboard's bus).

➤ In addition, ask what type of chipset the motherboard uses. You'll want one with a good, name-brand chipset, such as Intel, Chips & Technologies, IDC, Texas Instruments, and so on.

➤ Find out what type of expansion slots the motherboard uses, and whether they match the types of expansion cards you want to reuse. In addition, the number and position of expansion slots must match the slots cut into the back of your PC's case.

Get those standoffs! Make sure you receive several plastic or brass standoffs with your motherboard; you'll need them for proper installation. They look like oversized tuxedo shirt buttons, and act as posts that keep your motherboard fixed in place and separate it from your (metal) PC case.

➤ Because the BIOS comes with the motherboard, you'll want to make sure it supports the size hard disk you want to use, as well as other devices such as a CD-ROM, SVGA card, and so on. Most likely, this won't be any problem at all.

You'll pay around $200 for a new motherboard; for one with a CPU already attached, expect to pay between $300 and $1,200 (depending on the CPU's speed and type).

Fascinating Facts About Form Factors

The *form factor* of a motherboard describes its shape, the type of case it will fit in, the type of power supply it uses, and its general layout. There are several different motherboard form factors:

AT and Baby AT. You'll find full AT motherboards in old 386s. A foot wide, it simply doesn't fit into today's smaller cases. Baby ATs, which are only 8 1/2-inches wide and 10 to 13 inches long, were used in just about all computers until sometime in 1997. They usually include a single, full-sized keyboard connector built into the motherboard. The CPU and RAM are located at the front of the motherboard. (Long expansion cards float over this area, that is, if the fan/heat sink on the CPU doesn't block them.)

ATX and Mini ATX. The current form factor, especially in Pentium Pro and Pentium II computers. The ATX is 12 inches wide by 9.6 inches. The Mini ATX is 11.2 inches by 8.2 inches. Here, you'll find your serial and parallel port (and the PS2 mouse port) connectors soldered to the motherboard. You'll find the CPU and RAM located on the right side, in the back, near the power supply. The power supply, by the way, is connected with a single 20-pin connector, instead of the two 6-pin connectors used on an AT/Baby AT motherboard. Also, the power supply on the ATX motherboard is controlled not by the On/Off switch, but by software. So always treat the power supply in such a system as if it's on.

LPX and Mini LPX. Used in older slimline cases, its most distinguishing feature is the expansion card riser, a tower into which you plug your expansion cards (sideways). The LPX measures 9-inches wide by 11- to 13-inches long, and the mini LPX is 8- to 9-inches wide by 10 to 11 inches. Typically, the video graphics, parallel, serial, and PS2 mouse controller are built into the motherboard.

NLX. Used in newer slimline cases. The NLX measures 8- to 9-inches wide by 10- to 13.6-inches long. Again, you'll find a riser for the expansion cards. As a matter of fact, the floppy drive controller in the NLX motherboard attaches to this riser.

Doing the Deed

Well, if you're ready, I guess I am. First, back up your data, write down your CMOS, and update your emergency disk as usual. *You must write down the CMOS information because your new motherboard isn't going to know any of it.* See Chapter 3, "Now, Let's Find Out What Kind of Computer You Have," for help.

Before you start taking things apart, you may want to use masking tape to mark your cables and other parts of your PC, so you can remember what they're connected to. Discharge your static electricity on something metal, but don't use the PC. Again, if you've got a grounding strap, put it on and use it! Attach the other end of the strap to something metallic, not painted (bare metal), but not to the PC case.

If your tower case uses a removable mounting panel for its motherboard, remove it (and the motherboard). Unplug the two cables to your power supply, the speaker cable, system lock, reset and turbo switches, lights on the front of your PC, and battery.

Disconnect the cables that connect to the motherboard.

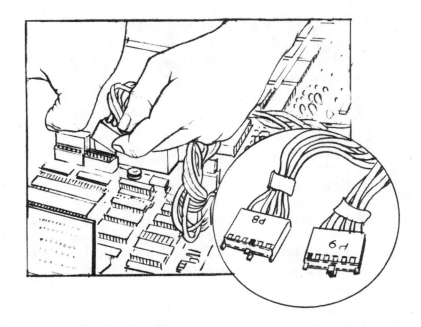

Disconnect the cables at the end of any expansion cards and unscrew the retaining screw holding them in. Lift each card out and place them on a static-free surface, such as a wooden or plastic desk (not metal). You may want to make a note of the order of your expansion cards—they don't have to be put back in the same order, but why risk it?

Techno Talk

Removable mounting plate? If you use a tower case, it has a removable plate on which the motherboard is mounted. Remove the plate, motherboard and all from the PC, *then* start removing memory chips and such. You'll find it easier than trying to work in the cramped quarters of your PC's case.

Unplug your memory chips or modules and put them on a static-free surface, too. Even if you can't reuse them, you may be able to trade them in for a reduction in the cost of new RAM chips.

Now that you've got everything off of your old motherboard, remove the screws holding it in place. Don't be surprised if there's only two or three. Again, make a note of where they go. Your motherboard's probably loose at this point, but not completely free. You probably need to move the motherboard to the left or to the front just a bit to release the standoffs underneath. You may even have to cut the standoffs off. Again, discharge yourself so you can lift the thing out (and be sure to hold the board by the sides to limit the chance of shorting anything out).

Get yourself a pair of tweezers and remove the standoffs from the old motherboard. Just pinch the top of each standoff and push it back down through its hole.

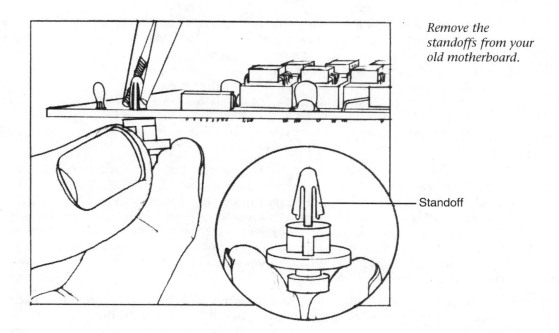

Remove the standoffs from your old motherboard.

Standoff

Discharge any static again and unpack your new motherboard. Look for damage, such as broken wires and such. Snap the standoffs up from the bottom into their marked positions on your new motherboard, so their pointed tips poke up towards you. If you need a standoff in a particular spot where a hole doesn't exist in order to support the motherboard, you can cut off the standoff's top, and simply rest the motherboard on it. Metal standoffs fit into threaded screw holes on the motherboard; plastic standoffs fit into 1-inch long holes that are narrower at one end. You need to support the motherboard with standoffs at every corner, and in the middle. Be sure to use a paper or plastic washer when screwing in the metal standoffs, if it looks like the screw head is wide enough that it might touch any part of the electric circuitry on the board.

Transfer the salvaged memory chips from your old motherboard (that is, if you can recycle them). If your old RAM chips, SIMMs, or SIPPs don't fit in the new motherboard, install your new memory chips now before you do anything else—see Chapter 19, "Make Mine More Memory," for help. Next, place your motherboard in the same spot that you lifted the old one out. The long expansion connectors on the new motherboard will be pointing directly to the expansion slots on the back of the PC case; that's how you'll know which direction is the right one. Make sure the standoffs line up with their slots in the PC case. These may not be the same slots you used with the old motherboard; many PC cases have more slots than there are standoffs, simply to accommodate as many sizes and shapes of motherboard as possible. Move the motherboard to the right until the screw holes line up and screw it in place—but not too hard—you may bend or crack it.

Check to see if you need to set any jumpers on the new board. You might need to do this if you added the CPU to the board yourself, if you're overriding any on-board controls (using an I/O *expansion card,* for example), or if you installed any additional cache RAM. The best procedure here is to check each and every jumper setting (using the motherboard manual), and make sure it is compatible with the CPU, cache, RAM, and so on that you are using. Check the jumper for the flash BIOS feature, and make sure it is off. Also, make sure the CMOS Clear jumper is set to the default (Off), so you can enter your CMOS settings and they will be saved. Incorrect jumper settings will cause bizarre problems that are hard to trace, so be careful here.

Replace the cables to your power supply (commonly called the P8 and P9 connectors)— *make sure the two black wires on each cable go next to each other, with the colored wires on the outside.* **You absolutely must get this part right—if you don't, you'll blow up your motherboard!** If you're using a new ATX form factor power supply, you'll have only one 20-pin connector. Connect the power cables to each device: CPU fan (unless it connects to the motherboard directly), hard drive, floppy drive(s), and power switch (unless you're dealing with an ATX form factor power supply, in which case you connect the power switch to the motherboard itself).

Next, replace the cables connecting your speaker, system lock, reset and turbo switches, lights on the front of your PC, and battery. The lights or LEDs and the system lock are typically connected together into a single 5-pin connector on the motherboard. The positive LED connector is placed in the first hole, the second is left open, the negative or ground LED connector is placed in hole number 3, and the positive and negative system lock connectors take up holes 4 and 5. The colored wire is typically the positive one, and the black or white wire is usually the ground. The speaker connector may only contain two wires, in that case, connect them to pins 1 and 4 of the motherboard header.

Keep in mind that you need to align the red wire on each cable with pin 1 on the connector, which is marked with a white "1" on the motherboard itself, right next to the pin. Reattach your drive controllers, again making sure you align pin 1 correctly. (Pin 1 might be marked with a "1", a notch, an angle on the connector, or a tab.)

Put your expansion cards back in the same order in which you had them originally and screw them in. Don't drop any screws! Screws that are accidentally forgotten can ruin your new motherboard when you turn it back on. It isn't the screw that makes the card work; but if you can get the screw in correctly, you're assured that the card is in correctly. Plug each card's cable back in (if any).

Plug your PC back in and turn it on. Do you get a response, doctor? If so, congrats on a successful surgery. Turn your system back off, and put your PC's case back together.

Upgrading Mistakes to Avoid

First, check simple things, such as whether the motherboard is touching anything (it shouldn't be). Make sure that the motherboard doesn't move around in the case, and that it's supported well.

If something's wrong, it's probably because you need to change the default CMOS settings for your new motherboard to match some of the ones from your old system. Good thing you wrote them down! See Chapter 27, "Fiddling with Ports, IRQs, Addresses, and Such," for help getting them into the CMOS of your new motherboard.

You might also want to turn the PC off and recheck all the connections, especially the power connections. Be sure that pin 1 is lined up correctly—it's especially easy to get the hard drive connector on backwards. Make sure also that all the pins are covered by all the holes in the connector, and that you're not one pin off. Check all motherboard jumper settings, especially the CPU jumpers: processor type, bus speed, clock multiplier, and voltage. Check to make sure you inserted the CPU and the memory chips correctly, and that you used the correct type of chips for your motherboard. Check the video card or video controller connector as well. If you have a problem with a particular part, check the appropriate chapter for help.

You can also set up a minimum system, and test it: You'll need a CPU, power supply, one full bank of memory, video card, and hard disk. Disconnect everything else and test the system. Then reconnect one thing at a time, until you locate the problem.

Replacing a Dead Battery

The battery in your PC keeps the CMOS chip charged so it can remember important stuff such as what day it is and what kind of hard disk your PC is supposed to be running. This battery is not the same as the power supply, which converts AC current into DC current to feed hungry PC parts. So when the battery starts to die and you turn the power off, the data in CMOS is lost, and as a result your PC gets a bad case of amnesia. When this happens, your PC will cry out, "Where am I?" with a message that looks like this:

```
Invalid system settings—Run Setup
```

In short, the battery is dead, and you're going to have to replace it. After that, you have to reenter the data that was in CMOS. Hopefully, back in Chapter 3, you copied down that data—because without it, there's a good chance your PC's going to be in a coma for a long, long time.

To replace the battery successfully, you've got to find the right kind of replacement. First, open up your PC; then, locate the battery. Sounds easy, but most of the time it's not because PC manufacturers are often ingenious at disguising things. Look for something attached to the power supply. You're looking for one of these things: a set of AA or similar sized batteries, two cylinders sealed in a red plastic sheath, a black and red box, a silver disk like a watch battery, or even a silver cube. If you don't find it near the power supply, check close to the keyboard connection.

> **Check This Out...**
>
> **Dead battery** A battery won't cost you much—between $3 and $15.

If you can't find the battery anywhere, you may need to look for a chip instead. Try to find something called Dallas, which is short for Dallas Real Time—it'll have a cute picture of a clock on it.

Can't remove? Some batteries are soldered onto the mother-board, and they can't be removed. They are replaced by a battery pack, which is connected to the external battery connector. A jumper near this connector must be reset to tell the motherboard that an external battery is going to be used from now on.

After you find the battery, or the chip, take a good look at it. Jot down a note about the way it's positioned—for example, which way the plus (+) and the minus (-) ends face. If the battery connects to the motherboard with small wires, make a note of their positions, too. You'll have to replace the battery *so it faces the exact same way*, or you'll blow up the CMOS chip. (And, because it's soldered to the motherboard, you'll have to replace the motherboard to fix it.) So take a good, long look.

When you're ready, make sure you discharge any static electricity by touching something like a file cabinet or a coworker. Now, remove the battery, or chip, and take it with you to the computer store so you can ask the clerk to get you another one just like it. Take the new battery or chip back to your dead PC and replace it so that it faces the exact same way as the old battery or chip. If the cable connecting the battery to the motherboard comes loose, replace it too, but make sure you position it in the exact same way it was before.

Put your PC back together and turn it on. Don't expect fireworks—you're not through yet. You still need to enter the CMOS info that was lost. See Chapter 27 for help.

Upgrading Mistakes to Avoid

If the PC won't boot, check to make sure you've connected the battery correctly. This is most likely the problem if the PC boots sometimes, but not all the time. If you are using an external battery pack, you should also make sure the jumper settings are correct.

Yes, You Can Replace Your BIOS!

The BIOS is like the PC's butler—performing the lowly tasks that the computer doesn't want to waste its time doing. This includes basic input and output stuff such as paying attention to the keyboard or the mouse, reading and writing files, or displaying information on the monitor.

One to four chips on the motherboard contain this BIOS, typically located in the vicinity of the expansion slots. You don't normally have to upgrade your BIOS—that's because it contains all the information it needs to run all the input and output devices in your system—for the most part, your keyboard, although the input coming from the mouse driver is important to the BIOS as well. What the BIOS doesn't handle (joysticks, for instance, or the mechanics of the mouse rather than its final input) is instead managed through the operating system. With both DOS and Windows, the operating system uses software-based *device drivers*, which supplement the computer's language skills. A device driver acts as the operating system's handle to a particular piece of hardware, such as a CD-ROM or high capacity storage drive. For example, if you add a CD-ROM drive to your computer, you need to add a device driver as well, so the BIOS can "talk" to it. Other devices that might cause you to upgrade your BIOS include 3 1/2-inch disk drives, large hard disks, CD-ROM drives, tape backups, and SVGA monitors. The operating system can handle most hard disk drives and all floppy disk drives on its own; no device drivers are required for those. Yet in the end, all of these input and output devices—whether they use device drivers or not— "speak" to the BIOS. So if the BIOS is incapable of interpreting what is being said to it, your only choices are to replace it, or if you happen to have a flash BIOS (see earlier sidebar), to upgrade it.

If you have an older system, you may notice when you add a fancy new part that its technology is so advanced that the old pokey BIOS just can't keep up. If you're told that you must upgrade the BIOS to get something to work right, then this section shows you how.

Flash BIOS

If you have a really fancy-schmancy PC, it may have something called *flash BIOS*, which means that you simply run a software program to upgrade it. Check for a disk that came with your PC, such as one marked Setup. Get the upgrade to your BIOS from your original manufacturer—you can usually just download it from their Web site.

After you have the upgrade, you'll need to flip some kind of switch or reset some jumper to enable you to reprogram the BIOS. If you're upgrading flash BIOS, the BIOS utility program will flip the BIOS into programmable mode for you. Check your manual for help.

Then restart the PC without loading any system drivers, and run the upgrade. With DOS 6.x, you can press **F5** during boot to bypass the configuration files. For earlier DOS versions, you'll need to rename the configuration files (CONFIG.SYS and AUTOEXEC.BAT) and reboot. With Windows 95 or 98, you'll need to press **Shift+F5** during boot to bypass the normal startup procedure.

It's not a speed thang Keep in mind that replacing your old BIOS won't make your PC faster. It just enables it to talk to some new fancy gadget such as a 3 1/2-inch disk drive, large hard disks, IDE anything, SVGA cards, and CD-ROM drives. A new set of BIOS chips, by the way, will cost between $20 and $80.

Shopping for Your BIOS

If there's anything more difficult than replacing the BIOS chips that are in your computer now, it's finding a source for the replacement chips in the first place. Today's BIOS chips are specialized for the motherboards in which they are installed. For this reason, retailers and direct sales outlets are unlikely to carry newer BIOS chips, because they can't order enough of one type in any significant quantity to either create or sustain the relatively low demand for that one type. (Some BIOS chips for older systems are simply unavailable.)

Service establishments take advantage of this new reality by performing the rough job of simply finding the right chipset and ordering it, and passing their costs directly on to you. As a result, some BIOS chipsets sold by service or repair shops may actually cost you more than a replacement motherboard containing that same chipset. Huh? That's correct; the entire motherboard might cost less *including* the BIOS chipset than just the BIOS parts alone.

Why? A few reasons: First of all, the manufacturer of the motherboard is the only party that can order the BIOS chips in high enough quantity to get them at low enough cost. You, on the other hand, would be ordering one and only one unit. You might be able to order this one unit directly from the BIOS manufacturer—major manufacturers do take orders online. But factor in shipping and handling charges, and you may have neutralized any savings you would have received from not ordering from the repair shop. Secondly, newer BIOS chipsets are those flash chips I mentioned a few paragraphs ago, whose ROM contents can be entirely rewritten through software. So you can download both the BIOS software-based patch and the program that implements that patch, from the BIOS manufacturer's Web site. This capability drives down the demand for replacement chips, which in turn raises their price.

If you're upgrading the non-flash BIOS chips on an older computer, the chips are more generic in nature, easier to obtain, and cheaper. A BIOS set for an IBM PS/2, for example, is more readily available. You can generally identify the chips you'll need from the make and model of computer you have, *if* that computer was manufactured before 1994. (But, with a computer that old, you may not want to bother upgrading it...sigh.) One way to learn more about your PC's BIOS is to use MSD (Microsoft Diagnostics). Just type **MSD** at the DOS prompt and press **Enter**. Click **Computer**, and you will see a screen telling you what you need to know. Make a note of the BIOS's manufacturer, version, and date. Of course, you typically have to have DOS version 6-something or Windows for MSD to be present.

Another way to discover what kind of BIOS your PC uses is to simply open it up and look. You're looking for anywhere from two to four chips located together, hopefully marked with something useful such as AMI BIOS. Sometimes the label on the chips matches what

MSD told you about the BIOS. You may discover a single BIOS chip all by its lonesome, but that's not what you're looking for—it's probably the video or the keyboard BIOS chip, not the system BIOS chip (yes, they're different).

But even looking directly at a BIOS chip might not tell you enough. You see, the machine that stamped the front of the chip when it was being manufactured did not know beforehand what type of motherboard the chip would go into. Before it was installed in that motherboard, the chip's own unique flash BIOS program was written into it by the motherboard manufacturer, not the chip manufacturer. This process changes not only the chip's ROM contents, but also its own serial number. You'll need this serial number—which is no longer on the front of newer BIOS chips—to find out how to replace that chip. Luckily, this number is not so difficult to obtain. Simply *turn on your computer*. When the very first screen shows up, telling you what brand of BIOS you have (and perhaps displaying the logo of the BIOS manufacturer), *press the pause key on your keyboard*. Then look on the screen (generally at the bottom) and you should see the serial number of your BIOS, its version, and date. You've paused the power-on-self-test (POST) mode of the computer, so you'll have time to jot this information down. Then press **Enter** to continue booting your computer.

After you know for sure what BIOS you currently have, you'll also need to know the name of your motherboard's manufacturer. That information is embedded somewhere within the serial number. Each manufacturer works a bit differently, so for an example, I'll use AwardBIOS, which currently claims 60 percent of the desktop Pentium market. Within the AwardBIOS serial number is an eight- or nine-character cluster—the third in the series, separated by dashes. The sixth and seventh characters in this cluster form a code which identifies the brand of motherboard. Go online with your BIOS manufacturer to find out where the codes are in their own serial number, and whose motherboards they point to. (Award's Web site is `http://www.award.com`.) A list of all the major, and most of the minor, BIOS manufacturers, along with links to both their home pages and their flash BIOS updates, is posted at `http://www.winfiles.com/drivers/bios.html`.

After you've located the manufacturer of your motherboard, you have at last found two vital things: 1) the *only* place where you can download flash BIOS updates, because BIOS manufacturers have made agreements with motherboard manufacturers not to provide user support for those motherboards' own unique versions of the BIOS; and 2) perhaps the least expensive source for BIOS chip replacements should you ever want or need them.

Replacing the BIOS

After you have your new chips, take the usual precautions (backing up, copying down your CMOS settings, upgrading your emergency disk, and so on) and open your PC. Locate your old BIOS chips. Make a careful note about which chip goes into which socket, and which way each one faces, because you have to put your replacement chips back in the exact same way. (Look for the location of the notch on the top of each chip.)

After you've written down everything you can about your existing BIOS chips and how they fit, you can remove them. First, check your static level by touching something metal. Now, if your upgrade kit included a chip puller (a large set of tweezers), use it to remove each chip. Otherwise, use a small flathead screwdriver to gently pry up one side of the chip a small amount. Then pry up the other side a small amount. Repeat until the chip comes loose. Don't play macho chip puller and try to remove the things in one step—you'll likely break off one of the legs. Just go slow and easy, and you should be fine.

Use your notes to help you place each chip in the right slot, facing the right direction. Line up the notch on one end of the chip with the same kind of notch on the chip's socket. To insert a chip, line up its little legs with the corresponding holes on the socket and apply a gentle downward pressure. You may want to straighten the legs out by pressing one side of the chip against your desktop before you insert the chip. Flip it over and press the other side against the desktop as well. This lines up all the legs so they are perpendicular to the chip.

Start up your PC and reenter the CMOS settings. Save them and then restart the PC.

Upgrading Mistakes to Avoid

After you have the chips in, just plug in the PC and start it up. You see a message during startup displaying the name and date of your new BIOS. If anything funky happens, turn the PC off and check the legs on each chip. One of them is probably sticking out. If so, remove the chip and gently bend the naughty leg back in place. Try inserting the chip again.

If you still run into a problem, then you may have inserted the chips into the wrong sockets. One BIOS chip is the leader, and the other is the follower. Switch their places and try again.

The Least You Need to Know

Replacing the motherboard, battery, or BIOS? Consider these things:

➤ Replacing the motherboard upgrades the CPU and BIOS at the same time.

➤ When you replace the motherboard, you may end up replacing other things as well so that they are compatible with the new motherboard—such as your RAM chips and video card.

➤ To replace a dead battery, you need to know your PC's CMOS information.

➤ Replacing a PC's BIOS is only necessary when your old one isn't compatible with new technology such as larger hard disks, SVGA cards, CD-ROM drives, and so on, or when a chip in the BIOS set is defective.

➤ Newer flash BIOS chips are easily upgradable through software, but are not as easily replaced, because their programs are peculiar to the motherboards in which they are installed.

Chapter 17

Powering Up the Power Supply

In This Chapter

➤ Time to replace the power supply

➤ Power toys for your power supply

➤ Your PC's biggest fan, and how to install it

Believe it or not, your PC does not work on regular household AC current. In fact, the 120 volts that AC current puts out would quickly fry all your wimpy (I'm sorry, I mean delicate) computer parts.

So your computer's power supply takes the AC current from the wall outlet and transforms it into low voltage (5-volt and 12-volt) DC current. The stuff in your computer then sucks what it needs from the power supply. Occasionally, the power supply peters out, or, in your upgrading frenzy, you may overtax it. If you're not sure whether your old power supply is cutting it, see Chapter 2, "What Makes Your Computer Tick, and What It Takes to Upgrade Each Component." When you decide you need to replace it, come back here for how-tos.

Going Shopping for a New Power Supply

Don't get zapped! When your power supply no longer works, you replace it. Under no circumstances should you try to fix it, because this can very well electrify you—even if the PC's unplugged.

Most of the PCs in stores today come with a 200-watt power supply, which is usually adequate for most people's needs. However, that's no guarantee that if you buy cheap, you won't get stuck with less. In any case, if you add a lot of stuff to your PC, or you're upgrading the motherboard/CPU to a Pentium Pro or a Pentium II, you may want to upgrade the power supply to 250 or even 300 watts. By the way, do not plug your monitor into the system unit, even if there's a socket. Instead, plug the monitor into your surge suppressor, next to the plug for the system unit itself.

The next factor in your selection is the number of power connectors (power plugs). Most power supplies come with four, which is adequate, but more is better. (There are such things as Y-splitters, which split one connector into two; but you don't want to have to rely on too many of these splitters for the same reason you shouldn't plug too many extension cords into one another.) Some devices, such as your 3 1/2-inch disk drive, use mini-plugs to connect to the power supply.

You also need to make sure that the two motherboard connectors coming off the power supply will work in your system: some motherboards require rectangular connectors, although others use square ones. In addition, some newer PCs have power supplies (called ATX power supplies) that use only a single, long connector. Your best bet is to simply open up your PC and take a closer look.

"Watt" it will cost · A 200 watt power supply costs about $20 to $35, and 230 or 250 watts run from $30 to $50.

Additional features to look for include extra fans (for cooling the PC—a good idea if you plan on cramming a lot of expansion cards and other components into the case), and a noise reduction system, which at least makes a valiant attempt at keeping the PC relatively quiet. It is the fans, after all, that produce nearly all the noise emitted by a PC that aren't beeps, .WAV files, or frying silicon.

Power supplies come in various sizes, so you may want to remove your old one and take it with you to the computer store, or at least take its measurements. Height is usually a critical factor in whether a power supply will fit in your PC's case. If you run into problems finding a compatible power supply, you may need to purchase one from your PC's manufacturer.

Power Toys for Your Power Supply

If you don't want to lose another power supply (or the PC itself), you need to invest in a good surge suppressor. When shopping for one, remember that you get what you pay for. In other words, if you spend only 10 bucks, you get only $10 worth of protection—which isn't bad, but it's not all that good either. Cheap surge suppressors offer only marginal protection against surges. More expensive surge suppressors meet much higher standards and are specifically rated for use with computers.

When comparing surge suppressors, look at several factors, including surge suppression capacity (measured in joules or watts/second)—obviously, the higher the capacity for protection, the better. Another feature to look for is EMI/RFI filtering, which reduces the impact of nearby electromagnetic fields or radio waves (uh, "line noise") on incoming current. Also, look for a surge suppressor that provides modem or fax protection. Overall, a UL 1449 rating is an excellent indicator of a good surge suppressor. Expect to pay around $40 to $80 for one.

A surge suppressor can't protect you against all power problems. For example, if your PC suddenly loses power due to a storm (or little Billy's fascination with wall outlets), then you lose whatever work you haven't yet saved.

If you can't afford to accidentally lose some work just because nature decides to play a trick on you, then you need to set up your program to automatically save your work for you at timed intervals, such as every ten minutes. If you still can't sleep at night even with such protection, you may want to think about adding a UPS (uninterruptible power supply). When the power goes off, a UPS (as opposed to a FedEx) kicks in and provides enough juice to your PC so you can save your work, log off, and grab a snack while you wait for the power to come back on. As an added bonus, a UPS also acts as a surge protector. The more expensive ones power down your system safely, even when you're not around.

A UPS will cost you around $90 to $450 for anywhere from 220 to 1000 watts. The wattage here needs to match your system's requirements. If you buy a UPS with higher wattage, however, you'll be able to keep the PC powered up a bit longer—for up to 25 minutes in some cases. More complete UPS systems with better surge protection and automatic shutdown systems run about $85 to $285 for 200 to 1000 watts.

If you ever need to add a device to your PC and you're out of power connectors (power plugs), you can purchase a Y-cable to split one of the connectors into two connectors instead. Plug one end of the Y-cable into the power plug, and, at the other end, there are two connectors—one for the device from which you originally stole the power plug, and a second one for your new device.

Your PC's biggest fan

If you've added several toys to your PC lately, you may want to think about adding a fan card. Yes, it's just what it sounds like—a fan mounted on an expansion card—and it's inserted just like any other expansion card. Your power supply comes with a fan, but it may not be able to keep things relatively cool, especially if you've crammed the inside of your PC with lots of stuff. A fan card adds extra circulation to problem areas, especially the motherboard in cases where a huge CD-ROM drive separates it from the power supply fan. See the section, "Upgrading the Fan," later in this chapter for help.

Installing a New Power Supply

Again, I feel compelled to remind you that if you try to open the power supply itself (even if you've unplugged it) the electricity that's built up inside can knock your socks off (and possibly kill you). However, there's no cause for alarm here—power supplies are perfectly safe *as long as you don't try to open them.*

Don't plug it in! Do not plug your new power supply into the wall to "test" it. A power supply, when it is on, *must be* connected to something it is intended to power, such as the motherboard and the hard disk as a minimum. If you simply plug the power supply into the wall while it's not connected to anything else, you may blow it up.

Start off by taking the usual precautions such as backing up your system (details in Chapter 4, "What You Need to Know Before You Open Your PC"). Turn off the PC *and unplug everything.* I can't say this one enough; most newer power supplies are turned on and off via the motherboard, and not the switch; as a consequence, they are "ON" as long as they are connected to a motherboard that's receiving power. In addition, power supplies retain a bit of power inside, so never, never, never (get the idea you shouldn't do this?) open one up.

Before you start ripping things apart, take a piece of masking tape to mark each plug so you can remember the device to which the thing connects. Remove each power plug from the power supply. The two big ones connect to the motherboard. The power plugs have six wires each, with a small white plastic connector at the end. Newer power supplies use a single connector that's roughly the size of the other two. To remove a plug, you rock it back and forth a bit so you can pull it loose. Just don't pull on its wires to remove a plug; instead, hold it by the white part, or use needle-nosed pliers. Some plugs have "keys" consisting of protruding clips that you must hold onto while rocking the plug.

Next, disconnect the on/off switch (some power supplies have built-in power switches, in which case, skip this step, pass go, and collect $200). After you disconnect the on/off switch, unscrew the power supply—you find the screws in the back, along the edges. Just be careful to unscrew the power supply, and not the fan inside—if you keep to the outer edges and stay away from the fan area, you're okay. Also, make sure you put the screws in a safe place so you can locate them again later.

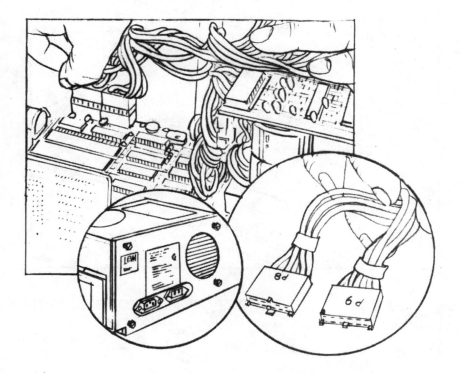

Unplug the devices connected to the power supply.

Clear a spot on your desk, lift the power supply out, and put it on the space you cleared on your desk. If your PC is a desktop unit, there are probably a couple of retainer tabs at the base of the case holding the power supply in place from the bottom. To release the power supply from these tabs, you need to lift the supply up just a bit and push the supply toward the front of the case. After you free the power supply, use a can of compressed dust remover to clean up the inside of your PC a bit.

Before you insert your new power supply, make sure it's set for the proper voltage (that's 120v for Americans, and 220v for Europeans and other metric-ites). You'll find a switch for this purpose along the back.

Now, look at the bottom of the power supply and note the position of the two holes. These two holes need to match up with those retaining clips at the bottom of your desktop case. Pop the new power supply into place, and then slide it toward the back of the case to engage the retaining tabs. After the power supply is in place, screw it in. Start each of the screws just a little, align the supply, and then screw each one in fully.

Push the power supply forward to release its retaining tabs.

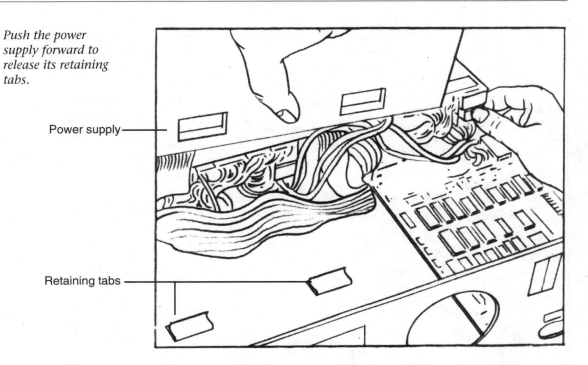

Power supply —

Retaining tabs —

Screw the new power supply in place.

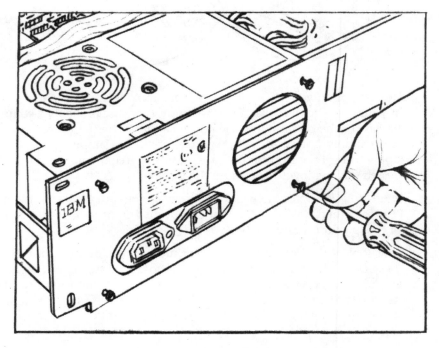

Finally, reattach each of the power plugs to its original device. Each device gets a power plug, but not any one in particular—in other words, there isn't a specific plug for the floppy drives, the hard disk, and so on. Your 3 1/2-inch disk drive will probably use a small mini-plug. Of course, the two big power connectors are reserved for the motherboard, thank you very much. These twins are usually marked P8 and P9. The power plugs can fit only one way because they are tapered, so don't force a plug—you may have it backward. By the way, as you connect the motherboard plugs, make sure that the dark wires on each connector cable lie next to each other—if you get them wrong, you can damage your motherboard when you power up.

Reconnect the power switch, plug in the power cable, and then turn the PC on to see if anything happens. If everything's okay, turn the power back off and put everything back together.

Upgrading Mistakes to Avoid

You should hear the fan when the power supply is on. If nothing happens when you try to restart your PC, then double-check all your connections, starting with the connection to the motherboard, and then the ON/OFF power switch. Check the power cable to the power supply, and make sure that it's not loose.

If you have the PC connected to a surge suppressor, make sure that it's ON. If one of the drives does not appear to be working, check its connection to the power supply.

Hopefully, you followed my earlier suggestion and you did not try to test the power supply without it being hooked up to at least the motherboard, and the hard disk drive. If you ignored this sage advice, your power supply may now be "locked up," and there is no real way to unlock it.

Replacing the Fan

Actually, you don't really replace the fan on your PC. That's because it's part of the power supply. If the fan should ever go out (which is doubtful, because it is designed to last many years), it's best to replace the power supply. You shouldn't try to open the power supply under any circumstances—it's just too dangerous.

You might, however, find yourself in a situation where you need an *additional* fan. If you add a lot of components to your PC, its case may become so crowded that good air circulation is impossible. Rather than let everything overheat, you should add another fan. This fan is in the form of an expansion card, so adding one is as simple as adding any other card to your PC. For help, see Chapter 4.

Another place where a fan is critical is on the CPU. If you have a Pentium, Pentium Pro, or Pentium MMX, you really must have a fan on it. Some CPUs come with a fan attached; if yours doesn't, don't despair; they are inexpensive (under $20) and easy to attach. Most clip onto the CPU itself; some are glued or taped on. See Chapter 15, "Getting Your PC to Go Fast with a New CPU," for information.

Upgrading Mistakes to Avoid

The only real problem you might have with a fan card is not inserting it properly, or forgetting to plug it in. So double-check both of these things before you get out your worry stone.

If you've added a fan to your CPU, make sure that its power line is connected to the power supply. If you don't have enough power connectors, you may need to purchase a splitter to split power going to some other device, such as the floppy disk drives. Do not split power going to your hard disk, because it's a high-priority piece of equipment, and you don't want it sharing power with anything.

If you find that your computer is still getting hot, you may want to rearrange the drives in your drive bays, placing the largest capacity (and therefore, the hottest) drive at the top of the stack, or in some bay farther away, where its heat can be more readily vented.

You can also clean the fan in your power supply by using a can of compressed air to blow the dust away. Of course, that means it will probably blow right onto the motherboard, but after you clean the fan, use the rest of the compressed air to blow the excess out of harm's way.

The Least You Need to Know

Obviously, your PC is nothing more than a boat anchor if it doesn't have a working power supply. Here's what you need to know:

➤ The power supply converts the high voltage electricity coming from the wall outlet into lower voltage electricity that won't burn up your delicate PC parts.

➤ *Never, ever, ever* try to open up the power supply to try to fix it. Even with the PC unplugged, opening up the power supply can kill you.

➤ If you're not sure whether the power supply is working, listen (or feel) for the fan. When the power supply is on, the fan is working.

➤ When shopping for a new power supply, take your old one with you. It's the easiest way to make sure that the new one will work with your PC.

➤ To protect your PC, you need to invest in a good surge suppressor, which costs between $25 and $100. To protect against data loss due to a temporary loss of power, invest in a good UPS (uninterruptible power supply).

➤ If you need to plug in a device and you don't have an open power plug on your power supply, you need to get a Y-cable to split one of the connections into two.

➤ Adding a fan to your computer will help keep its heat down. Additional fans come on cards which are inserted into an open expansion slot.

➤ Fans are also available for your CPU. They are placed on top of the CPU to vent its heat.

Chapter 18

Hands-On Hard Disk Replacement

In This Chapter

- ➤ IDE, SCSI, ESDI, and all the kids
- ➤ What to look for in a new hard disk
- ➤ Performing open PC surgery
- ➤ CMOSing, partitioning, and formatting a new drive

Recently, my husband and I moved into our first home, a nice, three-bedroom ranch located in a secluded neighborhood. Nice, that is, until we tried to stuff all our things into it. Now, if your hard disk is starting to look like my house, chances are you need to add more space. Before you hire an architect to design your new addition, however, try compressing your drive, as you learned to do in Chapter 8, "Fixing Hard Disk Hassles." In addition, if you've been having problems with the hard disk lately, it doesn't mean that the thing is going out. Try using CHKDSK or ScanDisk to ferret out the problem. Also, you may want to defragment your drive. See Chapter 8 for how-tos.

After trying all the tricks in Chapter 8, if you still feel like you need to "add on," then this chapter will lead you through the scary business of picking out a new hard disk and stuffing it into your PC.

First Things First: What Kind of Hard Drive Do You Have Now?

Before you go shopping for a new hard disk, you need to figure out what kind of hard drive your PC currently has (even if you plan on replacing it). Start by looking at your PC's manual. The next place to look is on the drive itself, on a sticker that has the manufacturer's name, the drive's specifications, and its date of manufacture. This sticker may be located on the top of the drive, or on the rear next to the data connectors. You might even call your PC's manufacturer if the sticker isn't there or if what it says doesn't make sense. In any event, it'll help the salesperson identify the type of hard disk you have.

Why is this so important? Well, the hard disk connects to a *drive controller*, and it's the controller's job to grab (read) data from the drive when the PC needs it. Likewise, the controller saves (writes) data to the drive when asked nicely. So your new hard disk will have to talk to this controller, because it's the controller's job to act as official interpreter between the PC and the hard disk. If you buy an incompatible drive, you'll have to spend some extra bucks on a new controller as well. If you're adding a drive and keeping your old one, too, you must buy a drive that's compatible with your old drive because you can only have one drive controller, and it has to be able to talk to both drives.

As you learned in Chapter 2, "What Makes Your Computer Tick, and What It Takes to Upgrade Each Component," there are basically four types of drive controllers:

ST-506. This is the oldest type of drive controller, introduced in 1980 by Seagate Technology. ST-506 controllers are used only in very old PCs, such as the original XT. The AT versions of this controller are called WD1002 and WD1003; but the standard here is the same, and so is the connecting cable. However, if you have a PC this old, you really shouldn't throw any more money in it. So I wouldn't mess around with upgrading it. (This type of drive, by the way, typically has two cables connecting it to the PC, one fat and one skinny, along with a third cable, which is the power cable.)

ESDI. Short for Enhanced Small Device Interface, Maxtor introduced this type of controller in 1983. ESDI was supposed to replace the ST-506 standard, and to some extent it did, but it's pretty much an antique today. Again, if your PC has this type of drive, think very seriously about replacing the computer instead of upgrading it.

IDE. Short for Integrated Drive Electronics, because the controller is built into the drive itself. By far, this is the most popular drive controller sold today. IDE is sometimes referred to as the AT Attachment interface. A new version of IDE, called EIDE (for Extended IDE, essentially ATA-2) is featured in most PCs today. EIDE allows you to add larger hard disks (over 528MB), and more of them. UIDE, or "Ultra IDE," is Quantum's brand name for its updated version of IDE using the ATA

(Western Digital) interface, or ATA-3. What's different is that *burst mode data rate* has been doubled to 33.3MB/sec. Wherever you see a hard drive where 33.3 is the reported burst mode rate, ATA-3 has been employed. You may also hear of Ultra ATA, Ultra DMA, DMA-33, or ATA-33 drives, which are similar to ATA-3 drives. Your BIOS must support these drives for you to use them. Don't be surprised to see ATA-66, a new standard supported by Quantum and Intel, with transfer rates of 66 megabytes per second (MB/sec, with a capital "M"), due out in early 1999. Meanwhile, the ATA-4 standard is still being worked on, but expect it to have similar transfer rates.

SCSI. Short for Small Computer Systems Interface, a SCSI controller can control several types of SCSI devices at once, including a hard disk, a CD-ROM drive, and a tape drive. Although it's pretty fast, SCSI drives are much more expensive than IDE. However, they are usually considered more reliable. Also, if you want to chain several SCSI devices (such as a hard disk, CD-ROM drive, and so on) to your new SCSI controller, you may run into problems, because lots of SCSI devices are incompatible with each other. However, if you stick with just SCSI hard disks, you should be fine.

I Know What Type of Hard Disk I Have. What Now?

Now that you know what type of hard disk controller your system uses, you can easily decide what type of drive to buy. By far, the easiest thing to do is to buy the same type of drive you're currently using, regardless of whether you're adding a drive or replacing one. So if your system uses IDE, get an IDE drive. If it uses SCSI, get another SCSI. If it uses ST-506 or ESDI and you still want to upgrade the thing, replace the controller with an IDE controller (adapter) and buy an IDE drive. It's the cheapest and easiest drive to install. (Don't fret; IDE controllers are cheap—under $20.)

Recall that for IDE disk drives, the actual drive controller is located on the drive itself rather than on a separate card (the "I" in "IDE" stands for "Integrated"). There is still a separate IDE adapter, however, which is either a separate card or a part of your motherboard. (The card is called a "controller" when you go out and buy it; the term is really a misnomer.) The IDE interface pairs a "master" component with a "slave"; in the enhanced EIDE version of the interface, as many as two masters are paired with as many as two slaves. The first drive in the pairing is the master, and acts as the controller for both itself and the next component in the chain. So if you notice a problem in the future with both your hard drive *and* your CD-ROM, perhaps its source is on the controller that's built into your hard drive, assuming it's acting as the master and the CD-ROM as the slave.

If your first drive is IDE, and you buy a new EIDE hard disk, you should get an EIDE controller to replace the IDE controller in your system. That way, you can take advantage of the EIDE enhancements: larger hard disks and greater speeds.

If your motherboard uses an EIDE adapter or adapter card, the type of component to which that card will connect is still considered IDE. There is no such thing as an "EIDE hard drive" or "EIDE CD-ROM," because the IDE versions of both components work with EIDE adapters. The only thing that changes in the EIDE scheme is the adapter, not the component; you can swap out an IDE adapter card for an EIDE adapter, and still keep your existing components.

If you end up buying a new controller card, make sure you buy one that fits the type of expansion bus your system uses. For example, an old XT type PC will need an 8-bit controller card, which is kinda hard to find. Most other systems will use a 16-bit controller, except for old MicroChannel.

General Things to Keep in Mind While Shopping

When shopping for a new hard disk, get the largest one that you can afford. Studies show that, with the rate at which the sheer size of software is skyrocketing, you're better off with a hard disk that's three times larger than the one you're using now, however large that might be. Sound ridiculous? Not when you consider how much room most programs consume: anywhere from 15–40MB *each*. If you use Windows, add another 40–125MB. And of course, if you create anything at all with these programs, you'll use up even more space. I added a 300MB hard drive to my system recently, which I compressed (DriveSpaced) for a total of 615MB. I installed Microsoft Office, Lotus 1-2-3, and a few other things, and I now have only 120BM left. You know your needs better than anyone else, so judge for yourself.

Square pegs and squarer holes

An important factor to consider when buying a hard disk is to get one that fits. Older computers have larger 5 1/4-inch drive bays, while modern PCs have smaller sized 3 1/2-inch drive bays. Don't despair; you can buy a mounting bracket to fit a smaller 3 1/2-inch hard disk drive into a fatter 5 1/4-inch bay if needed. The small drive screws into the larger mounting bracket, and the bracket mounts at the points where you bolt in a fatter drive.

In addition, very old systems use taller bays called full-height, although modern systems use half-height bays, which are about 1 1/2-inches tall. So make sure you get a drive adapter if your PC uses the older, full-height bays.

The True Tale of the Tape

When comparing hard drives, check their capacity (size) and speed (access time). Obviously, you want the largest hard disk you can afford. When you're comparing brands, take note of a figure that manufacturers tend to tout, called the *seek time*. The seek time tells you how long it takes for the hard disk to locate the first block of data you need; the lower the number, the faster the hard disk. Seek times range from 9.5–12 microseconds (ms). This number can fool you, however, because even though it takes only 9.5ms for the drive controller to locate the *first* block of data, it doesn't necessarily mean that reading the *rest* of that data will be faster than a drive with a seek time of 11ms.

A much more reliable gauge of a hard drive's performance is its *external transfer rate*—the speed at which data is transferred between the controller on the drive and the adapter attached to the motherboard. Equally important is the *track-to-track seek time*, which is the time it generally takes for the drive spindle to move from one track to the next. (Tracks on a hard disk platter are perfectly round, not spiral like on an LP record album.)

Seagate Technology and Maxtor contributed information for this chapter regarding their top-of-the line models. If you're looking at just seek time—the number that is usually given the spotlight—Seagate reports its Medalist series has a seek time of 11ms, and Maxtor reports the seek time of its DiamondMax series is just 9ms. A careless reviewer might report that DiamondMax is 22 percent faster than Medalist. But look at the more important numbers: Maxtor's DiamondMax series has an external transfer rate approaching 33MB/sec, and Seagate's Medalist series is rated slightly faster at 33 1/3MB/sec. This is a true rating of performance over a period of time, not just at the starting gate; so although Medalist takes a bit longer to get on its mark, it makes up more than DiamondMax's 2ms head start.

Does this mean Medalist is the better performing drive overall? Not if you take drive dynamics into account. While Medalist's track-to-track seek time is 2.5ms, DiamondMax's is less than 1ms. This means it takes DiamondMax only 40% of the time that Medalist consumes moving its spindle from track to track. How often does this spindle moving take place? Both drives are configured for 512 bytes per sector. For Medalist, there are 63 sectors in a track, for a total of 31.5KB (kilobytes) of data per track. That's roughly three one-hundredths of a megabyte; so a track is a pretty short thing by definition. For every megabyte of data being read, Medalist will switch tracks 32.5 times, for an expenditure of 81.26ms. This is time that the drive is spending *not* transferring data, scattered intermittently throughout the transfer process.

Now let's compare: At 200 sectors per track (minimum), DiamondMax has exactly 100KB of data on its track. For every megabyte being read, DiamondMax will switch tracks 10.24 times, for an expenditure of about 10ms. Ten versus 81 is a much more significant performance figure than 9 versus 11. This doesn't mean that DiamondMax will run at one-eighth the speed of Medalist overall, but it does explain one of the factors that make DiamondMax faster overall. But if you factor in overall price, you'll find the Seagate series is less expensive.

Another feature you might want to look for in your new hard drive is a cache. A *cache* (pronounced *cash*) stores the frequently requested data close at hand, so the hard drive can get to it more quickly. Not a lot of hard disks include a cache (sometimes called a buffer), but it's a worthwhile feature to look for.

Check This Out...

How much?
Nowadays, hard drives are cheap. Expect to pay only $160 to $180 for 2.5GB. Larger hard disks will cost you even less per megabyte.

When you finally buy your drive, make sure you buy the cables you need to connect it as well. You may think that the cables come with the drive, but in most cases, they're an extra item. If you're replacing your old drive with the same kind of drive, you can probably skip the cables and just reuse your old ones. If you're adding a drive, however, you will probably need a new cable, one that handles two drives. In addition, check to see if you need a power cable splitter, for connecting the new drive to the power supply.

Also, make sure your new drive has the brackets you need to slide the drive into the empty drive bay. For example, if your PC has 5 1/4-inch drive bays, you'll need a mounting bracket to make your new 3 1/2-inch hard disk fit. A mounting bracket is another item that not all manufacturers include with their hard drive kits as standard equipment. If you need one, make sure the kit has one or that you can get a hold of one; don't worry—they're cheap.

You may also need to get some adapters for your power connectors, if your PC uses the newer, smaller connectors, and the hard disk uses the standard 4-pin Molex connectors.

In addition, if you're switching drive types, you need a new controller card. Don't forget to pick one up, or you'll have to make two trips to the computer store. By the way, most newer PCs use an IDE or EIDE controller.

Check This Out...

Take control!

Actually, the IDE controller doesn't control anything—the controls for an IDE drive are built into the drive itself. The controller allows the drive to override the regular ST-506 controller that the motherboard expects to be there—an interesting bit of information you can toss about at your next dinner party. In any case, you still need an IDE controller (which, as I said before, is really an adapter) if you want to run an IDE drive.

If you're adding a hard drive where none has gone before, you'll most certainly need to upgrade the power supply. Keep this in mind before you start forking out big cash to upgrade something that's basically an antique. (Want a more accurate estimate of your power supply needs? See Chapter 2.)

You can also add an external hard drive, which is nice if you don't have any drive bays open, or you don't feel like messing around inside the PC. They cost a bit more, but it may be worth it. An external hard disk connects through a parallel port, so if you have a printer using your parallel port, you may need to add an I/O card that gives you an extra parallel and serial port (the ports, you recall, are the connectors on the back of your PC).

Another option, if you're out of drive bays but you do have space in your machine, is an internal mounting bracket attachment. It literally hangs onto something in your PC case and supports a 3 1/2-inch drive mechanism. All PCs are fairly different from one another, so this option may not work in your PC, but hey, it's worth a try.

In addition, "hard cards," which are hard drives on a card that fit into an expansion slot, are also available. Again, you pay a premium for not having to mess with a drive bay.

Can a Hard Disk Be Too Large?

Unfortunately, for some PCs, the answer is "Yes." Some older PCs have a BIOS that simply can't handle the large hard disks of today (those over 528MB). See Chapter 27, "Fiddling with Ports, IRQs, Addresses, and Such," for help in getting into the CMOS setup.

I got cheated!

After you install and format your hard disk, you may get the feeling that you got cheated somehow. For example, suppose you buy a 5.1GB drive, and then you check its size, and find out you have less than that: 4.86GB. You didn't get cheated; you just got a math lesson. The size of hard disks listed in catalogs and stores is computed in decimal (a ten-based numbering system), although the size you see in a directory listing is based on binary (a two-based numbering system). What's the reason for this? The same reason that "the best car you can buy for under $18,000" sells for $17,999: hard disk manufacturers want to make you believe that you're getting a really large hard disk, when, in computer terms, it's slightly less than that.

If your BIOS is older than 1994, then chances are you won't be able to use a large hard disk (one over 528MB) with it. How to tell? Well, you can look in your CMOS setup for signs of *disk translation*, a method that helps your BIOS keep track of all the tracks and sectors on large hard disks. Look for words like *translation, Logical Block Addressing (LBA)*, or *Enhanced CHS (ECHS)*. You might also find something called *Auto Detect*, although that doesn't guarantee that your BIOS can handle large hard disks. These fancy terms refer to modern technologies that enable a BIOS to interface with newer components; if these terms are missing from your CMOS setup, chances are your BIOS is not young enough to handle the big jobs. You might also encounter a problem with a slightly newer (and yet not quite new enough) BIOS that can handle hard disks larger than 528MB, but not over 2.1GB.

What are your options if you have an old BIOS? Well, you can upgrade it (see Chapter 16, "Replacing the Motherboard," for how tos). Or you can use an EIDE controller card, which comes with the drive translator on board. Or you could replace your motherboard, because most motherboards today have BIOS translation built-in. Or you can stick with a hard drive smaller than 528MB. (You can also get a software driver that will do the translating for you, but this isn't a good option because it may cause problems with Windows 95 or 98, or any of your programs.)

Wanna hear a funny story? (Okay, not so funny...) You could upgrade your BIOS and still run into a problem handling hard disks over 2.1GB. This time, the troublemaker is your operating system. Here, you can buy a hard disk less than 2.1GB, or use the latest version of Windows 95 (called OSR2) or Windows 98 and its FAT32 option to partition/format the hard disk for you. With the older version of Windows 95, Windows 3.1, or DOS that all use FAT16, you can partition large hard disks into multiple drives (C, D, E, etc.) of 2.1GB or less.

And the story goes on and on... As you move up the ladder to larger and larger hard drives, you may hit another barrier, known as the "8GB barrier," although it's really 8.46GB. This barrier, like the 2.1GB and the 528MB barriers, is also caused by your BIOS, and it's a tough nut to crack. The problem here is that even your BIOS has limits as to how many tracks and sectors it can keep track of, and 8.46GB represents its upper limit. So what do you do? Well, again, the simplest solution is to divide the hard disk into multiple partitions (logical drives such as C:, D:, and so on) that are no bigger than the limits of your BIOS. Another solution on the horizon is upgrading to a BIOS that supports what's called "13h extensions." This will, unfortunately, cause incompatibility problems with some of your programs, disk utilities, and so on. Windows 95 and 98 both support the 13h extensions, but some of the programs you run under these operating systems may not.

Performing Hard Drive Surgery

Before you scrub up, make sure you've done the usual: backed up your data, updated your emergency disk, and so on. See Chapter 4, "What You Need to Know Before You Open Your PC," for details. Also, and this is super important, make sure you copy down your current CMOS settings. (See Chapter 27.) In addition, make sure your emergency disk contains the FDISK and the FORMAT commands. You'll find them in the \DOS, \Windows, or the \Windows\Command directory.

Unpack your goodies and make sure you have a hard drive, cables, and brackets (if you're adding an additional drive, that is). If you're replacing your drive, you can steal the brackets from the old drive.

Also, before you move on, make a note of the parameters that are typically printed on the top of the drive. You'll need these to configure CMOS, something you'll do after you get the drive in place.

Techno Talk

Save time! You might want to invest in a little time saver called DriveCopy, a program that helps you copy everything (file allocation table, sector information, data, and so on) from one drive to another. Saves you the trouble of backing up, partitioning, and formatting your new drive, and it only costs $25.

Inserting the New Drive

Open up your PC and, as usual, get rid of any excess static. Remove the old drive if you're replacing it. To do that, first remove the cables. (Make any notes you want first.) You will find one or two data cables; these are ribbon cables that lead from the drive to the controller card. You'll also find a power cable; it has four separate wires leading from each end. Generally, to remove either cable, you just pull straight up or out. This doesn't take a lot of pressure, but just be sure to pull the cables by the plastic connectors and not by the wires.

Two drives?

If you're adding a drive to your system, you may want to remove the first drive, and follow the steps here to set up your new drive as the boot drive (drive C). By installing the new drive as drive C, and removing the other drive temporarily, you end up with only the new drive to test and get going. After you know your new drive is up and working, it's usually a simple matter to set the jumpers on the two drives to slave and master, and to reenter the CMOS settings, if needed, to make your old drive drive C again.

Remove the cables to free your drive.

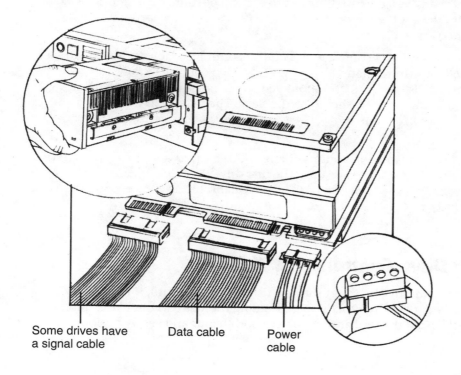

Some drives have a signal cable   Data cable   Power cable

After you get the cables off, remove the mounting screws that hold the drive in place. You may find them at the front of the drive, or along the sides. (You may have to remove other drives or cards to get to the screws.) After you get the screws out, the drive will slide out the front of the PC. If the thing is mounted on its side, push the drive out the back.

If you're replacing your old drive, transfer the brackets to the new one and then slide it into the old bay. If you're adding a second drive, add new brackets to it and slide it into an empty bay. (Your system may use a mounting box instead of drive rails, but the procedure is the same.) If needed, use your converter mounting bracket to fit a smaller drive into a larger drive bay.

Who's the boss?

If you're adding a second IDE drive to a system that already has one, you have to make the second drive the *slave*, which means that it shows up as drive D. To make your new drive a slave, you either have to set a DIP switch or move a small *jumper* (see Chapter 27 for details about jumpers).

Of course, you can make the new unit drive C, but it does mean having to change the old one from master to slave, which is no big deal. *You do not have to reformat the old drive C to remove its boot sector, so it can now act as a drive D.* This is good news, because the new drive you're installing as drive C will be found first, and the system will boot off it. The boot sector on the old drive C, which is now drive D, will never be found, so just leave it there.

If your system uses an EIDE controller or two IDE controllers, you can run up to four drives, although on two separate cables. On the second controller, the first connected drive (hard disk or CD-ROM) should be set up as the master for that pairing, and the second, if there is one, should be the slave. The master on this second connection will not be confused for drive C, which is the master on the first connection.

If you have an EIDE adapter on your motherboard or adapter card, then you'll have two connector plugs instead of just one. The first drive that you attach to the second connector will be the master of that particular cable. See the upcoming section, "Connecting the Drive Cables," for more info.

Adding a New Drive Controller (If Needed)

After you have the hard drive in, insert the new drive controller card, if needed. To insert a drive controller card, find a slot that's open. Holding the slot cover in place, unscrew the retaining screw. Hold the card at the top with both hands and gently position the edge connectors. Rock the card until it slips into place. (See Chapter 4 if you want more details about how to add an expansion card.) Add the connecting ribbon cables for your hard disk or floppy drives.

Cable Select Mode

Some IDE drives have a special setting marked "CS," for "cable select." Basically this means, let the plug on the cable be the designator for whether the drive is master or slave, rather than some specific jumper setting. For this to work, you need a special IDE cable different from the normal cable. On this special cable, the *middle* plug goes into the motherboard, then one end goes into the master and the other the slave. Both devices have to support Cable Select Mode, by the way, and there's usually a jumper involved in turning the mode ON.

The drawbacks are probably greater than the advantages here. First of all, the IDE controller has to support cable select specifically, and about the only way you know if it does is by trying to use the Cable Select Mode cable in the first place. The cable itself is more expensive than a regular cable, and it's actually *shorter* than the old one; so although you're saved from having to fiddle with the jumpers, the tradeoff is that you're stuck trying to allocate real estate for your drives inside the computer that's closer to the controller connection. Is it worth it? I don't think so.

If you're replacing your old drive controller, remove the cables from it and take the card out. To remove a drive controller card, unscrew the retaining screw, grip the card at the top with both hands, and pull straight up. Or, if your old drive controller is hard-wired onto the motherboard, check your manual for the location of the switch that disables it.

But there's more... Getting your new controller card to work takes more than just plugging it in. You'll have to fiddle with nasty things like IRQs and DMAs, whatever they are. Check out Chapter 27 for help in getting out of this mess.

Connecting the Drive Cables

Now, attach the data (ribbon) cables to your new drive. Remember that the red wire or stripe along the side of the cable aligns with pin 1 on the connector. Pin 1 is clearly marked with a "1." If you're adding a second ST-506 or ESDI drive to your system, the data cable is connected to the J5 slot-thing on the controller (drive C is connected to the J4 slot). With a data cable that connects two drives, drive D uses the connector that hangs in the middle.

Newer motherboards may have either two IDE adapters or one EIDE adapter with two connectors. What's the difference? For the purposes of plugging in your hard drives, *none*.

If your motherboard has two IDE or EIDE connectors, one primary and one secondary, then you can connect your second hard drive to the secondary controller with a data cable. In such a case, you won't need to worry about setting the second hard disk to "slave," as described in the previous section.

Da terminata

If you're connecting a SCSI drive, there's a bit more to it. You can link SCSI devices together, so you need to use something called a terminating resistor to indicate which device is the first and the last in the "chain." Typically, the SCSI host adapter is set to ID 7, at one end of the chain. The first hard disk is usually set to 0, which means it's at the other end, and you're done with this terminating business. However, if the drive is not the only SCSI device in your PC, and its ID number is set to something other than 1 (between the SCSI adapter's number and the other device's ID number), then you have to remove its own termination resistors or switches so the SCSI controller will know that it has to continue on from the hard disk to look for more SCSI devices. Yech.

Thankfully, this is pretty rare: in almost all cases, you'll want your drive to be set to 1, unless it's external, in which case, it will occupy some number *higher* than the SCSI adapter. Your setup would be, say, ID 2 = internal CD-ROM, ID 4 = SCSI host adapter, and ID 6 = external hard drive. In this setup, the CD-ROM and the external hard drive are terminated, and you remove the terminators from the SCSI adapter.

Usually all you have to do is identify these terminator critters and pull them off to disable termination of the daisy chain. (Of course, if your hard disk is the one and only SCSI device in your system, leave the termination thingies on.)

As you prepare to install your new hard disk, keep in mind that each SCSI device has to be given a number. Usually drive C is called device number 0, and drive D is device number 1, but check your manuals to be sure. And, the SCSI host adapter (the SCSI word for "controller") is usually given ID 7. Also, internal devices are typically given a number lower than that of the SCSI adapter, while external devices are given higher ID numbers. However, keep in mind that the numbers also set the priority of the device on the chain, with 7 being the highest priority, and 0 being the lowest. When practical, set slower devices such as tape drives and CD-ROM drives to the highest priority, so they won't get crowded out of the chain by the fast guys, such as your SCSI hard disk. Also, the manual will tell you how to actually set the device number. Some manufacturers give you a special SCSI device control program; others make it more difficult by forcing you to set the parameters manually on one line of your CONFIG.SYS file. Adaptec-brand controllers use a program in ROM (much like the one in your BIOS) that allows you to set the controller's internal parameters just after you boot your computer. If all your SCSI devices are Plug and Play, then you don't have to mess with this ID business, because each device is given its ID on-the-fly (Plug and Play also handles the termination business).

Now that you've prepared your drive, connect the power cable(s). Remember that these are cables with four separate wires. Generally, the white plug is shaped to fit only one direction; but in any event, the colored wires from the male end should plug into the same-colored wires on the female end.

Fastening the Drive in Place

Fasten the drive in place with its screws. Then, restore your PC to its former beauty and plug it in. Don't expect much when you start up the PC—you have to set up the hard disk before you can use it. This is the time when you may want to stop and bake those cookies so you can bribe some guru into helping you. If you don't know a guru, you can read the next section.

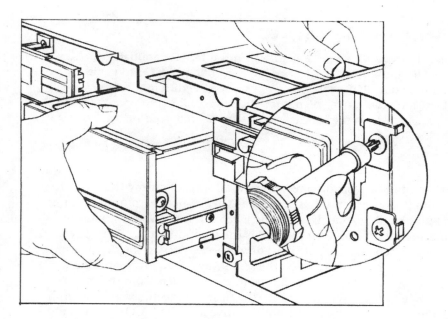

Fasten the drive in place.

Uh, Just a Few More Steps Before You Go

Well, the good news is you've got the drive in your computer, and you still have some skin left on a few of your knuckles. The bad news is, you're not done yet.

Telling CMOS About the New Drive

Before you can use your new hard drive, you have to get your PC to realize that it's there. You do that by changing the CMOS, which, as you learned in Chapter 3, "Now, Let's Find

Out What Kind of Computer You Have," is the thing that helps your PC remember mundane details such as what day it is and how much memory the PC has. Another detail that CMOS keeps track of is how many hard disks your PC has, and how big they are. So turn on your PC, and as it's booting, do whatever dance you usually do to get CMOS to show its face:

➤ Reboot your computer and press **Ctrl+Alt+Escape**. You can also try **Ctrl+Alt+Enter** or **Ctrl+Alt+S**.

➤ Reboot your computer and watch the screen for a message telling you what key to press for Setup. Then press it. (It may tell you to press **F1** or **F2** or even **Delete**.)

➤ Reboot your computer with its original manufacturer's setup disk in drive A. This is usually what you need to do for an AT-type 286 PC or PS/2, because it doesn't provide a friendly way to access CMOS.

IDE drive? No worries (maybe)!

If your new IDE drive has the same brand and internal parameters as the drive it replaced, then you might not have to change CMOS to get it to work, because your BIOS probably won't notice the difference. Of course, if you add a second IDE drive, even if it's the same brand and parameters as the first, all bets are off—which means that you better dig out your manual and start messing with CMOS.

To tell CMOS about your new drive, you have to know all sorts of creepy things such as how many *cylinders*, *heads*, and *sectors* it has, as well as science-fiction sounding things such as write protect and landing zone. If you're lucky, you'll find this information printed on the hard disk itself; if not, your manual is the second-best bet. Even if you don't understand what the terms mean, the hard drive specs listed on the drive or in the manual are listed the same way as the BIOS setup program lists them, so just type in the numbers from the manual or the drive sticker into the form onscreen. Or, better yet, if you're installing an IDE drive and the CMOS has an auto-detect feature, use it now. It'll save you tons of headaches. Jump to Chapter 27 for help in dealing with the CMOS monster.

What gives? After you enter the settings manually, CMOS will calculate the size of your hard disk. It may come up with a number that's a little off, such as 2112MB for a 2.5GB hard disk, but it shouldn't be way off, such as 1064MB.

Now, if you have to enter the parameters yourself, you may find that you are two parameters short, in terms of what the label on the hard disk told you. For *precompression*, use either **0** or **65535**. When in doubt, try **0** first. For *landing zone*, enter the number of cylinders minus one, which will usually be **1023**.

Setting Up a SCSI Drive

If you're setting up a SCSI drive, you have to run its software to add a driver to the CONFIG.SYS so your PC recognizes the drive. Next, you'll have to run the setup program that came with the SCSI controller in order for the controller to recognize the drive, too. The SCSI controller has to be able to recognize the hardware so it can "turn it on," and so in turn, you can have DOS high-level format the drive. Before using DOS, however, you may have to low-level format the SCSI drive. As a matter of safety, as long as your BIOS isn't controlling your hard drives anyway, you should set the BIOS up for *No Hard Drive* at all. This way, you won't accidentally use the BIOS to low-level format SCSI drives. Your BIOS thinks you're using something on the order of an ST-506 and doesn't have a clue about SCSI. Instead, to low-level format a SCSI drive, use the special program disk supplied by the manufacturer, or use utility software that's rated for SCSI drives.

Partitioning a New Drive (SCSI or IDE)

If you bought a large hard disk, it came with a disk that you need to run about now. Stick the thing in drive A and type **SETUP** at the A:\> prompt. The setup program takes care of the FDISK thing coming up, and FORMAT. It also checks your BIOS to see if you need to use a device driver so your computer will recognize the high capacity drive. Run the setup program if you have one, and skip gleefully over the next few paragraphs.

If your hard disk did not come with a Setup disk, then take your emergency disk with the FDISK and FORMAT commands on it, and read the next few paragraphs.

EZ-Drive Some drives include a software program called EZ-Drive, which makes setting up the drive a snap. If you can get your hands on a copy, it's well worth the effort, and hey, you'll get to skip the CMOS junk. Other drives include an Auto Configure option in their setup programs that does the same job.

Read this! Be very careful when using FDISK, because a simple typo could end up erasing the data of an existing drive. Be sure you are using FDISK on the correct drive letter, such as D, before you actually begin typing anything.

What Ma should have told ya

Do not, under any circumstances, attempt to low-level format an IDE drive. Turns the darn thing into a very expensive paperweight. High-level formatting, which you do with the FORMAT command, is not only a good idea, it's required.

After you've got the CMOS business over with, your next step is to *partition* your drive. Now, you don't officially have a hard drive yet, so you'll need to boot your system with your emergency disk in drive A. Although you can use this opportunity to divide a large disk into several smaller ones, you don't have to do this (unless your BIOS or your operating system forces you). You can, and perhaps should, have as few as one partition on your hard drive; but having more than one allows you to address one partition as "logical drive" C and another partition as "logical drive" D. If you really enjoy this type of confusion, be my guest and sign up for more than one partition.

The tale of the partitions

Sign up for only one partition, that is, *if you can*. As you learned earlier in this chapter, the BIOS of your PC, unless it supports BIOS translation, can only handle hard disks up to 528MB. If you have a slightly newer BIOS, it may be only able to handle hard disks less than 2.1GB. *Or*, if you're not using Windows 95 OSR2 or Windows 98 *and* FAT 32, you may still have a 2.1GB limit. If you can't get BIOS upgrades for either of these two conditions, and you don't want to use FAT32, then you'll have to partition the drive into chunks the BIOS can deal with. Even if you don't have to, you may still want to divide a large disk into at least two chunks, one for programs and one for your data, to make backups easier to do.

To partition your hard drive, type **FDISK** at the A> prompt and press **Enter**. You may be asked if you want to use FAT32 to partition the drive: What you'll see is a question such as `Enable large disk support`? If you want to use FAT32, then type **Y** for yes. Any partition you create that has over 528MB on it will then use FAT32 automatically. If you replaced your old drive, your new drive is the primary DOS partition. So choose **Create DOS partition or Logical DOS Drive** and then choose **Create Primary DOS Partition**. You can only have one primary DOS partition, by the way; that's the whole meaning behind "primary." You'll be asked if you want to use all available disk space for this partition. Type **Y** if you do, then press **Esc**, and you're done. Or press **N**, if you want to enter a smaller size amount, to create the first of several partitions for the drive. If you enter a size amount, press **Esc** to return to the FDISK menu. Next, you need to make this partition the active one, so press **2** (if needed), to select that option, then **1** to select partition 1. If you have additional partitions you need to create on drive C, press **Esc** to return to the FDISK menu, then select **1 Create DOS parition or logical drive**, and **2 Create Extended DOS Partition**. Press **Enter** to use what's left as your extended partition (don't worry, you can still divide this up into several logical drives). Press **Esc** to return to the FDISK menu, where you're prompted to enter the size of the next partition. You can use up what's left, or enter an amount, and repeat these steps to create as many partitions as you like. Press **Esc** when you're done with FDISK.

If you're adding a second drive instead, you need to partition drive D. So first of all, choose **Change current fixed disk drive** and then select **D**. *This is important, because you don't want to do anything to the data on your existing drive C.* Choose **Create DOS Partition or Logical DOS Drive**. Choose **Secondary DOS Partition** and press **Y** to partition it. Follow the steps given earlier if you want to divide drive D into several partitions.

After you finish with FDISK, your PC restarts (if not, reboot it yourself by pressing **Ctrl+Alt+Delete**). If you replaced your only hard disk, you need to insert your emergency disk. If you added a second hard disk, just smile and do nothing.

Formatting the Drive

After you partition the new drive, you have to high-level format it. Here's some strange-but-true advice: If you're setting up a multigigabyte drive, *after you've created the main bootable DOS partition for that drive using FDISK, reboot your computer* (with a boot disk in your A drive) *before* formatting your drive with FORMAT C:. Why? If you don't reboot, FORMAT will set your drive up for 528MB, no matter how big your drive or main partition really happens to be. After you reboot, your computer will see your drive for how big it really is.

If you replaced your old hard drive, then after you've rebooted, type **FORMAT C: /S** at the DOS prompt to format it and press **Enter**. The "/S" part will make it a "system" disk, so it can run DOS and boot itself without you having to put a DOS disk in drive A.

When the thing asks you for a volume label, you can type something clever, such as **MY DRIVE C**. If you added a second drive or if you partitioned your one hard disk into several logical drives instead, type **FORMAT D:** and press **Enter** to format it. You don't need the "/S" part here.

Which partition?

Be very careful when formatting your drives if you created several logical partitions, and you have an existing hard disk drive in your system. For example, you might have inserted your new hard disk and made it drive C, and then partitioned it into two drives. The second drive letter in this case will be E, not D, because D is already being used by your old hard drive. Get it? Good.

Again, when it asks you for a volume label, you can type whatever you want, up to 11 whole characters. (Repeat for additional logical drives, such as drive E: **FORMAT E:**.) Anyway, after you've formatted your new drive, everything should be okay. So remove any disks from their drives and restart your PC to test it out.

Done! Test your new drive out, then restore your old data.

Upgrading Mistakes to Avoid

If your new drive won't wake up, open up the PC again and check for obvious things like loose cables and such. Also check to make sure you didn't put the data (ribbon) cables on backwards. Remember, the red wire or stripe should match up with pin 1 on the data cable connector. Check the controller card as well, and make sure that it is seated properly.

Next, you might want to check the CMOS settings you entered to be sure you didn't make a typing mistake.

Check to make sure that you partitioned and formatted the thing okay. Type **FDISK** at the prompt, then read the partition table to see if the partitions are really showing up the way you intended. You should have one and only one primary DOS partition. And, one of the partitions must be made the active one, or you'll get the message, "No ROM Basic, system halted," or "No boot device found." If needed, just reboot with your emergency disk and use FDISK again. If you get the error message, "No operating system," you forgot the /S parameter when you used the FORMAT command on drive C.

If you're dealing with two IDE drives, they may not want to play together. You can try switching the slave and master drives with each other. If that doesn't work, you may have to take the new drive back and get a drive made by the same people who made the first one.

The Least You Need to Know

There's a lot to remember when shopping for a new hard disk. Here are some pointers:

➤ First, try compressing your current hard disk to see if you can avoid this whole business.

➤ Then make sure you have an empty drive bay in which you can put a new hard disk. If you're replacing a bad disk, this obviously isn't a problem.

➤ If you don't have any open bays, you can shop for a hard card or an external hard disk instead, or perhaps an attachment mounting bracket.

➤ For the easiest type of addition or replacement, shop for the same kind of hard disk you had before. However, if you're replacing an older ST-506 or ESDI drive, you may want to consider switching to IDE.

➤ Get the largest, fastest hard disk you can afford. (Keep your BIOS limitations in mind, along with the limitations of a system that does not use FAT32.)

➤ Make sure your new hard disk will fit into the open drive bay.

➤ If you switch standards, get a new controller card. Keep in mind that you may also need to replace the floppy drive controller if it is used by the old hard disk controller.

➤ Be sure to purchase cables and rack mounts if needed.

Make Mine More Memory

Random access memory, or RAM, is one of your PC's most precious commodities—it's also one of the most boring. That's because unlike your cool color printer, fax modem, or sound-like-thunder speakers, RAM just doesn't cause your friends to oooh and ahhh in admiration.

Yeah, memory's pretty boring—that is, until you run out of it. You see, before you can work with any kind of data on your PC, the PC must first place the data in RAM. In addition, the PC must copy into RAM any program you want to run before it can read and then carry out any of that program's instructions. So if your PC doesn't have a lot of RAM, and you try to run a memory-hogging program like a word processor to try to edit your 35-page corporate review, you're likely to get an Out of memory message. In English, this means you either have to get something out of RAM (close a document, stop a program, or something), or you have to add more memory to your PC. If you use Windows, it can shuffle things in and out of memory when you run out of RAM, but even Windows has limits. You see, when you run out of memory, Windows transfers stuff out of RAM and into *virtual memory*—a holding area on your hard drive. This whole process depends on you having spare room on your hard disk, which puts a crimp on your ability to create and save lots of documents. All this shuffling business can get on your nerves

My way or the highway Some PCs require that you purchase their RAM, and not any old generic RAM. Look in your manual; it should tell you whether you need to buy proprietary (name brand) RAM or not. Expect to pay a bit more, however.

after a while, too, such as when you make one tiny change to a document and then wait ten minutes for the computer to process it.

So how much RAM do you have right now, and how much more should you get? Good questions. Check out Chapter 2, "What Makes Your Computer Tick, and What It Takes to Upgrade Each Component," for the answers. Also, make sure to check your owner's manual to see what the limit is on the amount of memory your system can handle. RAM, by the way, will cost you anywhere from $50 to $200 for 16MB.

Get a device driver

If you're adding memory above 1MB for the first time, you need to install a device driver that can manage extended memory. Luckily, DOS versions 4.0 and higher, as well as Windows, come with HIMEM.SYS, a device driver that does just that. If you have a lower DOS version than 4.0, you may want to upgrade to get the HIMEM.SYS device driver so your PC can use memory above 1MB.

Sometimes, the memory above 1MB (extended memory) is converted into expanded memory using an expanded memory driver. This is rare because using memory this way is inefficient. You'll only need to worry about creating expanded memory if some program you use requires it.

Buying the Right RAM

Before you hit the shopping malls, keep this in mind: RAM prices fluctuate more than the price of gas. Shop around and don't hesitate to wait until you think the price is right.

Get the Right Kind

First, you need to know what kind of RAM chips your PC uses, such as DIPPs or SIMMs. In addition, if your PC uses SIMMs, you need to know whether they are 30-pin "low-density," or 72-pin "high-density" SIMMs (which are much wider than 30-pin SIMMs). Also, SIMMs come in parity checking or non-parity checking styles. If you want to know more, read the sidebar coming up. In addition, 72-pin SIMMs come in either single (1MB,

4MB, and 16MB) or double-sided (2MB , 8MB, or 32MB) varieties. The double-sided ones may also be composite SIMMs (especially if they are 32MB SIMMs), a special type that's wired slightly differently, and which may not be compatible with all double-sided SIMM systems. Some composite SIMMs may have a 16MB or even 64MB capacity. The 16MB ones are especially insidious, because by all rights, they should be single-sided. These 16MB composite SIMMs will not work in a normal 16MB system, so be careful when ordering your RAM.

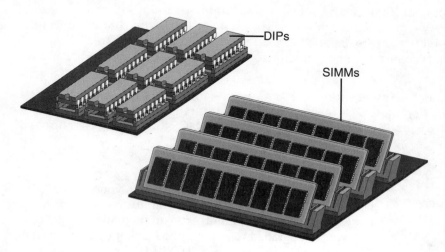

DIPs

SIMMs

Two flavors of RAM chips: DIPs and SIMMs.

Oh yeah, one last thing you need to know when shopping for SIMMs, they come in gold and silver. The ones with gold contacts fit into modules that also use gold contacts. Likewise, the silver contact SIMMs are designed for use in silver contact modules. So make sure you get the right metal for your system.

The newest PCs today (Pentiums, Pentium Pros, and Pentium IIs) use DIMMs, short for *dual inline memory module*. Although they are faster than SIMMs, DIMMs are much more expensive, so some PCs use a combination of the two. DIMMs look like SIMMs, but with 168 pins. They also come in different flavors: 3.3- and 5-volt (v), and buffered/unbuffered varieties—check your manual. Most systems use 3.3v unbuffered DIMMs. If you own a laptop, you may find that it needs a smaller version of a DIMM, called a SODIMM, or Small Outline DIMM.

Consider parity checking

If you're adding SIMMs to your system, there's another detail you need to consider, and that's parity checking. Your system either uses parity checking, or it doesn't. You have to match the right SIMMs (parity checking or nonparity checking) to your system.

Basically, SIMMs come in only a couple of styles, 30-pin or 72-pin. So first you need to get the right style to match the others in your system. The 30-pin SIMMs come in two versions: 9-bit (which are designed for parity checking) and 8-bit (which aren't). The 72-pin SIMMs come with a similar choice: 36-bit (which use parity) and 32-bit (which don't).

When talking about parity memory, you may also run into something called ECC memory, or *Error Correcting Code* memory. However, this type of memory will only work in computers specifically designed for it. (Check CMOS for a setting that turns on ECC mode.)

What about my SIPPs? Okay, if you have a very old system, it may use some memory chips called SIPPs, which are long and thin, with one row of pins. (If you want a picture, check out Chapter 2.) Anyway, you'll probably have quite a time trying to find these guys, so I would recommend (that is, if you're determined to upgrade your dinosaur) that you get a SIPP-to-SIMM adapter. It'll cost you a mere $6, but it'll save you $6 million in headaches. If you need help locating one, check out the Web address: http://www.lgr.lv/marshal/pcs/simmrcyl.htm.

If you're replacing your motherboard, and you would like to be able to use your existing RAM, you just got your wish. For example, if your old motherboard used 30-pin SIMMs, and you've upgraded to a motherboard that uses the newer 72-pin SIMMs, you can buy a SIMM adapter. The adapter fits into one of your 72-pin slots, and it has slots of its own into which you can insert your 30-pin SIMMs. You can, by the way, go the other route: If you're keeping your old motherboard but you would like to use the newer (and less expensive) 72-pin SIMMs, you can get an adapter that fits into a 30-pin slot and insert your 72-pin SIMMs into it. If you decide to use one of these adapters, keep in mind that you still have to fill a bank. So if the banks in your motherboard contain two slots, you have to fill them with the same amount of memory (for example, an 8MB SIMM in one slot, and an adapter with a total of 8MB). You can use two adapters in such a case, but they have to face away from each other so the SIMMs have room to breathe.

Get the Right Speed

After you know what kind of memory chips or SIMMs your PC uses, you also need to know their *speed*, or "access time," which is measured in nanoseconds (ns). The *smaller* the number, the faster the chip or SIMM. So a 70ns chip is faster than a 120ns chip. The speed is marked on the chip itself. In the following picture, the two numbers after the dash tell you that the speed of this chip is 10, which is an abbreviation for 100ns.

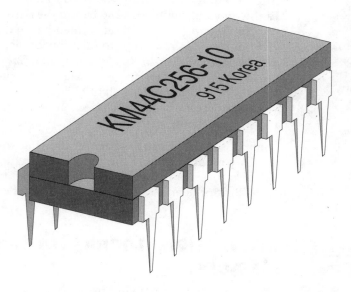

The numbers on the chip tell you its speed and capacity.

Here are some other abbreviations to know:

Number after the dash	Speed in nanoseconds
6 or 60	60ns
7 or 70 or 70SP	70ns
8 or 80 or 80SP	80ns
10	100ns
12	120ns
15	150ns
20	200ns

You'll most likely find 60-, 70-, or 80ns chips on newer 386, 486, and Pentium PCs. On ATs you'll probably find 100- or 120ns chips, although older PCs use 150- or 200ns chips instead. In any case, *you must match the speed to the other chips on your PC* (unless you decide to replace your existing RAM chips). In a pinch, you can substitute *faster* chips, but not slower ones. In situations where the faster chip becomes more mass-produced than the slower one, it can become the less expensive one as well; so it may be worth your while to shop for faster chips (which will run at the slower speed anyway), and save a bit of money.

Not a catastrophe, just a waste If you accidentally add RAM chips that are rated slower than the ones already in the PC, you won't blow up anything, but your PC won't recognize the new RAM chips, so you won't be able to use them, or the system will just run slower.

Get the Right Capacity

After speed, the next thing you need to look at is capacity. In the previous figure, the 256 before the dash tells you that the chip is part of a 256KB set. Remember that you need eight or nine of these chips to fill a row of memory so you actually get 256KB. *(All the chips in a row of memory must be the same speed and capacity.)* Why eight for some, and nine for others? Well, you need eight bits to make a byte, but if your computer uses parity to check memory, it needs one more bit, making the total nine.

Some PCs make this stuff easier by allowing you to use memory modules, where the eight or nine chips are all soldered together in a single unit of memory. Common capacities for DIP chips include 64KB, 256KB, and 1MB. SIMMs have larger capacities, ranging from 256KB to 64MB.

Faster chips aren't a cure-all Just because you install faster RAM chips, don't expect your PC to benefit from the speed increase. The speed at which RAM is accessed is set by the PC's internal clock, not the chips. Suppose you replace a set of old 100ns RAM chips with some new, slick 70ns units. If you then replace your system's CPU with one that has a faster clock speed, your system may benefit from both the faster CPU and the faster RAM.

Installation: Thanks for the Memory!

Get your PC tool kit, do your usual backup, update your emergency disk, and open your PC (see Chapter 4, "What You Need to Know Before You Open Your PC"). Take a look at the motherboard and check out the spot where you can add the new chips. If you've already decided that you have to add RAM through an expansion board, skip this step.

If your motherboard is full, you may have to yank some chips and replace them with higher capacity chips. A chip puller tool (which looks like large tweezers) is really handy if you find that you have to remove DIP chips. SIMMs don't require any tool to remove or insert.

Now, before you do anything, make sure that you discharge any static electricity. Here's a good job where a grounding wrist strap comes in real handy. Anyway, to remove a DIP chip, start with a small flat-edge screwdriver. Gently pry up one of the ends of the chip. Then move to the other end and pry it up a little. Repeat until the chip is fairly loose. You can use the chip puller or your fingers to extract the chip. Just be sure to pull the chip up, and not the chip/socket.

DRAM!

One more bit of memory stuff you should know about, especially if you start shopping for a new PC rather than upgrading. Your PC typically has one main core of memory, made up of chips called DRAM, or Dynamic RAM. (This is true whether you insert those chips separately or in a SIMM.) Anyway, DRAM is not exactly the fastest RAM chip manufactured, but it is the most cost-effective for use in large banks of RAM.

To speed up your PC, a lot of manufacturers include a RAM cache (an area in memory that holds the most requested data). This RAM cache is made up of SRAM (static RAM) chips, which beat standard DRAM chips hands down in the speed department. Static RAM, you see, doesn't degrade over time like Dynamic RAM (DRAM), so it doesn't need continual refresh cycles. This makes SRAM more expensive, but certainly fine for use in small RAM caches. By keeping the data you use most often in a cache, your PC can get to it quicker than searching regular memory for it.

Well, there's a different kind of DRAM chip on the market, and it's called EDO (extended data out) DRAM. Although they're not as fast as SRAM chips, they're faster than regular DRAM. Manufacturers are using them in place of standard DRAM chips to speed up regular memory. To keep costs down, these systems typically do not include an SRAM cache. That only slows them down by about 10 percent, by the way.

You may also run into a new kind of DRAM called SDRAM, or synchronous DRAM, which refers to the fact that it can synchronize its own clock with that of the CPU, thus reducing the number of latency periods. This eliminates normal waiting periods between when the CPU makes a request for data and when RAM supplies it—when RAM is synchronous with the CPU, it's like their dancing together in a perfect ballet.

When handling SIMMs, take care not to touch the connectors on the bottom. You want to keep these free of any grease or oils you may have on your hands. To remove a SIMM, first check to see how it's attached. You notice a clip at either end of the SIMM that holds the SIMM in place. To release the SIMM, press down on each clip to release it. The SIMM pops forward a bit. Hold the SIMM at its top edge and lift it out.

Yank the banks

If your motherboard is full, you can add memory on an expansion card, but some PCs don't enable you to do that. In this case, your only choice is to pull some RAM modules from the lower-numbered banks and replace them with higher capacity modules. Just keep in mind that memory chips work in *banks*, so you have to pull all the chips in one bank—which, if the PC in question has two banks of four rows each, means that you need to pull four of its eight SIMMs.

If the original banks were filled with 1MB SIMMs (for a total of 8MB), you could replace the four SIMMs with 8MB SIMMs for a total of 12MB. That is, if your motherboard thinks in twelves. Most motherboards are marked with the increments they can handle, which is usually something like 2MB, 4MB, 8MB, 16MB, and so on. In this example, you more than likely have to pull *all eight* 1MB SIMMs and replace them with 4MB SIMMs to get a total of 32MB. You can also replace them with 2MB or 8MB SIMMs if your motherboard supports a total of 16 (2MB × 8) or 64 (8MB × 8) megabytes.

Gently pry up the chip you want to remove.

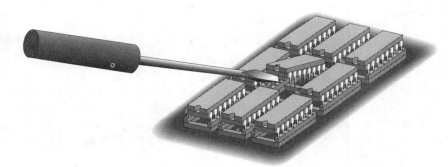

After you remove any old chips that you can't use, you're ready to insert your new chips. Make sure that you are thoroughly grounded before you pick up the chips. Keep in mind that memory is added in complete banks, and in order. Typically, the first bank of memory is called bank 0, and the second bank is called bank 1 (kinda like how the bottom floor of an office building is the basement, and the next floor up is numbered 1, and so on). Anyway, be sure to fill the banks in order, beginning with the first bank, and proceeding on.

To insert a DIP chip, first make sure that the chip's legs are straight. If needed, turn the chip on its side and press it gently against the side of a nonmetal table to align the legs perpendicular to the chip itself. Take a minute to use a can of compressed air to clean out any dust around the chip sockets.

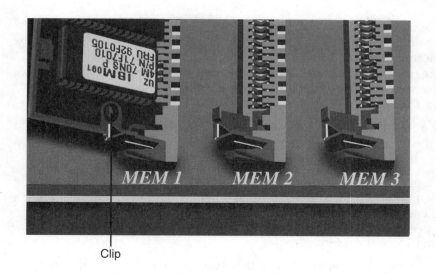

To remove a SIMM, release the clips holding it in place.

Clip

Next, look for a notch at one end of the chip. You have to match this notch up with the same notch on the chip socket, or with the "1" printed on the motherboard.

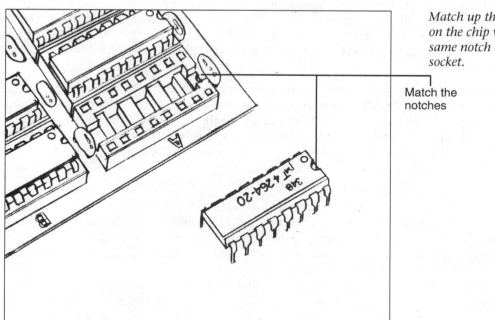

Match up the notch on the chip with the same notch on the socket.

Match the notches

293

Insert the chip, making sure that you don't accidentally bend any of the legs outside of the socket. Press the chip in place. If you're using an insertion tool (another one of those handy gadgets you find in most PC tool kits), place the chip in the tool. Insert the chip into the socket; the tool makes sure that the legs line up correctly with the holes. Press the plunger at the end of the tool's handle, and it applies an even pressure on the chip, securing it into the socket.

If you're inserting a SIMM, hold it at its top edge. Flip the SIMM so the notch at one end matches up with the same notch on the SIMM socket. Position the SIMM over the socket and gently insert it at an angle, as shown.

When you insert the SIMM, press it up gently until the tabs pop up to lock it in place. Don't force this; if it doesn't seem to want to work, you may have inserted the SIMM backwards, or not completely into the socket itself. Try again. You must insert some SIMMs at a 90-degree angle perpendicular to the socket and rock them backwards into a 10 o'clock position to lock them into place.

At first glance, a DIMM socket seems entirely different from a SIMM socket; it's black instead of white, its levers are gray plastic instead of silver metal. But the installation process is very much the same, except that a DIMM is inserted straight-down into the socket, instead of at an angle. A DIMM can only go into its socket one way, so if its pins aren't aligned with the connections on the socket, don't try to force it. With the pins aligned, you use the same process to insert the DIMM as you would for a SIMM. The gray plastic levers will catch on both sides when the DIMM is secure. Or you can tilt the lever up, and it will pull the DIMM down into the socket. Then tilt the other lever up to lock the DIMM in place.

To insert a SIPP, follow the general directions for a DIP chip. First, make sure that you didn't bend any of the SIPP's legs. Next, line up the legs with the holes in the SIPP socket. A SIPP doesn't have a notch to help you line it up right like a DIP chip does, so make sure that the number 1 pin on the SIPP aligns with the number 1 hole in the socket. Use other SIPPs on the motherboard as a guide so you can be sure that you're inserting the SIPP in the correct direction. Press the chip gently into place—if you press too hard, you could wreck the socket, and you'll have to replace your entire motherboard.

Finally, check your work to make sure that none of the chip's legs are hanging out. Check your PC manual to see if you have to either flip a DIP switch (which acts kind of like a small light switch), or move a jumper to "turn on" the new memory. Luckily, you'll probably only have to do this kind of nonsense on an old XT PC, which you probably wouldn't bother to upgrade anyway. If you find that you need to mess with DIP switches and you want help, check out Chapter 27, "Fiddling with Ports, IRQs, Addresses, and Such."

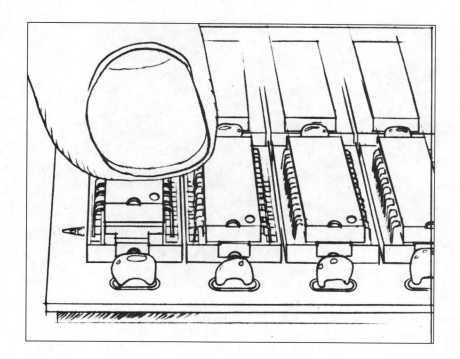

After you line up the legs, press the chip into place.

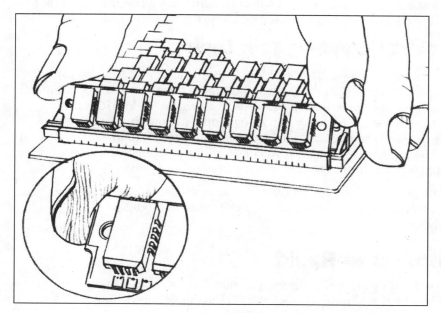

Hold the SIMM at the top edge to insert it.

Press the SIMM gently into place.

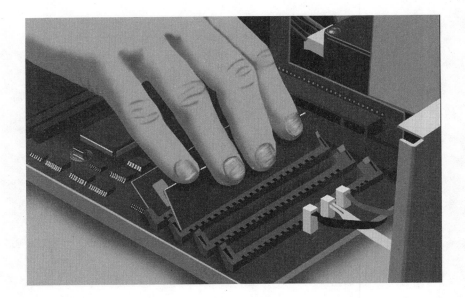

Put your PC back together and turn it on. Your PC will realize that you added some memory, but it'll be confused—you'll know because you'll see an error message. Don't panic—at least not yet. All you need to do is make sure the amount of memory recorded in CMOS is the correct amount. Newer BIOSes will automatically update this figure; but if it's wrong, you need to do it yourself. If you need help, see Chapter 27 again.

What to Do If You're Upgrading Your Laptop

First, make sure that you protect your data and then turn the laptop off. Getting into the system board of a laptop is not as simple a process as flipping open the hatch. With most laptops, all you have to do is remove a latch by pressing down and sliding it in the correct direction (like removing the battery hatch cover on a remote control). You may have to unscrew a small screw to open the latch. With others, you have to work a little bit harder; you may even have to unscrew the keyboard from the bottom of the case. Check your manual for complete directions on how to disassemble your laptop.

After you find the memory sockets, they pretty much work the same way as the ones you find in desktop PCs. Just make sure that you line up the memory modules correctly and push the chip gently into its socket.

Upgrading Mistakes to Avoid

If your PC doesn't recognize your new memory, you may have forgotten to flip the right DIP switch or to move the right jumper. Check the PC's manual to see what you need to do. Check your CMOS settings as well.

Remember that memory must fill a bank; you can't leave a bank half-filled. Each bank is numbered, beginning with 0. Look on the motherboard for the number of each bank.

You can also recheck the chips you inserted to make sure that each one is firmly in place. Also look for any pins that might not have made it into the right socket.

If you inserted a DIPP chip in the wrong direction, you may have burnt it out. If that's the case, you need to replace the chip. If you inserted a SIMM in the wrong direction, it's okay, but you'll need to insert it correctly to get it to work. Remember: The notch in the SIMM needs to match up with the corresponding notch on the slot.

If all this fails, then it's time to put your PC back like it was. Take out the new memory, put back any old memory chips in their old locations, then power on the system with your emergency disk in the drive. Remember, the AUTOEXEC.BAT and CONFIG.SYS files are on the emergency disk you created before the upgrade process. If you get a prompt and everything appears in order, the problem was evidently with something you added (or took away). If the problem persists, however, the problem was caused by the upgrade process itself, and it may be time to take the machine to the shop.

Two by two...

When dealing with this bank stuff, and making sure that you fill a bank, keep in mind that any Pentium motherboard that has a 64-bit memory bus (the part of the data bus that fetches memory from RAM) requires SIMMs to be installed in pairs *if* those SIMMS are 32-bit (72-pin) units. In some unusual (read: "Compaq") circumstances, 32-bit SIMMs have to be installed in *fours*. If a Pentium motherboard uses 64-bit DIMMs, pairing is not required. But many Pentium motherboards that use 64-bit *SIMMs* (not DIMMs) pair up modules to fill a bank anyway.

Now, you're probably thinking, "As long I know that I need to fill an entire bank, what should this pairing rule matter?" Well, true, if you fill a bank, you'll be following this pairing rule automatically, however, with some motherboards, although the banks exist, they're not marked. In such a case, the owner (that means you) is expected to simply *know* the pairing rule, either from having read the manual, or from watching smoke rise from the system.

The Least You Need to Know

Getting the right kind of memory for your system is probably the hardest thing to do. Here are some pointers to help you along the way:

➤ Buy at least enough memory so your PC has 16MB minimum (maybe 8MB if you're really on a budget). Buy more if you can afford it.

➤ Open up the PC to see where you can put more RAM chips. Adding memory through an expansion card is sometimes an option.

➤ While you've got the PC open, check out what kind of chips your PC uses: DIPs, SIMMs, DIMMs, or maybe even SIPPs.

➤ Also know the speed (in nanoseconds) of the RAM chips and their capacity.

➤ Check your manual to find out the maximum amount of RAM your PC can handle. Also, check to see if there are specific increments by which you can upgrade, such as 16MB, 24MB, and 32MB.

➤ Shop around when buying RAM chips; their prices change daily. You might also want to check for RAM prices online (on the Internet).

Chapter 20

Taking Advantage of Modern Video Capabilities

There are two pieces to your PC's video pie: the monitor and the video card. The monitor is in charge of displaying the best picture it can; it sets the upper limit of what you're gonna see. The video card, on the other hand, assembles the image you want to display; it determines the level of detail and the color palette that the monitor can use. To get the best picture, these two parts need to work together.

In other words, if you have a lousy monitor, buying a super video card isn't going to make you happy. On the other hand, you'll be equally displeased with the combination of a super-expensive monitor and a dime-store video card. So match the capabilities of both to get the best results.

Keep it in good shape

One of the simplest things you can do to keep your new monitor in good running order is to turn it off every once in a while. Monitors are magnetic creatures, and as such, they are sensitive to magnetic forces, such as (stop me if you've heard of this one) *gravity*. To prevent the buildup of such forces from throwing off the sensitive magnetic guns inside the monitor, most monitors demagnetize (degauss) themselves every time they're turned on (some monitors have a degauss button in the back, which you yourself are expected to press every once in a while). In any event, if you never turn your monitor off and just leave it as it is all the time, degaussing will never happen. So do yourself a favor and turn your monitor (and your computer, too, for that matter) off at least once a week, if not every day.

On another note, be sure you protect the *electronics* of your monitor by plugging it into a good surge protector. Of course, this goes for your computer as well.

Do you really need it?

You may be wondering, "Is it worth it?" I mean, if you have to replace both the graphics card and the monitor on your current system, is it worth going all out and getting a good monitor. I've got only one word for that, and that's a big "Yes!" If you spend a lot of time on your computer, you owe it to your eyes to get the best, brightest, and biggest monitor you can afford. And if your kids use your computer, you owe it to them, too.

Now you may be thinking, "Sure, I'd like a good monitor, but I only use my computer at night and on weekends." That may be true, but isn't that when you're the most tired, or at least, when your eyes are under the most strain—after a full day's work? Why add the extra stress when good monitors are relatively inexpensive anyway? Also, because the monitor is probably the only thing you'll keep when you eventually move from this computer to a new one, making the investment now is definitely worth it.

So What Should I Look For?

When shopping for a monitor, the salesperson will throw a lot of goofy-sounding words at you, trying to confuse you into letting go of your wallet. Here's some information you should take with you for self-defense:

Resolution. Look for the higher resolutions such as 1024×768 (good), 1280×1024 (better), and even 1600×1200 or 1600×1280 (best). Expect to pay bigger bucks for higher resolutions. A standard VGA monitor supports one resolution—640×480, but you can't buy them anymore, so who cares? The SVGA monitors sold today support multiple resolutions and are for that reason called "multiscan" monitors. Besides, it's a cool, sci-fi-sounding term.

Screen resolution

Resolution, you may recall from Chapter 2, "What Makes Your Computer Tick, and What It Takes to Upgrade Each Component," is the number of pixels (dots) that comprise the images on your screen. The more dots, the better defined that image can be. At low resolutions such as 640×480, there are fewer pixels to fill the screen, so they are bigger and fatter, and images are less well-defined. At higher resolutions such as 1280×1024, the pixels are smaller and images are sharper and more finely detailed.

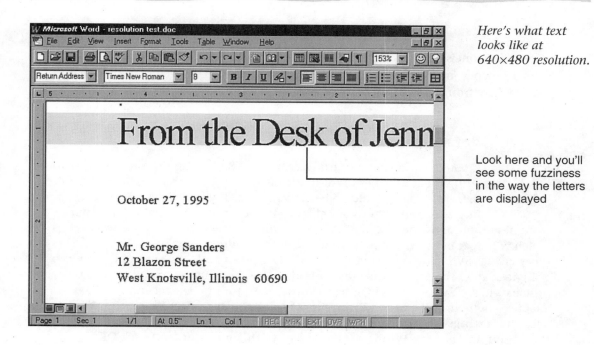

Here's what text looks like at 640×480 resolution.

Look here and you'll see some fuzziness in the way the letters are displayed

Here's the same text at 1024×768 resolution.

At higher resolutions, you don't get the fuzz

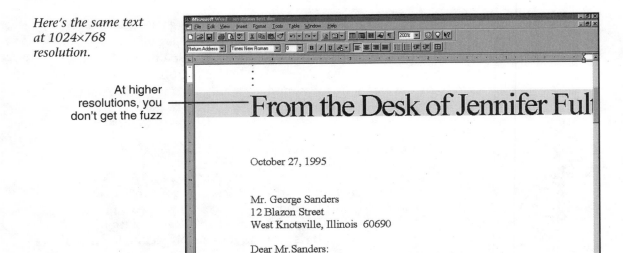

Size. This one's easy; it's the size of the viewing area. Monitors today are usually 14 or 15 inches (measured diagonally), but, for a price, you can get a monitor that's anywhere from 17 to 21 inches.

Got more than one monitor?

If you do, and you're running Windows 98, you can use a new feature to string them together to form one big picture that stretches across both monitors. Why would you ever want this? If you're a designer or architect, you could have your blueprints appear on one monitor and your word processor on the other. You'll only have one mouse pointer, by the way, which will float between the two monitors. Both monitors must be of the same type, such as SVGA. (Or you could use a PC monitor and a TV monitor, plugged into a single adapter that has connectors for both.) After hooking one monitor into the primary video adapter, and plugging the other monitor into the secondary video adapter, you're ready to begin. Right-click the desktop and select **Properties**. Then click the **Settings** tab, and select the secondary monitor by clicking its icon. Select the option, **Extend my Windows desktop onto this monitor**, and click **OK**.

Dot pitch. Basically, this is the onscreen distance between those little pixels. A good number to look for here is .28mm (millimeters); the lower this number is, the sharper the image onscreen. Each pixel on a low dot-pitch monitor is less fuzzy around its edges, so color pictures are crisper. This is because there's less fuzz in between the colors.

Refresh rate. Sometimes called the scanning frequency, this tells you how often the electron beams (cathode rays) update the image onscreen. The faster the refresh rate, the less flickering you'll see. 70Hz is a decent speed for 1024×768, while 60Hz is average for a higher resolution like 1280×1024. (At higher resolutions, it's normal for the refresh rate to go down.) Multiscan monitors (monitors that support multiple resolutions) that alter their refresh rates for added clarity at the lower resolutions are called "multisync" monitors (another cool, sci-fi–sounding term).

Match the refresh rates

The refresh rate your monitor uses must match at least one of the rates your video card supports. (If you buy a multisync monitor which is capable of supporting multiple refresh rates, making a match between it and a video card is easier.) If you mismatch the two, you can wreck your monitor. On the back of each video card's package is a list of resolutions and corresponding refresh rates which the card supports. Finding the refresh rates for a monitor isn't as easy; you'll need to ask a salesperson or support representative to supply you with literature from the manufacturer. You'll need the monitor's information later when setting up your video card, so it's worth the trouble to get it.

Video bandwidth. This is the maximum frequency at which the monitor is capable of operating. It's the same as the maximum horizontal resolution multiplied by the maximum vertical resolution multiplied by the maximum refresh rate. In short, it's the size of the biggest video signal the monitor supports. The higher, the better; 65MHz–75MHz is about average. (Compare that to 3.58MHz for the standard North American TV signal.) The video bandwidth of any resolution probably averages out close to this maximum value; as resolution increases, the refresh rate proportionally decreases.

Interlacing. An interlaced monitor paints an image onscreen by first updating all the even-numbered rows (starting with the first, row "0"), then skewing the electron guns by half-a-pixel and updating all the odd-numbered rows in-between. It's like painting an American flag starting with all the red stripes, then filling in all the white stripes. The first multiscan monitors had to support interlacing to produce 800×600 and 1024×768 images, because they weren't really capable of scanning a single image at these high resolutions. Interlaced video can result in an annoying flicker that can strain your eyes. Most monitors today are non-interlaced, which means they paint the image onscreen sequentially, resulting in an image with less flicker, and which is much easier on the eyes.

Surface. This is the second easiest, second least-technical issue on this list. Average monitors, like average television sets, are ever-so-slightly convex (curved toward the viewer). Sony patented and then licensed the patent for picture tubes with a *flat screen*; its contents aren't distorted by the shape of the tube. You pay more for a flat screen, and you may not notice the difference in the store—but just use one for an hour or two and ask your eyes how they feel.

Energy Star, EPA, or DPMS. Your monitor is the most energy-consuming part of your PC, so getting an energy-smart monitor (one that carries the Energy Star logo) can save you about $75 a year on your electric bills.

Multiscan, multisync, multimode. This kind of monitor can switch between several kinds of video modes easily, making it simpler to get your monitor to work with your video card. Technically, a multiscan monitor is one that supports several resolutions. A multisync monitor can adjust its refresh rates for all the various resolutions it supports. A multimode card is capable of "fudging" older video modes such as CGA or Hercules Mono if for some reason you're using a program that requires such a mode.

DDC. Monitors with DDC (Display Data Channel) can communicate to your graphics card, basically telling it exactly which resolutions/number of colors the monitor supports. This extra bit of communication ensures that you are presented with valid options when you attempt to configure your monitor within Windows. DDC-2 is essentially the PnP version of this same technology.

When shopping for a monitor, by all means, test it! First, go into Windows and look at all the icons. Are the ones at the middle of the screen as crisp-looking as those at the edges? Can you read the text in the title bars without a lot of effort, even at 640×480 resolution? Look at the edges of the lines onscreen. Do they bend slightly at the edges, or are they sharp and crisp?

Start a word processor such as Write or WordPad. Type a few words in a small font and look at the letters. Are they fuzzy, or sharp and easy to read?

Go into a graphics program such as Paintbrush (which comes with Windows 3.1) or Paint (which comes with Windows 95/98) and draw a big circle. If it looks like a circle and not a flat tire, the monitor probably works well with graphics. Finally, play with the monitor's controls. Does the image jump as you turn the brightness up and down? If so, that's a sign of a cheap monitor. If your monitor passes all these tests, you'll probably be very happy with it.

Shopping for a Video (Graphics) Card

The main thing to keep in mind when you shop for a new video card is that it must match the capabilities of your monitor. Otherwise, the card may not even work at all. To do that, you should look closely at the resolution capabilities and refresh rates of both the monitor and the video card.

Check This Out...

Monitor prices Expect to pay anywhere from $100 to $2,000 for a monitor. You can probably get a decent 15-inch monitor for around $230 to $300. Expect to pay $250 to $300 more for a 17-inch monitor.

Techno Talk

Watch out if you have local bus video!

Some PCs with local bus video have the video stuff built into the motherboard. Before you can upgrade, you have to disable the video thing on the motherboard and then add the video card you want to use. To do this, you have to flip a DIP switch or move a jumper on the motherboard, or change some setting in your CMOS setup. Check out your PC's manual for help on what to do—if you need help setting the DIP switch or jumper, see Chapter 27, "Fiddling with Ports, IRQs, Addresses, and Such."

Also, keep in mind that a few PCs have been given a so-called "all-in-one" design, which is not always convenient. Some such designs do not allow you to disable their onboard video. This means you will not be able to install your own video card.

When you go shopping for a video card (sometimes called a graphics card), don't let all the techie terms throw you:

Accelerator. Accelerators used to be separate, but video cards today all "accelerate," which means they have on-board chips that take over the responsibility of handling the video from the CPU. This makes the process of keeping your screen updated a whole lot faster.

VESA or VL-bus. Fits into a VL-bus expansion slot, that is, if your PC has one. A *local bus* slot provides a super fast pathway to the CPU, kind of like driving down one of those "Ride Share" lanes on the highway during rush hour—the video signal avoids the other computer "traffic" and gets to the CPU much faster. VESA local bus used to be the most common, but it has been replaced by PCI bus.

PCI. Fits into a PCI expansion slot, which you'll find on Pentium-type PCs. Like VL-bus, PCI provides a similar "super fast highway lane" to shuttle video information to the CPU as quickly as possible. PCI was not designed exclusively for video, so you can use a PCI bus slot for something other than your video card if you want.

Video RAM. On-board memory allows the video board to assemble the image before passing it on to the monitor. It also controls the amount of colors the video card can produce. Get a card with some on-board RAM—at least 2MB. If possible, get a card that uses VRAM (video RAM) memory, not DRAM (dynamic RAM), which is slower. VRAM chips are cheap and don't use parity checking. (Remember that term from Chapter 19, "Make Mine More Memory?")

AGP support. AGP is short for Accelerated Graphics Port, a special data channel that's a variation of PCI. The purpose of AGP is to allow the graphics controller to access memory directly and perform its own calculations, so it can display graphics on your monitor more quickly—especially important for 3D graphics and full-motion video. For AGP to work, your computer must have a Pentium II that supports AGP (not all do), a built-in AGP port, Windows 95 OSR/2 or 98, and of course, a video card that supports AGP.

Cheaper DRAM

There are some new DRAM chips on the market that approach VRAM performance at a lower cost. The latest PCs are all being sold with them. Certainly this is a good way to get fast, fast, fast video at an incredible price. Here they are, arranged by order of speed: EDO DRAM (Extended Data Out), VRAM, WRAM (Windows RAM), synchronous DRAM (SDRAM), Rambus DRAM (RDRAM), Multibank DRAM (MDRAM), and Synchronous Graphics RAM (SGRAM)—which is four times faster than DRAM.

8-bit, 16-bit, 24-bit, and so on. These are the number of bits used in one "word" of information in VRAM. Here's a little formula you can play with on your calculator—at the video card's lowest supported resolution, 2 raised to the number of bits equals the total number of colors the video card can display; anywhere from 256 colors to 16.7 million (2 to the 24th power). Cards that advertise 64 bits and higher don't provide more colors—they use the extra bits for faster storage and retrieval of the video image.

3D video. These graphics cards are especially designed to handle 3D graphics, such as the ones you'll find in most computer games sold today. 3D is also useful when you visit virtual reality Web sites. When these programs invoke certain functions that generate 3D images, the 3D acceleration hardware built into these cards takes over from the software, and handles the rendering job on its behalf. So-called "3D accelerators" are either built into the graphics card itself (for instance, STB's Velocity 128) or a separate card that connects to the existing SVGA graphics card by way of an auxiliary cable.

VFC or VAFC connector. These connectors allow you to add on a daughter card (a card that connects to your video card) for MPEG decoding, TV input, and so on. Nice feature if you think you'll need it.

One other important factor you need to consider when shopping for the perfect video card is whether or not that card will work with the programs you want to use. If you use Windows or OS/2 Warp, make sure the card supports that program. If you want to upgrade to Windows 95/98, make sure that it works with that, too—it should support Plug and Play (PnP). If you use DOS only, you'll have to make sure the card supplies a *driver program* to help it talk to the specific programs you run, such as AutoCAD, Microsoft Word, Lotus 1-2-3, and so on.

What's it gonna cost me? A video card costs anywhere from $35 to $300, depending on the card's capabilities. You can probably find a pretty decent one for around $120 to $200.

Shopping for a Graphics Accelerator

STB Systems, Inc. graciously supplied information and assistance for this chapter. STB's Velocity 128 is a graphics adapter whose acceleration hardware shares the same card. Included on the card is a generous supply (4MB minimum) of 128-bit SGRAM (Synchronous Graphics RAM), which is as valuable as 8MB of standard 64-bit VRAM.

Velocity 128's hardware is designed to support a Microsoft standard for graphics rendering, called DirectX 5. Software that specifically uses DirectX 5 for its rendering will receive the greatest benefit from Velocity's accelerators, whose programs run on very fast hardware instead of software in your computer's RAM. The rest of your ordinary Windows software benefits less, but still measurably, by virtue of Velocity's very high bandwidth (1600Mb/sec) and very fast memory. (If you see an accelerator card that mentions something called Direct3D, it is an integral part of DirectX 5, referring to the 3D rendering division of the software.)

You might consider investing in a dedicated adapter/accelerator like Velocity 128 if the applications you run are graphics-intensive (for instance, 3D Studio Max as opposed to just Excel), and if animation is important to what you do. Yeah, yeah, it makes for really cool-looking real-time gaming; you already know that. Do you sacrifice anything by switching to a card like Velocity? Very little, if anything. At Velocity's highest available resolutions, the output signal to the monitor is a slightly slower refresh rate than other non-accelerator cards may produce (only 60Hz); however, at lower resolutions, the output signal has a significantly faster refresh rate (120Hz). What came as a surprise to me—and may even surprise some at STB—is the fact that, with the most recent version of STB's own software drivers, Velocity 128 outperforms the resolutions and color palettes listed on its own box. Although both the box and STB's Web site state that Velocity 128 doesn't support 24-bit color, its drivers clearly make it support *32-bit color* at resolutions as high as 1152×864! The lesson here is that it helps to check out the recent magazine reviews of accelerator cards and other hardware prior to your purchasing it, for you may be able to find capabilities even the manufacturers don't know exist.

My husband tested Velocity 128 with a game designed to support this and other specific accelerator cards: Activision's Battlezone. Suffice it to say that somehow our marriage remains intact, even though I'm beginning to see less and less of him. The game has you driving a hover-tank that does battle with evil forces on the lunar surface. Battlezone renders this surface with genuine craters and valleys, based on NASA maps of the moon, in real time. The game's frame refresh rates, he says, approximate that of video tape. The accelerator card really does change the experience of the game, by giving the computer the tools to employ specific light sources at specified angles that cast definitive shadows, and that change the shading of the object in motion. Any "cartoon-ness" the virtual world may have had is eliminated.

Some of the more graphics-intensive games support a different kind of rendering standard called 3Dfx, which is neither DirectX nor a replacement for it. STB does make an accelerator card that supports 3Dfx graphics, called BlackMagic 3D. It, too, acts as both adapter and accelerator; although for BlackMagic, those functions split the card's real estate rather than share it, so the rendering and accelerating divisions of the card each have their own dedicated RAM. The result is a graphics card that is not only faster than even Velocity 128, but is substantially more expensive.

Separate, but equal

Separate accelerator cards (cards that connect to your video graphics card through a cable) come complete with their own on-card memory. How come, if the adapter card uses its own VRAM? Because if a processor on your computer does not have access to your main memory (through Direct Memory Access), and especially if a processor needs faster memory than main memory, then it needs direct access to its own memory. Think of a graphics accelerator as an associate who works with you to accomplish the job at hand. Think of memory as analogous to a "desk," where either your associate shares a desk with you or has a desk of his own. In either situation, your associate needs some space where he can perform his job. A graphics accelerator needs its own space, somewhere, where it can "sculpt," if you will, the form of the 3D image. If the graphics adapter and accelerator are on the same card, like STB's Velocity 128, then not all of its memory is used for generating the final image; some of it is being used by the accelerator hardware for 3D-rendering purposes. But if the cards are separate, then the adapter has all of its memory to itself, and the accelerator has its own separate memory bank.

Connecting a New Monitor (Difficulty Factor –10)

Connecting a monitor to a PC is not terribly difficult. First, however, you may have to put the monitor together. That is, you may have to attach the base to the monitor.

To attach a swivel base, you start by flipping the monitor over. You may notice some slots into which you can slip the connectors on the base. Do that and flip the completed monitor back over.

To connect your monitor to the PC, make sure that its power switch is off. Plug the monitor's connector into the back of the video card. Now, take the power cord for the monitor and plug that into the wall.

Plug the monitor into the back of the video card.

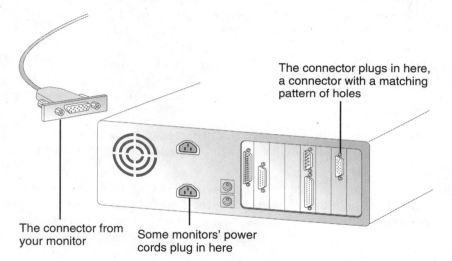

The connector plugs in here, a connector with a matching pattern of holes

The connector from your monitor

Some monitors' power cords plug in here

Adding Your New Video Graphics Card

Adding your new video (graphics) card is similar to adding any new card to your PC. Before you start, take the usual precautions: Do a backup, update your emergency disk, and so on. (See Chapter 4, "What You Need to Know Before You Open Your PC," for help.) And before you begin to work, make sure you discharge built-up static by touching something metal, such as a metal desktop or filing cabinet, or better yet, use a wrist grounding strap. Ready? Then take the cover off the PC.

First, remove the old video card. To do that, disconnect the monitor from the card. Lay out some paper on your

Plug it into the system unit instead Some older style monitors don't plug into the wall, but instead plug into the system unit. So if your monitor's plug doesn't fit into the wall outlet, don't force it. It's probably one of the types that you need to connect through the system unit. Of course, if your monitor is really that old, you should consider replacing it.

desktop. Unscrew the retaining screw holding the card in place. Once again, make sure to discharge any static before continuing. Grasp the video card at the top and gently pull it straight up. Lay the old video card on the paper for now.

Change your Windows driver first

Before you start taking everything apart, you may want to change the display driver to something friendly, such as its generic VGA driver. This keeps you from seeing junk when you start Windows (this applies no matter what version of Windows you use). Later on, you can switch to the new video driver you install. If you need help, see Chapter 26, "Getting Windows to Recognize Your New Toy."

If your PC doesn't have a video card per se (its video is handled by a special chip on the motherboard), you have to turn off your old local bus video chip first. Check your manual; this usually requires some switch setting and jumper pulling, or possibly some CMOSing. If you need help, see Chapter 27.

Next, unwrap your new video card. Before you touch it, discharge any built-up static and then remove the video card from its static bag. You can put the old card into this bag to keep it safe, if you want.

If you're putting the card into a different slot than the previous card (for instance, into an unused VL-Bus or PCI slot), then set it down on the paper for now. Restore the slot cover for the old slot and screw in its retaining screw. Remove the retaining screw from the slot you want to use with your new video card and remove the slot cover. There! Now you can insert the new video card.

Hold the video card at the top with both hands and position its connectors over the expansion slot. Press down slowly until the video card slips into place. Screw the retaining screw back in.

Connect the monitor to the card and turn the PC on to test your connection. If everything works right, turn the PC back off and put its cover back on. Now you need to install your *driver*; you'll find this on the disk that came with the video card. The driver is the program that helps your PC talk to the video card so it can translate its signals properly for the monitor. If you need help installing the driver for DOS or Windows, see Chapter 26.

Adding a Dedicated Adapter/Accelerator Card

Installing a dedicated adapter/accelerator card is not much different from installing an ordinary SVGA adapter card. STB's Velocity 128 provides you with a CD which you play *before* you begin the installation. This CD features a digital manual (actually an Adobe

Acrobat file) that gives you a tour of what you are about to do, before you start. You leave the CD in the drive as you take apart the computer and replace the card (using the procedure described earlier). When you turn the computer back on, Windows' Plug and Play will load Velocity's drivers from the same CD.

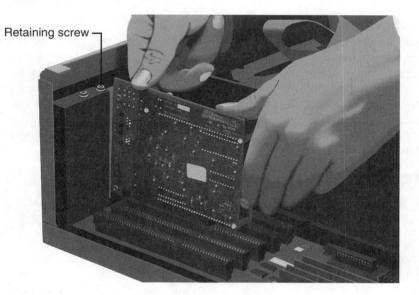

Retaining screw —

Push your video card into place.

Adding a Separate Accelerator Card

Although it isn't always obvious even from looking at the box, some so-called "graphics accelerator cards" are designed to be *supplements* to your existing graphics card rather than replacements for it. Both cards occupy separate positions on your computer's PCI bus, but a separate cable outside of the bus connects the graphics adapter to the graphics accelerator. But for this to work, your existing graphics adapter card needs the capability for something called a "pass-through cable" to be installed. (Modern adapter cards, such as those made by Creative Labs and STB Corp., have this pass-through capability.)

You don't need to remove any of your existing hardware before you add your new stand-alone accelerator card; it plugs into any open PCI slot. But there will be one pass-through cable that connects the adapter card and the accelerator card, whether it's inside or outside of the computer. An inside cable will be a gray ribbon cable, like the one used to connect your drive controller to your drives. Your graphics adapter card will need to have a series of pairs of metal posts that the ribbon cable will clamp over, equal in size and shape to the connector on the accelerator card. Not all adapter cards have this digital extension connector, and for those that don't, the inside cable connection won't work.

Graphics adapters that support an outside pass-through cable to connect it to an outside accelerator are generally manufactured by the same company as the outside accelerator.

Creative Labs brand adapters, for instance, are built to support Creative Labs brand accelerators. In such a situation, after you've inserted and secured your accelerator card and affixed the retaining screw, there's a short, round patch cable that plugs into the outside of your accelerator card. The other end of this cable goes into the pass-through connection on the outside of your adapter card, which is the plug on the adapter card where the VGA monitor cable is *not* plugged in.

Many brands of both graphics adapters and accelerators have worked out a method where some other device from the outside can have access to the card on the inside. One end of a converter cable is threaded through a small round hole in the metal slot at the back of the card. Inside, the cable is plugged into the digital pass-through connector (again, a series of pairs of metal posts sticking up). Outside, the cable may be plugged into some other cable, or into a plug adapter that accommodates some other cable, which leads to the device seeking direct access to the card—perhaps a digital camera (which I talk about in detail later in this chapter).

Upgrading Mistakes to Avoid

If you're having trouble with the monitor, first check to make sure that you properly connected it to the PC, and that none of the pins on the connector are bent. This is usually the trouble if your monitor suddenly starts showing one color, or no colors at all.

Check to make sure that the card fits properly in its slot. If necessary, take the card out and put it back in again. Check to see if there are any switches or jumpers on the card that you have to set to make it work. PCI video cards usually take their IRQ assignment from the particular slot they are in; so you might try re-slotting the card if you end up having an IRQ conflict.

If you just added a video card and it doesn't work, make sure you've disabled any on-board video controller. If yours is a VESA local bus/PCI combo system and you're trying to use a VLB card, take it back and try a PCI video card instead.

If you use Windows 3.1 and you've set your system to a high color depth, you may run into problems if you have too many icons in a single group. At high color resolutions, each icon takes up a lot of video memory—which, under Windows 3.1, isn't very large. So video memory gets eaten up quickly, and you're left with some funny-looking (often completely black) icon-squares. Try upgrading Windows or cutting down on the number of icons you place in each program group.

If you are always adjusting the size and position of the onscreen image, there may be something wrong with the timing of your graphics card. You can usually adjust this using the setup program that came with the card itself.

If you use Windows and you're having a reoccurring problem with your video, such as the system locking up or a junky display, you may have an outdated video driver. Check online (on the Internet) or with the manufacturer for an update.

If your screen seems to flicker and you have a non-interlaced monitor, the problem could be that the refresh rate is set too low. Sometimes, however, you have to change to a lower resolution (for instance, down to 800×600 from 1024×768) to get a higher refresh rate. Check your monitor's manual for details. You can set the refresh rate higher using either the video graphics setup or the Display icon in the Windows Control Panel. While you're there, make sure that Windows has the correct monitor type listed. If not, your video card may think your monitor is more limited in its refresh/resolution settings than it actually is. In addition, make sure you installed the most current version of the video driver for your video card.

Adding a Digital Camera or a Video Capture Board

With a digital camera, you could capture a still image and import it into your computer. Once there, you could manipulate that image (color correct it, blend or distort part of it, and so on), then print it out on a specially designed color printer. Or you could include the image in an email message, a document, or a multimedia presentation. But the most popular use of digital cameras is to supply photos for inclusion on Web pages. For example, a real estate agent could take pictures of all her clients' homes and put them out on the Web to increase their marketability. So if you're into Web page creation, a digital camera is pretty essential nowadays.

Of course, you could take a picture with a standard camera and use a scanner to bring it into your computer, but you would waste a lot of time taking the picture, having it developed, and then scanning it in. With a digital camera, you can do all these things in a few simple steps, and of course, the "processing" is free. (Some cameras even let you record sound with your images!)

Of course, there are limits: a digital camera captures images and saves them with a particular *resolution*. You remember resolution from our earlier discussion about monitors; it refers to the number of pixels (dots) that make up an image. The more pixels, the more distinct and better defined an image appears. So a digital camera that captures 1024×768 images has a higher resolution and better quality images than a camera that uses 640×480 resolution. This comes at a price, however. The cameras that offer higher resolutions can store fewer images than the lower resolution cameras. Why? Because images with less detail take less memory to save. Most cameras come with removable cards that you can use to store additional images. Of course, keep in mind that you only have to store the images until you can download them into the computer—so being able to capture more images at one time, but in a lesser resolution, may not be such a big benefit to you.

Also, some cameras offer JPEG compression, which enables them to store digital images in less space. Making an image smaller for JPEG format requires the computer to use a technique called *lossy compression*. Unlike ZIP or the compression technique used for GIF, you lose some of the image's quality; so this is not necessarily a good thing, unless your goal is to capture lots of photos. Most cameras allow you to select the level of compression (if any) that you want, usually through some button, or later, through your computer software.

313

Digital cameras, by the way, plug into either a serial, parallel, or SCSI port (depending on the brand), and some even use USB (Universal Serial Bus) and FireWire ports as well (see Chapter 3, "Now, Let's Find Out What Kind of Computer You Have," for details).

To install a digital camera, you run the setup program that comes on the accompanying disk. Then you select the compression level you want on the camera, select the level of zoom (if applicable), and shoot your picture(s). To upload the images to your PC, connect the camera to the proper port on your computer (such as the serial port), then use the accompanying software to transfer the images to your PC's hard disk. Once there, you can adjust the images as needed, then print them out if you like. Clear the images from the camera's memory, and you're ready to start again.

Cool. How much?

Digital cameras range from $300 to $1,900, depending on their resolution, onboard memory, and extras such as sound capture capability, JPEG compression, flash, and zoom. Don't be fooled into trying to get by with the camera that's typically included in a video conferencing kit; these digital cameras are definitely not the take-it-with-you kind. They're often made to sit on top of your monitor, and generally take fuzzy, black-and-white images that are suitable for video conferences, which is okay, because that way, the other party can't see that you aren't wearing any pants.

Most photo quality printers will run you anywhere between $200 and $2,000, with the medium-quality printers costing about $500.

Video capture boards run from $100 to $300, depending on whether they capture still or full motion video.

With video capture boards, you have a choice of capturing still images from a video source (such as your video camera or the TV) or capturing full-motion video. Capturing full-motion video (think: movie) takes up a lot of hard disk space and memory, so it's not for everyone. But they do make a cool addition to your Web pages.

In addition, there are low-end video capture boards specifically designed for video conferencing—here, the point is not to capture high quality video images, but to transmit a usable picture across phone lines to your colleagues far away.

To install a video capture board, follow the procedure outlined in Chapter 4: Take the normal precautions for opening your PC (perform a backup, update your emergency disk, and so on), then locate an empty expansion slot and insert the card. Just like many cards, a video capture board contains jumpers or switches that let you set its IRQ; this, of course, can't conflict with some other device's IRQ. See Chapter 27 for more info.

Check This Out...

Since when are all movies silent movies?

Many people invest in a high-quality video capture device and a graphics card that outputs to a TV or VCR, only to forget that the best movies (at least, the best ones produced in the last 70 years) have sound. Video cards have nothing to do whatsoever with sound. To use your computer to capture, digitally edit, and output to video tape a movie that has sound, you need a more-than-adequate *sound card* to handle the job of processing the sound. An ordinary 8-bit beepity-beep-beep sound card made for such games as "Dueling Fat Worms" will not be appropriate. As long as you're making the investment, you may as well look into a good wavetable sound card (see Chapter 24, "Sensational Stereophonic Sound," for details).

Upgrading Mistakes to Avoid

With digital cameras, keep in mind that the number of pictures you can store in the camera is directly related to the level of compression you select. *And* the level of compression you select controls the quality of the image you capture. The higher the level of compression, the less precise the image.

In addition, the level of compression controls the maximum size of the printed image, because the level of quality goes down as the compression goes up. So if you choose a high level of compression for an image, you will not be able to reprint that image in as large a size as you might like. Check with the camera's documentation for specifics.

If you have problems getting your video capture board to work, it may be conflicting with other devices in your PC. See Chapter 27 for help.

If you notice the playback on your captured video is rather choppy, the problem may not be with your video card. When Windows accesses your hard disk drive, it has to "lock down" certain resources that other devices (for instance, certain video capture cards) might share. So if you've set up Windows to defragment your hard disk in the background, the resources used for capturing video segments may be "locked down" while Windows is moving bits of your hard disk around—a bit like diverting traffic on the major streets while the President's motorcade passes through. When you're capturing video, make certain your operating system isn't otherwise occupied, to assure you of the best quality clips.

Adding TV to Your Screen (TV Input)

With a TV tuner card and Windows, you can display TV images onscreen, in a tiny window. You can also watch TV in a full-screen display (which is handy for when your boss is out of town). (Some tuner cards only output to a full screen; so if that's inconvenient for you, be careful when you're shopping for tuner cards.) If you like to keep tabs on CNN or C-SPAN or even the weekly soaps, you can do it, without leaving your precious PC. You can also use one of these cards to capture live video images from the TV input. Some video cards, such as the Stealth64 Video TV card, combine the features of a sound card with TV input. In addition, a lot of cards allow you not only to watch TV but to listen to FM radio; your choice.

Most TV input cards attach to the VFC/VFAC connector on your video graphics accelerator card. To play the sound that accompanies the TV video, you'll need to connect the card to your sound card through its line-in connector. Of course, you will also need to connect the card to some kind of TV input, such as your cable, or even your video camera.

With the software that comes with your TV input card, you can typically channel surf, scan closed-captioned text for keywords, and capture video images.

What'll it cost me? A decent TV input card will run you about $100 to $200.

Most TV tuner cards are installed the same way you would any other expansion card. Make sure you take the normal precautions before opening up your PC—make a backup, update your emergency disk, and so on. Then open the PC and insert the card as explained in Chapter 4.

Connect the card to the your video graphics card, then run a cable from the audio out to the line-in connector on your sound card. Connect the video source to the video-in adapter on the TV input card. Then run the setup program that comes with your TV input card.

Some TV tuner cards actually aren't "cards" at all in the traditional sense. Instead, they are attachments to the *outside* of your existing graphics card. Installation is almost too simple to be printed in this book: You unplug your SVGA monitor cable from the back of the adapter card, then plug the TV tuner contraption into that connector. You then attach the monitor to one side of the TV tuner, and your coaxial cable to the other side. End of story.

Upgrading Mistakes to Avoid

Because video signals degrade quickly, make sure that the PC is located fairly close to the video source. Add an inline amplifier to the video input if needed to boost the signal.

If you're not getting any sound, double-check your connection to the sound card.

Adding PC to TV (TV Output)

With PC-to-TV, you can send what's normally displayed on your PC monitor to a television screen, enabling you to present your data to a larger audience. You can get a PC-to-TV converter for your desktop or your laptop, allowing you to give dynamic, multimedia presentations anywhere, even in a client's office. You can also record your presentations onto video tape if you like, so you can replay them anywhere. In addition, most PC-to-TV converters include a remote that enables you to zoom in, pan, and freeze particular parts of your presentation.

The TV converter is not a card; in fact, it doesn't even require one. Instead, it's a box that intercepts the signal that would normally go from your graphics adapter card to your monitor, and instead sends it to at least one, sometimes as many as four (depending on the box), TV output devices. To install your PC-to-TV converter, connect it to your computer, then to the TV. Most converters do not even require you to run a setup program—set the TV to channel 3 or 4, like you would when using a VCR. Then connect the converter to a power source (some connect to your keyboard input and steal power from your PC), and you should be ready to play!

Upgrading Mistakes to Avoid

If you're not seeing any image at all, make sure the converter is getting power, then double-check the connections. Also make sure the TV is set to channel 3 or 4.

When you turn on the TV, your monitor may get out of whack; that's because the video signal is being adjusted to a different frequency for proper TV viewing. You won't really be able to do much about this, except maybe replace the monitor with one that can handle a larger range of frequencies. Until then, turn the monitor off.

The Least You Need to Know

When choosing a new monitor and video card, remember these things:

➤ Make sure your monitor and video card will work together. Compare resolutions and refresh rates.

➤ *Resolution* is determined by the number of pixels that appear—the higher the resolution, the more pixels. *Dot-pitch* is the distance between pixels. The closer the pixels are, the better the image.

➤ *Refresh rate* is the rate at which the screen image is refreshed, or updated. The faster that's done, the less flickering you're likely to see.

➤ *Interlacing* is a process where the image is updated by painting the even rows of pixels first, then painting the odd rows.

➤ A *multiscan* or similar monitor can handle several different types of video resolutions, which makes it easier for you to find a video card that will work with it.

➤ Most video cards today are accelerators; they include a chip which takes over the PC's video business so the CPU doesn't have to bother with it.

➤ *VL-bus* is a special kind of expansion slot that enables the video signal to shoot straight from the video card to the CPU. This makes things appear onscreen faster.

➤ *VRAM* is a special kind of RAM chip that is faster than ordinary DRAM chips. It is used exclusively in the memory of a video card.

317

Chapter 21

Replacing a Floppy Drive

In This Chapter

➤ Adding a new drive to your system

➤ Replacing drives you can't fix

➤ What to look for when shopping for a drive

➤ Installing the darn thing

Disks come in two basic sizes: 5 1/4-inch and 3 1/2-inch. Older PCs typically contain only one 5 1/4-inch floppy drive which is pretty inconvenient these days; most people use 3 1/2-inch disks because they hold more data, and they fit more neatly into a shirt pocket. To be able to install certain driver programs supplied by expansion hardware manufacturers, and to share data with coworkers, your PC will need a 3 1/2-inch drive. (Actually, to install most application programs and to be really cool, your PC must have a CD-ROM drive, too—but that's another chapter.)

Is it still alive? Before you give up on an existing drive, see Chapter 11, "Easy Repairs for Peripherals," for ways in which you might be able to save it.

Of course, even if your PC has a 3 1/2-inch drive, that doesn't guarantee that your troubles are over. That's because the darn things not only come in different sizes, but also different *capacities*. Low-density drives can only read and write low-capacity "double-density" disks, which means that if your PC uses a 3 1/2-inch low-density drive, it can read only disks with a capacity of 720KB. (Low-density 5 1/4-inch disks have a capacity of only 360KB.) Low-density drives can't read high-density disks, such as 5 1/4-inch 1.2MB disks, or 3 1/2-inch 1.44MB disks. So if your PC has only low-density drives (which, admittedly, is pretty rare), you'll want to upgrade to high-density drives soon. (Yes, you read right, "double-density" is the lower of the two.) Oh yeah, even more rare are ED, or extra density 3 1/2-inch drives. They read 2.88MB floppies, but they never caught on. If your PC has one of these drives, you'll know it because the disks are expensive and nearly impossible to find.

If you're not sure whether your drive is high-density, format a disk and see how much free space is listed after the formatting is done. If you have a disk that you know is double-density (it's marked "DD" or "2D" someplace) and you can't format it using just the plain vanilla FORMAT command, chances are you have the high-density floppy drive—which, if you'll remember, is a good thing. Another way you can tell: Take a look at the disks your drive normally uses. High-density 3 1/2-inch disks are usually marked HD someplace, and they have two tiny holes, one on each side of the disk. A high-density 5 1/4-inch disk *does not have* a colored ring (a hub ring) around the inside edge of the circle that's located in the middle of the disk.

Shopping for a New Drive

Assuming you need to add a new floppy drive after looking at the pros and cons listed in Chapter 2, "What Makes Your Computer Tick, and What It Takes to Upgrade Each Component," and also assuming that you're not trying to add one to a laptop (which is pretty darn near impossible), then it's time to go looking for your new toy. Before you go shopping for your drive, however, take a scout team and assess the situation:

➤ *Does your PC have an open drive bay?* If not, you can replace your existing 5 1/4-inch drive with a combo (dual) drive that crams both a 5 1/4-inch drive and a 3 1/2-inch drive in the space that one drive normally takes up. Or, you can add an external floppy drive that sits on your desk and attaches to your PC through a parallel port (the same kind of connector that you use to attach a printer—of course, this option works only if you have two parallel ports, or if you don't have a printer). As a third (and perhaps a bit radical) option, you could simply remove the 5 1/4-inch floppy drive—you probably aren't using the thing anyway.

The cost

A new high-density 3 1/2-inch floppy drive runs about $45 to $50. A combo (dual) drive runs about $90, and features both sizes of disk crammed into one drive. External floppy drives cost around $180.

If you're running out of drive bays and you're thinking about adding a tape backup at some point, you may want to consider the new 3 1/2-inch disk drive/tape drive combos that are new on the market. They retail at around $200. Both disk and tape drive parts use the same floppy drive controller, so for a tape drive, they're relatively easy to install, provided of course, you're not already using the extra floppy controller for a second floppy disk drive.

➤ *Do you really need a floppy disk drive?* Sounds silly, but as large as some files are these days, you might be happier with larger-capacity drives, such as these:

Iomega Zip™ and SyQuest EZ™ drives, which use relatively inexpensive magnetic disk cartridges about the size of a 3 1/2-inch floppy disk to record around 100–230MB worth of data. These are actually more like single-platter hard disks, so they're less volatile than tape cartridges.

Magneto-optical "MO" drives, which use a magnetic head to store data that is read optically from a shiny optical disk enclosed in a cartridge. Because an MO is read optically like a CD-ROM, your backup data is non-volatile (less likely to degrade over time). In the 3 1/2-inch drive, an MO drive can store either 128MB or 230MB (or both), though the cartridges for both types are different. In the 5 1/4-inch drive, an MO drive may use any of several capacities of cartridge, ranging from 600MB to 2.6GB.

No assembly required (or wanted) When shopping for an external floppy drive, make sure you buy one that is already assembled, with a built-in power supply. Look for a connecting cable, too. Also, it should come with a disk that contains software for updating your BIOS if needed. (An external floppy drive, by the way, will not be bootable.)

LS-120 drives, which do use a laser but, surprisingly, not for reading or writing data. The "laser servo" (what the "LS" stands for) is used to position the drive's read/write head over the *magnetic* (not optical or MO) disk, allowing for more accuracy and much higher storage densities. An LS-120 drive can read both 120MB floppies, and standard 3 1/2-inch floppy disks. However, if you want this drive to act as drive A, and you'll need to boot from such a drive, you will most likely have to upgrade your BIOS to a version that is flexible enough to register 1736 tracks on a device that normally reports 80. If your computer uses a so-called "IDE floppy controller" (which is *not* the IDE hard drive controller) then you can replace your existing floppy with the LS-120 without replacing any other hardware. If your existing floppy controller doesn't meet the IDE standard, however, you will have to install a special LS-120 controller in place of your floppy controller.

➤ *What size are your drive bays?* Most drive bays today are half-height, which means they are half the height of the older bays like the ones you find in an XT or some AT-type PCs. Half-height bays are about 1 1/2 inches tall, although a full-height bay is 3 inches. If you have a full-height drive, you'll need to get a cover plate and adapter kit to help you adapt today's half-height drives to fit it. The good news is that these cover plates are not terribly expensive.

➤ *How are your drives mounted?* Do your current drives ride rails, or are they held in place by some screws along the side? If your drives use rails, then you'll need to make sure the drive you purchase has its rails included in the box. Otherwise, you'll need to purchase them separately. (If you're replacing a drive, you can reuse its rails to mount your new drive—no need to get new rails.)

*How are the drives
attached to the PC?*

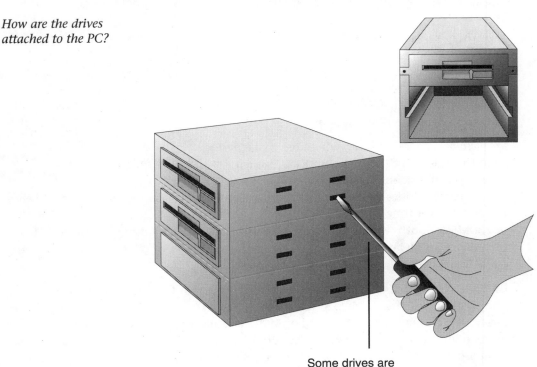

Some drives are
screwed directly into
the drive bay

➤ *Will your floppy controller cable accommodate your new drive?* While you have the PC open, check to see if your existing floppy controller has an additional connector for a second floppy drive (most do). Look at your current floppy drive; there you find a fat ribbon cable leading from it to the floppy controller that is located either on the motherboard or on an expansion card. If you see a connector located in the middle of this cable leading nowhere, then you have the connector you need for your new floppy drive. Otherwise, you need to replace this cable with a *standard floppy controller cable*; if you get this, you'll have the two drive connectors you need. Also, keep in mind that your new floppy may have either a pin connector (a connector with two rows of holes into which the drive connector's pins are inserted) or an edge connector (a connector that has a slot instead of holes, into which the flat-edged drive connector fits—it's similar to the bottom edge of an adapter card). The cable in your PC needs to support the type of connector on your floppy drive; otherwise, you need to get a converter (most drives include such a converter in case you need it, but ask if you're not sure). Some cables contain both pin and edge connectors.

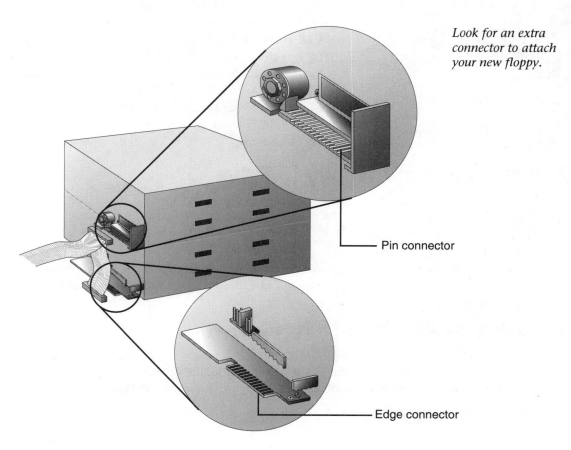

Look for an extra connector to attach your new floppy.

Pin connector

Edge connector

323

PS/2 and Compaq drives If you own a PS/2 or a Compaq PC, chances are that it requires you to buy that brand of floppy disk drive, and *no other*. These PS/2 and Compaq drives will probably cost you a bit more than generic drives—but they're the only ones that will work in your system. You can probably find used ones quite cheap.

You may be out of luck Adding a high-density 5 1/4-inch drive to an older PS/2 may prove impossible: Its BIOS does not support it, and finding a replacement BIOS is difficult.

➤ *Is there an open power connector?* Check your power supply and locate an open power connector. Running from the power supply are several connectors, each with four tiny wires and a white plastic tab at the end. Look for an open one to connect to your new floppy. In addition, make sure the open connector is the right size—most new floppy drives use smaller, mini-connectors. If you don't find an open power connector, you have to get a *Y-adapter* to split the power connection to the existing floppy drive in two so you have an open connection.

➤ *Check your DOS and BIOS.* I mentioned this in Chapter 2, but it's worth mentioning again. To control a 3 1/2-inch drive, you'll need at least DOS version 3.3 or higher—but if you want one that uses ED (extended density) 2.88MB disks, you'll need at least DOS 5.0. You can check your DOS version by typing **VER** at the DOS prompt and pressing **Enter**. If your PC is really, really, old, there's a small chance you'll have to upgrade your BIOS to run a 3 1/2-inch drive. (Of course, with a PC this old, why upgrade it at all?) Check the owner's manual, call the manufacturer, or check CMOS to see what floppy drive options your PC can handle.

Putting Your New Floppy in Drive

After you bring your new floppy drive home, it's time to connect it. To install an external floppy drive, you usually connect its cable to an open parallel port. Then connect the power cable, turn it on, and you're set (except for running the setup software, that is).

To install an internal drive, prepare your system in the usual way, following Chapter 4's instructions: Run a backup, update the emergency disk, and so on. Then turn the power off, open up the PC, and discharge any static electricity you've built up, or strap on your grounding wrist strap.

Removing the Old Drive (If Needed)

Now, if you're replacing a drive, remove the old drive by disconnecting its data cable and then its power cable. The data cable is a wide, flat ribbon cable, and the power cable is made up of four separate wires with a small white connector on the end.

Drivers: dream or nightmare?

Using a driver to update your BIOS may sound like a dream—after all, you don't have to mess with CMOS or the BIOS chips themselves. Using a driver creates certain problems, however. For example, your computer has to load the driver into memory first, before it can activate the drive. Therefore, you can't use a driver for drive A, because then you can't boot from A in an emergency. The drive doesn't "exist" until the driver is loaded, and that doesn't happen until you boot the computer.

Also, a lot of backup and utility programs take over total control of floppy drives when you activate them, and they ignore any driver programs in memory. This makes them incompatible with your driver–run floppy disk drive. As a final irritant, driver programs usually assign some bizarre letter to the floppy drive, such as E: instead of what you expect, such as B:, which makes working with them a headache. In addition, the drive letter they assign can change if you add another hard drive or IDE device or logical partition.

However, sometimes a driver is the only thing that will get your new floppy to work in your system. Because of this, most floppy drives come with a software driver that you can install if needed.

Remove the cables from your old floppy drive.

Next, remove the four screws along the sides of the drive that hold it in place. Slide the drive out the front of the PC. Remove the two rails on the drive (if any) and attach them to the replacement drive.

Preparing the New Drive

If you're not replacing a drive but simply adding a new one, then you still need to do some preparation. First, remove the faceplate or bezel that covers the empty drive bay. You can usually do this by gently prying it off with a flathead screwdriver. Keep the faceplate; it makes a great bookmark, or it may actually come in handy later if you ever remove the drive. If the bay uses rails to connect the drive, attach a set of rails to either side of your new floppy drive. You may find a pair of rails in the open drive (some manufacturers have thought ahead here), or you may have to purchase a set yourself. Other drives don't use rails at all; instead, you screw the drives directly in place. In that case, ignore this rail business. Some drives have you attach a mounting plate to the bottom of the drive, other PCs have removable cases or metal boxes in which you place the drive, prior to placing the entire case into the system unit.

If your new drive is of the 3 1/2-inch variety, you need to mount it into an adapter so that it fits into your regular 5 1/4-inch drive bay. (Of course, if your PC has a 3 1/2-inch bay, you can dispense with this nonsense.)

Attach the drive adapter to your 3 1/2-inch drive.

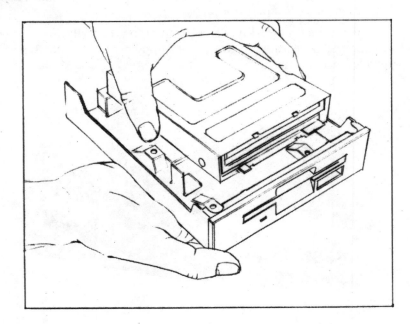

Next, you have to deal with the cable adapter that converts the drive's pin connector to an edge connector, so it works with the rest of your system. This usually entails simply connecting the cable on the drive adapter to the pin connector on the 3 1/2-inch drive. Sometimes it gets a little harder, and you have to plug a converter board into the back of the drive. In any case, after you connect the converter, screw the drive into the adapter.

You get the best success if you screw in each of the screws just a little and then adjust the drive so you can easily insert and eject a disk out the front. After the drive is set properly, tighten each of the screws. Attach drive rails (if needed) to the drive adapter assembly.

Now, if your new drive is drive B, then remove the terminating resistor. It's not too hard to find; it's usually marked TR or T-RES. Look for either a lone chip, a jumper, or a set of DIP switches. If the drive is a 3 1/2-inch drive, forget the terminating thing because it doesn't come off. You only have to remove the TR from a 5 1/4-inch drive that's acting as drive A. In other words, remove the TR only if the drive is *not* located at the physical end of the cable, which is drive B's usual position.

Connecting the Cables

Okay, now that's over, so slide the drive about halfway into its bay and connect the power cable and the data (ribbon) cable. One end of the data cable has a twist in the ribbon itself; this connector identifies drive A. The other non-twisted cable connects to drive B. If you're adding a dual drive (combo drive), connect it as drive A. Make sure that you don't connect the ribbon cable backwards—align the striped edge with the number 1 pin on the connector. (If you look at the numbers on the connector, you see that there are lower numbers at one end.)

> **Techno Talk**
>
> **Swapping drives?** If you want your new drive to act as drive A, it's easy to do. First, make sure you cable the two drives properly—the twist in the data cable must be connected to drive A. Then change your CMOS info. Some newer CMOS menus actually have a swap floppies option, which allows you to keep the data already entered for your original drive A, and swap it with the info on the new drive. This saves you the trouble of reentering the data for both drives.

If you don't have an open power connection, disconnect the power connector from the existing floppy drive and connect a Y-cable to it so you now have two connectors. Reconnect the power to the existing drive and then use the remaining open connector on the new drive. If needed, attach the converter to the power connector so it can be attached to the smaller mini-plug on your 3 1/2-inch drive. Again, make sure that when you connect any data cable, you align the striped edge of the ribbon with pin number 1 on the connector. In any case, the power connector is *keyed*, which means it can only go on one way (assuming, of course, that you don't try to force the issue).

Screwing the Drive in Place

After the drive is in place, slide it the rest of the way into the bay and screw it in. Now's a good time to make sure you don't mount the drive upside down. The door on a 5 1/4-inch drive closes downward; a 3 1/2-inch drive doesn't have a door; but it has a release button located on the lower left. Most drives have four screws (two on each side). If the drive is not mounted on rails, this can get a bit tricky; just line up the holes on the drive with the holes on the side of the bay and turn each of the four screws just a little. This gives you a little "play" so you can line up everything okay. After you correctly line up the drive, screw everything in the rest of the way.

Connect your new drive.

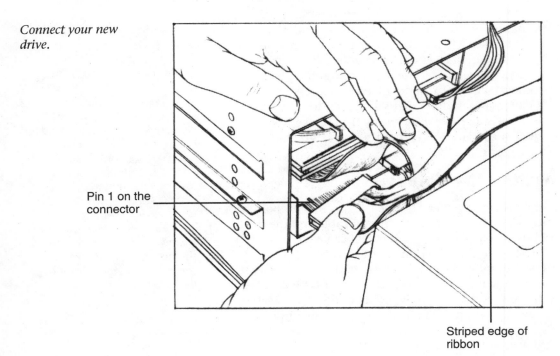

Pin 1 on the connector

Striped edge of ribbon

Messing with CMOS and Testing Your Drive

Now that it's connected, test your drive. Turn the power back on and see if it can read a disk. If you added a *new* drive, you probably have to flip a switch, move a jumper, or mess with CMOS so that the PC acknowledges it first—see Chapter 27, "Fiddling with Ports, IRQs, Addresses, and Such," if you need details. After everything's okay, turn the power back off and close up your PC.

Upgrading Mistakes to Avoid

If your new drive doesn't work, don't panic. First, check the connections and make sure they're tight. Also, check to make sure you didn't flip the ribbon data cable and connect it upside down—the striped edge of the ribbon aligns with pin 1 on the connector. In addition, make sure that none of the pins is bent, and that all of them are inserted properly into the connector.

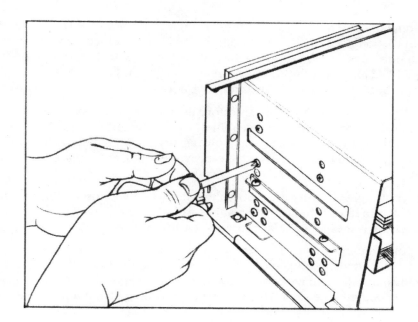

Screw your drive into place.

·After checking the cabling (Is it backward? Is it inserted correctly?) and the position of the twist in the ribbon cable (the cable with the twist is for drive A), you should check your CMOS information to make sure you entered it correctly.

If drive A and B are reversed, you need to swap the data (ribbon) connectors of the two drives to straighten things out. (To test which drive is A, go to a DOS prompt and type: **DIR A:** and press **Enter**. The A drive will light up.) Remember that the data cable with a twist in the ribbon connects to drive A. For example, if you want your new 3 1/2-inch drive to be drive A, then place the connector with a twisted cable on drive A, and use the other connector on the data cable to connect drive B.

If neither drive is working now, you may have accidentally set them up with the same letter. Usually, this nonsense is taken care of by the twist in the ribbon cable; the drive closest to the twist in the cable is assumed to be drive A. This twist reverses the DS (drive select) setting on the drive. Normally, each drive comes from the factory set up as drive B. When you plug the cable with the twist in it into your first drive, it changes to become drive A.

When you work with a PC that is designed to have only one floppy drive, and you add a cable to create a second connection, neither cable has a twist in it. So both drives become drive B. To fix this problem, make sure that drive A has its DS jumper or switch set to the lowest setting, which is usually 0 or 1. Set drive B to the second DS setting, which is usually 1 or 2.

If you installed a dual or combo drive (one of those thingies with both a 5 1/4-inch and a 3 1/2-inch drive in it), you need to do some fiddling to tell the PC which one is supposed to be A and which one's B. (If you need help telling which one is which, jump to the DOS prompt and type **DIR A:** and press **Enter**. The A drive will light up.) Look in the manual for help on this one, but it'll probably tell you to move a jumper on the drive somewhere.

If you notice that the drive keeps showing a directory listing of an old disk, and not the current one, you may have set the disk change (pin 34) setting incorrectly. Again, you need to enable this setting for all drives except a low-density 5 1/4-inch drive (it has a jumper on it). Also, this could be a sign of a data cable gone bad. Get a replacement and try again.

If you notice that your higher-density drive doesn't realize when you insert a low-density (double-density) disk into it, or it has trouble reading and writing to low-density disks, the media sensor setting is messed up. Make sure the setting is *enabled* (on).

If your PC's really old, you may have to update its BIOS so it will recognize the new drive. If you have a software upgrade, run its setup program to update the BIOS. If you bought some new BIOS chips, install them with the help you find in Chapter 16, "Replacing the Motherboard." If you bought a new controller card, you need to install it and connect the new drive.

The Least You Need to Know

When you go out shopping for a new floppy disk drive, here's what to look for:

➤ Before you go shopping, check to see if you have an open drive bay. If you don't, consider replacing your current floppy with a combo drive, or adding an external floppy disk drive.

➤ If you have older full-height drive bays, you need a cover plate and adapter to fit the new half-height drives into it.

➤ If your drives ride the rails, be sure to get a pair of rails when adding a new drive.

➤ Check to see if you have an open connector on the floppy drive data (ribbon) cable. If not, replace that cable with a standard floppy connector cable.

➤ Check also to see if there's an open power connector. If not, again, you should get a Y-adapter.

➤ If you're adding a high-density 3 1/2-inch drive, check to see if your DOS version is at least DOS 3.3.

➤ Check your PC's manual to see if the BIOS accepts newer 3 1/2-inch drives.

➤ Keep in mind that some PCs, such as Compaqs or PS/2s, require that you buy their specific drives, and not a generic one such as Teac.

➤ Adding a floppy drive to a laptop is pretty difficult. Avoid doing this if possible.

Adding a CD-ROM or DVD-ROM Drive

In today's market, a CD-ROM drive is basically a necessity. It's becoming darn near impossible to find programs that you install using 3 1/2-inch disks, because it costs manufacturers a lot less to put their programs on a single CD-ROM, rather than a billion disks. When you do find a program that's sold in both disk and CD-ROM, the CD-ROM versions often include extras you don't get in the disk version; so it's worth your while to add a CD-ROM drive for that reason alone. If you need more incentive, when you're not installing software, you can use your CD-ROM drive to entertain you with music while you work.

Check This Out...

Can this old drive be saved? If you're looking to replace a CD-ROM drive, see Chapter 11, "Easy Repairs for Peripherals," for ways in which you might be able to get some more life out of it.

Check This Out...

So what'll it cost me? You can find a good CD-ROM drive for $45 to $90, depending on its speed: from 16x to 32x (x represents the spin rate of the first CD-ROM drive; 16x is 16 times that speed). Portable CD-ROM drives run from $300 to $400. CD-R (recordable) and CD-RW (rewritable) drives cost from $285 to $500, again depending on their speed—from 2x to 4x.

Shopping for a CD-ROM Drive

There are a lot of options to think about when buying a CD-ROM. First, you have to decide if you want an internal one that fits into an empty drive bay, or an external one that sits next to the PC. In addition, Sony offers a portable CD-ROM drive that looks like a personal CD player, but acts like an external CD-ROM drive—so your choices are wide open.

Internal or External?

To be able to use an internal CD-ROM drive in your PC, you need to make sure you have an open drive bay to use. Also, you may need to purchase drive rails that connect to the drive and enable it to slide into your drive bay. These should be very inexpensive items; don't get rooked into paying $15 or more for so-called "bay adapters." CD-ROM drives sold today are designed to fit into standard half-height drive bays, but if you have an older PC with a full-height bay, you'll need drive rails to hold the CD-ROM drive in place. If you don't have an open drive bay, you can buy a combo floppy drive (which combines a 5 1/4-inch and a 3 1/2-inch floppy drive into one unit) or a combo floppy and CD-ROM drive (which combines a 3 1/2-inch floppy drive with a CD-ROM drive in one unit). Combo drives save you a drive bay, and they also save you a bit of money, too. You could, of course, dump your 5 1/4-inch drive, because they're not much use anymore anyway.

An external drive doesn't require an open drive bay, but it will cost you a bit more, so there's your wallet to consider. But an external drive is a lot easier to install, and you can also share it with your coworkers. In addition to an open drive bay, you'll need to make sure your PC has an open power connector for the drive. If it doesn't, then you can get a power splitter (y adapter), and split the power going to some other drive (but not your hard disk—that would be a very, very, baaad idea.) You may also need to upgrade your power supply, if you're adding a CD-ROM drive and a sound card to an already taxed system. See Chapter 17, "Powering Up the Power Supply," for more info.

If the size of your wallet is the most important factor

If cost is the most important factor for you when purchasing a CD-ROM drive, then consider getting a multimedia package, which includes a sound card, speakers, and a CD-ROM drive at one low price. But beware if you decide to get a sound card with a connector for a SCSI CD-ROM: If you want to upgrade your sound card later on, you'll be limited to a sound card that can run your particular SCSI CD-ROM drive. If you can't find such an animal, then you'll need to purchase a separate SCSI adapter card to run the CD-ROM drive.

If you buy a multimedia package that includes a sound card with a connector to an IDE CD-ROM, you won't have a problem if you upgrade the sound card later on. First of all, your IDE CD-ROM will be compatible with any sound card you get that has an IDE connector. And if you decide to purchase a sound card with a SCSI connector instead, you can always connect the CD-ROM to the "slave" end of the IDE connector, where drive C: acts as your "master."

If you're thinking about DVD, now may be the time. DVD players can also play CD-ROMs (albeit at slower speeds than the current 12x average), saving you money with a single all-purpose drive. But DVD-ROM discs have substantially higher capacity; and, with some extra software, they can play DVD movies on your PC monitor. For more information on DVD, see the upcoming sections later in this chapter.

What Speed?

Next, decide what speed you can afford to buy: currently, CD-ROM drives come in 16x, 18x, 24x, and 32x speeds. A 16x drive is 16 times as fast as the original CD-ROM drives were. A 32x drive is twice as fast as that. (Kinda. See the sidebar for the real details.) Of course, they cost more too. Another way to increase drive speed is to include a cache, which allows it to access frequently used data quicker. Most drives come with a 128KB or 256KB cache.

What about my laptop? If you have a laptop and a desktop PC, consider an external CD-ROM drive designed for use in both. These usually come with a PCMCIA connector for a laptop, and a SCSI connector for your desktop PC.

How fast is X?

The x in 16x and 4x refers to the spin rate of the CD; the first CD-ROMs spun at the same speed as conventional audio CDs. So 4x is four times this speed. Because a 1x drive transfers data at 150Kb/sec, then a 4x drive transfers data at 4×150Kb, or 600Kb/sec. This is pretty dependable way to compare drives, at least those 12x and under. You see, CD-ROMs under 12x spin at variable rates, so they can *transfer data at the same rate,* regardless of whether that data is located at the inner or outer most edge of the CD-ROM. This is a good thing generally speaking, as long as you can ignore the noise the drives make as they constantly adjust their speed.

CD-ROMs over 12x use a *constant velocity*, which means that they don't speed up when the read/write head is over the outer edge, as opposed to the center of the disc. Because of this, data transfer rates fluctuate: with a 16x drive for example, you'll get a lot less than 16x data transfer speed whenever the drive's reading data at the center of the disc (something like 6x). Unfortunately, data is placed on a CD-ROM from the center out, so unless the disc is full, you won't *ever* achieve 16x speed. Yech! The best solutions to this problem are the combo drives, such as the 12x/24x drives, which combine both speed technologies to get the fastest overall data transfer rates.

When comparing two drives of similar speed, you should look at all factors: transfer rate, access time, and seek time, as explained in the next sidebar. By the way, the drives being advertised today as 100x are definitely not that, but 12x drives using a hard disk cache, which is something you could set up for any drive, provided you had enough free hard disk space.

Words, words, words

When you go shopping for a CD-ROM drive, salespeople will throw a lot of terms at you, such as *data transfer rate*, *access time*, and *seek time*. Well, the data transfer rate is the rate at which the PC can receive data from the CD-ROM, usually measured in kilobytes per second—here, the higher the number, the better. The seek time of a CD-ROM drive is a measure of how long it takes (on the average) for the PC to find stuff on a disc—not to read it, just to find it—obviously, the lowest seek time is most desirable. Access time (average seek time) is how long it takes for the drive to respond to the PC's request for data by finding that data and sending it on to the PC (the lower, the better).

Other Options to Look For

One option to look at is whether or not the drive includes software that enables your PC to play audio CDs. This may not be a big factor, because Windows 95 and Windows 98 includes just such an item, called CD Player, accessible through the Accessories menu. In addition, Windows 3.1 includes a program called Media Player.

You may also be interested in asking whether the drive supports Kodak Photo CDs. For example, you can have your travel photos and such put on a Photo CD, so you can view them onscreen, use them as a background in Windows, or import them into a word processing document or an email message. A Photo CD is not just for fun and games; it's a pretty nice feature for a real estate agent who wants to use it to store photos of homes for sale, or for someone who works with lots of graphics. Most CD-ROM drives can display photos placed on a CD in a single session. However, to be truly compatible with the Photo CD format, a drive must be listed as XA compliant.

Should I look for Plug and Play?

If you're using Windows 95 or Windows 98, you may want to make sure that your CD-ROM drive is Plug and Play–compatible, which guarantees that Windows 95/98 can work with it. (Most drives today are PnP, so I wouldn't worry too much about this.) Plug and Play (PnP) is a system that enables operating systems like Windows 95 or Windows 98 to automatically recognize a new device as soon as you plug it in and, at least for the most part, "install" that device's supporting software. Don't let PnP be the deciding factor, however; lots of CD-ROM drives work perfectly well with Windows 95/98 even though they are not listed as Plug and Play. In particular, if you buy an IDE CD-ROM, it will automatically identify itself to your BIOS (you'll learn more about this feature later in this chapter). Also, keep in mind that Plug and Play requires three elements to work: an operating system such as Windows 95/98, a Plug and Play device, and a BIOS that supports PnP. If your PC was manufactured prior to 1994, chances are it does not have a PnP BIOS. Of course, you can always upgrade the BIOS, too (see Chapter 16, "Replacing the Motherboard," for the details).

When choosing your new CD-ROM drive, consider whether or not it includes a *caddy* for loading. The cheaper ones don't, making them a bit less sturdy, but perfectly fine (they use a tray into which the CD is placed, instead). The main consideration here is if you plan on mounting the drive vertically, rather than horizontally. In that case, a caddy is needed to support the disc so it can be read consistently. So if you plan on mounting the drive vertically, spend the bucks to get a caddy-loaded CD-ROM drive. A caddy is also helpful in faster drives, which benefit from the extra stability.

CD-ROM drives that use a loading tray are sturdy.

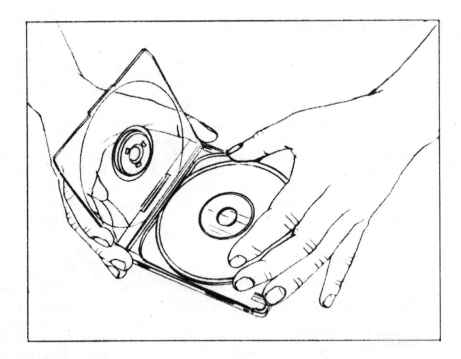

If you want to give multimedia presentations that use lots of CDs, you may want to consider a drive with a CD-ROM changer. A changer holds several discs at one time and switches between them as programmed, without making you switch discs yourself all the time. Of course, this feature makes the CD-ROM drive cost quite a lot more: from $100 to $265 for a 4–5 disc changer with a speed of 12x or 16x.

The Business of Which Interface to Choose

An important feature to consider is the type of interface the CD-ROM drive uses to communicate with your PC. CD-ROMs sold today typically follow one of two interface schemes: either SCSI or IDE (sometimes called ATA IDE, ATAPI IDE, PCI IDE, or EIDE—for an explanation of some of the differences between these standards, see Chapter 2, "What Makes Your Computer Tick, and What It Takes to Upgrade Each Component"). So how do you choose? (External drives, by the way, may use a parallel port, or if designed for a laptop, a PCMCIA port.)

SCSI

Well, if you choose SCSI, you'll need to make sure that the CD-ROM drive comes with a SCSI adapter to connect your CD-ROM drive to your PC. Sometimes you can kill two birds with one stone by getting a sound card that supports SCSI and then connecting your SCSI CD-ROM drive into it. If you plan on using your CD-ROM with an existing

SCSI controller, make sure the two are compatible. Many aren't. Just keep in mind that of the two, a SCSI adapter is gonna cost you more than an IDE adapter.

IDE

Now, before you run out and choose an IDE CD-ROM drive, there are some other factors to consider, some of which may send you running back for SCSI. Modern day CD-ROMs have adapters which meet the specifications of EIDE, which means that they are an enhanced version of typical IDE (Integrated Drive Electronics). IDE, you may recall, is the most common type of hard disk available, so chances are pretty high that you've got one of them in your PC right now. IDE can support up to two devices, so if you only have one hard disk, you can plug your EIDE CD-ROM drive into the open connector, and you won't even have to worry about buying any kind of extra card.

EIDE

An EIDE adapter on your system does not make your IDE or EIDE CD-ROM any faster than it already is. If you purchase an EIDE CD-ROM, you can install it on your IDE-based system with no problem. Part of what makes EIDE "enhanced," however, is its inherent wider bandwidth for devices that will eventually come along to support such bandwidth. Only now are CD-ROMs being manufactured whose maximum transfer rates or "burst rates" approach those of the fastest hard disk drives (33.3MB/sec). These are the so-called "100x" CD-ROMs. Originally, "1x" was roughly equal to 150KB/sec; but if you do the math, you find that the meaning of the "x-factor" in CD-ROMs is gradually being lost. At any rate, CD-ROMs only sustain these maximum transfer rates for short periods of time anyway; their average, or "sustained," transfer rates are somewhat slower, and are often disproportionate to their burst rates.

The final quarter of 1997 saw the rise of the first CD-ROMs whose sustained transfer rates actually bumped against the maximum supported transfer rates of the IDE interface. So you will not feel as much of a benefit with a so-called 100x CD-ROM on a standard IDE interface adapter as you will with an enhanced IDE (EIDE—especially an ATA-3) adapter. That is, if you're timing your applications with an atomic clock. But an EIDE CD-ROM will work because it is compatible with IDE on all levels.

It's certainly a simple matter, however, for you to get a new EIDE adapter to go along with your new drive. You'll spend between $50 to $120 for the adapter; the more expensive models have extra cache memory. The new adapter will allow you to take advantage of the speed of your new CD-ROM, while also allowing you to plug up to four total devices into it. You see, besides speed, EIDE also improved on the old IDE limit of only two devices. Make sure you get an EIDE adapter that supports four devices, because believe it or not, there are slightly cheaper EIDE adapters that only support two devices anyway.

One more alternative

Instead of buying an EIDE adapter, you can purchase a so-called IDE sound card and plug your CD-ROM drive into it. (IDE has nothing to do with the sound card, just the connection *on* the sound card.) You might also want to purchase the two together in a multimedia kit to save even more bucks. But again, if you connect your CD-ROM to a sound card, you're tied to it. Upgrading your sound card later on may be a pain, because you'll have to find one that supports your CD-ROM drive. If you already have one EIDE adapter on your system that supports four devices, the IDE adapter on your sound card will most likely not work; you'll probably need to disable it with a jumper setting.

If your PC already has two IDE hard disks, well, then you'll have to get the EIDE adapter card whether you like it or not.

Anyway, after you get the adapter, you'll have to disable your old IDE hard disk controller and reconnect your IDE hard disk(s) to this new adapter card. That's because your PC can't handle two hard disk controllers (the EIDE card and your old IDE controller) at the same time. This assumes that you can disable the IDE controller; on some older PCs, there's no way to do it. So for some, this whole IDE business may be more trouble than it's worth, and you're better off with SCSI. On the other hand, IDE CD-ROM drives are usually less expensive than their SCSI counterparts, so it's worth a minute or two of investigation before you decide.

PCI IDE

Also, if you have a newer PC that features a PCI IDE local bus, then a matching IDE CD-ROM drive (sometimes called EIDE) may be a better choice for you than SCSI, because it can hook into your local bus and run fast, fast, fast.

Aaaiiii! More letters!

IDE, you may recall, is a standard for controlling hard disk drives. Well, it's been adapted into a local bus scheme that enables it to "drive" just about any device you plug into it at a faster rate than a VL-bus (VESA local bus). As a local bus, PCI IDE costs more, so you won't find it on your PC unless you've got a 486 DX4 or a Pentium, Pentium Pro, or Pentium II. If you have an older 486, you'll probably find a VL-bus instead.

Do You Need to Record Anything?

CD-R drives are capable of recording data on a CD-ROM disc *one time*. This makes it effective for archiving your data files, especially large graphic files (if you happen to work with them, that is). CD-Rs hold about 650MB of data.

You'll be able to find a CD-R drive that is compatible with both IDE (EIDE) and SCSI interfaces. A CD-R drive is installed the same way as regular CD-ROM drives, so just follow the same steps as you would for an ordinary CD-ROM. You can even find CD-R drives that connect to your PC's parallel port.

If you want to use and reuse a disc you create, then you need a CD-RW ("Re-Writable") drive instead. You could use a CD-RW drive as your backup solution, copying (and recopying) your important data onto it at periodic intervals. For now, your CD-ROM drive cannot read discs that you've recorded with CD-RW, and vice versa; the formats, contrary to what the name seems to imply, *are not compatible. Yet.* By the time this book goes to press, Philips and Hewlett-Packard will be introducing its new CD-RW standard, called MultiRead, which changes the way future CD-RW discs are written so existing CD-ROM drives can read them. Problem is, this technology is built into the next generation of CD-RW drives, and it doesn't appear the present generation can be retrofitted.

Get on the same bus

To reduce the amount of errors you may encounter when trying to record (burn-in) a CD-ROM, try to place both the hard disk that contains the data and the CD-ROM drive on the same controller. This reduces the possibility of contention problems from other computer activities.

The exception here is if you plan on copying data from a CD-ROM onto the disc you're creating. In such a case, put the two drives on *different* controllers.

Now That You've Bought One, Here's How to Install It

The way you install a CD-ROM drive depends, of course, on whether that drive is an internal or external one. Also, if you're replacing a busted drive, you'll have to remove the old one first. To remove a CD-ROM drive, make sure you prepare your system following the instructions in Chapter 4, "What You Need to Know Before You Open Your PC." Then, turn the power off, open up the PC, and discharge that darn static electricity.

Now, to remove the old drive, start by disconnecting its data cable first (that's the wide, flat ribbon cable). Next, remove the audio cable if there is one; it's the small cable on the left. Finally, remove the power cable; it's got four separate wires with a small white connector on the end. It might be kinda hard to remove, but just wiggle it back and forth a little, and it should come out fine. Just don't pull the power cable by its wires; pull it by the white connector instead. Next, unscrew the drive and slide it out the front of the PC. If the old drive uses drive rails, remove them and screw them into the new drive.

Well, now that you've got that out of the way, there's one more thing to do before you can install the new drive.

Installing the CD-ROM's Controller Card

Whether your drive is an IDE or a SCSI CD-ROM drive, it must connect to some type of *controller*. This will be either an EIDE adapter, a SCSI card, or a sound card, depending on the drive that you chose.

Second controller If you plan on connecting your CD-ROM drive to your PC's secondary IDE controller, make sure you run your CMOS setup, and enable the second controller.

Follow the usual presurgical procedures: Make a current backup, update your emergency disk, and get rid of any static electricity. Then open your PC.

Setting Up a SCSI Controller

Before you insert the card, make sure that it's set up properly. For a SCSI card, this may mean setting a jumper or two to set the IRQ, DMA address, and SCSI ID. Usually, you should not change anything at all, but instead, jot down the default settings and compare them to similar settings for your other devices. If you find an IRQ conflict, for example, then you need to change the IRQ setting in the SCSI card. I can't help you much on this one; you've got to figure out what IRQs other devices are currently using and then select a unique one for this drive. See Chapter 27, "Fiddling with Ports, IRQs, Addresses, and Such," for more help.

If you're installing a sound card with your CD-ROM drive, well, skip to Chapter 24, "Sensational Stereophonic Sound," for details.

Setting Up an EIDE/IDE Controller

If you're installing an EIDE card, make sure that the switches are set correctly. Usually you can leave the first set of switches as is; but the second set of switches controls the second connector, so you may want to mess with them. You see, even if you're connecting just one hard disk and one CD-ROM drive to the EIDE card, you'll probably want to use both connectors, because the slowest of the two devices on a cable determines the speed of both devices. There's no sense slowing down your hard disk just because the CD-ROM drive can't keep up, so put them on separate connectors. If you're using two hard disks and a CD-ROM drive, put both hard disks on the first connector, and the CD-ROM drive on the second.

Anyway, to turn on the card's second connector, the last set of switches must be set to "on."

I don't have an EIDE card, but I have an EIDE drive!

Uh, before you get too confused, you might not have an EIDE card unless you elected to buy one. You see, if your system only has one IDE hard disk, you can attach your CD-ROM drive to the extra connector, and you're done.

If you did buy the EIDE card, then you have to disable your original IDE controller. Open up your PC and grab the data cable for your hard disk—it's not hard to spot; it's the flat, wide ribbon cable attached to the hard disk. Follow it back to wherever it leads—either to a multifunction expansion card, or to the motherboard itself. Somewhere near this location is (hopefully) a jumper that you can pull to disable the IDE controller connector. You definitely need to check the manual for help with this one—you don't want to pull the wrong jumper and end up disabling something else. You may be able to disable the IDE controller through CMOS.

If you can't find a way to disable the IDE controller, then you're out of luck. Better pack everything back up and trade it in on a SCSI CD-ROM drive.

Installing the Controller Card

To install the card, unscrew the retaining screw for the slot you want to use and remove the slot cover. Hold the card at the top with both hands and position the edge connectors on the bottom of the card over their slots. Gently press the card into place with just the right amount of downward pressure. (Don't force the card into its slot.)

Installing an Internal CD-ROM Drive

Now, you're finally ready to install the drive. Again, before you touch any part of your PC, make sure you've banished the static guy by grounding yourself first. With the cover off, remove the faceplate for the drive bay you've chosen. It's sometimes part of the cover, and other times, it's part of the case itself. You can usually stick a flathead screwdriver just under the rim of the faceplate to pry the thing off.

If You're Installing a SCSI CD-ROM

If your new drive's a SCSI, you've got to set its switches. These things control the SCSI address for each device in the SCSI chain (number 0, 1, 2, and so on). Just set the drive to a number that doesn't match that of any other SCSI devices in your PC. By the way, the adapter has an ID too; it's usually set to ID 7, so choose something else for your drive, such as 6. (You may be able to set the ID number for the SCSI adapter through its software setup program.)

Gently press the expansion card into its slot.

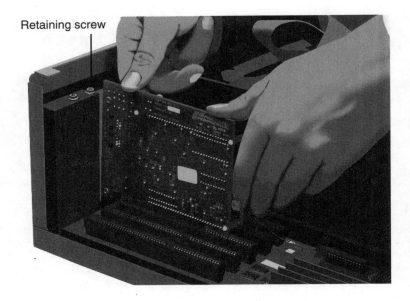

Retaining screw

Also, you've got to remove the terminator on this SCSI drive if it's not the last one in the chain. You see, each SCSI device in your PC connects to the same SCSI controller card. One end of the SCSI chain is at the controller, and the other end terminates with the last device. Between the controller and this last device (whatever it is) there may be up to six other devices.

Now, SCSI devices come with something called a *terminating resistor*. Nothing fancy; just a little plug-thing—but it's there to stop (terminate) the SCSI signal at the end of the chain. If your CD-ROM drive is one of these middle guys, you've got to remove its terminating resistor for the SCSI signal to continue to other devices further away from the controller. You're looking for a jumper or a chip called T-RES, or just TR. After you find it, just pull the T-RES plug off of the drive. Of course, if your CD-ROM drive is the last guy you plugged into the cable leading from the controller, then leave the terminating resistor *on*.

If You're Installing an EIDE CD-ROM

If your new drive's an IDE drive, then you may need to change some settings before you insert it. You need to set a jumper on the drive to designate whether this one's a master or a slave. The master in this case is the first IDE drive, while the slave is drive number two. If you plan on putting your hard disks on one connector cable and the CD-ROM drive on another, then your CD-ROM drive can remain set as "master" even if one hard disk on the other connector is also a master, because the CD-ROM drive is the only device on that cable. If you connect the hard disk and the CD-ROM drive to the same cable, then set the CD-ROM drive to "slave." Check the manual for details, but this usually involves moving one simple jumper.

Some devices have a Cable Select Mode (CSM) option, which you can use with a special Cable Select Mode cable, to avoid having to jumper each drive as master or slave. Both drives on the same cable must support this, however. Also, the cable costs more, and you may have to set a jumper to enable Cable Select Mode, so the whole thing is rather silly, really.

Connecting the Cables

After you've got it all set up, slide your spankin' new CD-ROM drive into the open bay. Don't bother to screw it in yet; you've got to plug the thing in first.

There are three cables you've got to plug in. Start with the power cable (the one with the white connector). You probably have a free power cable running from the power supply. If not, you'll need to get a Y-adapter to split one connection into two. Make sure you connect the power cable correctly; if you don't you can do serious damage to your new drive. Luckily, the power connector is usually notched so it can only go in one way.

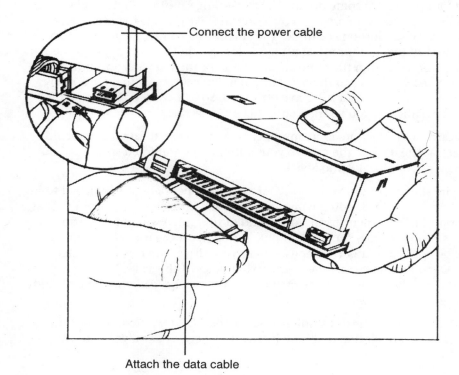

Connect the power cable

Attach the data cable

Plug in your CD-ROM drive.

343

Next, connect the data (controller) cable (the big fat one). The other end is attached to whatever card you're using to control the CD-ROM drive: SCSI card, sound card, or EIDE controller. The red-striped edge of the cable should match up with the pin marked 1 on the connector. Some thoughtful manufacturers use a triangular arrow to show you which way is "up." Be careful; on a lot of sound cards, there are multiple data connectors, keyed to specific brand CD-ROM drives, so check with the sound card's manual for help.

Finally, if your CD-ROM drive has an audio cable, plug it in. The other end goes into your sound card (you do have one, don't you?), or into the audio connector located at the upper-right corner of the EIDE card. Although this is officially a cable, by the standards of other such cables that you've installed thus far, it's really nothing more than a covered wire. It's often in blue or brown spaghetti sheathing, and is about as flimsy as these wires can possibly get. There are tiny plugs on both ends. The plug that has the clip on it goes into the CD-ROM, generally in a tucked-away corner. Look at the top of your CD-ROM drive for a diagram that tells you where this sound plug is located. If there's no diagram, look for two or four tiny metal prongs in a row, generally on the back end. You might find both two *and* four prongs on some drives. The two-prong set is for digital audio connection; the four-prong set is for analog. You won't mistake one for the other, and your sound card will only support one of these. The clip on the connector going into the drive will face up. A set of two or four metal prongs is located on the sound card. Where the tiny colored wires emerge from the main sheath, look for the red wire, and turn the connector so the tiny red wire faces to the *left*. Although you can't blow up anything by plugging this cable in wrong, you can still have no sound. So as a word of advice, don't bolt down your PC cover before you've tried out a CD on your speakers.

Beware: The EIDE card can't function as an amplifier, so you'll have to run a patch cord from the output jack at the back of the card to your amplifier or amplified speakers. You can find a patch cord at your local Radio Shack.

If you see a *green* wire sticking out of your CD-ROM and that's permanently attached to it, *that's not the sound cable*. It's a grounding wire that, while not crucial to its operation, may be crucial to its survival in a thunderstorm. At the end of this green wire is a brass antenna lead, which is simply a brass "O." Pick a spot, any spot, on the unused portion of the metal cage inside your computer that houses all of your drives, then place a small screw through the O, and screw it into one of the fixing holes of this cage. Next time you forget to ground yourself during an upgrade operation, you may be glad you remembered to screw down this grounding wire.

Good job. The patient's alive (at least, I think so). Screw the CD-ROM drive in place and close up the PC. But don't attach the final bolts to the back yet until you've heard the sound of music.

Wait, you're not finished yet

After you install your new drive, you should start your PC and run the setup program for your card (if you added one) and then run the setup program for your drive. The setup program for your IDE CD-ROM drive should install two drivers in your configuration files: MSCDEX (a Microsoft driver for your CD-ROM's file system), and the specific driver that runs your CD-ROM drive. Without these two drivers, your CD-ROM won't work. If you use Windows 95 or Windows 98, it doesn't need the MSCDEX driver, so it will automatically remove it if it finds it. In addition, when you go into CMOS to tell it that it has a new baby drive, and you select the option **autotype** your IDE CD-ROM drive will respond by telling Setup that it's a CD-ROM. If your BIOS is old, it won't have this option, and you'll need to try calling your drive a type "0," which should be enough to tell it that the drive is a CD-ROM. Some BIOSes are stubborn, however, and they force you to enter information such as the number of tracks and sectors manually, which in the case of a CD-ROM, are equal to 0.

If you're installing a SCSI drive, you'll still need to run some kind of setup program to install the SCSI adapter driver (for the SCSI controller card) and the SCSI CD-ROM driver.

Also, if you use Windows 98, Windows 95, or Windows 3.1, there are some additional last-minute things you'll need to do to get Windows to acknowledge your new drive. See Chapter 26, "Getting Windows to Recognize Your New Toy," for help.

Installing an External CD-ROM Drive

Adding an external CD-ROM drive is rather simple, because you don't have to get your hands dirty opening up the PC's case. Of course, you might have already had it open to install the controller card for your CD-ROM drive. Oh, well.

In any case, with your PC closed up, attach the cable to your CD-ROM drive. Then run the cable to the connector on the card, be it sound, IDE, or SCSI. Actually, because a SCSI cable can accommodate multiple devices, you may only have to attach your SCSI drive to any open connector on the existing SCSI chain.

Also, if your drive's a SCSI, then you'll need to set its SCSI address (device 0, 1, 2, and so on). That's done by moving a simple jumper or switch on the back of the drive. See the manual for help. Also, depending on the drive's location along the SCSI chain, you may need to remove the drive's terminating resistor. Basically, if your CD-ROM drive's not at the end of the SCSI chain, you remove its resistor. See the details on installing an internal SCSI drive for more help with this one.

Connect your drive to its controller card.

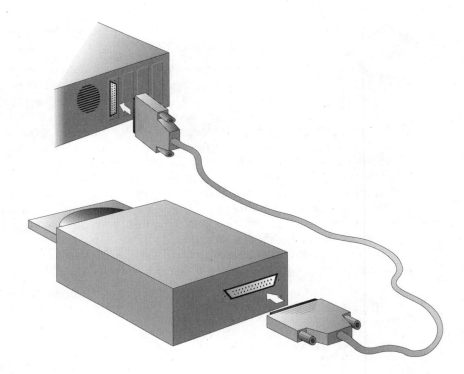

If you're installing an external IDE CD-ROM drive, you'll need to install an external connector in place of the retaining clip covering one of your unused expansion ports. You see, IDE wasn't originally supposed to be used externally; external IDE drives are a new thing. The ribbon cable part of the connector adapter stays inside your computer, and either plugs directly into your IDE or EIDE controller, or into your IDE ribbon cable at the point where an internal drive would go. Outside your computer, a 37-pin DB cable, looking a lot like your printer cable, attaches the affixed connector adapter to your external drive. This cable comes with your external drive.

If your CD-ROM is the third IDE device in your system, you'll need to replace or override your existing IDE controller with a new EIDE adapter card. Your existing IDE controller may be located on the motherboard or on a multifunction card. Also, make sure that you've set your external IDE CD-ROM drive to be a master because it'll be the only device running on its particular connector. There is no slave to an external IDE device.

Finally, plug your drive's power cord into a surge protector and turn it on. (This is especially important if you're installing a SCSI drive, because the PC won't recognize it if you don't turn it on first.) Start your PC and run the setup programs for the card and the drive. In addition, you may need to make changes to your CMOS, if it doesn't automatically detect the new drive. See Chapter 27 for help there. Also, if you use Windows, you need to do some setup stuff to get Windows to acknowledge your new drive. See Chapter 26 for how-tos.

Upgrading Mistakes to Avoid

➤ If the drive's not working, make sure that you've connected it correctly, and that you've chosen the right IRQs and such. See Chapter 27 for help.

➤ If you're installing an IDE CD-ROM drive and you've connected it to your sound card, but it doesn't work, try connecting the CD-ROM drive to the second IDE connector on your hard disk cable. Some PCs have trouble dealing with two IDE controllers (in this case, the one on your sound card and the one that runs your hard disk), so putting both IDE devices (the hard disk and your CD-ROM drive) on the same controller solves the problem. Go figure.

➤ If you're using an external CD-ROM drive, make sure that it's turned ON before you turn on the PC.

➤ If the drive's still not operating, make sure that you've run the setup program for the drive. When you start your PC, does it load the drivers correctly, or do you see an error? If the drivers are trying to load into high memory through the CONFIG.SYS or the AUTOEXEC.BAT, try taking out the LOADHIGH or DEVICEHIGH command so they load into conventional memory instead. See Chapter 26 for help.

➤ Gotta problem running an audio CD? Make sure you have a program that enables your CD-ROM drive to play audio discs. Have you installed your sound card, and did you remember to connect your CD-ROM drive to the sound card? Did you turn on the external speakers, and play with the volume knob? Are you using the software program that enables your CD-ROM to play audio CDs? Windows 95 and Windows 98 come with CD Player, which will do just that.

➤ Many of the games you'll play on your PC are still DOS-based, regardless of the preponderance of Windows. For that reason, you'll want to install the so-called *real mode drivers* for your CD-ROM, so it will be a recognized device when you exit Windows and go to your DOS prompt. But it might be a mistake for you to install those drivers while you're in Windows, because the commands which invoke those real mode drivers will be added to the AUTOEXEC.BAT and CONFIG.SYS files that are run each time you start Windows. Your Plug and Play CD-ROM drivers—which Windows 95 and Windows 98 *will* run to recognize your CD-ROM—should override any real-mode drivers that CONFIG.SYS may happen to include. But sometimes, the real mode driver and the PnP driver will conflict with one another, causing the operating system to crash.

➤ Maintaining startup files for DOS mode that are separate from Windows was supposed to be one of Windows' key features; but for some reason, not every Windows 95 does this, and Windows 98 absolutely does not. What Windows 95 will do, guaranteed, is execute any commands you add to the DOSSTART.BAT file each time you exit to DOS. DOSSTART.BAT is located in your \WINDOWS directory. You can use Notepad to edit this file; and if it's not there at all (who's to say?) you can use Notepad to create it. Any real mode drivers you need for DOS to understand your devices—for instance, MSCDEX, which indexes your CD-ROM, or your mouse drivers—can be loaded by this DOS batch file. The command that calls up your real mode CD-ROM driver should be added here; but here's another problem: Most real mode drivers are .SYS files, designed to be invoked by CONFIG.SYS at startup. Batch files such as DOSSTART.BAT cannot invoke .SYS files—only .EXE, or pure executable, files. So you need a real mode CD-ROM driver that is an .EXE file, whose command can be appended to DOSSTART.BAT. If your CD-ROM didn't come with one, you'll need to download it from its manufacturer's Web site. Creative Labs' new .EXE version of the real mode driver for CD-ROMs, attached to its Sound Blaster cards, can be downloaded from

```
ftp://ftp.ctlsg.creaf.com/files/creative/patches/ctload.exe
```

For instructions on how to install Creative Labs' real-mode driver, point your browser to

```
http://www.ctlsg.creaf.com/wwwnew/tech/faqs/ctload.html.
```

By the way, your real mode CD-ROM driver command should go on a line *before* MSCDEX in the DOSSTART.BAT file. This is because MSCDEX cannot index a CD-ROM device that, from its point of view, isn't there. Your driver will make it "there."

What's real mode?

This is a throwback term to the days when Windows ran "on top of" MS-DOS, as an environment that enhanced the features of DOS. For Windows back in the mid-1980s to perform true multitasking, it had to invoke a memory management feature of Intel 386 CPUs called *protected mode*. But because not all computers were 386s, Windows had to have a fallback mode for running under pure DOS. This was real mode. Today, all driver programs that follow the rules of old MS-DOS without breaking into exclusive Windows territory are still called real mode drivers.

➤ Sometimes, by loading a driver through the CONFIG.SYS file for DOS, you'll throw Windows 95/98 out of whack, and it won't recognize the CD-ROM at all. If you suspect this, REM out the driver command in CONFIG.SYS and try rebooting to see if Windows recognizes the drive. If so, then leave the driver commented out. Then, go to the Properties dialog for the icon that represents your game or other DOS program, and click the **Program** tab. Click **Advanced**, and select **MS-DOS Mode**, then select **Specify a new MS-DOS configuration**. Make the modifications here to load the CD-ROM driver. With this setup, the driver will only load when you start that program from Windows.

➤ Some CD-ROM drives won't work by themselves on their own IDE channel, so you may have to place the drive as the slave on the primary IDE channel with the hard disk as the master. (This is usually due to a conflict with PCI bus mastering and Windows 95/98.) You can also try unloading the bus mastering drivers.

➤ Another thing to check is the length of the cable; IDE cables should not be any longer than 18 inches in length, or you'll get intermittent problems with any devices attached to them.

➤ Some CD-ROM drives encounter problems running under Windows 3.1, if the 32-bit access option is enabled.

➤ Some computers that use dynamic drive overlays for larger hard disks do not like it when you place a CD-ROM drive on the same IDE channel as the hard disk itself. Move the drive to its own channel, and try again.

If You Have Trouble Recording a CD

If you're having trouble recording a CD-ROM with your CD-R or CD-RW drive, consider these things:

➤ The best way to burn in a CD-ROM is to first assemble the data on the hard disk, then start the copying process.

➤ Make sure that the source hard disk has been defragmented before you start.

➤ Use your recording software to run a test first, before you begin the burn-in.

➤ Set up the BIOS of the SCSI host adapter for the CD-R drive to "enable disconnect," which means that if some other device in the SCSI chain wrests control of the SCSI bus (the SCSI word for the circuit connecting SCSI devices) or if it loses the bus altogether, it won't stop the CD-R from completing the recording operation in progress. If the CD-R can complete the job at hand, your disc may be saved, and you might not have to start the recording process over from scratch just because someone turned off a SCSI device elsewhere. Also, concurrent SCSI operations intended for other devices can cause a data-writing to pause, and even hang indefinitely, if it doesn't have the capability to "yank itself loose," if you will, from its SCSI bus.

➤ Don't perform any tasks while the burn-in is taking place. You want the copy process to proceed uninterrupted.

➤ Restart the PC before you begin the burn-in, *especially* if you use Windows. Then shut down any programs that may have started automatically.

➤ If you use Windows 95 or 98, disable the auto detect feature for the CD-ROM drive: open the **Control Panel**, double-click the **System** icon, then click the **Device Manager** tab. Select the CD-ROM drive, and click **Properties**. Click the **Settings** tab and *turn off* the **Auto insert notification** option.

Other problems you might have with a CD-R or CD-RW drive:

➤ Some CD-R and CD-RW drives are confused as WORM drives by the operating system. This causes the drive not to be recognized. Typically, all you need to do is get an updated driver from the manufacturer of the drive.

➤ If you're having trouble reading discs in your drive, again, you may need a driver update.

Shopping for a DVD-ROM Drive

DVD (Digital Versatile Disc or Digital Video Disc, depending on whom you ask) drives have only recently hit the market—so you won't need to do a lot of shopping because there are very few drives to choose from. Currently, only DVD players are available, but expect DVD-R (recordable) drives to arrive soon.

Play it again, DVD A DVD drive can also play CD-ROM and audio CDs (and maybe eventually, CD-R and CD-RW), so you don't need to add both drive types to your system. Of course, the CD speed is not the same as the faster CD-ROM drives, but it's still pretty darn good, currently anywhere from 8x to 20x speed.

A DVD disc is similar in size to a CD-ROM, but it holds a lot more data—between 4.7GB and 17GB—versus 650MB for CD-ROM! DVD drives run anywhere from $250 to $440, and are available for both IDE (EIDE) and SCSI interfaces.

To take advantage of the multimedia capabilities in commercial DVD discs, your PC will also need a sound card capable of handling the three DVD audio formats. In addition, your PC's video card will need to support MPEG-2, the DVD video standard.

As good as it sounds, don't upgrade to DVD for the *wrong* reason. You see, since the first attempts by Sony and Philips to found the DVD standard in 1995, there has been considerable in-fighting among the companies making investments in this new technology, most notably involving Toshiba (which made an end run around Philips and tried to make a DVD standard of its own), and the movie studios that have considerable funds tied up in DVD. Perhaps you've noticed that none of the DVD movies released up until the first quarter of 1998 were made by Paramount.

What does all of this have to do with upgrading? If you're investing in DVD-ROM to be able to play movies on your computer, don't expect the abundance of movie titles that you currently have with your VCR. In fact, there may never be such abundance as long as the movie studios and technology companies continue to fight amongst themselves. Meanwhile, software manufacturers—especially game producers—will be releasing more and more titles on DVD-ROM over the next several months. One caveat: DVD video has been divided up into several regions:

No MPEG audio DVD drives do not currently support MPEG-1 audio.

➤ Canada, United States, and U.S. territories

➤ Japan, Europe, South Africa, and Middle East

➤ Southeast Asia and East Asia

➤ Australia, New Zealand, Pacific Islands, Central America, South America, and Caribbean Islands

➤ Former Soviet Union, Indian Subcontinent, Africa, North Korea, and Mongolia

➤ China

You can only play videos with the regional code that matches the regional code of your DVD player. So don't expect to buy a DVD player in Japan and play U.S. movies on it, or vice versa. The regional codes do not affect computer software or DVD-audio, although they might someday.

How DVD-ROM Installation Differs from CD-ROM

That's included! Some DVD drives come with their own controller cards; for others, you'll need to shop around.

All the real differences between a DVD-ROM drive and a CD-ROM drive are hidden inside the drive. On the outside, the DVD-ROM looks, feels, weighs, and even *installs* like a CD-ROM drive. Use the installation instructions for a CD-ROM drive given earlier in this chapter, and you'll be fine.

However, if your PC does have an MPEG accelerator card, or a graphics accelerator that performs MPEG acceleration, then it's possible that your DVD-ROM drive can play movies by overlaying its "movie screen," if you will, on top of the image of the Windows desktop being sent to your monitor. To be more precise, the image from Windows is being sent digitally by your graphics adapter card, which may or may not include an accelerator of its own. An MPEG accelerator acquires this image directly from the cable that would otherwise connect directly to your monitor, and overlays it with the analog image of your DVD movie. The movie won't show up in a window, but rather in an otherwise undecorated corner of your screen, or on the entire screen.

So you will need to connect an external VGA loop-back cable between the MPEG accelerator (or whatever card performs that function) and your graphics adapter. It's a simple process: Unplug your monitor from the adapter card, then plug one end of the loop-back cable into the monitor connector. Plug the other end into the 9-pin port on the MPEG accelerator, then plug the monitor into the 15-pin port on the MPEG accelerator.

Because a DVD-ROM has one, if not two, audio plugs, and a DVD can have movies on it, you may be wondering where the video plug is. Consider the standard data cable the video plug, because DVD movies are digital, and designed to be decoded by a program running *outside* of the DVD player. By contrast, digital CD music is decoded *inside* of the CD player, so the sound comes out of that box through an audio cable—digital or analog.

Upgrading Mistakes to Avoid

If your DVD game is not making any sounds, double-check the connection between the DVD drive and your sound card. (Remember, like a CD-ROM, you must run an audio patch cable between the drive and your sound card's Audio Out connector.)

If you can't start your system after installing the drive, double-check the connectors (especially the pin 1 thing) and make sure that you've set up the drive to be a slave, if it's the last drive on an IDE connector, or a master, if it's the first drive on the second IDE connector. If it's a SCSI DVD drive, make sure you've set the ID and the termination correctly.

An error message, `Mobius hardware not detected`, indicates that the external VGA loop cable is not installed properly. Double-check your connections.

If you detect too much red color when playing movies, try lowering the contrast on your monitor. That should fix the problem.

The Least You Need to Know

When shopping for a CD-ROM drive, you face an enormous number of choices. Use this list to help you sort them out:

➤ To save money, buy a CD-ROM in a multimedia package that includes a sound card and speakers.

➤ If you buy an internal CD-ROM drive, you'll need an open 5 1/4-inch drive bay.

➤ An external drive costs more, but it's easier to install.

➤ CD-ROMs come in several speeds. To compare the speed of various drives, check out their data transfer rates, access times, and seek times.

➤ If speed is a factor, make sure your CD-ROM drive uses a cache of at least 256KB.

➤ Make sure your drive plays audio CDs. You might also want to check that the drive is Photo CD–compatible.

➤ If you use Windows 95 or Windows 98, you might want a Plug and Play–compatible drive.

➤ CD-ROM drives that include a caddy are more stable.

➤ A nice feature to look for in more expensive drives is a CD changer, which can store several CDs and switch between them easily.

➤ If you plan on adding DVD at some time in the near future, you might not want to mess with adding a CD-ROM drive, because a DVD drive can play CD-ROM discs.

CHACKA CHACKA

Chapter 23

Maxi-Infra-Mega Storage Solutions

In This Chapter

➤ Installing a cool Zip drive

➤ Installing a cooler Jaz drive

➤ Getting your tape backup drive to work

Hard disks today have reached almost mythic proportions—some over 16GB (*gigabytes*). Hard to believe what someone might do with that much room—that is, until you load a few programs on your own hard disk and discover you barely have enough room left over for your data.

But after you upgrade your system to one of the newer maxi-mega-infra hard disks, you're faced with an even bigger problem: how to *back up* all the information that's stored on it. Or you may simply have a desire to place sensitive data on some kind of *removable* storage that you can lock up. In this chapter, I present you with two simple solutions to protecting your data: Zip/Jaz drives, and tape backups. There are other solutions you might use, although the two discussed here are by far the most popular.

There are alternatives?

In addition to Zip/Jaz drives and tape backups, you might want to consider LS-120 drives (which use disks that store 120MB each), MO or *magneto-optical* drives (which store data optically on disks that store from 600MB to 4.6GB of data), CD-R or CD-RW (a CD-ROM drive that can write data onto disc), and Syquest drives (similar to Jaz drives, but with greater capacity at 2.3GB).

Shopping for a Zip or Jaz Drive

Iomega makes two very popular large capacity disk drives: Zip drives and Jaz drives.

What do they cost?

Zip drives run $135, and ZipPlus drives cost $200. Jaz 1GB drives cost $300 to $400, depending on whether you get an internal or external version. Jaz 2GB drives run from $550 to $650. Zip discs (which hold 100MB of data, or one-tenth or one-twentieth the amount of a Jaz disc) cost about $10–$12, and Jaz 1GB discs cost $125, and 2GB disks cost $170. Although Jaz discs currently cost you more per megabyte, they're more convenient, because you have to change them less often when doing a backup, and of course, you can store more of your larger files on them.

A Zip drive can conceivably replace your floppy disk drive, and in fact, on some of the newer systems being sold today, it does just that. A Zip drive uses 3 1/2-inch disks that store 100MB each. The disks look similar to conventional 3 1/2-inch disks (which have a storage capacity of 720KB or 1.2MB, depending on their density), except they are slightly fatter. *A Zip drive cannot use conventional 3 1/2-inch disks*. Also, you can boot to a Zip drive if needed, which means that you could replace your current drive A with one, if you like.

You can get Zip drives in both internal and external versions, depending on your needs. An external Zip drive can be connected to a SCSI or a parallel (printer) port. If you want to use the drive on any PC, get the external parallel version, because most PCs do not come with a SCSI port. The parallel drive is slower, but real easy to install. Also, if you get the parallel drive, you won't have to purchase a SCSI adapter, because there's a very good chance your PC doesn't have a SCSI port.

An internal drive can be connected to a SCSI or an IDE controller, just like a hard disk. That means you'll have the same concerns here if you decide to go with what Iomega dubs an "insider." Check to make sure you have an open drive bay, an open power connector, and an open data connector to either a SCSI or an IDE controller. If your PC has an IDE controller, you can only control two devices on it. If you have a hard disk, and a CD-ROM hooked up to it, you're stuck. In that case, upgrade your system to EIDE, which supports up to four devices. If you decide to go SCSI and your system does not yet have a SCSI controller, Iomega sells some that are designed to work with their cables, which might save you an extra step.

Iomega has recently released an updated version of their drive, called the ZipPlus. The "pluses" are many, including increased performance and decreased power consumption. And, in case you were wondering, ZipPlus drives use the same Zip disks as standard drives.

A Jaz drive is basically a souped up version of a Zip drive, and with its larger capacity (up to 2GB), it is very versatile. You can use it to backup even the largest hard disks with ease; you can even use it as a sort of "removable hard disk" if you want. Jaz drives come in two flavors: original (which use 1GB disks) and jazzier (which use 2GB disks). The "jazzier" drives are also faster, by the way: for comparison, try these numbers: Zip drives have a sustained transfer rate (both read and write) of 1,063kbps (*kilobits* per second, not kilo-bytes), although Jaz drives have a rate of 5,098kbps. So Jaz are a little under five times faster.

Jaz drives are available in both internal and external versions, however, they can only be connected to a SCSI port. So if your PC doesn't have one (which it probably doesn't), you'll need to get yourself a SCSI controller card in addition to the drive.

Both Zip and Jaz drives come with their own software for formatting their disks. Of the two, the Zip drive is probably the easiest to install, because you can get a version that connects to your printer port (can't get any easier than that). Your printer, by the way, connects to the Zip drive, so don't go thinking you'll have to give up printing.

Installing an External Zip/Jaz Drive

Installing an external Zip/Jaz drive is fairly easy, especially because it means you won't have to get your hands dirty opening up the PC. First, turn off the PC. Then disconnect your printer cable from the back of your PC. Next, connect the Zip drive's cable to the printer port. Connect your printer cable to the back of the Zip drive, to the second port.

Finally, connect the power cord to the back of the drive, and then to an outlet on your surge suppressor. Turn on the drive, then turn on your PC. All you gotta do then is run the setup program that comes with your drive, and you should be ready to fly.

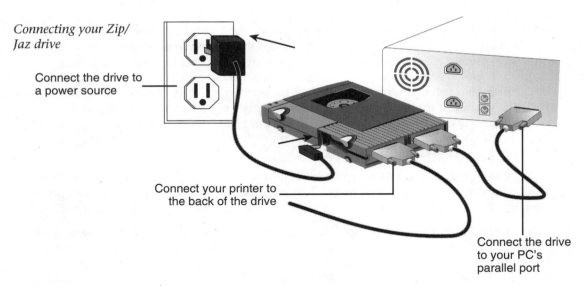

Connecting your Zip/ Jaz drive

Connect the drive to a power source

Connect your printer to the back of the drive

Connect the drive to your PC's parallel port

Techno Talk

blah blah blah blah blah blah blah

But I don't have a SCSI connector! If you don't have a SCSI connector on your PC, you'll need to get a SCSI controller card and install it. (Yech.) See Chapter 4, "What You Need to Know Before You Open Your PC," for steps on how to break open your PC and insert an expansion card.

Installing an external SCSI Zip or Jaz drive takes a few more steps. First, the drive is designed to connect to a SCSI-2 connector which has 50 pins. If your PC has a SCSI-1 (it also has 50 pins, but in addition, it has little clips on either side of the connector) or a 25-pin SCSI connector, you'll need to get a compatible cable to connect the drive to your PC. After you get the right cable, connect it to your SCSI port, and to the first SCSI connector on the back of the Zip/Jaz drive.

Next, connect the drive to a power supply using the cable that came with it. After the drive's connected, you can power it up and check it out. It may or may not work; there could be more you have to do, depending on whether you have other SCSI devices in your PC, and on how they're set up. See the next section for help there. If you pass Go and your drive is recognized okay at startup, then run the setup program from Iomega, get yourself a cup of coffee, and have some fun—you're done.

Installing an Internal (Insider) Zip/Jaz Drive

To install an internal drive, you'll need to follow the same basic steps as you would for installing a hard disk, or an internal floppy drive. So, scrub for surgery, then back up your important data, update your emergency disk, copy your CMOS settings, and so on. See Chapter 4 for how-to's.

When you're ready for surgery, open up the PC, and locate the empty drive bay you've decided to use. The drive will require a full width bay (6 inches wide), not one of those fancy schmancy mini bays some systems use. The bay should also be half-height, or 1 1/2 inches tall, or you'll need an adapter to use the drive. Get the drive ready by attaching the mounting bracket if needed (some drive bays are super small, and you might not need the bracket). In addition, set the SCSI switches on the drive as needed; the first switch sets the SCSI ID to either 5 or 6, and the second switch sets the termination. (For an explanation on these two switches, see the section, "Upgrading Mistakes to Avoid.")

If you're installing an Insider IDE Zip drive, you'll need to set it's master/slave switch to the proper setting. If you're placing the drive on the same controller as your hard disk, then you need to set the Zip drive to slave. If you're placing it by itself on the second IDE controller (that is, assuming you have two), then make sure the drive is set to master. Setting the drive to slave or master is usually done through a jumper; check your manual for details.

Cable select mode

Through the use of a special Cable Select Mode cable, and two drives that support Cable Select Mode, you can skip this master/slave jumpering business and let the system figure out which drive is which. There may be, however, a jumper setting you have to change to enable Cable Select Mode on each drive, so is it worth it? I don't think so.

Installing a SCSI or IDE/EIDE Controller Card

Discharge your excess static before doing anything inside the PC. Then, insert your SCSI or IDE/EIDE controller card, if needed.

If you're adding an EIDE controller, *and* if you plan on using both controllers, you'll need to set the second set of switches to ON, to enable the second connector on the card. You could connect two devices to the first controller, and just leave it at that, but you might not want to, because the slowest device on the controller determines its speed. So, whenever possible, connect the hard disk to the first controller (because it's the fastest device), and other IDE/EIDE devices such as a CD-ROM, Zip/Jaz drive, or your tape drive to the second controller. (Remember, with EIDE, you can run up to four devices—two on each of the two controllers.)

Get that second controller going If you plan on connecting your drive to your PC's secondary IDE controller, run your CMOS setup to enable it. See Chapter 27, "Fiddling with Ports, IRQs, Addresses, and Such," for help with CMOSing.

In addition, before you can add your EIDE controller, you'll need to disable the IDE controller already in your system. The easiest way to locate the IDE controller is to follow the data cable from your hard disk back to its source. The data cable is the widest one connected to the hard disk. After you locate the controller, look for a set of switches or a jumper nearby that you can set to disable it. You may possibly be able to disable the controller through CMOS (You may need some help from your computer manual for this.) Of course, if you can't disable the IDE controller, you're kinda out of luck, and you'll need to either connect your tape drive to it (that is, if you don't already have two devices connected to the IDE controller), or you'll have to trade in your tape drive for a SCSI version.

Techno Talk

Setting IRQs, DMAs, and so on When adding a new controller, whether IDE or SCSI, there's some setup you need to do to get the thing to work, which means messing around with IRQs and DMAs and other letters. See Chapter 27 for details.

If you're adding a SCSI card, it too requires a bit of set up. SCSI controllers have switches for all sorts of techie things like IRQ and DMA. See Chapter 27 for help with IRQs, DMAs, and other letters of the alphabet.

In addition, you need to set the adapter's SCSI ID. The SCSI ID determines where in the SCSI food chain your new drive will fall. ID 0 is for a bootable device, such as your hard disk. The other IDs (1–7) are for the rest of your SCSI devices, such as the adapter card, a CD-ROMs Zip/Jaz drive, and so on. The adapter card is usually set to ID 7, so don't change it unless you have to.

To install the card, remove the slot cover. Hold the card at the top and gently press the card into place. (Don't force the card into its slot.)

Connecting the Cables

Connect the drive's data cable to the controller. Make sure the red wire or stripe that runs along one side of the cable aligns with pin 1 on the connector. Also, make sure you use the right connector on the IDE cable; the first connector is for the master boot drive (which is probably your drive C), and the second connector is for a slave device on that IDE channel. The third and fourth connectors on the data cable are for the master and slave devices on the second IDE channel (if there is one.)

Next, connect the power cable—it's the white plug with four wires hanging off it. You'll find a bunch of power cables running from the power supply. Unfortunately, these guys are sometimes all used up, so if needed, get a Y adapter to split an existing power connector so you can run your new drive. Just make sure you split power with something that doesn't run all the time, such as one of your floppy disk drives. Don't split the power running to a hard disk. The power cable is designed to plug in only one way, but if you're trying to be careful, make sure you match up the colored wires when connecting the two ends of the power cable.

Inserting the Drive

After you've got the thing cabled, you're ready to slide the drive into place. Secure the drive in its bay with screws. You can now test your drive by powering up the PC and then running the setup program. (If you've just installed a SCSI controller, run *its* setup program first, then run the setup for the Zip/Jaz drive.) If you're satisfied that everything's hunky dory, turn off the system again, and then go ahead and close up the PC case.

Upgrading Mistakes to Avoid

If you can't print after installing a parallel Zip drive, make sure the printer cable hasn't come loose from the back of the drive. If it has, reconnect it, and then lock it tight using the screws on either side of the connector. Your Zip drive *does not* have to be ON in order for the printer to work, so don't worry about that.

With a SCSI drive, you may run into conflicts with other SCSI devices, if you have any. There are two switches on the back of the drive that might help: The first switch allows you to change between ID 5 and ID 6. You see, each SCSI device attached to your PC is given a number, from 0 to 7. All you gotta do is make sure that some other device isn't hogging the number you want to use with the Zip/Jaz drive. So, if something else is using ID 5, you can throw the switch to change the drive to ID 6. That should solve the problem. How do you find out what ID numbers are assigned to which SCSI devices? Well, you can use the utility that came with the SCSI card or the drive. Or, in Windows 95/98, you can use the Device Manager (which you can get to through the System icon in the Control Panel) to solve the mystery.

Now, before you go assigning IDs, check out the numbers you're currently using, and then place your new drive somewhere in the middle if possible. Usually, the hard disk is 0, and the SCSI adapter is 7, but not always. External devices are given ID numbers that are higher than the SCSI adapter, so if your hard disk is external, it'll have some number like 6, and the SCSI adapter might have some number like 4. If you set your Zip/Jaz drive to 5, you've got it made.

The second switch or jumper enables you to terminate the SCSI chain. Think of an invisible chain linking all your PC's SCSI devices together. There can only be one beginning, and one end to the chain; thus you need a terminator at each end of your SCSI chain. So, if your PC already has SCSI devices in it, it's likely that the chain has been terminated at one end by some other device. (The high end, SCSI ID 7, is typically used by the SCSI host adapter, which also terminates that end of the chain.) If that terminating device has an ID lower than your Zip/Jaz drive, then you're cool. (This is usually the case with a SCSI hard drive, which is typically set to 0.) If however, the device that terminates the chain has some number like 63, then the SCSI host adapter won't look below ID 6, so it won't find your Zip/Jaz drive if you use ID 5. If you have a SCSI hard disk, it most likely will be ID 0, and if it's the only SCSI device, it will also be the terminator. That's cool, if the other end of the chain is terminated at ID 7, the SCSI host adapter.

If your Zip drive falls at one end of the chain however, you'll have to remove the terminator from the old terminating device, and turn on the terminator on your Zip/Jaz drive by throwing that second switch. See Chapter 18, "Hands-On Hard Disk Replacement," for help with removing the terminator from a hard disk; see the appropriate chapter for help with other devices, such as Chapter 22, "Adding a CD-ROM or DVD-ROM Drive."

If you're dealing with an insider drive that won't work at all, open up the PC again and check for the obvious, such as loose cables. Then make sure you didn't put the data (ribbon) cables on backwards. Remember, the red wire or stripe should match up with pin 1 on the data cable connector. Check the controller card as well, and make sure that it is seated properly.

Shopping for a Tape Backup

One way to protect your important data is to back it up on tape. There are many, many tape drives from which you can choose, including:

➤ QIC (Quarter Inch Cartridge)

➤ Travan

➤ DAT (Digital Audio Tape)

➤ DLT (Digital Linear Tape)

➤ Iomega Ditto

What'll it cost me? 4mm DAT drives cost from $475 to $1275. 8mm DAT drives run from $900 to $2,700. Travan/QIC drives cost anywhere from $100 to $450. DLT drives range from $2,300 to $6,800. Ditto and Ditto Max drives run from $150 to $290.

And, as if this isn't confusing enough, some of these so called "standards" have spawned many variants, as you'll soon see. If you want some sort of guideline for deciding which tape drive to buy, then go for one that has a capacity large enough for you to store your data on a single tape, whenever possible. This just seems to make things easier. Just keep in mind that the capacities listed in most ads assume some type of *data compression*, using the software that comes with the drive.

Software brings up another issue, one of compatibility. Make sure the drive comes with software that will run under the operating system you use, such as Windows 95. Or, if you already have a backup program you like, make sure the drive you purchase is compatible with it.

Data compression

Tape drives usually list their capacities in compressed format, assuming that you're going to be able to compress your files with a ratio of 2:1. This just doesn't happen in the real world, where depending on the contents of the files you're backing up, you may experience only 1.5:1 up to 1.8:1. In English, this means a drive that advertises a capacity of 2GB may only give you 1.5–1.8GB of actual stored data.

Speed isn't really a big concern when shopping for a tape backup, because you can usually schedule the backup to occur when you're not around, such as overnight (this assumes, of course, that all your data will fit on a single tape). If speed is an issue, then DAT or DLT drives will probably suit your needs the best, because they are the fastest. There is such a thing as too fast, however, at least when it comes to tape backups. If your PC is slow (such as a 486SX 33), then a high-capacity tape backup drive (one that can back up 15GB on a single tape, for example) might not work well with your PC. Ask the manufacturer if they recommend the drive you want for your particular PC.

Price, on the other hand, probably *is* a concern (unless you're a Rockefeller). But remember to compare not only the price of the drive, but the price of the tapes as well. When comparing tape prices, look at the cost per megabyte. Shop around when pricing tapes—you'll find that vendors can be pretty competitive, especially if you buy in bulk.

Make it easy on yourself

The easiest way to speed up your backups is to *simplify* them. And the easiest way to do that is to have two drives (or to partition your one hard disk into two drives) and then to place your programs on one drive, and your data on another. By the way, if you have two physical drives in your system, this is a great way to protect your data against hard drive failure—of the two, drive C is more likely to fail, so with your data on drive D... You get the picture.

The last issue of course, is whether you can get the thing to work in your system. Here, you're looking at issues that are similar to adding any other drive, such as whether you want an internal or external version, whether you have a compatible drive controller or if you'll need to add one (some tape drives come with their own adapter card, eliminating this problem), whether your PC has a free drive bay (and if you need drive rails to make the tape drive fit), and whether you have a free power supply connector (or if you'll have to buy a splitter).

If you are out of power supply cables, you'll need to get a Y-splitter.

Y-splitter—

Floppy drives? Some tape backups connect to your floppy drive controller. These drives are not terribly fast, but that may be a plus for a slower computer. Tape drives connected to the floppy drive controller are compatible with QIC-80, TR-1, TR-2, and sometimes, with TR-3 tape cassettes.

QIC Drives

There are several QIC standards, but the most popular is QIC-80, which stores 80–120MB of data on a single tape cassette. Even with compression, that isn't enough space to hold all the data on today's large hard disks, so there are newer QIC formats, including QIC-3010, QIC-3020, QIC-3080, QIC-3095, and QIC 3220, whose capacities range from 340MB–10GB uncompressed.

Sony made a slight alteration to the standard when it widened the tape from .25 inches to .315 inches, creating QIC-Wide. QIC also comes in larger data cartridges (5 1/4 inches wide) called DC for short, as in DC-2000 tapes. Standard-sized mini cartridges (3 1/2 inches) are called MC instead.

With all these different variations in QIC technology, how do you choose a tape drive? Well, your first concern is backward compatibility, that is, if you've got some old QIC-40 or QIC-80 tapes lying around that you still need to be able to access. Otherwise, pick a tape drive whose capacity fits your needs, and whose tape costs fit your budget.

Travan Drives

Travan is actually just another quarter-inch tape standard, introduced by 3M. Travan drives accept both Travan tapes and certain QIC tapes as well. Of course, there are several Travan standards: TR-1 (originally called T-1000) is compatible with QIC-80, but with more storage capacity—400MB uncompressed. TR-2 (or T-2000) tapes are compatible with QIC-3010, but they hold 800MB uncompressed. TR-3 (or T-3000) tapes are similar to QIC-3020, with an increased storage capacity of 1.6GB uncompressed. TR-4, the latest Travan standard, was never called T-4000, for whatever reason. It's compatible with QIC-3095, and can hold up to 4GB of data. TR-5, expected soon, will be compatible with QIC-3230, and it will store up to 10GB.

Floppy drive standard QIC-40 and QIC-80 are known as the floppy drive standards, because these drives were designed to be hooked up to a floppy drive controller. Newer, high-capacity QIC drives are connected to higher bandwidth drive controllers such as IDE/EIDE and SCSI.

If you like quarter-inch technology, then a Travan-compatible drive is your best bet, because they are backwards compatible with QIC. If this is an issue, be sure to look for a drive that will read the specific type of QIC tapes you already have on hand. Speeds for TR-4 drives range from .5–1MB/sec. You'll find Travan drives in all flavors: parallel, SCSI, and IDE, so you shouldn't have a problem locating a drive that's compatible with your system.

DAT Drives

Short for Digital Audio Tape, DAT drives come in two flavors: 4mm and 8mm tapes. 4mm drives are more common, because they are a lot less expensive, and relatively fast (up to 2.4MB/sec). 8mm drives are typically faster (up to 6MB/sec), but they cost a lot more. For that reason, you'll find most likely find 8mm drives attached to network servers, and not to personal PCs.

DAT drives use something called *helical scan technology* to record information on tape, resulting in large storage capacities, from 2–12GB for 4mm DAT tapes, and 1.5 50GB for 8mm DAT tapes. There are two DAT storage formats: DDS (Digital Data Storage) and Data/DAT. Most drives support the more standard DDS format: DDS-1 (2GB uncompressed), DDS-2 (4GB uncompressed), and DDS-3 (12GB uncompressed).

If you want to use a DAT drive in your system, you're going to need a SCSI-II connector, which may mean that even if you have a SCSI port, you may need to upgrade to a newer controller card.

Techno Talk

Helical scan Helical scan technology isn't magic; it's the same technology used to record VCR tapes. Data on DAT tapes is stored diagonally across the width of the tape.

Both Travan and DAT drives are similar, both in tape drive technology, and in price and performance. However, currently, DAT drives have an advantage in that they can perform verification of the data as it's being written—Travan drives check data in a second pass, causing longer backup times. (Of course, this process does tend to make your backups more reliable, and that is the *point*, after all.)

In case you're wondering, can DAT backup drives read and play music from DAT audio cassettes? The answer is no; although the tapes are the same, the storage mechanisms and formats for audio and backup DAT tapes are incompatible.

DLT Drives

Short for Digital Linear Tape, DLT was developed by DEC. DLT drives use 1/2-inch cartridges that store between 15 and 35GB of data, uncompressed. Expensive but fast (1.5–5MB/sec), DLT drives are cost effective for backing up large networks, but you won't be able to afford one for your own PC.

DLT drives are available for SCSI controllers only, so keep that in mind if you decide to shop for one, because it will probably mean that you'll need to add a SCSI controller to your system.

Iomega Ditto Drives

The original Ditto tape drives from Iomega were simply Travan drives. The Ditto 800 was a TR-1 drive, and the Ditto 3200 was a TR-3.

With the introduction of their Ditto Max line of tape drives, Iomega has forged its own variation on Travan technology. The Ditto Max 2G stores up to 2GB of compressed data on Ditto tape cassettes. The cassettes are made by many different tape manufacturers, so you'll be able to find a competitive price for them. The 2G drive can read several tape formats, including QIC-80, QIC-80W, TR-1, TR-2, TR-3, and QIC-3010.

The 7G drive stores up to 7GB of compressed data, and it is able to read TR-3 and QIC-3020 tapes, so there is some compatibility with other Travan drives. Like the other Ditto Max drives, it can only use Ditto tapes, however.

If you need more capacity, try the Ditto Max 10G. Like its brother, the 10G can read TR-3 and QIC-3020 tapes, but it can only write data onto Ditto tapes. The speed of the Ditto Max 10G is 36MB/min. The internal versions of both drives come with a special Ditto Dash accelerator, which reads and writes the special Ditto format. You can, however, also get an external version that connects to your parallel port.

Installing a Tape Backup

Installing an internal tape backup is similar to installing a hard disk, floppy drive, or CD-ROM drive, so if you've done any of these things before, you're a couple steps ahead. In any case, prepare for computer surgery by following the steps outlined in Chapter 4: Do a backup, update your emergency disk, and so on. Then open the PC case.

First, discharge any static electricity you may have built up, or better yet, put on a wrist grounding strap. After you're protected, you're ready to begin working.

Installing the Controller/Adapter Card

If you bought an internal tape drive, you'll be connecting it to any of the following: an IDE or a SCSI controller, a floppy drive controller, or an adapter card that came with the drive. If you're inserting a new controller for your tape backup, jump back to the section, "Installing a SCSI, IDE/EIDE Controller Card," for the nasty details.

If your backup drive came with its own interface card, installing that card should be no different than installing any other standard card. It will go into an open ISA (not PCI) expansion port. A ribbon cable will connect this interface card with the backup drive; but to make it easier on you, attach the cable to the connector (a row of pairs of open metal posts) *after* you've secured the card in the port and screwed down the retainer clip. The other end of the cable, naturally, goes into the back of the backup drive.

Setting Up the Drive

If your tape drive uses an IDE interface, it may have to share the same EIDE/IDE controller with some other device, so you'll have to set a jumper on the drive to designate it as a slave. The "master" is the first IDE device connected to a controller, and the slave is device number two. If you're putting the tape drive on its own controller, then you can leave it set as master, because it's the only device on that cable. Check your manual for details. (Also, see the earlier sidebar on the Cable Select Mode issue, if you're interested.)

If you're installing a SCSI drive, you've got to set its SCSI ID. As you remember, the adapter has an ID too; it's usually set to ID 7, so choose something else for your drive, such as 6.

Besides making sure that each device has a unique ID, you also need to make sure that the device that has the highest and the lowest number (and *only* those two devices) are set to terminate the chain. One end of the SCSI chain is usually the controller (set at ID 7), and the other end terminates with the last device. Between the controller and this last device (whatever it is) there may be up to six other devices. To terminate a device so to speak, you add a jumper or set some switch; see the instructions that came with your tape drive for help. Also, if the tape drive is the new terminator, then some other device was terminating the chain, but no longer needs to. That means you must change the setting on that device so it doesn't terminate the SCSI chain at itself.

There may be other switches to set as well, for controlling such things as parity checking, compression, and tape detection. See the manual that came with the drive for additional information.

Connecting an Internal Tape Drive

First, remove the faceplate or bezel for the drive bay you've chosen. If needed, stick a flathead screwdriver just under the rim of the faceplate to pry it off. Then install any required drive rails or other mounting hardware, as needed.

Connect the data cable (the largest connector) and the power cable (the small, white connector). The power cable will only go in one way, but with the data cable, you need to make sure that the red-striped edge of the cable matches up with the pin marked 1 on the connector. Also, make sure that you use the *right* connector on your IDE cable: The first connector is for the boot drive (drive C), and the second connector on the cable is for a slave device on the first IDE channel. The third and fourth connectors on the data cable are for the master and slave devices on the second IDE channel (if your computer has one.)

Attach the data cable to your tape drive.

Align the striped edge with pin 1

If you're connecting a floppy controlled tape drive, then disconnect the floppy drive cable from its controller. Next, connect the data cable that came with the tape backup drive to the back of the tape drive. Match up the side of the cable with the red stripe to pin 1 on the connector. Then connect the other end of this cable to the floppy drive controller (the drive B connector), once again doing the stripe/pin 1 thing. There's an extra connector on the tape drive cable; connect the floppy drive data cable to this extra connector.

Connecting an External Tape Drive

To connect your external tape drive, run its data cable to the correct port on the back of your PC: SCSI, parallel, or special adapter. (Soon, you may even be able to connect one to an external IDE adapter.) Then connect the power cord. Simple, eh?

Oh yeah, one more thing: if you're using a parallel drive, connect the printer to the pass-through port on the back of the tape drive.

Running Setup

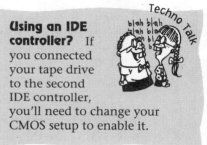

Using an IDE controller? If you connected your tape drive to the second IDE controller, you'll need to change your CMOS setup to enable it.

Last thing to do is to test the drive by powering up, and then running its setup program. First however, if you've got a SCSI drive, run the setup program for the controller card (if you just inserted one). Then run the setup for the tape drive itself.

If the drive came with some backup software, be sure to install it as well. In addition, if you use Windows, there are some other things you'll need to do to get Windows to acknowledge the tape drive. See Chapter 26, "Gettng Windows to Recognize Your New Toy," for help.

Backing up Windows backup

The Backup program that comes with Windows 95 and Windows 98 uses disks as its backup medium of choice. It was supposed to automatically recognize the installation of your tape backup drive. However, it often doesn't. Don't try to make it recognize your backup drive (in other words, don't follow directions) because it won't. Sometimes, the program locks up trying to find the single model of ethereal backup drive that it knows how to look for.

Your backup drive may come with its own version of Microsoft Backup custom-tailored for that drive, *or* it may come with another program that works even better. If you have neither, you can find specialized versions of Microsoft Backup for download from Microsoft's Web site (http://www.microsoft.com/win95).

To test the drive, do a backup, and then verify the backed up files against the real ones on your hard disk.

Upgrading Mistakes to Avoid

Here's a list of mistakes you might encounter when upgrading storage devices:

➤ If the drive's not working, make sure you've connected it correctly, and that you've chosen the right IRQs and such. See Chapter 27 for help.

➤ If you're using an IDE tape backup, make sure that it's not in conflict with the IDE controller on your sound card (that is, if you use an IDE sound card). Disable the controller on the sound card if possible—this usually involves changing some jumper setting. See your sound card manual for help.

➤ If you placed the tape drive on the secondary IDE channel, then make sure that the channel is turned on through CMOS. Also, make sure you've set your master/slave jumpers correctly.

➤ If you're having problems with an external tape drive, make sure you've turned it on.

➤ If you're using an external SCSI tape drive, make sure it's turned ON before you turn on the PC. Also, if you have more than one SCSI device, it may be interfering with the tape drive by causing the SCSI controller to reset when it detects that they are idle. Go into the SCSI controller's setup to enable disconnection, which will allow the tape backup to disconnect from the SCSI chain when it's busy backing up.

➤ If you notice that the tape backup drive seems to be spinning the tape back and forth for long periods of time, then your PC may be too slow for the tape backup. Sometimes you can slow the drive down through it's software setup, however, you may not be able to do that with all drives.

➤ If the drive is still not operating, make sure you've run the setup program for the drive. When you start your PC, does it load the drivers correctly, or do you see an error? If the drivers are trying to load into high memory through the CONFIG.SYS or the AUTOEXEC.BAT, try taking out the LOADHIGH or DEVICEHIGH command so they load into conventional memory instead. See Chapter 26 for help.

➤ If you've installed a QIC-compatible drive and it's not working, try turning off any of the following Windows 95/98 Device Manager options: High Speed Burst Transfers, Concurrent Hard Disk Access, and/or Concurrent Video Update.

➤ Some external drives may have problems if you install a software utility with a backup program such as Norton Utilities. The driver that comes with the utility program may attempt to override the driver that came with the tape drive, causing a problem. In that case, you may need to edit Windows' configuration files to remove the utility program's backup driver.

➤ You should also operate your external tape backup at least 18 inches from your monitor to avoid EMF interference.

The Least You Need to Know

When shopping for a storage/backup solution, keep these things in mind:

➤ Consider your needs: Do you want a convenient, inexpensive way to save large files to disks? Or are you looking for a way to backup all your data?

➤ Will you need to run the backup overnight? If so, you must find a system that does not require you to change tapes/disks.

➤ What controller will you be using: IDE/EIDE, SCSI, or parallel? Will it work in your system (can you add another IDE/EIDE or SCSI device, or are you maxed out?)

➤ Is speed an issue? If so, you'll be happier with a SCSI or an EIDE drive.

➤ Is price an issue? Then DLT is probably out.

➤ Do you need to share the drive with another PC? If so, you're looking at an external drive.

Chapter 24

Sensational Stereophonic Sound

In This Chapter

➤ Shopping for a great sound card

➤ Tips for getting good speakers

➤ How to install the darn things

One of the most popular PC buzzwords is "multimedia." What that means varies, but most people generally include at least two elements in their definition: graphics and sound. Graphics, which require typically large, complex files, are usually stored on CD-ROM discs. So a CD-ROM drive is essential in the quest for a true multimedia system (see Chapter 22, "Adding a CD-ROM or DVD-ROM Drive," for how to buy and install one). A sound card is also a must.

Sound cards exist at two levels: The more affordable versions provide good quality sound for casual use, such as playing CD-ROM games and audio CDs. The more expensive sound cards appeal to the true sound artist, such as a musician, or to the multimedia maniac. In this chapter, you'll learn how to find the ultimate sound card for your needs.

Before You Buy, Here Are Some Things You'd Better Consider

The first consideration you will face when shopping for a sound card is really the matter of price. Cards come in 16-bit, 32-bit, and 64-bit styles. The higher the number of bits, the more detailed and accurate the resulting *waveform*, or sound, will be. The number of bits here does not refer to the number of bits your expansion slots can handle; in other words, you can shove most sound cards into any standard 16-bit ISA slot. You can also find sound cards that fit PCMCIA slots on laptop computers. Having trouble determining what kind of slots your PC uses? See Chapter 2, "What Makes Your Computer Tick, and What It Takes to Upgrade Each Component," for a quick refresher.

Check This Out...

So what'll this cost me? A 16-bit card runs between $25 and $50. 32-bit sound cards cost from $75 to $100. Multimedia kits with 24x CD-ROM drives and 32-bit sound cards cost about $150 to $300.

Most sound cards support only a limited variety of CD-ROM drives, *and some low cost sound cards do not have an IDE/SCSI interface at all.* So if you plan on connecting your CD-ROM drive to your PC *through* your sound card, that's something to keep in mind. Also, each card only supports a particular kind of interface, either IDE or SCSI, which definitely limits your choice of a CD-ROM drive (see Chapter 22 for more info). A simple way to defeat this problem is to buy a multimedia kit (which contains a sound card, a CD-ROM drive, and speakers) for one low price. Getting these items together ensures compatibility, while also saving you money.

Sound Card Standards

You need to make sure your sound card is compatible with the programs you want to run it with, most notably Windows. "Sound Blaster" compatibility is a good thing to look for because most programs support some form of the Sound Blaster standard. When a sound card or a program mentions Sound Blaster compatibility, it generally means that it can accept the same sound instructions meant for an 8-bit Sound Blaster card (the oldest and least expensive of the Creative Labs product line, and thus the "least common denominator"). Exceptions include game programs manufactured after 1996, many of which default to the 16-bit Sound Blaster 16 standard. Also, if you use Windows 95/98, look for the PnP (Plug and Play) compatibility symbol.

Sound cards follow one of two standards for re-creating sound: *FM synthesis* and *wave table synthesis*. The less expensive technology, FM synthesis, creates sounds by combining pure tones of varying frequency and strength to produce a synthesized sound.

But I don't know if I'll want the best sound

If you're not sure if you'll really need the high-quality sound that a wave table sound card can provide, no problemo. Just shop for a sound card with a Wave Blaster-compatible expansion slot. Then if you decide to upgrade later on, you can buy a wave table daughterboard and connect it to the sound card. A daughterboard, by the way, is a small expansion board that fits into the slot next to the sound card.

Sound cards that use wave table synthesis (sampling) contain a large table of exact digitized waveforms for various sounds. For example, a sample note is taken from an instrument and then stored in a table as a digitized waveform. These waveforms are exact duplicates of their real-life sounds, so a wave table sound card reproduces sound more accurately than FM synthesis—but at a higher cost. (Some sound cards are wave table-upgradable, which allows you the freedom of upgrading them later on, when you have more cash.)

Not all wave table cards are the same; look for a minimum of 2.5–4MB of sample RAM (the area in which the samples are generated). The best-sounding (thus most expensive) sound cards support several wave tables for different octave ranges, so synthesized instruments sound more true-to-life. In other words, the best wave table sound cards contain multiple tables with several samples from each instrument, instead of just one.

Are You into Games?

If you want to play games and really hear the sound, make sure your sound card is Sound Blaster- and General MIDI-compatible. (General MIDI is what most games require for the background music.) Incompatibility with General MIDI makes a lot of high-end sound cards not suitable choices for game use. You might be surprised to learn that an expensive sound card, when playing the soundtrack of a game programmed just for Sound Blaster compatibility, may sound like an elementary school band practice session compared to the simple Sound Blaster the soundtrack was based on. Another feature to look for in a good sound card for games is 3D and special effects compatibility (a kind of stereo surround sound), which adds a special dimension to game playing. Also, you might be interested in whether or not your sound card has a game port, a place into which you can plug a game control such as a joystick.

What's a MIDI? A MIDI device is a digital electronic instrument (such as an electric keyboard) that supports the MIDI (Musical Instrument Digital Interface) standard. MIDI enables an electronic musical instrument to communicate with your digital computer. You can use your computer to compose a musical score with multiple instruments, and your MIDI instrument set can play it.

Techno Talk

Great composer Most sound cards include a MIDI port, which is suitable for a joystick if you don't intend to use it as a MIDI port; however, to use a MIDI device in such a port, you'll need a separate break out box. If you're a professional musician, you might want to look for a sound card that supports either Roland GS or Yamaha XG, both of which extend the General MIDI palette.

Some Terms You'll See As You Shop

Here are some other terms you'll encounter while shopping for your sound card:

Audio line input Special input for recording sound off of a stereo, TV, VCR, or CD-ROM. This is not the same as a microphone input, which is usually monophonic and not stereophonic.

Full duplex This means the sound card can record sound and play it back at the same time.

3D A 3D sound card is capable of altering the sound you hear (assuming you put your speakers in the proper place) so it sounds to you like the sound is coming from a broader area, such as a big stage, a battlefield, or a distant planet.

Voice The number of tones used in the composition of parts (instruments) on a sound card. The more the better. For FM, a good number is 20, allowing five-part harmony from well-formed, four-voice parts. It usually takes four FM voices to comprise one tone, so 20 voices allows for up to five-part harmony of four tones. Wave table cards may require fewer voices per part, because its individual voices are more true-to-life.

Polyphony The number of notes a card can play at the same time. Six-timbre (or six-voice) polyphony can reproduce orchestral sound.

Multitimbrality The number of different voices that a sound card can play at the same time.

DSP Short for Digital Signal Processor, the on-board chip that performs the task of rendering sound waves (or any type of waveform, for that matter) in a format most closely approximating analog, or true-to-life sound.

A Note About Speakers

The depth of sound from speaker to speaker varies a great deal. When shopping for a set of PC speakers, look at the frequency response range. This tells the range of high to low sounds the speaker can reproduce. The best speakers can reproduce a range close to that of human hearing (20Hz–20kHz). Some speakers add a 3D sound effect, which is a cool addition to role-playing games. These speakers' effects are best felt with a 3D sound card installed.

You should also make sure your new speakers contain their own amplifiers to help boost the signal coming from the sound card. Most do, so this shouldn't be a major factor.

However, you should look at the total power wattage of the speakers, because the sound card produces a fairly weak signal that needs to be amplified by your speakers. Low-cost speakers offer only 4–7 watts, while the best offer as much as 100 watts of power output. Although I'm talking about power, keep in mind that most speakers run off of two or more lowly C batteries. You might want to seriously consider investing in an AC adapter, which will prevent unnecessary trips to the store when you're in the middle of an intense dog fight. (Some speakers come with a built-in AC adapter plug.)

The term *total harmonic distortion* refers to the amount of distortion (noise) level that occurs when a sound is amplified. Look for .1 percent or less.

Another feature to watch out for is the number and type of control knobs the speakers offer. Most come with a volume control, but the better ones also allow you to adjust the amount of bass, treble, and super bass (dynamic bass boost).

Sounds nice You don't have to spend big bucks on PC speakers if you've already spent lots of dollars on a nice home stereo system. You can easily run the output of your sound card through your stereo system. Just get the right adapter to fit the jack on the card, and the jacks on the AUX inputs in your stereo. If that sounds like just too much trouble, invest in a good set of headphones instead; at least they're cheaper!

Also, if your PC has a USB (Universal Serial Bus port; see Chapter 3, "Now, Let's Find Out What Kind of Computer You Have," for more details), then you might want to look for speakers that support USB.

Keep in mind that most speakers contain magnets to create their sound. Make sure your speakers have adequate protection around their magnetic parts—especially if you're going to put the speakers anywhere near your monitor, which is especially sensitive to magnetic fields. This warning applies to your disks as well as other magnetic media. (What does this mean for speakers that are *built into* the monitor—for instance, Compaq Presario? There's enough shielding between the monitor and speakers that interference is not a problem. *Weight*, however, is.)

One final word: If you plan on putting your speakers far away from your PC (or if you use a tower case), make sure your speaker cables are long enough.

Installing Your Sound Card

Installing a sound card is not difficult, but getting it to work correctly often is. The main problem centers around choosing the right IRQ, DMA, and I/O addresses. The easiest way to determine which settings to use is to figure out what settings your other devices are using. Back in Chapter 3, you hopefully completed a listing of your PC's components; well, guess what—all that hard work is about to pay off.

Before you install your sound card, you should make a note of its IRQ, DMA, and I/O address settings, compare them to the settings used by other devices on your list, and change them as needed so you end up with one big, happy computer family. You'll have to look in the manual for the location of these switches. This is a total yech, but at least you're not alone—there's more help for you in Chapter 27, "Fiddling with Ports, IRQs, Addresses, and Such." Some sound cards are considerate and enable you to change their settings through software, a much more pleasant experience.

Change the sound card's settings as needed before you insert it.

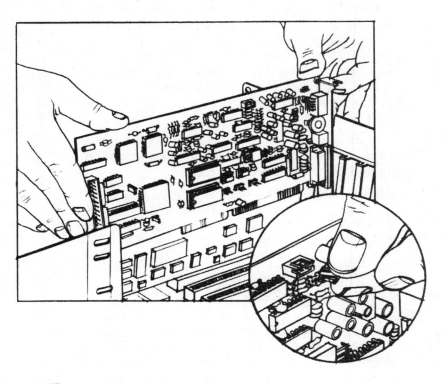

That's a shocker! Before you remove your sound card from its static bag, clear an area on your desk. Lay down some paper to put the card on, then discharge any static you may have built up shuffling around, waiting for your sound card to arrive. Then pull the sound card from the bag and place it on the paper. Change the settings as needed.

When you're ready to install your card, make sure you prepare your system by doing a backup, updating your emergency disk, and so on. See Chapter 4, "What You Need to Know Before You Open Your PC," for how-to's. Then make sure you've discharged any static and open up your PC.

To install the sound card, pick out the slot you want to use and unscrew its retaining screw. This slot should be located as far away as possible from noisy components such as the hard disk and the power supply. Remove the slot's cover, but keep the thing; if you dump your sound card later, you can use it to cover up the hole. Make sure you pick up the card at its top with both hands. Then position the edge connectors at the bottom of the card over their respective slots. Press the card into place, but don't force it—you could bend it.

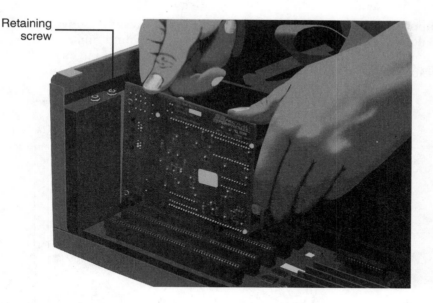

Retaining screw

Gently press the expansion card into its slot.

Secure the card in place with its retaining screw. If you're connecting a CD-ROM drive to your sound card, plug its connector cable into the correct slot on the card. Keep in mind that many cards come with several connectors, one for each of the specific types of drives they support. These different connectors are usually well marked so you can't make much of a mistake, but check with the manual if you're not sure which one to use. You'll also want to connect the CD-ROM drive's audio cable to the sound card. See Chapter 22 if you want more help with your CD-ROM drive.

Your sound card typically comes with several outside connectors: a microphone connector, a headphone connector, an external speaker connector, and a joystick or MIDI connector. First, connect your two speakers. If your speakers come with two strands of speaker wire, then you use one strand to connect one speaker to the other speaker, and another to connect the right speaker to the sound card. If you instead have one strand of speaker wire with a connector in the middle, connect the middle part to the right speaker, one end to the other (left) speaker, and the other end to the sound card. If you want to connect your sound card to your home stereo, it's no trick, but you'll need an adapter that has a 1/8-inch mini stereo connector at one end (to fit your sound card) and regular RCA sound plugs at the other.

> **Check This Out...**
>
> **Blown away** The first time you use your stereo with the sound card, turn the volume to low, to keep from accidentally blowing the speakers.

Now you can mess with the extras, such as a microphone (for recording all those wise tidbits you come up with every day) and a joystick or MIDI device. By the way, you can connect more than one MIDI device to your sound card by running the output of one

379

device into the input of the previous one in the chain. See, MIDI devices connect to one another like SCSI devices—in a daisy-chain. So if you have a MIDI multi-timbre module, a MIDI sequencer, and a MIDI drum unit, you can connect them in a chain in any order by using 5-pin DIN cable and then connecting one end of the chain to the MIDI card.

You can easily connect your sound card to your stereo system.

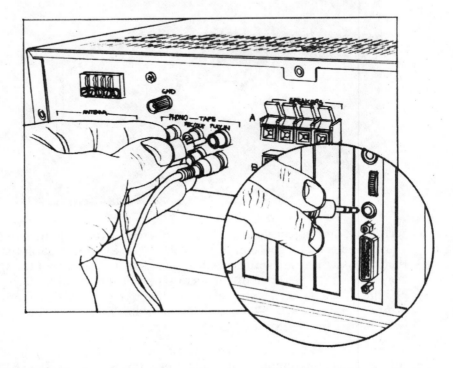

After you connect your card, close up the PC and turn it on. Next, you need to run the sound card's setup program to install the card's device driver. The device driver, you may recall, is what allows the PC to communicate with the sound card. If you use any DOS games, you'll need to select your sound card from each game's own setup program. You'll have to do some messing around in Windows, too, if you use it. See Part 5, "Getting Your PC to Figure Out What You've Done," for help.

Upgrading Mistakes to Avoid

The main problem you'll run into when you add a sound card to your system is IRQ, DMA, and I/O address conflicts. Keeping an accurate list of the channels your other devices are using is the only real way to solve this problem. See Chapter 27 for help.

If you can't hear sound in a particular game, run its setup program and make sure that your sound card (or a compatible model that your card emulates or imitates) is selected. Also, some games only support Sound Blaster compatible cards, set at the default settings of DMA 1, IRQ 7, and I/O address 220. Games that support *two* DMA channels instead of one have a Sound Blaster compatibility mode running on a separate channel. Your game may identify these as the "low channel" and "high channel." Obviously, the lower number identifies the low channel. If you can hear digital sound—such as people speaking or bogeys crashing—but you can't hear the music you're expecting, the MIDI base address might not be set up properly in your game. Usually this address is 0388h (or just 0388).

To DMA or not to DMA?

Many Plug-and-Play sound cards, such as ESS AudioDrive, let Windows determine what DMA addresses to use. So when you're setting up a game to play on your sound card, and that card supports AudioDrive explicitly rather than just its fallback mode of Sound Blaster 16 compatibility, you'll notice that the DMA setting gadget is either disabled or absent. Don't worry; that means that the program doesn't have to be told what the card's DMA addresses are.

If you still can't hear the sound, make sure your speakers are on, and their batteries are working. Check the mixer program and make sure the master volume is set high enough. In Windows 95, you can get to the master volume control by double-clicking the speaker icon on the taskbar. You can also test the volume by running the sound card's diagnostic program and playing a test sound file. If you bought cheap speakers, they might not be amplifying the sound enough. Try connecting the sound card to your stereo to see if that solves the problem. You could also try plugging some headphones into your sound card and bypassing the speakers altogether.

Check those settings Many 16-bit sound cards prefer using DMA channel 5, 6, or 7. Others prefer DMA 3. For true Sound Blaster compatibility, you may want to use DMA 1. Sound cards with Sound Blaster 16 use two DMA channels, generally 0 and 3. The first is exclusively for the compatibility mode, while the second is for the card's native sound generator. When there's a conflict with the sound card's settings and the settings of other devices, you may get a parity error, or your PC may "lock up."

Another way to resolve a sound problem is to restart the PC and make sure that the sound card's driver loaded properly. Next, you might want to check the CONFIG.SYS settings to see if the initial volume for the driver is set too low. You should also check the volume knobs on the speakers (and the power ON switch).

One last thing to check is the cable that connects your speakers to the sound card. Make sure you use a stereo speaker cable if your sound card is stereo. If you accidentally use a mono cable, you'll either get sound of a very low volume, or no sound at all.

If you get sound but it's pretty scratchy, make sure your sound card is not too close to the hard disk or the power supply. The signal that a sound card sends to your speakers is an analog signal, which is susceptible to radio frequency distortions. These are constantly created by things like your power supply, your hard disk drive, and a hyperactive dachshund on a really tight leash. You might also want to move your speakers farther away from your monitor—unless the speakers are shielded heavily against electrical interference, your monitor may be causing a disruption.

When there's nothing left to try

Sometimes your PC's BIOS may be the reason why your sound card won't work, especially if it handles its DMA channel differently than your card expects. Thankfully, this typically occurs in only very old systems. If the BIOS' DMA timing can be changed (slowed), this usually clears up the problem. You can get to this setting through CMOS. Time to call in the nerds (and Chapter 27) for help with this one.

The Least You Need to Know

Shopping for a sound card can be a confusing experience. Here are some tips to remember:

➤ Buying a multimedia package that includes a sound card, CD-ROM drive, and speakers saves you money and ensures that you won't run into any compatibility problems. However, you won't get the best quality components.

➤ When choosing a sound card, get one that's at least 16-bit. Get a 32-bit sound card if you can afford it, because it provides a better-quality sound. A 64-bit sound card provides professional (and expensive) quality.

➤ Of course, before you buy any sound card, check the programs you want to run with it and make sure they are compatible with the sound card you choose.

➤ You should also make sure that the card you buy is Sound Blaster-compatible, because most programs support Sound Blaster sound cards. If you like to play a lot of games, look for compatibility with General MIDI, too.

➤ Sound cards that use FM synthesis are less expensive, but they don't provide as nice a sound. Wave table cards are a better choice.

➤ If you want a high-quality sound card, pay particular attention to voice, polyphony, and multitimbrality. Also check to see if the sound card includes a DSP chip.

CHUGA
CHUGA
BEEP

FAX

Chapter 25

Adding a Fax Modem

In This Chapter

➤ Talking that modem jive

➤ What to look for in an ideal modem

➤ Installing an internal modem

➤ Installing an external modem

A *modem* is a device that takes digital junk coming out of your PC and changes it into analog beeps and buzzes to send over a conventional phone line. At the other end, the receiving modem unscrambles this beeping, buzzing nonsense and converts it back into digital computer data. A communications program at each end controls the whole exchange.

With a modem, you can send or receive files and electronic messages. You can even connect to an online service, bulletin board service, or your company's network. But I won't kid you—installing a modem and getting it to work is not always easy. After you get it up and running, however, a modem can be pretty useful and a lot of fun.

Most modems sold today are fax modems, because fax machines truly are modems in the first place. It's almost impossible these days to locate a new modem that doesn't have the capability to send and receive fax. But where's the paper scanner? A fax modem doesn't need one. Its image of the page being transmitted exists within your computer's own RAM, and is managed by your computer's operating system.

Talking Modem Jive

Now, when you're shopping for a modem, the salesperson is gonna use words like "error correction" and "data compression" whether you want him to or not. Here's a brief list you can use to decipher his modem-speak:

➤ *Online service.* A pay-for-use subscription service that allows its users to send and receive files or email, shop online, "chat" online with other users, and search for answers to puzzling problems. You also get access to the Internet through customized screens that provide an easy way to locate what you need. Popular online services include America Online and The Microsoft Network.

➤ *Internet.* A group of interconnected computer networks that spans the world. You connect to the Internet through your modem by way of an Internet service provider (ISP), which charges you a fee for the access; or from an online service, such as America Online. You then jump from Internet site to Internet site to find the information you need. One warning, however: No one is actually responsible for the Internet as a whole, so "surfing" the Net is kind of like riding the New York City subway—you never know exactly what you're going to see.

➤ *Uploading.* Uploading is the process of sending a file.

➤ *Downloading.* Downloading is the process of receiving a file.

➤ *BBS.* Short for *bulletin board service*. A BBS is kind of like an electronic bulletin board, but the members of a BBS can leave messages and exchange information electronically. A BBS is similar to an online service, but on a smaller scale—usually locally owned and operated, sometimes in a local storefront, occasionally in someone's closet. Most BBSs are devoted to a particular topic, such as sailing, computers, gardening, and so on. You can dial up a local BBS directly by phone. Also, you can access a distant BBS through a local BBS if the local BBS supports "BBS Express," or you can sometimes reach a BBS through the Internet.

➤ *FTP.* Short for *File Transfer Protocol*, FTP is one process by which data files are uploaded or downloaded from the Internet. Your Web browser (such as Netscape Navigator or Internet Explorer) has FTP capability built in.

➤ *bps.* Short for *bits per second*. It is a way of measuring the speed of a modem. Sometimes called *baud rate*, although that's technically incorrect.

➤ *Baud.* The amount of frequency changes per second during a transmission. With early modems, this was the same as the number of bits per second, but that's not the case with today's high-speed modems.

Thinking about a 56Kbps modem?

If you've been considering a 56Kbps modem, you may have been holding off, waiting for some kind of standard to be declared. Well, good news—as of February 1998, there is now a standard to which all 56Kbps modems can comply: V.90. Make sure that any 56Kbps modem you buy uses V.90, so you'll be compatible with everyone else. (You can read more about this issue in the section, "Shootout at the 56K Corral," coming up later in this chapter.)

➤ *UART*. Universal Asynchronous Receiver/Translator. This is the heart of your modem. Like a CPU, it is one chip, often surface-mounted to the modem card. Rockwell and Lucent (formerly part of AT&T) are the leading producers of UART chips for all brands of modems.

➤ *COM port*. Your PC has up to four serial ports called COM ports. A port is a route through which a device communicates with the CPU. Your modem uses one of these COM ports.

➤ *Protocol*. A set of standards that governs how two modems communicate with each other, and how to detect errors in transmission.

➤ *Parity*. The procedure for determining when an error occurs. A protocol will use either even or odd parity, where a ninth bit is added to the eight bits (which make up a character) to make the total number of 1 bits either odd, or even. If even parity is being used, and a modem receives the nine bits 010010111, then it'll know there's some kind of mistake because there are five 1 bits—an odd number.

➤ *Error correction*. The protocol (sorry, uh, *method*) that a particular modem uses to discover whether an error occurs during transmission.

➤ *Data compression*. The method the modem uses to shrink the data before transmitting it, so it takes less time. Popular protocols that include both error correction and data compression are V.42 and Microcom Network Protocol, or MNP, (actually, V.42 is an implementation of MNP).

Things to Consider When Shopping

Probably your top consideration when buying a modem is its speed (and the cost, of course). The speed of a modem is measured in *bits per second*, thankfully abbreviated as bps. Common speeds for modems sold today include 28,800, 33,600, and 56,200bps (these are also abbreviated, showing up on modem ads as 28.8, 33.6, and 56.0Kbps, with the latter often abbreviated again to "56Kbps"). A 28.8 modem is still available—very cheaply—but not for long. But a 33.6 modem may save you money in the long run if you use an online service (such as AOL) or the Internet a lot.

Faster connection not!

Just because you spend the bucks and get yourself a high-speed 56Kbps modem, that does not guarantee that you'll actually connect at that speed. Many factors come into play when you connect to your online service or Internet service provider: First of all, are you connecting to a modem that's as fast as yours? Because 56Kbps is just now becoming a standard, many ISPs are using 33Kbps baud modems to connect to your modem on their end. So if you connect to one of these, your 56Kbps modem will "slow down" to 33Kbps mode. Even if you connect to another 56Kbps modem, excessive line noise caused by atmospheric conditions (uh, storms) and poor quality phone lines can slow down the speed of data transfer, because the two modems may have to resend data several times before it's received correctly.

With a faster modem, you'll use less connect time—usually. Many dial-up access lines for online services are limited to 33.6Kbps, even if you have a 56Kbps modem. This is because, until February of 1998, there wasn't an international standard for 56Kbps transmission. Now, there is—the V.90 standard—so this state of affairs is likely to change.

If you're buying an external modem Most external modems don't include a serial modem cable, which you need to connect the external modem to your PC. COM ports come in two sizes: 9- and 25-pin, so make sure you get the right cable to fit your needs. Don't accept imitations—make sure the cable says that it's appropriate for use with modems.

Modems come in both internal and external types; an external modem plugs into a spare serial port, so make sure you have one. If you've inherited an external modem from a buddy, but you don't have an extra serial port, you can add one with something called an *I/O*, or *multifunction card*. You can share an external modem with your coworkers, or use it with your laptop PC, if it has a spare serial port or a serial I/O PCMCIA card. If you have a laptop, however, you might prefer a modem that fits into a PCMCIA connector. But be sure to get one with its own power supply, so it won't drain the laptop's main power; or plug the laptop into an outlet to bypass its battery supply.

What'll it cost me?

The 28.8Kbps modem is almost no longer available; if you find any, you might pay as low as $30, or no more than $60, for it. Because the 56Kbps standard was just approved, the price range for both 33.6Kbps and 56Kbps modems is similar, beginning at $45, and going all the way up to $200 for a full-feature set (such as voice, fax, and pager support). But expect to see a big price drop in 33.6Kbps modems, with most 56Kbps modems staying up in the $100 to $200 range, and 33.6Kbps modems dropping well below $100. A PCMCIA PC card-based modem costs anywhere from $30 to $100 more than a regular modem.

Just keep in mind that you get what you pay for. Some cheap modems are so hard to install and to get working that they're just not worth the $10 or $20 you'll save by buying them. The modem you buy should be Hayes-compatible, an industry standard which deals with the way your computer (or more accurately, your software) communicates with your modem. Popular brands include Hayes (duh), Cardinal, USRobotics/3Com, Boca Research, Supra, Practical Peripherals, and Zoom. (Some Cardinal and all Practical Peripherals models are now manufactured by Hayes.)

One feature you won't have to worry much about when choosing a modem is faxing—all modems today are capable of faxing (sending a facsimile electronically, just like a fax machine). Of course, you'll need a software program to handle the faxing details for you, but most modems include that, too. With your fax modem and the proper software, you can send a document created with your PC to either another fax modem, or to an actual fax machine. When shopping, the standard you want to look for here is called CCITT Group 3 Fax; about 98 percent of all the fax modems will support Group 3, but at least you can weed out those built on the island of Outer Gamzabia that don't.

Something you might be interested in (especially if you work in a small office or at home) is a modem that supports voice mail and caller ID, commonly called a *voice modem*. Along with the proper software, these modems enable you to set up one of those fancy voice mail systems where callers can leave messages for particular people by pressing the right button. Software made for voice modems allows digital messages, recorded by you and stored in your computer, to be played through the modem so the human caller can hear you. This way, your computer becomes a sophisticated answering machine, capable of directing tone-dialed calls through to specific "mailboxes," or to your fax program. A voice modem can also record messages from the caller, so your software can store those messages to your hard disk as .WAV files. Of course, this means you must leave your computer and your modem on all the time, so you can receive messages. Also, these voice message files can get quite large, so you better check your messages often and delete them.

Check This Out...

Why you want a fast modem

Modems have to talk to each other at the same speed to communicate. But don't worry; a fast modem can always talk to a slower one, because after connecting, it automatically slows down to the speed of the other modem. But in general, the faster your modem is, the less money you will spend on connect-time to online services (assuming, of course, that you are charged a different rate based on the amount of time you spend online), and the less time it will take you to download stuff.

Shootout at the 56K Corral

Although 56Kbps modems have been sold through retail channels since late 1996, for the lion's share of their history, they have not been supported by an international standard in the way V.34 has supported 28.8Kbps transmission. As a result, the market was split down the middle between two competing specifications. On one side, Rockwell and Lucent Technologies, the two leading producers of UART chips in the world, supported a specification called K56Flex (perhaps named after a soft-rock FM station). Meanwhile, 3Com, the owner of USRobotics, which is the best-selling modem brand in the world and already a standard-bearer with its HST high-speed technology, joined with Texas Instruments to found a specification called X2. The technical differences between the two sets of specs are just that, technical.

In February of 1998, the International Telecommunications Union of the United Nations announced its intention to launch a true 56Kbps standard, to be dubbed V.90. Both sides in the 56Kbps wars claimed victory, which generally means that neither side got entirely what they wanted. The V.90 standard will be officially ratified in September of 1998, according to the ITU. In the meantime, V.90 modems have already gone on sale.

But what happens if the ITU changes a few dots on its i's or crosses on its t's between now and September? Won't these pre-ratification modems (perhaps what my husband, an Oklahoman, would call a "Sooner," after those who jumped the gun during the Land Run of 1889) be outmoded? Hayes and several other manufacturers already selling V.90 modems ahead of time are equipping those modems with their own flash ROMs. This way, if the instructions for how to support V.90 change, the manufacturers can post those changes on their Web sites. You would then download their patches, and use their software to upgrade your modem yourself without having to open your computer up. Existing 56Kbps modems with their own flash ROMs will be upgradable to V.90 in the same fashion, *although not all 56Kbps modems have this luxury*. This was the danger that owners undertook when purchasing their 56Kbps modems before a true standard was announced.

With what appears to be a settlement on the 56Kbps standard finally at hand, Internet service providers are now compelled to begin working on upgrading their infrastructure, so modems can at last dial in at rates faster than 33.6Kbps. People who own 56Kbps modems can now take advantage of them.

Cross Your Fingers, It's Time to Install

Hayes Microcomputer Products, Inc. graciously contributed information to this chapter on installation and troubleshooting techniques.

Before you install your modem, make sure that you change its COM port setting to the COM port you want to use. Usually you set the COM port by changing some DIP switches. DIP switches are kind of like light switches; they're either set on or off. By setting these switches to certain positions, you select COM1, COM2, and so on. (Of course, before you touch anything, make sure that you've discharged that darn static.) Some modems are more intelligent, and they let you change their settings using software.

Any port in a storm

Before you install your modem, you'll need to decide which COM port to use. Newer PCs have four COM ports; older ones have only two. Don't get too depressed, because if you own a computer with an ISA bus, it can only use two COM ports at the same time anyway (there are some PCs that try to provide three COM ports). In other words, it can use only COM1 and COM2, or COM3 and COM4, at any one time.

Trouble is, with only two COM ports to choose from, your modem is pretty likely to bump into some interference from other serial devices such as your mouse, a serial printer, or scanner. In addition, a serial port (even if it doesn't have anything attached to it) can cause a conflict unless it's disabled, which you do in CMOS.

Installing an Internal Modem

When you're ready to install your modem, go through the usual steps to prepare your system. (If you need hints, see Chapter 4, "What You Need to Know Before You Open Your PC," for help.) Take a moment to get rid of that nasty static cling and then open up your PC.

Unscrew the retaining screw of the slot you've picked out. Remove the slot cover and then, using both hands, pick up the modem at its top edge. Make sure the card's edge connectors are positioned over their respective slots. Gently press the card into place. Be careful not to force the modem in—you could bend it.

Press the internal modem into its slot.

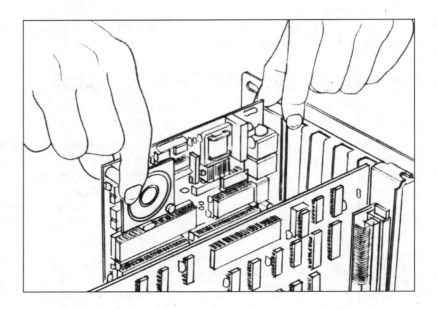

After you have the modem in, connect the phone line. Just leave the PC open if you want; you still need to test the modem, and it's easier to correct problems if you still have access to the problem maker (uh, the modem). Fax modems connect to one telephone line, so you'll need to be ready to facilitate fax and data transmission capabilities through the same phone number. On the back of the modem, you'll see two connections—you need to use the one marked "To Line" or "To Wall." Connect the cord into a regular telephone jack, preferably one that's in a surge protector (many surge protectors come with a protected phone jack—use one to avoid damage to your modem from electrical surges).

If you've got only one phone jack, don't fret—you won't be able to use the modem and the phone together, but you can still get them to share. Just disconnect your phone from the wall and then connect it to the phone jack marked "To Phone." Now, when you're using one phone line for both your phone and your modem, you should get rid of extras like "call waiting," which wreak havoc on the modem's capability to send and receive data undisturbed, or disable call waiting by adding the prefix *70 to any number you dial (you can do this in the modem's setup program).

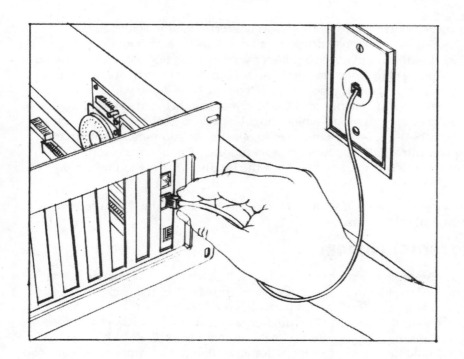

Plug in the telephone line.

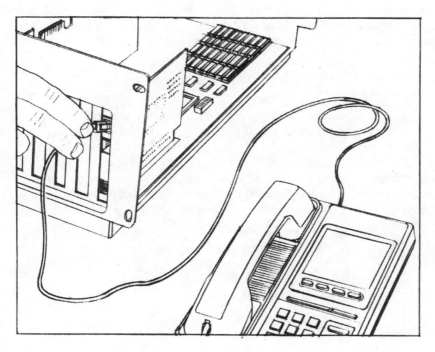

You can connect your phone to the modem if you have only one line.

Some specialized voice modems, such as Hayes' Accura series, enable you to attach a special type of device called an *electret microphone* that lets you use your modem as, well, a telephone. Granted, all modems give you a plug for your existing telephone. But with an electret microphone plugged in, your modem becomes functional as a digital telephone. Software on your computer takes the place of the telephone console, so you can use day-planner or office-organizer software not only to store your numbers but also as a substitute for speed-dial. An electret headset—which looks like a diamondless tiara with a tube pointing to your mouth—leaves your hands free to operate the computer; so the transition of your computer into a fully functional speakerphone with digital answering is complete. You can also use this setup to chat over the Internet with a good telephony program.

Well, that's over. Leave the cover off so you can test this thing (see the "Testing Your Modem" section later in this chapter).

Installing an External Modem

There's not a lot to installing an external modem, thank goodness. Just take your serial cable (you did remember to buy one, didn't you?) and connect it to the back of the modem. Connect the other end to the COM port you chose on the back of your computer. Your serial cable needs to be a DB25, which means it should have 25 pin connections. The connectors on the cable should be "male" on both ends. Preferably, the COM port you plug into should have a 25-pin connection as well; but if the only open slot is a 9-pin connection, it's easy to get a 25-to-9 converter for your cable. Your external modem may come fully equipped with a DB25 cable and a 25-to-9 converter. The 25-to-9 converter that came with your serial mouse will not work, because its genders aren't right.

You call that a shield?

When shopping for a serial cable to connect your external modem, you should check the level of shielding that protects your modem from nasty electrical surges. Now, just about every serial cable you'll find on a store shelf has the word "shielded" written on it someplace. As far as you know, the manufacturers may be calling that cable "shielded" because it has rubber over the wires. If the cable says "RF shielded," now that means something! This tells you that the cable is completely shielded from radio frequency interference.

Better yet, if you see the familiar "UL" label, and the cable says "RF shielded," that's the manufacturer's way of saying, "If we're lying, then we have to pay you a lot of money."

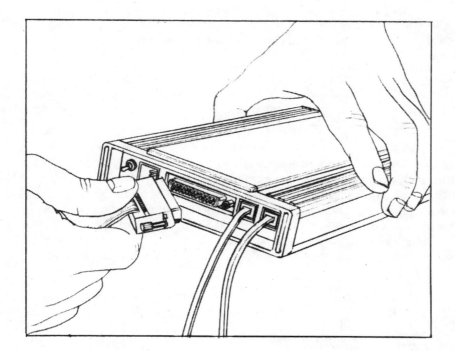

Use a serial cable to connect your external modem.

Next, plug in the power cable and connect it to a wall outlet, or preferably, a surge protector. Then connect the phone line. You'll see two telephone-type connections: use the one marked "To Line" or "To Wall." If you don't see the labels, turn the modem over. Sometimes they're on the bottom. Connect the phone cord and then plug it into a telephone (RJ11) jack, preferably in a surge protector. If you have only one phone jack, disconnect your phone from the wall and connect it to the other phone line connector on the modem—the one marked "To Phone." Of course, you won't be able to use your phone and the modem at the same time! By the way, if your modem has only one phone jack, buy an adapter, as shown below. Then plug the adapter into the wall jack and plug both your phone and your modem into the adapter.

Okay. That went pretty well. Now it's time to test the darn thing.

Testing Your Modem

Power up the PC. If you have an external modem, turn it on. Now, some modems come with software that you can use to test the thing; if you don't have any other way to test the modem, just type **ECHO ATDT>COM1** at the DOS prompt and press **Enter**.

Of course, if you connected your modem to COM2 instead, then type this: **ECHO ATDT>COM2**. You should hear a dial tone. If you do, then everything's fine so far. You can turn off the PC and close it up now. If something's funky (such as an unconnected modem, or one which is connected to the same COM port as another modem) then DOS will respond with the error message, `Write fault error writing device COM1. Abort, Retry, Ignore, Fail?`. Press **A** for abort and check out the next section for help in determining what's wrong.

As a final step, you need to install your communications program such as ProComm Plus or CrossTalk, and select your brand of modem in the process. There are some additional things you need to do in Windows to get your modem to work, too. See Part 5, "Getting Your PC to Figure Out What You've Done," for help.

With your communications program installed, you can give your modem the next phase of tests. At the terminal screen, you should see the letters `OK`. This message is coming from your modem, not from DOS and not from your communications software. Type **ATDT**, then press **Enter**. This time, you should not only hear a dial tone, but you should also see another `OK` message. Finally, type **ATZ**, and press **Enter**. The dial tone should cease, the phone should hang up, and you should see another `OK`. If anything's wrong, you'll see the message `ERROR`, in which case, you'll need to go back and check your connections once again. But if you see three `OK` messages at this point, your modem has passed the basic tests.

Use an adapter if your modem provides only one phone jack.

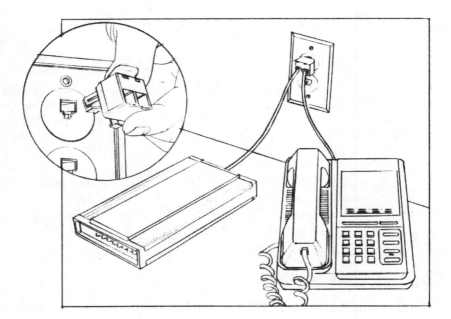

Upgrading Mistakes to Avoid

When testing your modem from the DOS prompt, if you get the error message: `Write fault error writing device COM1 (or COM2)`, then either you forgot to turn the modem on, or there's something wrong with the connection. If you're using an internal modem, turn off your computer, and then try taking it out and reseating it again.

If you run into problems after you've already got your modem up and running, there could be a COM port conflict with some other device, especially if your mouse (or whatever) begins acting up, too. A conflict might also result in the modem stopping in the middle of transmission.

Better safe than sorry

To protect your modem from damage, you should plug both its power cord and its incoming telephone line into a surge protector. Electric surges and spikes from both of these are capable of "zapping" your modem should they get struck by lightning. As a matter of fact, you should place all your valuable electronics on surge protectors, such as your TV, stereo, and telephone answering machine. Not all surge protectors have outlets for telephone lines. If your surge protector has nothing to plug a phone line into, you can get a separate phone surge protector that plugs into one of the power outlets in your existing protector. Why would the phone protector need to plug in there? Not because it needs power, but to ground it using the ground wire in your electric system.

If your PC is old, it may not have a fast enough UART chip for your external modem to keep up. (Internal modems come with their own UARTs that override anything your PC already has.) Run MSD as described in Chapter 4 and click **COM Ports**. Your chip should be a 16550 or higher. Older chips such as the 8250 just can't keep up. If you're getting only partial transmissions, this may be the culprit. Replace the I/O board that's connected to your external modem with something less dusty.

The Least You Need to Know

When shopping for your new communications buddy, consider these tips:

➤ Buy the fastest modem you can. It'll pay for itself in a few months, with savings on long-distance phone and online service charges.

➤ If you opt for an internal modem, make sure that you have a free slot, hopefully away from noisy devices like your hard disk or the power supply.

➤ If you buy an external modem instead, make sure you have a serial port available. Check the UART chip used by your serial port; if it's old, you'll need to buy an I/O card to update it.

➤ If you get an external modem, be sure to buy a modem cable with which to connect it.

➤ Error correction is the method by which the modem can detect errors in transmission. Data compression is the method the modem uses to compress the data prior to transmitting it.

Part 5
Getting Your PC to Figure Out What You've Done

Unfortunately, it's not enough to sweat off ten pounds in a nerve-wracking contest between you and your PC. You've installed your new device, but chances are pretty good that it's not ready to work just yet. That's because in order to get most gadgets to work, you've got to install an interpreter called a device driver, which is fluent in Windows-speak. The device driver then takes over the job of translating the device's requests to and from Windows, enabling them to get along quite nicely.

Chapter 26

Getting Windows to Recognize Your New Toy

In This Chapter

➤ How to let Windows 95 and Windows 98 know that you've installed a new toy

➤ Telling Windows 3.1 about your new keyboard, mouse, video card, and monitor

➤ Introducing Windows 3.1 to a new printer or other gadget instead

Installing a driver for DOS through the CONFIG.SYS and AUTOEXEC.BAT configuration files just isn't good enough for Windows. No sir. That's because Windows has its own configuration files: WIN.INI, SYSTEM.INI, and (in the case of Windows 95/98) the gargantuan System Registry. It takes a DOS device driver to make your new device officially part of the computer; but Windows needs a device driver specifically designed for Windows before it can become aware of your new toy. For most new devices, you'll need to install a Windows device driver as well. I know this is like learning you have to fill out your tax forms twice in the same year, but did you really expect your computer to be easy?

Most devices include a Windows driver on the disk with the DOS driver, but if they don't, you'll find additional drivers on the Windows setup disks—you know, the disks you used to install Windows in the first place.

If you've got Windows 95 or Windows 98, it's pretty easy to let it know you've added a new device. See the following section for details. If you've decided to stick with Windows 3.1 a little longer, skip ahead to the section "Telling Windows 3.1 What You've Added Instead" later in this chapter.

Telling Windows 95/98 About the New Hardware

After you install your new toy and restart your Windows 95 or Windows 98 PC, the operating system may or may not recognize that something is different. That's because Plug and Play (the automatic part of Windows that's supposed to figure out on its own that you've added something new) doesn't work without its other two parts: a Plug-and-Play BIOS, and a Plug and Play device.

In other words, if you've just added a Plug and Play modem, and you're using a Pentium Pro, or Pentium II PC, or at the very least a 486DX PC with an updated BIOS chip, your PC automatically recognizes your new modem and begins the installation process as soon as you turn on the PC and start Windows.

If you don't own a Plug and Play computer, or if you didn't buy a Plug and Play device, no big deal—Windows is pretty good at installing your new device anyway. It just needs a little shove in the right direction.

Adding Just About Anything

When Windows doesn't automatically welcome your new toy, here's how to tell Windows about it.

First, open the **Start** menu, select **Settings**, and then select **Control Panel**. Double-click the **Add New Hardware** icon. The Add New Hardware Wizard appears. Not much to do on this first screen, so click **Next.**

Getting Windows 95 to search for your new device is easy.

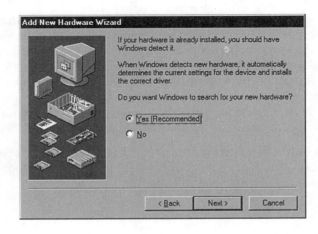

The easiest way to handle this is to sit back, relax, and let Windows do all the work. When it asks you if you want Windows to search for and detect your new hardware, by all means, click **Yes**. Then click **Next**.

Before you continue, close all your programs. Then click **Next**. This whole detection thing will take a few minutes, so feel free to put your feet up while you wait. Meanwhile, Windows will start sniffing around, looking for something new. When Windows finds your new part, it displays the name of that part (or at least what Windows believes that part to be) in a box. If the guess is right, just click **Finish**, and Windows installs the proper device driver. You may be asked to provide additional information, or to perform additional steps—for example, if you're installing an external modem, Windows will ask you to turn it on. Then it will ask you to enter your phone number and the COM port you're using.

If Windows doesn't find your new toy, or if it guessed wrong, you'll see a message telling you to give it another try. Click **Next**. You'll see a list of hardware types. Select your hardware type from the list. If you don't see your hardware type listed, choose **Other devices**. Click **Next**.

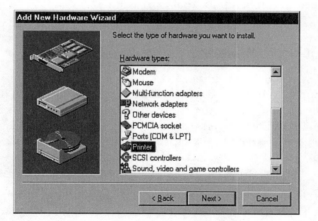

The manual method of telling Windows 95 about a new device.

You'll see a list of manufacturers for your particular device. For example, if you select **Printers**, then you'll see a list of common printers. Click the name of the manufacturer that made your printer (such as Hewlett Packard), and you'll see a list of HP printers. Pick your model from the list and click **Next**. Windows installs the driver for your new part.

If you still can't find your new part in a listing anywhere, then Windows did not come with a driver for it. Click **Have Disk** and insert the setup disk supplied by the maker of your new gadget. Select the driver file from those listed (there'll probably only be one file listed) and click **OK**. Windows installs the driver.

After you've installed your new part under Windows, you can start using it right away— that is, right after you boot your system, so Windows will recognize the new device.

If you want to change any of your choices later on (for example, you want to change your modem's phone number), just return to the Control Panel and click the appropriate icon, such as the Modem icon.

Telling Windows 3.1 What You've Added

After you install your new device, and DOS actually recognizes it, you'll need to perform a few extra steps to get Windows 3.1 or Windows 3.11 for Workgroups to recognize it. Thankfully, these steps are not terribly complex, as you'll soon learn.

New Mouse, Keyboard, or Monitor? Step Right Up!

If you replace your old mouse, keyboard, or monitor with the exact same mouse, keyboard, or monitor you had before, you don't have to do a thing in Windows. You can just go ahead and start using the new device. You see, DOS and Windows need drivers to recognize a particular brand and model of device, but there's nothing particular about one video card that differentiates or distinguishes it from another card of the same make and model. If you replace a defective XYZ Model 12 Card with a working XYZ Model 12 Card, you don't need to run Setup for that card again.

But what about my video card?

Suppose you have an old VGA monitor and a standard VGA card running Windows' generic VGA driver, and you buy a new video card, but not a new monitor. Chances are you don't have to do a thing to your Windows drivers, because your old monitor is less likely to be able to take advantage of the new card's capabilities anyway. In most cases, you really need to upgrade both the video card and the monitor, because they work as a team. See Chapter 20, "Taking Advantage of Modern Video Capabilities," for help.

So again, the only time you need to change display modes with this procedure is if you upgrade *both your video card and your monitor* to a higher standard, such as upgrading from VGA to Super VGA.

If you upgrade to a higher quality monitor, or if you change the brand of mouse or keyboard you use, however, chances are you have to do something to tell Windows about it. Whether you need to do anything at all depends on whether you bought a device that operates under a different *mode*. For example, in the Windows 3.1 Setup program, under Mouse, you have only two choices: Microsoft mouse, or another brand of mouse. So you only need to change mouse modes if you switch from a Microsoft mouse to a Logitech mouse, or vice-versa. In some cases, however, you may need to install a driver for your mouse.

In any case, the safest thing to do is go through this upgrade procedure, if for no other reason than to make sure that you're currently operating in the right mode. Be sure to get out any disks that came with your new hardware before you start; you may need them. You may also need your Windows disks as well, so find them and dust them off before you start.

Read this before you change your Windows setup

Before you attempt to change your Windows Setup, do yourself a big favor and copy the WIN.INI and SYSTEM.INI to the emergency disk you created in Chapter 4, "What You Need to Know Before You Open Your PC." If you accidentally change anything that makes it impossible to start Windows, you'll be able to quickly copy the original .INI files back to the Windows directory with the emergency disk so you can get into Windows and try something else.

This is especially important to do before you change video modes, because if the current Windows selection is not compatible with your system, you won't be able to see a darn thing.

Now, before you start, exit all programs, because Windows is going to restart the PC at the end of this business. Now, open up the Main window and then double-click the **Windows Setup** icon. The Windows Setup dialog box pokes up its head. Open the **Options** menu and select **Change System Settings**.

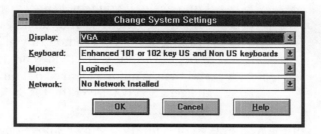

Changing Windows settings.

Click the down arrow next to the item you want to change. For example, to change your mouse, click the down arrow to open up a drop-down list of mouse options. Scroll through the list until you find your particular brand of mouse, click your mouse's brand name, and click **OK**. If your particular brand of mouse isn't listed, select the **Other** option at the bottom of the list—this means you'll need the disk that came with your new part. Windows will read a list of (hopefully) only one mouse driver from that disk, but you'll still need to select your one mouse brand from that one mouse list.

Feeding Windows.

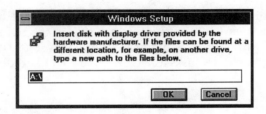

Feed Windows the appropriate disk and then click **OK**. Windows copies the device driver to the hard disk. When asked, click **Restart Windows** so the new driver can take effect. Your new toy is ready to play.

Changing Windows Setup from the DOS Prompt

But Windows didn't ask me for a disk! If your new part is similar to the old one, Windows may already have installed the proper driver. That's because in most cases Windows installs several drivers at once to make it easy for you to switch modes for a device. But if Windows allows you to install the driver that came with the new device, by all means, do so—it'll be more current than any driver that Windows might provide.

If you change the display driver or whatever, and now Windows 3.1 doesn't work, you can run the Windows Setup program from DOS to correct your mistake. Here's what to do:

1. First, change to the Windows directory by typing **CD\WINDOWS** and pressing **Enter**.

2. Type **SETUP** and press **Enter** to start the Windows Setup program.

3. Use the up-arrow key to select the item to change and then press **Enter**.

4. Make a selection from the list that appears and press **Enter** again. If you're not sure what to select, pick something generic so you can at least get Windows running again. For example, if you selected what you thought was the correct video driver for your system and then Windows blanked out on you, change to the generic VGA driver (that is, if you use VGA) and try again.

5. Finally, highlight the **Accept the configuration shown above** option. The Setup program will probably ask you for some disks, so oblige it. After it installs the device driver, the Setup program dumps you out at the DOS prompt.

You should now be able to start Windows. If not, try running the Windows Setup again.

Adding a Printer

To install a printer under Windows 3.1, you use a slightly different method than you use to change your monitor, keyboard, or mouse. First, open the Main window and double-click the **Control Panel** icon.

Double-click the **Printer** icon. The Printers dialog box pops its head up. Click the **Add** button, and the dialog box expands, as shown.

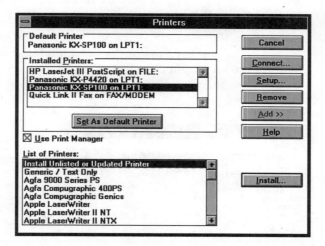

The Printers dialog box expands so you can choose your new printer.

Select your new printer from the List of Printers list box and then click **Install**. If you don't find your printer listed, select a compatible printer instead (a printer that your printer *emulates*, or mimics).

Dig out the Windows disk that Windows asks you for and click **OK**. Windows copies the printer driver to the hard disk. When you get back to the Printers dialog box, select your new printer from the **Installed Printers** list and click **Set As Default Printer**.

You can remove your old printer driver after the new one's working—it'll save you a bit of hard drive space. Just select your old printer from the **Installed Printers** list and click **Remove**.

> **Fallback position** Many printers have at least one "emulation mode," or fallback mode, that allows a newer brand of printer to behave, for the computer's sake, like an older, more common brand—at least until that new brand becomes more common. If you're not sure what your printer's emulation mode is, check its specifications as listed in the manual that comes with it.

Use the newest driver Whenever possible, use the disk that came with your new gadget to install the Windows device driver. Even if Windows already has a copy of the driver, chances are pretty good that the driver is really old.

Adding Other Junk

So far, you've learned how to install your monitor, mouse, keyboard, and printer under Windows 3.1. To install other devices, you use the generic Drivers utility.

First, open the Main window and then click the **Control Panel** icon. Double-click the **Drivers** icon. The Drivers dialog box appears onscreen. Click **Add** and you see the Add dialog box.

Scroll through the list until you find the brand name for your new toy. If your device's brand isn't listed, select the **Unlisted** option at the bottom of the list and get the disk that came with your new part because you're going to need it.

Select your brand.

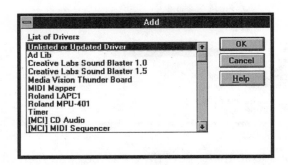

After you've selected your new toy from the list, click **OK**. Feed Windows the appropriate disk and click **OK**. Windows copies the device driver to the hard disk and then asks you if it's okay to exit Windows and restart it. Click **Restart Windows**, and Windows restarts so the new driver can take effect. Your new pal is ready to play.

Editing Your Configuration Files Manually

When you start your PC, it opens its eyes, stretches a bit, and yells for somebody to tell it what day it is. After that, it reaches for its configuration files—AUTOEXEC.BAT and CONFIG.SYS—so it can get set up for the day. Among other things, these files tell your computer to load device drivers so your computer can "talk" to the various stuff you've added, such as a sound card or a CD-ROM drive.

At least this is what happens when you start DOS. If you start Windows 95 or 98, your system may not even have an AUTOEXEC.BAT and a CONFIG.SYS. For the most part, the configuration settings (and the locations of device drivers) are stored in the Windows configuration files, WIN.INI, SYSTEM.INI, and the System Registry.

So why mess around with AUTOEXEC.BAT and CONFIG.SYS? Well, in the real world, you may still find yourself using DOS, even though you really do Windows. For example, if you decide to run a game, it's more than likely that the game must run at the DOS prompt. But if you don't have an AUTOEXEC.BAT and CONFIG.SYS, then when you exit Windows and start DOS, your devices (such as your CD-ROM or your sound card) may not work. That's because no one was there to tell DOS to load the appropriate driver (called a real mode driver). So, after following the steps given earlier in this chapter to install the device driver for your CD-ROM under Windows, follow these steps to install another driver for DOS.

What's the difference?

The CONFIG.SYS was designed as a way for the user to customize DOS to a certain extent; with the CONFIG.SYS, you can: add device drivers for peripherals that DOS was not originally intended for, change the number of files a program can open at one time, change the maximum number of recently opened files in memory, and enable your computer to use memory more efficiently.

The AUTOEXEC.BAT was designed like Windows' Startup folder: to run programs automatically when the computer is booted. Because, like most people, you probably skip DOS and go straight to Windows, you won't need the AUTOEXEC.BAT for much. There are, however, some device drivers that are programs instead of just files (they end in EXE or COM), and they need to be loaded through the AUTOEXEC.BAT, instead of through the CONFIG.SYS. For example, your mouse driver is often loaded this way. Also, a device may place special "notes" to itself in the AUTOEXEC.BAT through something called the SET command.

Running the Setup Program for Your New Device

As I mentioned before, the PC's BIOS handles the job of talking to the computer's basic parts, such as the hard disk and memory. When you add other devices such as a sound card, tape backup, CD-ROM drive, printer, video card, or modem, then you have to run some kind of setup program to configure the new device and to install a program called a *device driver*. The device driver's role is to help the BIOS talk to the new device.

Before you run the setup program Make sure you've followed the steps in Chapter 4 to update your emergency disk. That way, if the setup program makes changes that render your PC helpless, you'll be able to undo them.

Your new piece of hardware usually comes with a disk or two that includes its setup program. Typically, you'll run these setup programs under Windows. But occasionally, you'll run them at the DOS prompt instead, to load a real mode driver.

To run most setup programs, install your new device, then turn the PC on. If you end up in Windows 95/98, then exit to DOS. Next, insert the setup disk into drive A, type **A:SETUP** at the DOS prompt, and press **Enter**. (Some programs have you type **A:INSTALL** instead.) At this point, you'll be treated to several screens that might ask you interesting questions such as "What COM port do you want to use?" or "Do you want the device driver loaded into high memory?" For the most part, just go with whatever option the program suggests. You can always rerun the setup program if you change your mind later on.

Don't forget! After you edit a configuration file, you'll have to restart the computer to test your changes. The easiest way to do that is to press **Ctrl+Alt+Delete** or your computer's **Reset** button.

If the program asks you if you want it to make changes to the AUTOEXEC.BAT and CONFIG.SYS files, by all means answer **Yes**, because you don't really want to operate on these files all by yourself if you can help it.

After the setup program is done, restart your PC so the changes it made to the configuration files will take effect. The computer can't really see these changes until it has actually read them, and it doesn't read those files at any time other than at startup.

Fixing What the Setup Program Did

If you restart your PC after using the setup program only to run into a problem (like the PC won't start), use your emergency disk. Just stick it in drive A and restart the PC again. Then edit the configuration files to either remove or change what the setup program did, so your PC and the device will work. The new changes will be easy to identify, because they'll be things you won't recognize, but you can always check the manual to be sure. Or you might just copy back to the hard disk the unchanged versions of your configuration files that you put on your emergency disk just prior to installing the new device.

First, start with the manual that came with your new toy. It might suggest some changes that will help the device to work in your system. If worst comes to worst, you can always edit the files yourself to remove part or all of the changes one at a time until you find the culprit. Use Windows Notepad to edit the files.

Don't forget the PATH

If you add a command to a configuration file and you expect DOS to carry it out, you better make sure you give DOS enough information. For example, if you want to include a command that loads a device driver, you better make sure that you also include the driver's location or *path*.

A path is made up of three parts: the drive letter where the file is located, followed by a colon, followed by a backslash (\) and the name of the directory in which the file is kept. Finally, this nonsense is followed by another backslash and the name of the file.

So if you want to include a command to load the device driver MAXSOUND.SYS, make sure you also include its location as part of that command, like this:

```
DEVICE=C:\BLASTER\MAXSOUND.SYS.
```

The Least You Need to Know

After you install a new device, you have to get Windows to recognize it. If you use Windows 3.1, you install the DOS device driver and a separate one for Windows. If you use Windows 95 or Windows 98, you may be able to let Windows find and install the proper device driver for you, by way of its Plug and Play system. You might need to install a DOS device driver, too, if you intend to use the device when you exit Windows and go to DOS.

➤ Windows 95 may automatically recognize and install your new device, if it's Plug and Play-compatible, and you're using a Plug and Play computer. Otherwise, you'll need to use the Add New Hardware icon in the Control Panel to install your new device.

➤ Before you install the driver for your new gadget under Windows 95, close down your other programs, because you'll need to restart Windows for the changes to take effect.

➤ Before making any changes to your setup under Windows 3.1, update your emergency disk.

➤ Also exit any programs before starting, because you'll have to restart Windows 3.1 for the changes to take place.

➤ You'll need either your Windows 3.1 disks or the disk that came with your new gadget to install its driver.

Fiddling with Ports, IRQs, Addresses, and Such

When you install some new gadgets in your PC, they bring wine, flowers, and candy, eager to be loved by all the other parts. Other parts bully their way in, steal Dad's favorite chair, and refuse to behave.

I'm guessing that you just installed one of these brutes, or you wouldn't be boring yourself with this chapter. Here, you'll learn to tame your beast and get everyone working happily together again.

Before you mess inside

Before you take the cover off your PC to mess with jumpers, switches, and other junk, take out some insurance in the form of an emergency disk. See Chapter 4, "What You Need to Know Before You Open Your PC," for details.

Sound card alert

If you are configuring some device and you have a conflict with your sound card, you're usually better off if you change the resources of the other device, *and not those of the sound card*. Why? Well, if you're like me and you play a lot of games (uh, only when my work is totally done, really), then you probably play games that run under DOS and not Windows. DOS games are notorious for trying to work directly with the sound card, and expecting it to be using certain resources. So if you change the parameters for those resources, you'll most likely have problems with your games.

How do I know I have a resource conflict?

Unfortunately, Windows 3.1 gives you no help in detecting these problems; you'll really need a DOS utility such as MSD. However, for Windows 95/98 users, just go into **Device Manager**, choose Computer at the top of the list, and then click the **Properties** button. The Computer Properties dialog box shows IRQs, I/O addresses, DMA addresses, and reserved RAM blocks. If conflicts do exist, Device Manager points them out on its main list, by flagging the sources of the conflict with a black-on-yellow exclamation point icon.

A Word About Plug and Play

As you already know (or you wouldn't be reading this chapter), getting all your system's devices to play together nicely is hard work. In an attempt to relieve you of this potentially hair-pulling, mind-numbing experience, Microsoft came up with an answer it calls Plug and Play (PnP). PnP is built into Windows 95 and Windows 98.

What it does (or attempts to do) is dynamically assign resources such as DMA addresses and IRQs to each PnP device as the system starts. (Actually, it starts with a list of previous assignments, and only tries to find resources for new devices.) In theory, this is a terrific idea; however, in practice, it's a bit less than that. When dealing with a system that contains both PnP and non-PnP devices, Plug and Pray (sorry, I mean Plug and Play) doesn't always come up with the best allocation of resources.

Hands off?

You can, in theory, take control away from Plug and Play if needed. Just go into **Device Manager** and pull up **Properties** for one of the listed devices, and then click the **Resources** tab, and you'll see a list of the current settings. PnP checks the box for "Use automatic settings." To change any of these settings, uncheck the box; and that is *supposed* to tell PnP, "Hands off, I'll take care of this." However, sometimes even when you do this, PnP can (although not always) put its little hands back on right after your next reboot. It depends on the device; newer devices seem to have fewer problems. On the other hand, the first PnP video and sound cards were murder to control this way. But for some good news: PnP has been improved with Windows 98, so maybe you'll have less reason to try to wrest control from it in the first place.

Fiddling with Jumpers and Switches and Such

Back in the days of cave men and stegosauruses, PCs got most of their configuration information from tiny pins called *jumpers*, or small switches called *DIPs*. But even with all their fancy-schmancy hardware, some computer parts still prefer this primitive method of communication.

A jumper is made up of two or more parallel pins, which are part of a circuit. If the pins are sticking up in the air, then obviously the circuit is open, which is the same as having a switch turned off. To turn on an electric circuit, you need to close, or complete it; with a jumper, you close the circuit with a little rectangular doodad called a *shunt*, which you slip onto a pair of pins, as shown. The pins are labeled; check the device's manual to find out which pins the jumper is supposed to be put on.

For example, if you're installing a modem and the manual tells you to set the jumper to J5 to set the modem to COM2, then remove the shunt from its current resting spot and place it over the two J5 pins. As if this junk isn't hard enough, some jumpers are set in a row and not in pairs. Here you place the shunt over two numbered pins, such as pins 4 and 5. The number points to the pair of pins that together form the jumper; you have to be careful here, because one pin can be part of two jumper pairs. For instance, you might find three pins (not four) in one row, with markings for J1 and J2. The J1 pair will most likely be the top pair (the first and second pin from the top), and J2 will probably be the bottom pair (the second and third pin).

Place the jumper over the correct pins to change the setting of the device.

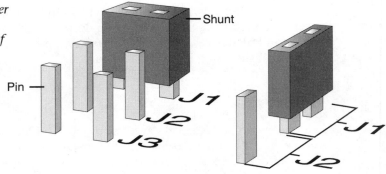

Shunt

Pin

J1

J2

J3

J1

J2

If you need to remove a shunt, let it hang over one pin, like this, so you don't lose it

To remove the shunt from the jumper, just pull up. If the shunt is stuck, you may find tweezers or threats helpful. Be careful not to let the metal tweezers touch anything it might short out. Most people rest the shunt over a single pin, which doesn't do anything, but it does give you a good place to keep the thing should you ever need it again.

Don't remove under penalty of law

Don't remove a shunt entirely from a card even if the manual tells you to; you're likely to lose the little guy. Instead, leave the shunt hanging over one of the two pins, as shown in the figure. (A jumper is formed and works by joining two pins with a shunt, so putting it over one pin will have no effect.) That way, it'll be easier to find the next time you need to change the gadget's settings.

DIP switches (sometimes called rocker switches) are like tiny light switches: they can only be set to on or off. By setting the correct switches to either on or off, you can reconfigure a device. Oh, in case you care, DIP is short for *dual in-line package*. Yes, it's the same DIP as in "DIP chip"; the term refers to the way the item is mounted to the circuit board. You'll notice two (thus the "dual") rows of prongs (thus the "inline") sticking out of opposite sides of both a DIP chip and a DIP switch set. They could've called it "two row package" but then the acronym would have been "TRP chip," and you'd have to pronounce it "trip" or "twerp." Although "twerp chip" sounds fitting, it doesn't have that whole double entendre thing going for it.

Before you rock

You may want to write down the device's switch settings before you start messing with them, so you can at least go back to the original settings if things go wrong. It might not be what you want, but hey, at least it works.

To change a DIP switch, use a ballpoint pen—your fingernails will thank you. Flip the switch to the side marked on (sometimes marked with just an arrow symbol) if you want to activate it, or to the other side to turn it off.

I'm feeling a bit left out

Don't be bummed out if your PC doesn't use old-style jumpers and DIP switches. A lot of modems let you set the jumpers for the COM port selection using the software program included with the modem.

What to Do When Your COM Ports Start a Fight

Various serial devices—modem, mouse, scanner, and serial printer—use COM ports to communicate with your PC. All's well and good, as long as you only use two of these critters, and you set them to use different COM ports.

But if you install a new serial device and it grabs somebody else's COM port as its own, you're gonna have what's commonly called a mess. Sorry—I mean a COM port conflict.

These aren't Grandma's rockers.

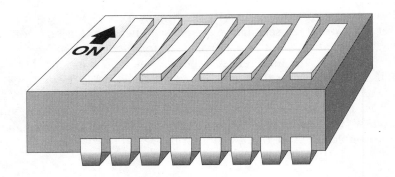

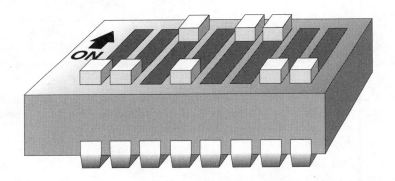

Another fine mess

The easiest way to avoid this problem is to write down the settings your gadgets use. Then, before you install anything new, just choose some settings that aren't being used. You can use this method to avoid not just COM port conflicts, but also IRQ and DMA conflicts.

Most PCs can support up to four COM ports, but you can use only two of them at any one time, at least on most systems (see the upcoming sidebar). That's because COM1 and COM3 both use the same *interrupt* to talk to the CPU. (More on interrupts in a minute.) Same goes with COM2 and COM4. (Windows 95 and Windows 98 will register this in their Device Manager programs as official conflicts, although there's no way for you to fix them.) You can use all four COM ports simultaneously; in some cases, you might not have a choice. But be aware that the operating system is taking efforts to distinguish which device is actually invoking the interrupt, when two COM ports do share that interrupt. So conflicts can arise, and Murphy's Law has a tendency to play a big role when it comes to conflicts in Windows.

Two or three COM ports?

Most systems have allocated two IRQs for use with serial devices, namely IRQ 3 and IRQ 4. The problem with Windows in the past was, although there were four logical COM ports, COM1 through COM4, only two could be made active because only two could be given firm interrupts. Now, IRQ 4 is shared by COM1 and COM3, and IRQ 3 is shared by COM2 and COM4. But some newer systems have set up three IRQs instead of two for annexing among the serial devices, so maybe you'll have fewer conflicts.

I don't think I have a COM3 or COM4

Some devices don't want to use the higher COM ports, so you can't set them to COM3 or COM4 even if you want to. Likewise, some PCs, such as old XTs or those that use a DOS version earlier than DOS 3.3, don't support COM3 or COM4.

Now, most PCs come with two serial ports on the back, marked COM1 and COM2. It's important to remember that these two ports are active, *even if you have nothing connected to them.* So if you insert a serial device such as a modem, it'll conflict with one of these two. To deactivate a COM port, you usually remove some jumper, or make some change in your CMOS setup. Check your PC manual for help.

It's still not working!

If you set up one device to COM1 and the other to COM2, and they're still not working, switch them. (Some devices just don't like being number two.)

To change the COM port an external device uses, plug it into a different serial port. To change an internal device, you usually have to flip some silly DIP switches or move a stupid jumper. (If you're lucky, you get to use software for this nonsense instead of setting the COM port through switches.)

After changing COM settings, reset the device by turning it off and then back on, so the new settings take effect. If the gadget's an internal one, restart the PC to reset it.

Fixing What IRQs You

When a child wants to get someone's attention, he usually yells. When a boss wants an employee's attention, she usually yells. (Notice the trend...) When a computer part wants to get the CPU's attention, it uses an *interrupt*, or *IRQ*. You see, your computer's CPU is busy all the time. If some device needs immediate attention, it sends an S.O.S. along its private interrupt. For example, if you start pressing keys on the keyboard, the keyboard controller sends an interrupt signal to the CPU so it knows that someone's pressing keys. If two devices are accidentally assigned the same interrupt, the CPU doesn't know what device actually needs its attention, so either of two catastrophic things can happen:

➤ The CPU just ignores any messages it gets, or in the case of two PCI devices which share the same interrupt, the CPU will just "schedule" them for processing, one behind the other.

➤ The CPU processes one device's message as though it came from the other device.

PCI does its own thing

PCI cards, which are connected to the PCI bus (a high-speed bus that connects directly to the CPU, to speed up the devices connected to it), do their own thing when it comes to IRQs. PCI cards still use them, but they are usually called A, B, C, and D, so they won't get mixed up with the regular system IRQs. If your PC has more than four PCI slots, then they share IRQs.

These four PCI interrupts are mapped to the regular system IRQs, typically one or more IRQs (whatever's available), from IRQ 9–12. In Windows 95 OSR2 and in Windows 98, PCI interrupts are handled by PnP (Plug and Play) instead, using something Microsoft calls PCI steering. The whole idea is to avoid interrupt conflicts by assigning interrupts to devices at startup. If you go into Device Manager (through the Device icon in the Control Panel) you'll see PCI steering listed as an extra entry under each PCI device, but don't think it means you have some kind of conflict.

Imagine what can happen when the CPU thinks that someone's typing "DELETE *.*" on your printer.

So what you need to do is assign a unique interrupt to each device. Sounds simple, but it's not, because most of the interrupts are already taken by the PC's inner few. Here's a list of the various IRQs and what normally occupies them:

Interrupt	What Owns It	Problems
IRQ 0	System timer	
IRQ 1	Keyboard controller	
IRQ 2	Controller for IRQ 8–15	If you have an old XT, then this one's available. (IRQs 8 through 15 don't exist in older PCs.) If you own a newer PC, you can sometimes set a gadget to IRQ 2 (but it actually ends up using IRQ 9).
IRQ 3	COM2 and COM4	This is what can get you into trouble using COM2 and COM4 at the same time. Besides modems, your mouse, sound cards, network cards, and tape backup accelerators may use this IRQ.
IRQ 4	COM1 and COM3	This is what can get you into trouble using COM1 and COM3 at the same time. Besides modems, your mouse, sound cards, network cards, and tape backup accelerators may use this IRQ.
IRQ 5	LPT2	The most common interrupt used by sound cards. Some newer modems allow you to set them to IRQ 5. In addition, LPT3 uses this interrupt, along with some network cards, tape accelerators, and the hard disk controller on the very old PC/XT.
IRQ 6	Floppy disk drive controller	Tape accelerator cards also try to use this interrupt.

continues

continued

Interrupt	What Owns It	Problems
IRQ 7	LPT1	This is usually taken by your printer. LPT2 can also use this interrupt, in addition to some modems using COM4, sound cards, network cards, and tape accelerators.
IRQ 8	Clock	Clock
IRQ 9	Controller for IRQs	Because IRQ2 is used as a controller for IRQ 8–15, the computer automatically switches any device set to IRQ 2 to IRQ 9. A network card often grabs it, or your PCI cards, a sound card, or SCSI host adapter.
IRQ 10	Unused	Some gadgets don't support an IRQ this high. What you will typically find here are your PCI devices, AGP video, network cards, sound cards, SCSI host adapters, or the secondary IDE channel.
IRQ 11	Unused	Some gadgets don't support an IRQ this high. What you will find here includes PCI devices, network cards, sound cards, SCSI host adapters, VGA video cards, and maybe your tertiary IDE channel.
IRQ 12	PS/2 mouse	Typically used by the mouse, however, network cards, sound cards, SCSI host adapters, VGA video cards, and even PCI devices might also slug it out for this one.
IRQ 13	Math coprocessor	Even if your PC doesn't have a coprocessor, you can't use this because it's not wired to the expansion slots.

Interrupt	What Owns It	Problems
IRQ 14	Primary IDE channel	Hard disk controller, Primary IDE channel, or SCSI host adapter.
IRQ 15	Secondary IDE channel	Some gadgets don't support an IRQ this high. But your secondary IDE channel uses this one, in addition to network cards, and SCSI host adapter.

As you can see, the only way you're going to get out of this mess is to know what IRQs your other devices are using. See the list you created in Chapter 3, "Now, Let's Find Out What Kind of Computer You Have," for help in figuring out what's what.

To assign an interrupt to a particular device, you usually need to move a jumper or two, or a series of switches. If you need help with these monsters, see the first section in this chapter. By the way, some civilized devices actually enable you to assign the IRQ through software, which makes guessing a bit easier.

Messing with DMA Address Junk

First, the good news: Not every device needs a DMA channel. Now, the bad news: There aren't that many of them. Good news again: Although there aren't that many DMA addresses, hardly any of them are taken; this means they're up for grabs by the first device that claims them.

DMA is short for *direct memory access*, and it's the technique that your peripheral devices (mainly your expansion cards) use to address your computer's main RAM. Standard DMA is used by the devices that are attached to the ISA bus—those devices that need DMA, that is. Devices that have their own RAM—for example, your laser printer—don't need DMA. Your video card doesn't need DMA (although it might use DMA through the PCI bus) because it has its own VRAM on board. But your sound card uses DMA because it composes its sound waveforms within main RAM. Your floppy disk controller has DMA channel 2 reserved exclusively for it. In addition, most tape drives require a DMA channel, and so does the use of a ECP (Enhanced Capabilities Port) parallel port. Some CD-ROM drivers may require a DMA channel, although most modern units do not, because they are mostly controlled by the IDE interface, which does not use DMA.

PCI devices do not use standard DMA either; instead, they use a different kind of DMA scheme called *first party DMA*, which involves *bus mastering*, where the device actually handles—or, more accurately, *marshals*—the transfer of data between itself and main memory. Bus mastering is required here, because the device needs to wrest temporary control of the expansion bus for this transfer to work. First party DMA allows for much higher transfer rates than standard DMA. With standard DMA, the DMA controller handles the transfer operation. Typically, modern hard disks use bus mastering, and so do SCSI cards, some network cards, and even some video cards.

Again, the best way to figure out this nonsense is to make a list of the DMA addresses that your gadgets are using and then select an unused one for your new toy.

DMA Address	What Owns It
DMA 0	Memory refresh.
DMA 1	Sound cards typically use DMA 1, but SCSI host adapters, ECP parallel ports, tape accelerator, network cards, and voice modems also use it.
DMA 2	Floppy disk controller.
DMA 3	Could be anything, from ECP parallel ports, SCSI host adapters, tape accelerator cards, sound cards, network cards, voice modems, or the hard disk controller for an old PC/XT.
DMA 4	DMA controller.
DMA 5	Sound cards that can use DMA channels 5–7, also SCSI host adapters, and network cards.
DMA 6	Again, only sound cards that can use 5–7, SCSI host adapters, and network cards.
DMA 7	Again, only sound cards that can use 5–7, SCSI host adapters, and network cards.

Expansion cards that are only 8-bit (they use only one slot of the two slot ISA connector) can only access one of the first three DMA channels. 16-bit cards can access any of the seven channels that are available.

To change a device's DMA address, again, you resort to flipping switches or pulling jumper shunts. Some nice toys enable you to set this nonsense with software, but if you're stuck with switches and jumpers, see the first section in this chapter for help.

Playing Around with I/O Addresses

Just about every device uses an I/O address, which is their home place in memory. Devices shuffle input and output through this tiny space in memory. The size of the I/O address varies by device; typically, a device that handles a lot of data at one time, such as a network card, has a large I/O address space—others, such as your keyboard, use a small address area in memory for their input/output. What happens is this: When a device receives some kind of data, such as a keypress, it places it in memory where the CPU, when it can get around to it, can retrieve the data and process it. The I/O address channel works the other way too; in cases where the CPU needs to return the data to the device, it places that data in the designated I/O address (you can think of it as a private mailbox).

The I/O addresses for devices can come into conflict just like those other addresses, DMAs. Video cards, disk drive controllers, sound cards, SCSI adapters, network cards, and the COM and LPT ports all use I/O addresses. Here's a listing of I/O memory addresses (shown in hexidecimal notation), and their common uses:

I/O Address	Typical Use
000-00Fh	DMA controller for channels 0–3
010-060h	System
060h and 064h	Keyboard controller and PS/2 mouse
070h - 0C0h	System
0C0-0DFh	DMA controller, channels 4–7
0E0-130h	System
130-14Fh and 140-15Fh	SCSI host adapters
170-173h	Secondary IDE controller's master drive
1F0-1F3h	Primary IDE controller's master drive
200-203h	Joystick port
220-22Fh	Sound cards, and some SCSI host adapters (220-23Fh)
240-24Fh	Optional address for sound cards and network cards (240-243h), or NE2000 network cards (240-25Fh)
260-26Fh	Optional address offered by sound cards and network cards (260-263h), or NE2000 network cards (260-27Fh)
270-273h	System
274-277h	Plug and Play
278-27Fh	LTP2
280-28Fh	Another optional address for sound cards and network cards (280-283h), or NE2000 cards (280-29Fh)
2A0-2BFh	Network cards (2A0-2A3h), or NE2000 cards (2A0-2BFh)
2E8-2EFh	COM4
2F8-2FFh	COM2

continues

continued

I/O Address	Typical Use
300-30Fh	Default for most network cards (300-303h) or 300-31Fh (NE2000 network cards), however, 300-301h is optional for MIDI port on most sound cards
320-32Fh	Talk about a slugfest: 320-323h (network cards), 320-33Fh (NE2000 cards), and 320-327h (hard disk controller on old PC/XT systems)
330-35Fh	330-331h is default for MIDI port on sound cards, 340-343h (network cards), 320-33Fh or 340-35Fh (NE2000 network cards), 330-34Fh or 340-35Fh (SCSI host adapters)
360-37Fh	Another slugfest: 360h or 370h (tape accelerator cards), 360-363h (network cards), 360-37Fh (NE2000 network cards), 376-377h (Secondary IDE controller's slave drive), and 378-37F (LPT1)
389-38B	Sound card's FM synthesizer
3B0-3BBh and 3C0-3DFh	Used by VGA cards
3E8-3EFh	COM3 (3E8-3Efh), tape accelerator card (3E0h)
3F0-3FFh	Floppy disk controller (3F0-3F7h), COM1 (3F8-3FFh), tape accelerator cards (3F0h), and slave drive of the primary IDE controller (376-3F7h)

So how do you assign an I/O address? Through that device's setup program. As you can see here, most devices allow you to select from various I/O addresses that they support. This should hopefully allow you to resolve any conflicts you encounter. Check with the device's manual for more specific information about the addresses it will support.

Resolving Upper Memory Address Problems

As if you didn't have enough problems...yes, there is one more area in which you might encounter a conflict. Between conventional memory (0-640KB) and extended memory (the stuff above 1MB) lies a lonely area of memory called *upper memory*. This area is basically used by the system, which is why it doesn't get much press.

Upper memory is also used by some devices for their own BIOSes, which is why I feel compelled to bore you with this topic. Basically, we're talking about SCSI host adapters, VGA video BIOS, IDE hard disk controllers, and network cards. You set the upper memory addresses that a device may reserve for itself through that device's setup program.

Here's the lowdown of what's what:

Address	Device That Uses It
F0000-FFFFFh	System BIOS
C0000-C7FFFh	VGA video BIOS
C8000-CBFFFh	IDE hard disk BIOS, SCSI host adapter
D0000-D7FFFh	Alternate SCSI host adapter address
Check the manual	Network cards, if used to boot the network

In addition, EMM386, a device manager that manages extended memory (memory above 1MB), will usually allow programs to use any unused sections of upper memory for their own purposes. To prevent any potential conflicts, you can add one or more *X* parameters to the EMM386 launch statement in CONFIG.SYS to block off the areas that other devices need to use. Here's an example where two segments of memory are blocked off with X parameters: `DEVICE=C:\WINDOWS\EMM386.EXE RAM HIGHSCAN I=B000-B7FF X=A000-AFFF X=B800-C7FF.`

Here, the I parameter tells the operating system to *include* a region of memory that would normally be blocked off automatically (in this case, for an older version of Windows) as part of main RAM.

Dealing with CMOS

As you learned in Chapter 3, CMOS is kind of like your PC's reminder pad, keeping track of important stuff like how much memory the computer has, how large the hard disk is, how many floppy drives there are, and so on.

Techno Talk

CMOS protection

Because the information in CMOS is irreplaceable, you should make a copy of it. Follow the steps here to start CMOS and then print the information out by turning on the printer and pressing the **Print Screen** key on your keyboard.

When you upgrade certain basic PC parts, you need to upgrade the information in CMOS too, or your computer's gonna be mighty confused. You see, each time you start your system, the BIOS checks the information in CMOS and uses that to test each basic component to see if it's awake and functioning. If something in the CMOS doesn't jive with reality, then the BIOS gets real mad and flashes some kind of nasty message onscreen.

By the way, if you own an old XT or earlier type PC, then it doesn't use CMOS. Instead, it uses a more primitive system of jumpers and DIP switches. Jump back to the section "Fiddling with Jumpers and Switches and Such" for help in how to deal with them.

To change the CMOS, exit Windows or any other program. Then try one of these tricks to start CMOS:

➤ Reboot your computer and watch the screen for a message telling you what key to press for Setup. Then press it. Most likely, it'll tell you to press **F1**, **F2**, or **Delete**.

➤ If that doesn't work, try rebooting your computer and pressing **Ctrl+Alt+Escape** or **Ctrl+Alt+S**. You can also try **Ctrl+Alt+Enter** or **Ctrl+Alt+Insert**.

➤ If you own a 286 PC or PS/2, restart your computer with its setup disk in drive A.

After you have CMOS up and running, change whatever information you need. If you've just changed the battery, whatever was in CMOS is gone; use your printout to restore the settings.

To move from item to item, you usually press the Tab key or the down arrow key. You typically use the left or right arrow key to change a setting or to move from page to page. Just follow the tips provided at the bottom of the screen.

When you're done making changes, be sure to save them. Usually you just press **Esc** and select **Yes** to save the changes. You'll end up at the DOS prompt. Restart the computer so your changes take effect.

The Least You Need to Know

Some devices refuse to play well with others. Here's how to deal with them:

➤ To move a shunt from a jumper, pull it off the two pins it currently occupies and slide it back on top of two other pins.

➤ Flipping a DIP switch is similar to flipping a light switch: the switch itself is either on or off.

➤ You can't set two devices to the same COM port. Also, COM1 and COM3 conflict, and so do COM2 and COM4. So you can't set devices to conflicting ports.

➤ COM ports (serial ports) are active, even when nothing is connected to them.

➤ An IRQ (hardware interrupt) is a way for a device to get the CPU's attention.

➤ A DMA channel is a high-speed channel for data transfer to the CPU.

➤ CMOS keeps track of important info, such as the number and type of floppy disk drives, the size of hard disks, and the amount of memory.

Quick Fix Guide

If something goes wrong with your PC, why not try to fix it, rather than simply chucking the troublesome part? Yes, it may take a little more than your Mom's chicken soup (or Campbell's) to nurse an ailing part back to good health, but the process is usually easier than you might think.

Use this table to identify the troublemaker, then jump to the appropriate chapter for help.

Problem	See Chapter(s)
Bad command or filename	8
Bad or missing command interpreter	5
Battery dead	16
Beeping noise from keyboard	11
Burned-in image onscreen	11
Can't capture video	20, 27
Can't connect to the Internet	10, 11
Can't find the Windows desktop	6
Can't hear my CD	11, 20, 22, 23, 24, 27
Can't hear the modem dialing	10, 11, 13, 25, 26, 27
Can't print	11, 14, 23, 26
Can't print digital image in the size I want	20

continues

continued

Problem	See Chapter(s)
Can't print envelopes or labels	11
Can't read my disk	11
Can't read/save files	8, 15, 17, 18, 22, 23, 27
Can't read my printout	11, 14
Can't read what's onscreen	11, 20
Can't record CD	22
Can't record sound	11
Can't take another picture on my digital camera	20
Can't tell which key is which	11
Can't write data to a low-density disk	21
Capturing video doesn't work	20, 27
CD-ROM isn't playing music	11, 20, 22, 23, 24, 27
CD-ROM isn't working	11, 18, 22, 23, 26, 27
Choppy video playback	20
CMOS RAM error	5
Computer acting strangely	5, 8, 11, 16
Computer keeps losing track of time	16
Computer locks up (crashes) often	6, 20
Computer making noise	17
Computer starts sometimes	16, 17
Computer too hot	5, 17
Computer too slow	6, 8, 11, 15, 16, 20
Computer won't respond when I press a key	5, 11
Computer won't start	5, 8, 9, 16, 17, 22, 27
Cordless mouse not working	11, 13
Dead battery	16
Desktop in Windows is hard to get to	6
Digital camera won't take enough pictures	20
Digital image the wrong size	20
Directory listing doesn't update	21
Dirty PC	5
Floppy disk drive doesn't work	11, 21, 27

Problem	See Chapter(s)
Floppy disk won't format	11
Drives A and B are reversed	21
DOS program won't start	7, 22
Envelopes chewed up in printer	11
Faint image onscreen	11
FILE0001.CHK in root directory	8
Fonts the wrong size onscreen	9
Games are slow and jerky	20
Game doesn't work	22
General Protection Fault	6
Graphics are slow	20
Hard disk making noise	8
Hard disk not reading/saving files	8, 15, 17, 18, 22, 23, 27
Hard disk slow	8
Headphones don't work	11
Inkjet printer out of ink	11
Internet connection doesn't work	10, 11
Invalid media	11
Invalid system settings	16
Jerky video playback	20
Keyboard beeping	11
Keyboard cable is torn or frayed	11
Keyboard is dirty	5, 8, 11
Keyboard not found	11
Keyboard not working	5, 8, 9, 12, 26
Labels peel off when I try to print them	11
Lost mouse pointer	11
Low-density disks don't work in my floppy drive	21
Microphone won't record	11
Mobius hardware not detected	22
Modem isn't dialing	10, 11, 13, 25, 26, 27
Modem won't connect	10, 11
Modem won't hang up	11

continues

429

continued

Problem	See Chapter(s)
Monitor has burned-in image	11
Monitor is blank	5, 11, 20
Monitor is dirty	5
Monitor is making noise	11
Monitor shows wrong colors	11, 22
Mouse doesn't work in a program	13
Mouse doesn't work in Windows	9, 13, 26, 27
Mouse is dirty	5, 11
Mouse not responding	5, 11, 13, 25, 26, 27
Mouse pointer jumping around	11
Music coming through speakers when I use my headphones	11
My fonts are the wrong size onscreen	9
My game doesn't work at all	22
My game is 3D	20
My game is too slow	20
My program won't print	11, 14, 23, 26
My windows don't update	9
Nonsystem disk or disk error	5, 11
No image on TV monitor	20
No sound	11, 20, 22, 23, 24, 27
Not enough hard disk space	6, 8
Not enough memory	6, 7, 11, 19
Not ready reading drive X	11
One of my speakers isn't working	11
Out of hard disk space	6, 8
Out of memory	6, 7, 11, 19
Out of toner	11
Paper jamming in the printer	11
Parity error	19
PC acting strange	5, 8, 11, 16
PC keeps losing track of time	16
PC locks up (crashes) often	6, 20
PC makes noise	17

Problem	See Chapter(s)
PC starts sometimes	16, 17
PC too hot	5, 17
PC too slow	6, 8, 11, 15, 16, 20
PC won't respond when I press a key	5, 11
PC won't start	5, 8, 9, 16, 17, 22, 27
Printer doesn't work at all	11, 14, 23, 26
Printer doesn't work in a particular program	14
Printer is too slow	11
Printer out of ink	11
Printer prints half a page	11
Printer won't print digital image in the size I want	20
Printout is illegible or light	11, 14
Program won't respond	5
Program won't start	5, 7
Programs crashing often	6
Programs sluggish	6, 7, 8
Protect a disk	11
Quality of digital image is low	20
Reading files doesn't work	8, 15, 17, 18, 22, 23, 27
Registry too big	6
Resources low	5, 6 ,7
Ribbon in printer needs replacing	11
Running out of Windows resources	5, 6, 7
Saving files doesn't work	8, 15, 17, 18, 22, 23, 27
Screen doesn't update	9, 20
Screen doesn't work when TV is on	20
Screen image always needs adjusting	11, 20
Screen image burned-in	11
Screen is blank	5, 11, 20
Screen is jerky	20
Screen is slow	20
Sector not found	11

continues

continued

Problem	See Chapter(s)
Size wrong for digital image	20
Speakers don't work	11, 20, 22, 23, 24, 27
Startup takes too long	6
Static on monitor	5
Static on speakers	11
Stereo speakers don't work with my PC	11, 20, 22, 23, 24, 27
Strange noises	5, 11, 17
Surge protector making noise	5
System locks up	6, 20
Takes too long to open, save a file	8
Tape drive not working	18, 22, 23, 27
Time is wrong on my computer	16
Toner cartridge needs replacing	11
Too many TEMP files	6
TV doesn't show what's on my PC	20
TV image is slow	20
Video capture board not working	20, 27
Video is jerky or choppy	20
What I type doesn't appear onscreen	11
Windows desktop is hard to get to	6
Windows doesn't like my mouse	13
Windows hates my printer	14
Windows in Windows don't update	9
Windows locks up (crashes)	9, 20
Windows Registry too big	6
Windows startup takes too long	6
Windows too slow	6, 8, 20
Write fault error writing device COMx	11, 13, 25
Wrong colors on monitor	11
Zip/Jaz drive not working	18, 22, 23, 27

Index

443

453

X-Z